Lecture Notes in Computer

T0230184

Commenced Publication in 1973
Founding and Former Series Editors:
Gerhard Goos, Juris Hartmanis, and Jan van Leeuwen

Kokichi Futatsugi   Fumio Mizoguchi
Naoki Yonezaki (Eds.)

Software Security – Theories and Systems

Second Mext-NSF-JSPS International Symposium, ISSS 2003
Tokyo, Japan, November 4-6, 2003
Revised Papers

 Springer

Volume Editors

Kokichi Futatsugi
Japan Advanced Institute of Science and Technology (JAIST)
1-1 Asahidai, Tatsunokuchi, Nomi, Ishikawa 923-1292, Japan
E-mail: kokichi@jaist.ac.jp

Fumio Mizoguchi
Tokyo University of Science, Information Media Center
2641 Yamazaki, Noda, Chiba, 278-8510, Japan
E-mail: mizo@ia.noda.tus.ac.jp

Naoki Yonezaki
Tokyo Institute of Technology
Graduate School of Information Science and Engineering
Department of Computer Science
2-12-1-W8-67 Ookayama, Meguro-ku, Tokyo 152-8552, Japan
E-mail: yonezaki@cs.titech.ac.jp

Library of Congress Control Number: 2004114314

CR Subject Classification (1998): C.2.0, D.4.6, E.3, D.3, F.3, K.6.5

ISSN 0302-9743
ISBN 3-540-23635-X Springer Berlin Heidelberg New York

Springer is a part of Springer Science+Business Media

springeronline.com

© Springer-Verlag Berlin Heidelberg 2004
Printed in Germany

Typesetting: Camera-ready by author, data conversion by Scientific Publishing Services, Chennai, India
Printed on acid-free paper   SPIN: 11340331   06/3142   5 4 3 2 1 0

Preface

Following the success of the International Symposium on Software Security 2002 (ISSS 2002), held in Keio University, Tokyo, November, 2002, ISSS 2003 was held in the Tokyo Institute of Technology, Tokyo, on November 4–6, 2003. This volume is the collection of the papers that were presented at ISSS 2003. The proceedings of ISSS 2002 was published as LNCS 2609.

Although the security and reliability of software systems for networked computer systems are major concerns of current society, the technology for software security still needs to be developed in many directions. Similar to ISSS 2002, ISSS 2003 aimed to provide a forum for research discussions and exchanges among world-leading scientists in the fields of both theoretical and systems aspects of security in software construction.

The program of ISSS 2003 was a combination of invited talks and selected research contributions. It included the most recent visions and researches of the 9 invited speakers, as well as 11 contributions of researches funded by the MEXT grant-in-aid for scientific research on the priority area "Implementation Scheme for Secure Computing" (AnZenKaken). We collected the original contributions after their presentation at the symposium and began a review procedure that resulted in the selection of the papers in this volume. They appear here in final form.

ISSS 2003 required a lot of work that was heavily dependent on members of the program committee, and staffs and graduate students who participated in AnZenKaken. We sincerely thank them for their efforts and time.

June 2004

Kokichi Futatsugi
Fumio Mizoguchi
Naoki Yonezaki

Organization

Program Committee

Kokichi Futatsugi (Co-chair)	JAIST
David Gilliam	Jet Propulsion Laboratory
Masami Hagiya	University of Tokyo
Fumio Mizoguchi (Co-chair)	Tokyo University of Science
Aloysius Mok	University of Texas at Austin
George Necula	University of California at Berkeley
Mitsuhiro Okada	Keio University
John Rushby	SRI International
Etsuya Shibayama	Tokyo Institute of Technology
Andre Scedrov	University of Pennsylvania
Naoki Yonezaki (Co-chair)	Tokyo Institute of Technology

Organization Committee

Kokichi Futatsugi	JAIST
Fumio Mizoguchi	Tokyo University of Science
Mitsuhiro Okada	Keio University
Benjamin Pierce	University of Pennsylvania
Andre Scedrov	University of Pennsylvania
Naoki Yonezaki	Tokyo Institute of Technology
Akinori Yonezawa (Chair)	University of Tokyo

Sponsors

Japanese Ministry of Education, Science and Culture (MEXT)
National Science Foundation (NSF)
Japanese Society for the Promotion of Science (JSPS)

Table of Contents

Part 4: Secure Execution Environments

Part 5: Secure Systems and Security Management

Verifying Confidentiality and Authentication in Kerberos 5*

Frederick Butler[1,3], Iliano Cervesato[2], Aaron D. Jaggard[1,4],
and Andre Scedrov[1]

[1] Department of Mathematics, University of Pennsylvania,
209 South 33rd Street, Philadelphia, PA 19104–6395 USA
scedrov@saul.cis.upenn.edu
[2] ITT Industries, Inc., Advanced Engineering and Sciences,
2560 Huntington Avenue, Alexandria, VA 22303 USA
iliano@itd.nrl.navy.mil
[3] Department of Mathematics, Armstrong Hall, P.O. Box 6310,
West Virginia University, Morgantown, WV 26506-6310 USA
[4] Department of Mathematics, Tulane University, 6823 St. Charles Avenue,
New Orleans, LA 70118 USA
adj@math.tulane.edu

Abstract. We present results from a recent project analyzing Kerberos
5. The main expected properties of this protocol, namely confidentiality and authentication, hold throughout the protocol. Our analysis also
highlights a number of behaviors that do not follow the script of the protocol, although they do not appear harmful for the principals involved.
We obtained these results by formalizing Kerberos 5 at two levels of
detail in the multiset rewriting formalism MSR and by adapting an inductive proof methodology pioneered by Schneider. Our more detailed
specification takes into account encryption types, flags and options, error
messages, and a few timestamps.

1 Introduction

Over the last few years we have pursued a project intended to give a precise
formalization of the operation and objectives of Kerberos 5 [1–3], and to determine whether the protocol satisfies these requirements. Our initial results were
reported in [4]. A detailed and complete account of this work can be found in [5].
This paper is instead intended as a high-level summary of the goals, methods
and outcome of the overall project.

* Scedrov, Butler, and Jaggard were partially supported by the DoD University Research Initiative (URI) program administered by the Office of Naval Research under
Grant N00014-01-1-0795, and by NSF Grant CCR-0098096. Cervesato was partially
supported by NRL under contract N00173-00-C-2086. This paper was written while
Cervesato was visiting Princeton University.

K. Futatsugi et al. (Eds.): ISSS 2003, LNCS 3233, pp. 1–24, 2004.
© Springer-Verlag Berlin Heidelberg 2004

We adopted a hierarchical approach to formalizing such a large and complex protocol, and gave a base specification and two orthogonal refinements of it. These may be thought of as a fragment of a family of refinements of our base specification, including a common refinement whose detail would approach that of pseudocode. Notably, we were able to extend the theorems and proofs for our most abstract formalization to one of our more detailed formalizations by adding detail.

Our base specification, which we refer to as our 'A level' formalization, contains enough detail to prove authentication and confidentiality results but omits many of the details of the full protocol. The first ('B level') refinement of the A level specification adds selected timestamps and temporal checks to the base specification; while these are an important part of the protocol, the B level formalization did not yield as many interesting results and is omitted from further discussion here. See [5] for details. We refer to our second refinement of the base specification as our 'C level' formalization, although it neither refines nor is refined by the B level formalization. The C level description of Kerberos adds encryption types, flags and options, checksums, and error messages to the core exchanges included in the A level.

Our analysis concentrated on the confidentiality of session keys and on the data origin authentication of tickets and other information as the main requirements at the A and C levels. The initial report [4] of this work included some of these properties for the A level; we have extended this work both to other parts of the A level and to parallel theorems in the C level formalization. We also found various anomalies—curious protocol behaviors that do not appear to cause harm, and that do not prevent the protocol from achieving authentication. We summarize those findings here, including details of an anomaly not noted in [4].

Background. Kerberos [1–3] is a widely deployed protocol, aimed at repeatedly authenticating a client to multiple application servers based on a single login. Kerberos makes use of various tickets, encrypted under a server's key and unreadable the user, which when forwarded in an appropriate request authenticate the user to the desired service. A formalization of Kerberos 4, the first publicly released version of this protocol, was given in [6] and then extended and thoroughly analyzed using an inductive approach [7–10]. This analysis, through heavy reliance on the Isabelle theorem prover, yielded formal correctness proofs for a specification with timestamps, and also highlighted a few minor problems. A simple fragment of the more recent version, Kerberos 5, has been investigated using the state exploration tool Murφ [11].

Methodology. We used the security protocol specification language MSR to formalize Kerberos 5 at the various levels of abstraction we intend to consider. MSR [12–15] is a simple, logic-oriented language aimed at giving flexible specifications of complex cryptographic protocols. It uses strongly-typed multiset rewriting rules over first-order atomic formulas to express protocol actions and relies on a form of existential quantification to symbolically model the generation of nonces, session keys and other fresh data. The framework also includes

static checks such as type-checking and data access verification to limit specification oversights. In contrast to other meta-security systems, MSR offers an
open and uncommitted logical basis that makes it possible to reason about and
experiment with a wide variety of specification and verification techniques in
a sound manner. While MSR resembles the inductive method used to analyze
Kerberos 4 in that both model state transitions in a protocol run, MSR is tailored to specifying protocols because of its primitive notion of freshness and its
formal semantics that captures the notion of transition. It is thus of interest to
connect this specification language to methods of proof; indeed, this project was
also intended as a test-bed for MSR on a real-world protocol prior to embarking
in a now ongoing implementation effort, and to explore forms of reasoning that
best take advantage of the linguistic features of MSR. The experience gathered
during this project was very positive.

The verification methods we used were inspired by Schneider's notion of rank
function [16] and also influenced by the inductive theorem proving method Paulson et al. applied to the verification of Kerberos 4 [7–10]. For each formalization of Kerberos 5 that we analyzed, we defined two classes of functions, rank
and corank, to capture the essence of the notions of authentication and confidentiality, respectively. Our experience with these functions suggests that their
(currently manual) generation might be automated and that they might be embedded in an MSR-based proof assistant.

Results. We proved authentication properties for both tickets (Ticket-Granting
and Service) used in Kerberos 5 and the associated encrypted keys that the client
sends with each ticket in a request to a server. In doing so, we used separate confidentiality properties that we proved for the two session keys generated during
a standard protocol run. We have proved the confidentiality and authentication
properties for the first key and ticket in both our A and C level formalizations,
and we have shown that the parallel properties for the second key/ticket pair hold
in our A level formalization; we expect these to also hold in the C level formalization. Table 1 (in Sect. 4.1) shows which property statements here correspond
to the two property types and two protocol exchanges. In this report we state
the protocol properties in language that is applicable to both formalizations;
for those properties proved in both, deleting details from the corresponding C
level theorem gives the A level theorem statement, and the proofs show similar
parallels.

We also uncovered a handful of anomalous behaviors, which are interesting
curiosities rather than practical attacks: in the A level "ticket switch" anomaly,
an intruder corrupts a ticket on its way to the client but restores it as it is about
to be used. This was refined to the "anonymous ticket switch" anomaly at the C
level. The "encryption type" anomaly is found only in the C level and has to do
with the intruder hijacking requests by manipulating their encryption type fields.
After these anomalies were reported in [4], we found the "ticket option anomaly,"
whose effects generalize those of the anonymous ticket switch anomaly although
the actions of the intruder are simpler than those originally described for the

anonymous ticket switch anomaly; we describe this anomaly here in addition to reviewing the other anomalies that we found.

Organization of This Paper. We start in Sect. 2 with a high level description of Kerberos 5 and a discussion of which details are included in our A and C level formalizations. Section 3 outlines MSR and the definition of the rank and corank functions that we used in our analysis. In Sect. 4.1 we turn to our positive results on confidentiality and authentication in Kerberos 5; Sect. 5 discusses curious protocol behavior we have seen in our work. Finally, Sect. 6 outlines possible directions for extensions of this work.

The appendices contain MSR rules comprising our formalizations of Kerberos 5. Appendices A and B give the A level description of behavior by honest protocol participants and the intruder, respectively. Appendices C and D do the same for our C level formalization.

2   Overview of the Kerberos 5 Protocol

2.1   Intuitive Description

A standard Kerberos 5 run provides a client C with convenient means to repeatedly authenticate herself to an application server S. To this end, she obtains a *service ticket* from a third party known as a *Ticket Granting Server* or TGS. For added flexibility, authentication to TGS is implemented by presenting a *ticket granting ticket* to a fourth party, the *Kerberos Authentication Server* or KAS.

Therefore, the core of the protocol consists of a succession of three phases outlined in Fig. 1 (the color conventions and the various fields will be explained shortly). We will now describe them in succession:

- In the first phase, C sends a request KRB_AS_REQ to a KAS K for a ticket-granting ticket TGT, for use with a particular TGS T. K replies with a message KRB_AS_REP consisting of the ticket TGT and an encrypted component containing a fresh *authentication key* $AKey$ to be shared between C and T. TGT is encrypted using the secret key k_T of T; the accompanying message is encrypted under C's secret key k_C.
- In the second phase, C forwards TGT, along with an *authenticator* encrypted under $AKey$, to the TGS T (message KRB_TGS_REQ). T responds in KRB_TGS_REP by sending a service ticket ST encrypted under the secret key k_S of the application server S, and a component containing a *service key* $SKey$ to be shared between C and S, encrypted under $AKey$.
- In the third phase, C forwards ST and a new authenticator encrypted with $SKey$, in message KRB_AP_REQ to S. If all credentials are valid, this application server will authenticate C and provide the service. The acknowledgment message KRB_AP_REP is optional.

A single ticket-granting ticket can be used to obtain several service tickets, possibly for several application servers, while it is valid. Similarly, one service

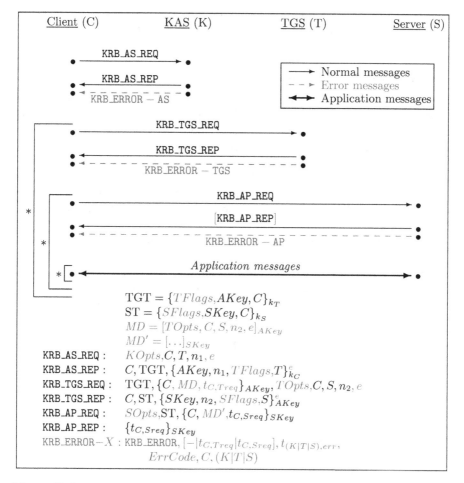

Fig. 1. Kerberos 5 Messages in the A level and C level Formalizations of Kerberos 5

ticket can be used to repeatedly request service from S before it expires. In both cases, a fresh authenticator is required for each use of the ticket.

The protocol run described above is very similar to that of Kerberos 4. The primary difference between the two versions (aside from some options available in version 5 and not in version 4) is the structure of the KRB_AS_REP and KRB_TGS_REP messages. In version 4 the ticket-granting ticket is sent by the KAS as part of the message encrypted under the client's secret key k_C, and the service ticket sent by the TGS is likewise encrypted under the shared key$AKey$. In version 5, we see that the ticket-granting ticket and the service ticket are sent without further encryption; this enables the cut and paste anomalies which we describe below.

Note that the Kerberos 5 protocol has changed since the initial specification [1]. Here we use version 10 [3] of the revisions to [1]; changes include the addition of anonymous tickets, although these may or may not be present in future revisions of the protocol [17]. The description of the protocol is an IETF Internet Draft, each version of which has a six month lifetime. The current version is [18].

2.2   A and C Level Formalizations

The fragment of Kerberos 5 we adopt for our A level specification consists of the minimum machinery necessary to implement the above presentation. It is summarized in black ink in Fig. 1 (please ignore the parts in gray) and fully formalized in [5], with salient features reported in App. A.

We adopt standard conventions and use the comma "," to denote concatenation of fields, and expressions of the form $\{m\}_k$ for the result of encrypting the message m with the key k. We do not distinguish encryption algorithms at this level of detail. We usually write n, possibly subscripted, for nonces, and t, similarly decorated, for timestamps.

Our C level specification extends the A level by adding additional fields and messages, displayed in gray) in Fig. 1. These additions include error messages, option fields (used to by the client in her requests), flag fields (used by servers to describe the options granted), keyed checksums, and explicit consideration of encryption types. The C level formalization is explored in App. C.

3   Protocol Analysis in MSR

MSR originated as a simple logic-oriented language aimed at investigating the decidability of protocol analysis under a variety of assumptions [12, 15]. It evolved into a precise, powerful, flexible, and still relatively simple framework for the specification of complex cryptographic protocols, possibly structured as a collection of coordinated subprotocols [14]. We will introduce the syntax and operations of MSR as we go along.

A central concept in MSR is that of a *fact*—protocols are expressed in MSR as rules which take multisets of these objects, whose precise definition we omit for the moment, and rewrite them as different multisets. MSR facts are a formal representation of network messages, stored information, and the internal states of protocol participants. Protocol runs are represented as sequences of multisets of facts, each obtained from the previous one by applying one of the rules in the formalization of the protocol.

3.1   Protocol Signature

A protocol specification in MSR requires type declarations classifying the terms that might appear in the protocol. We include the types KAS, TGS, and server for authentication, ticket-grating, and applications servers, respectively; these interact with clients, the fourth type of protocol participant. Each of these is subtype of a generic principal type, and the names of each may be used in network messages. Thus principal <: msg and KAS <: principal, *etc.*

Other types we use include nonces, timestamps, and keys. We use some auxiliary types to allow shared keys to be included in messages while prohibiting long-term database keys from being sent over the network. For example, given C : client and T : TGS, the shared key type shK $C\,T$ is a subtype of msg while the database key type dbK C is not.

Our C level formalization uses an expanded signature which includes options (subtypes of Opt), which a client uses to modify the default request to a server, and flags (subtypes of Flag), which describe the options actually granted by a server. The C level also adds encryption types, which allow a client to specify the encryption method(s) she would like to use; in this formalization, the encryption type is an additional parameter to the different types of keys.

Syntactically, A level non-atomic messages are either the concatenation m_1, m_2 of two other messages or the result of (symmetrically) encrypting another message m_1 with a key k; we denote the resulting message by $\{m_1\}_k$. As noted above, the C level formalization includes message digests (cryptographic hashes). The digest and encryption of m_1 using k are both parameterized by an encryption type e and denoted by $[m_1]_k^e$ and $\{m_1\}_k^e$, respectively; here k and e must be compatible, e.g., k : shK$^e\,C\,T$ or k : dbK$^e\,C$. We will keep the encryption type implicit unless we are specifically discussing it. In our present formalizations, we only use shared keys and not database keys to construct message digests.

3.2   State and Roles

Intuitively, MSR represents the state of execution of a protocol as a multiset S of ground first-order formulas (the 'facts' mentioned earlier). Some predicates are universal: in particular, $N(m)$ indicates that message m is transiting through the network. Other predicates are protocol-dependent and are classified as memory or role state predicates. *Memory predicates* are used to store information across several runs of a protocol, to pass data to subprotocols, and to invoke external modules. The intruder I stores intercepted information m in the predicate $I(m)$. We will encounter other memory predicates as we go along. *Role state predicates*, of the form $L(\ldots)$, allow sequentializing the actions of a principal.

Principals cause local transformations to this global state S by non-deterministically executing *multiset rewriting rules* of the form $r = lhs \longrightarrow rhs$, where lhs is a finite multiset of facts and some number of constraints (which are not facts). These constraints are used by principals to check system clocks or determine the validity of requests via external processes not explicitly modelled here. Whenever the facts in lhs are contained in S and the constraints are all satisfied, rule r can replace these facts with those from rhs. The actual definition is slightly more general in the sense that rules are generally parametric and rhs may specify the generation of nonces or other data before rewriting the state.

The rules comprising a protocol or a subprotocol are collected in a *role* parameterized by the principal executing it. Rules in a role are threaded through using role state predicates declared inside the role.

3.3   Rank and Corank Functions

Inspired by Schneider's analysis of the amended Needham-Schroeder protocol [16], we defined rank and corank functions on facts and multisets of facts. We used rank to authenticate the origin of a message whose construction involved encryption or message digestion, and we used corank to prove the confidentiality of data. Here we give a high-level overview of these classes of functions; the complete inductive definition of rank and corank for MSR terms is given in [5].

Given a key k and message m_0, the k-rank relative to m_0 captures the maximum number of nested encryptions (or keyed message digestions in the C level formalization) of the message m_0 using the key k which appear in a term; the innermost encryption/digestion must be exactly $\{m_0\}_k$ or $[m_0]_k$, i.e., m_0 encrypted/digested using k. We then define the rank of a fact $P(t_1, \ldots, t_j)$ to be the maximum value of the rank of the t_i; intuitively, the number of times m_0 is encrypted by k to obtain this fact can be obtained by looking at the arguments to the predicate P. The rank of a multiset of finitely many distinct facts is the maximum rank of a fact in the multiset.

We authenticated the origin of $\{m_0\}_k$ or $[m_0]_k$ by showing that a specified protocol participant may create a fact F of k-rank 1 relative to m_0 but that no other participants, including the intruder, can rewrite a multiset M of facts so that the resulting multiset M' has greater k-rank relative to m_0 than M did. If no facts at the beginning of the trace had positive k-rank, then the appearance of a fact of positive k-rank in some multiset of the trace implies that the protocol participant created F at some point in the trace.

For a set E of keys and atomic message m_0, the E-corank of a term relative to m_0 is the minimum number of decryptions using keys from E needed to extract the message m_0 from the term. We then define the corank of a fact $P(t_1, \ldots, t_j)$ to be the minimum corank of an argument t_i that may be placed back on the network; this allows, e.g., protocol participants to store keys in memory without using facts whose corank equals 0. Corank is defined for a multiset of facts as the minimum corank of a fact appearing in the multiset.

Note that the fact $I(m_0)$ that corresponds to the intruder's knowledge of m_0 has E-corank equal to 0 relative to m_0 for every set E of keys. We thus used corank to prove the confidentiality of some m_0 by showing that for some set E of keys, no facts of E-corank 0 relative to m_0 ever appear in a protocol trace.

4   Properties of Kerberos 5

4.1   Overview

We have established *confidentiality* and *data origin authentication* properties for Kerberos 5. The latter are particularly important because Kerberos claims to provide authentication; the former are used in proving authentication and are also important because some of the session keys which we show to be confidential may be used for additional (post-protocol run) communication between protocol participants.

These types of properties hold in both the Ticket-Granting and Client/Server exchanges. As these sub-protocols have similar structure, it is unsurprising that the properties are expressed and proved in very similar ways. Table 1 shows the parallel relationships between the properties that we have established—each exchange has a corresponding confidentiality property and a corresponding authentication property. The confidentiality properties give conditions under which an intruder never learns certain information, while the authentication properties state conditions under which, if certain messages appear on the network, then these messages originated with specific principals. These properties are described in more detail for the Ticket-Granting Exchange in Sec. 4.2 and for the Client/Server Exchange in Sec. 4.3. Throughout this work, we assumed the presence of a Dolev-Yao intruder. Additionally, we did not intentionally leak keys to this intruder as was done in [7–9].

Table 1. Properties established for Kerberos 5

	Confidentiality	Authentication
T-G Exchange	Property 1	Property 2
C/S Exchange	Property 3	Property 4

Here we give intuitive statements of these properties; we state them precisely—in terms of MSR facts and rules—in [5]. Those more formal statements and their proofs are related in much the same way that our formalizations themselves are related—removing some information from the C level version gives the more abstract A level version. As a result, we are optimistic that the properties shown for the Client/Server Exchange may be extended to our C level formalization.

4.2   Properties of the Ticket-Granting Exchange

As the Ticket-Granting Exchange is closer to the beginning of the protocol run, these properties are slightly simpler than for the Client/Server Exchange below. We have proved these properties for both the A and C level formalizations.

Confidentiality of $AKey$. The first property that we have established for Kerberos 5 is the confidentiality of the session key generated by the Authentication Server, *i.e.*, that the intruder does not learn this key.

Property 1. If the intruder does not know the long term secret keys (k_C and k_T) used to encrypt the session key $AKey$ generated by the authentication server K for use by C and T, then the intruder cannot learn $AKey$.

Authenticity of the Ticket-Granting Ticket and Authenticator. The second property of Kerberos 5 is data origin authentication of the ticket and authenticator used in the client's request to the ticket granting server.

Property 2. If the intruder does not know the long term key used to encrypt a ticket-granting ticket TGT and this ticket didn't initially exist, then if the TGS processes a request, ostensibly from a client C, containing the ticket-granting ticket TGT and the session key $AKey$, then some Authentication Server created the session key $AKey$ for C to use with the TGS and also generated TGT. Furthermore, if the intruder does not know the long term key that the authentication server used to send $AKey$ to the client, then the authenticator was created by this particular client.

4.3   Properties of the Client/Server Exchange

We now move to properties of the Client/Server Exchange; as this exchange parallels the Ticket Granting Exchange, the properties parallel the properties we have proved for that exchange. These properties build on those stated above and may be viewed as the main positive results that we have obtained. We have only proved these properties for our A level formalization, although we expect these to hold for the C level formalization as well.

Confidentiality of *SKey*. The first property for the Client/Server Exchange is that the session key shared by the client and server is not know to the intruder.

Property 3. If the intruder knows neither the long term secret key used by a TGS to encrypt the service ticket ST containing a new session key $SKey$ for a client to use with a server nor the session key used by the client to request the service ticket, then the intruder cannot learn $SKey$.

Authenticity of the Service Ticket and Authenticator. The second property in this exchange is the data origin authentication of the ticket and authenticator included in the client's request to the server.

Property 4. If the intruder does not know the long term key used to encrypt a service ticket ST and this ticket did not initially exist, then if a server S processes a request, ostensibly from a client C, containing the service ticket ST and the session key $SKey$, then some Ticket Granting Server generated the session key $SKey$ for C to use with S and also created ST. Furthermore, if the intruder never learns the session key which the Ticket Granting Server used to encrypt $SKey$ when replying to the client's request for a service ticket, then this client created the authenticator.

5   Anomalies

5.1   Overview of Anomalies

In our analysis of Kerberos 5, we found four anomalies that we review here. Three of these were described in [4]; we give a more detailed description of the fourth in Sect. 5.2. While this behavior deviates from the intended protocol behavior, these anomalies do not compromise the security of the protocol. As noted by Jeffrey [19], some implementations of Kerberos 5 do not sufficiently guard against replays, allowing an intruder to force repeated generation of fresh credentials by replaying requests from a client. This concern is separate from the anomalies noted here, and we leave further discussion of it to the more detailed report [5] of our work.

The first anomaly can be realized in our A level formalization, while the remaining anomalies require the detail of our C level formalization. The ticket option anomaly further requires the detection of replays; this is not explicitly included in the C level, although generic error detection is.

In the 'ticket anomaly' an intruder I intercepts the KRB_AS_REP message from some KAS K and replaces the ticket-granting ticket with an arbitrary bit string. I then intercepts subsequent KRB_TGS_REQ messages from the client and restores the original ticket, allowing the protocol to proceed normally. This behavior is undetectable by the client because she expects to be unable to read the encrypted ticket. However, she has false beliefs about the data in her possession, namely that she holds a valid ticket when in fact she does not. While the origin of the ticket and authenticator may be authenticated, unlike in Kerberos 4 [7] we cannot prove that the entirety of a valid KRB_TGS_REQ message originated with the client.

In the 'anonymous ticket switch anomaly' a client requests two service tickets, one anonymous and one non-anonymous, from a TGS T for use with a server S. An intruder I may intercept the two KRB_TGS_REP messages and switch the tickets, forwarding the resulting messages to the client. Exactly one of the tickets the client receives contains her identity (the other is anonymous), but the client is mistaken in belief about which of the tickets this is. The client then sends two KRB_AP_REQ messages to S, one with and one without her name (but matched to the wrong ticket) and not requesting mutual authentication in either one. The intruder intercepts both of these messages and replaces the authenticator without the client's name with the other authenticator, forwarding the resulting messages to S. S may read both tickets, but only the key from the non-anonymous ticket opens the accompanying authenticator. S then accepts the request with the non-anonymous ticket and rejects the request with the anonymous ticket, returning an error message to the client. I may tamper with this message so that it contains the client's name; she then correctly believes that exactly one of her requests was accepted, but incorrectly believes that S has not seen her name.

The 'ticket replay anomaly,' described in more detail below, has effects similar to the anonymous ticket switch anomaly. Again the intruder intercepts an KRB_AP_REQ messages to a server S, but now she simply replays it to produce a replay error from the server; she may then tamper with this error message at will, essentially using the server to unpack the timestamp from the request to make the new error message appear authentic. If this is done in conjunction with intercepting a second KRB_AP_REQ message from the client to S, the client might believe (as in the anonymous ticket switch anomaly) that S has accepted exactly one of her requests but have an incorrect belief about which one.

These first three anomalies all involve separating tickets from the rest of the message containing them. This was not possible in Kerberos 4, where the tickets were included with other data encrypted by a server for the client. This change in message structure between the two versions of the protocol allows these anomalies but does not affect the basic authentication provided by Kerberos.

In the 'encryption type anomaly' we assume that a client C has different long-term keys for use with different encryption methods, that one of these has been learned by the intruder I, and that C knows this key has been compromised. When sending a KRB_AS_REQ message to some KAS K, C would then request that the response be encrypted using an encryption method other than the one corresponding to the lost key. As this message is unencrypted, I may change the encryption type field to specify the encryption method corresponding to the lost key. K's response will then be encrypted using the lost key and thus be readable by I, who may then impersonate C. While I could do this anyway knowing C's long-term key, we see that such impersonation is possible even if C takes steps to avoid using the lost long-term key.

5.2   Ticket Replay Anomaly

We now examine the ticket replay anomaly in detail; similar discussions of the other replays we found are given in the detailed report of our work [5].

Figure 2 updates Fig. 1 to show the message flow in this anomaly. The client C initiates and completes the Authentication Service Exchange with a KAS K, obtaining a ticket-granting ticket TGT for the TGS T. She then uses this ticket to make two requests for service tickets for a single server S, requesting different options for these two service tickets.

T receives these two requests and grants two different service tickets ST and ST' with associated session keys $SKey$ and $SKey'$; we assume that the options actually granted by the TGS are different for these two tickets. Recall that the TGS sends a copy of the granted options along with the new session key (both encrypted under the session key shared by the client and the TGS), so the client associates the different granted options with these different keys. The client then sends two requests to the server, one with ST and an authenticator encrypted using $SKey$ and containing a timestamp t and other with ST', $SKey'$ and t', respectively. We assume that in both requests, the client does not request mutual authentication from the server, so she expects a response only in case of an error.

The intruder I intercepts these requests. She duplicates the request containing ST, $SKey$, and t and forwards these to the server, who accepts the first and rejects the second because of the replayed authenticator. This prompts an error message, containing t, from the server, which the intruder may intercept, modify, and send to the client. The intruder does not send the second request, containing ST', $SKey'$, and t', to the server.

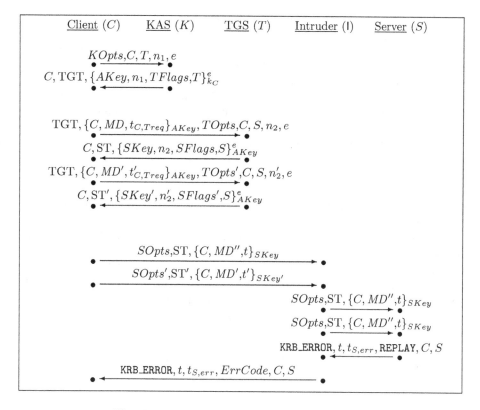

Fig. 2. Message flow in the ticket replay anomaly

As a result, the client receives an error message containing the timestamp t but no response to her request containing ST', $SKey'$, and t'. She might assume that her first request was rejected while her second was accepted, while the reverse is actually true. This is potentially worrisome because the options on the tickets are different; in the case of anonymous tickets, the client might erroneously assume that her identity has not been seen by the server (if the error is tied to a non-anonymous ticket).

It is unclear whether this anomaly is of practical concern. It does highlight the interactions between the ticket options and other traces; for the anonymous ticket option, these may be particularly undesirable.

Note that in our C level formalization, application servers do not explicitly save authenticators and check for replayed authenticators. Thus the trace in Fig. 2, which includes an error message for a replayed authenticator, cannot be realized in this formalization. However, the MSR rule changes needed to realize this anomaly in the C level formalization are minor; in particular, they do not require any change to the C level protocol signature.

6   Conclusions and Future Work

In this paper, we have summarized the results of a project specifying and analyzing the Kerberos 5 suite [3]; our initial report on this work was given in [4], and a detailed discussion is contained in [5]. We have concentrated on a subset of this protocol that takes into account encryption types, checksums, flags and options, error messages, and a few timestamps on top of the core message exchange. We have formally shown that, at this level of detail, Kerberos 5 complies with the confidentiality and data origin authentication requirements. We have also observed anomalous behaviors that deviate from the expected script of the protocol, but do not appear to have the potential of causing harm to the principals involved. In order to produce these results, we paired the MSR security protocol specification language [13, 14] with an inductive proof method inspired by the work of Schneider [16].

This work may be extended in two directions. First, our formalizations of the Kerberos 5 may be refined by adding more options (in particular renewable or postdatable tickets), more timestamps and temporal checks, and the seldom analyzed optional subprotocols that comprise the suite (in particular the KRB_SAFE and KRB_PRIV exchanges and the mechanisms for distributing and updating long-term keys). Second, we may refine the tools used in the analysis to cope with the increasing complexity and the necessity to assess requirements that go beyond confidentiality and authentication. A first step is the ongoing implementation of an MSR environment that will help manage complex specifications and assist with their development. Another part of this is the further development of our verification methods in order to reuse previously proved results as guidelines for new proofs in more refined specifications of Kerberos 5. We are also looking at automation to help for this purpose.

We have received encouraging feedback from the IETF Kerberos Working Group [17, 20].

Acknowledgments

We are grateful to Alan Jeffrey, John Mitchell, Clifford Neuman, and Ken Raeburn for a number of helpful comments on our earlier work.

References

1. Kohl, J., Neuman, C.: The Kerberos Network Authentication Service (V5) (1993) Network Working Group Request for Comments: 1510.
2. Neuman, B.C., Ts'o, T.: Kerberos: An Authentication Service for Computer Networks. IEEE Communications **32** (1994) 33–38
3. Neuman, C., Kohl, J., Ts'o, T., Raeburn, K., Yu, T.: The Kerberos Network Authentication Service (V5) (2001) Internet draft, expires 20 May 2002.

4. Butler, F., Cervesato, I., Jaggard, A.D., Scedrov, A.: A Formal Analysis of Some Properties of Kerberos 5 Using MSR. In: Proceedings of the 15th Computer Security Foundations Workshop, IEEE Computer Society (2002) 175–190

5. Butler, F., Cervesato, I., Jaggard, A.D., Scedrov, A.: A formal analysis of some properties of kerberos 5 using *MSR*. Technical Report CIS-MS-04-04, University of Pennsylvania, Department of Computer and Information Science (2004) 59 pages. Available from `ftp://ftp.cis.upenn.edu/pub/papers/scedrov/ms-cis-04-04.[pdf|ps]`.

6. Bella, G., Riccobene, E.: Formal Analysis of the Kerberos Authentication System. J. Universal Comp. Sci. **3** (1997) 1337–1381

7. Bella, G.: Inductive Verification of Cryptographic Protocols. PhD thesis, University of Cambridge (2000)

8. Bella, G., Paulson, L.C.: Using Isabelle to Prove Properties of the Kerberos Authentication System. In Orman, H., Meadows, C., eds.: Proc. of DIMACS'97, Workshop on Design and Formal Verification of Security Protocols (CD-ROM). (1997)

9. Bella, G., Paulson, L.C.: Kerberos Version IV: Inductive Analysis of the Secrecy Goals. In: Proc. of ESORICS '98, Fifth European Symposium on Research in Computer Science. Number 1485 in Lecture Notes in Computer Science, Springer-Verlag (1998) 361–375

10. Bella, G., Paulson, L.C.: Mechanising BAN Kerberos by the Inductive Method. In: Proc. of CAV98 – Tenth International Conference on Computer Aided Verification. (1998)

11. Mitchell, J.C., Mitchell, M., Stern, U.: Automated Analysis of Cryptographic Protocols Using Murφ. In: Proc. of the IEEE Symposium on Security and Privacy, IEEE Computer Society Press (1997) 141–153

12. Cervesato, I., Durgin, N.A., Lincoln, P., Mitchell, J., Scedrov, A.: A Meta-notation for Protocol Analysis. In: Proc. of the Twelfth IEEE Computer Security Foundations Workshop. (1999) 55–69

13. Cervesato, I.: Typed Multiset Rewriting Specifications of Security Protocols. In: Proc. of the First Irish Conference on the Mathematical Foundations of Computer Science and Information Technology–MFCSIT'00, Elsevier ENTCS 40 (2000)

14. Cervesato, I.: Typed MSR: Syntax and Examples. In: Proc. of the First International Workshop on Mathematical Methods, Models and Architectures for Computer Network Security — MMM'01. Springer-Verlag (2001) St. Petersburg, Russia, 21–23 May 2001.

15. Durgin, N.A., Lincoln, P.D., Mitchell, J.C., Scedrov, A.: Multiset Rewriting and the Complexity of Bounded Security Protocols. Manuscript, 63 pages. (2002)

16. Schneider, S.: Verifying Authentication Protocols in CSP. IEEE Transactions on Software Engineering **24** (1998) 741–758

17. Neuman, C.: (2002) Personal communication.

18. Neuman, C., Yu, T., Hartman, S., Raeburn, K.: The Kerberos Network Authentication Service (V5) (2004) Internet draft, expires 15 August 2004. `http://www.ietf.org/internet-drafts/draft-ietf-krb-wg-kerberos-clarifications-05.txt`.

19. Jeffrey, A.: (2002) Personal communication.

20. Raeburn, K.: (2002) Personal communication.

A   Abstract Level Protocol Formalization

We now give a more detailed description of the A level formalization of Kerberos 5. Some of the MSR roles and rules comprising this formalization are shown in the black type in Figs. 3—6; as noted below, we omit some of the roles from the full A level formalization given in [5]. We believe that the A level formalization contains the minimum amount of detail needed to capture the Kerberos 5 protocol. Although our proofs related to this formalization do not rely on nonces, omitting them would remove the connection between the KRB_AS_REQ and KRB_AS_REP messages.

A.1   Authentication Service Exchange

Recall that the Authentication Service Exchange allows a client C to obtain from a KAS K credentials to be used in the Ticket Granting Exchange with a TGS T. C's actions in this exchange are formalized in Fig. 3, K's in Fig. 4. Note that K's rules fill in the gaps between C's rules; for the later exchanges of the protocol, we will omit the various server rules because they are essentially recoverable from the client rules.

$$
\begin{array}{l}
\forall C{:}\text{client} \\[4pt]
\exists L : \text{client} \times \text{KOpt} \times \text{TGS} \times \text{nonce} \times \text{etype}. \\[6pt]
\begin{array}{llll}
\forall T : \text{TGS} & & & \exists n_1 : \text{nonce} \\
\forall K : \text{KAS} & & \overset{\alpha\delta_{1.1}}{\longrightarrow} & N(KOpts,C,T,n_1,e) \\
\forall KOpts : \text{KOpt}. & & & L(C,KOpts,T,n_1,e) \\
\forall e : \text{etype} & & &
\end{array} \\[14pt]
\begin{array}{llll}
\forall \ldots & & & \\
\forall k_C : \text{dbK } C & N(C,X,\{AKey, & & \\
\forall AKey : \text{shK } C\,T. & \quad n_1, TFlags,T\}_{k_C}) & \overset{\alpha\delta_{1.2}}{\longrightarrow} & Auth_C(X,TFlags, \\
\forall X : \text{msg} & L(C,KOpts,T,n_1,e) & & \quad T,AKey) \\
\forall n_1 : \text{nonce} & & & \\
\forall TFlags : \text{TFlag} & & &
\end{array} \\[14pt]
\begin{array}{llll}
\forall \ldots & N(\text{KRB\_ERROR}, t_{K,err}, & & ASError_C(\\
\forall ErrorCode : \text{msg}. & \quad ErrorCode,C,K) & \overset{\delta_{1.2'}}{\longrightarrow} & \quad \text{KRB\_ERROR}, t_{K,err}, \\
\forall t_{K,err} : \text{time} & L(C,KOpts,T,n_1,e) & & \quad ErrorCode,K)
\end{array}
\end{array}
$$

Fig. 3. The client's role in the Authentication Service Exchange

C asks K for credentials for the server T using rule $\alpha_{1.1}$, sending a KRB_AS_REQ message with her name C, the name T of the TGS for which she wishes to obtain credentials, and a fresh nonce n_1, and storing these in the role state predicate L. Rule $\alpha_{1.2}$ allows C to process the KRB_AS_REP message which K sends in response to her initial request. This message is expected to contain C's name, an opaque ticket X to be passed on to T and, encrypted under C's long-term key k_C, a session key $AKey$ for use with T, the nonce n_1 from the original request, and the name T of the TGS. If the message is of this form and if C, T, and n_1, match the data from the original request (stored in L), C removes the KRB_AS_REP message from the network, deletes the role state predicate L, and stores the relevant data in the persistent memory predicate $Auth_C$. In the abstract formalization, C does not process any other (*i.e.*, error) messages which K may return as defined in [3].

$$
\begin{pmatrix}
\forall C : \text{client} & . & & & & \forall K : \text{KAS} \\
\forall T : \text{TGS} & . & & & & \\
\forall n_1 : \text{nonce} & . \; \mathsf{N}(KOpts,C,T,n_1,e) & & & \exists AKey : \text{shK } C\,T & \\
\forall k_C : \text{dbK } C & . \; Valid(KOpts,C, & & \alpha\delta_{2.1} & \mathsf{N}(C,\{TFlags, & \\
\forall k_T : \text{dbK } T & . \quad T,n_1,e) & & \longrightarrow & AKey,C\}_{k_T}, & \\
\forall AKey : \text{shK } C\,T . \; SetAuthFlags(KOpts, & & & \{AKey,n_1, & \\
\forall KOpts : \text{KOpt} & . \quad TFlags) & & & TFlags,T\}_{k_C}) & \\
\forall e : \text{etype} & . & & & & \\
\forall TFlags : \text{TFlag} & . & & & & \\
\\
\forall \ldots & \quad \mathsf{N}(KOpts,C,T,n_1,e) & & & & \\
\forall ErrorCode : \text{msg}. & \; Invalid(KOpts,C, & & \delta_{2.1'} & \mathsf{N}(\text{KRB\_ERROR}, t_{K,err}, & \\
\forall t_{K,err} : \text{time} & \quad T,n_1,e) & & \longrightarrow & ErrorCode,C,K) & \\
 & \; Clock_K(t_{K,err}) & & & &
\end{pmatrix}
$$

Fig. 4. The authentication server's role in the Authentication Service Exchange

If there is a KRB_AS_REQ message from C on the network, and if it is valid (as determined by the external process $Valid$), rule $\alpha_{2.1}$ allows K to generate a fresh session key $AKey$ for use between C and T and to send this key in a KRB_AS_REP message to C. This message consists of C's name, the ticket for T, and, encrypted under k_C, the key $AKey$, the nonce n_1 from C's request, and the name T of the TGS. The ticket for T is encrypted with T's long-term key k_T and contains $AKey$ and the name C of the client.

A.2   The Ticket-Granting Exchange

The third and fourth messages shown in Fig. 1 comprise the Ticket-Granting Exchange. Here the client C presents credentials previously obtained from an authentication server (via the Authentication Service Exchange) to a TGS T in order to obtain a service ticket for an application server S.

The client's actions in this exchange are formalized in Fig. 5. If, as indicated by the memory predicate $Auth_C(X,T,AKey)$, the client C has completed the authentication service exchange to get credentials for the TGS T, rule $\alpha_{3.1}$ allows her to initiate an exchange with T to obtain credentials for the application server S. In doing so, she chooses a new nonce n_2 and sends a KRB_TGS_REQ message to T consisting of the previously obtained ticket X, an authenticator (C encrypted under the session key $AKey$), her name C, the name S of the server for which

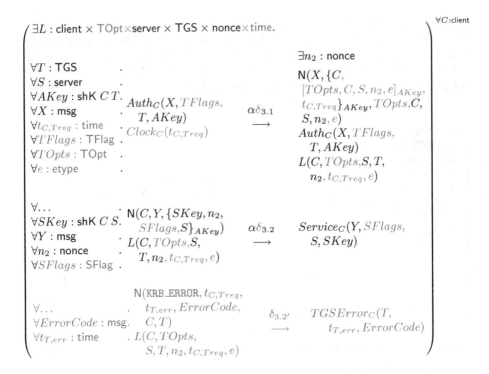

Fig. 5. The client's role in the Ticket-Granting Exchange

C wishes to obtain credentials, and the new nonce n_2. C stores the information about this request in the role state predicate L, and retains the memory predicate $Auth_C$ for use in future exchanges with T.

The client's second rule, $\alpha_{3.2}$, allows her to read a KRB_TGS_REP message that matches her request to T. This message consists of C's name, an opaque ticket Y to be passed to the application server, and, encrypted under the session key $AKey$, a session key $SKey$ for use by C and the application server, the nonce n_2, and the application server's name S. C, S, and n_2 must match the stored information about the original request to T in order for C to process the KRB_TGS_REP message. If C does process the message using $\alpha_{3.2}$, she stores the ticket Y, server name S, and session key $SKey$ in the memory predicate $Service_C$.

Because of its close correspondence to the rules in Fig. 5, we omit TGS role here. If a KRB_TGS_REQ message, such as that in the right-hand side of rule $\alpha_{3.1}$, appears on the network, the TGS rule allows the TGS T to read it from the network and process it; this includes a validity check that constrains the firing of the rule. In firing the rule, T produces a fresh session key for the client to share with the server named in the KRB_TGS_REQ message and places a KRB_TGS_REP message (like that in the left-hand side of rule $\alpha_{3.2}$) onto the network.

A.3   The Client/Server Exchange

The fifth and sixth messages in Fig. 1 form the Client/Server Exchange. Here the client C presents credentials, previously obtained from a TGS, to the application server S. In the abstract level formalization we assume that mutual authentication is requested by C; thus the sixth message (of type KRB_AP_REP) is required for the protocol to finish.

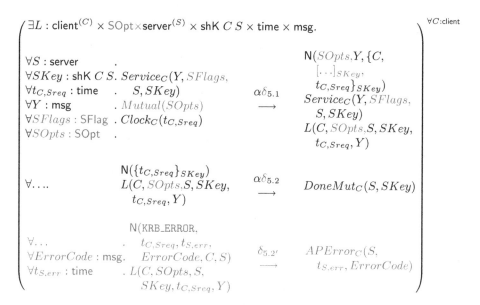

Fig. 6. The client's role in the Client/Server Exchange with mutual authentication

Figure 6 shows the role of the client C in the exchange. If she has previously obtained credentials (a ticket Y and session key $SKey$, stored in the memory predicate $Service_C$) for use with S she may fire rule $\alpha_{5.1}$. This places a KRB_AP_REQ message containing the ticket and an authenticator (obtained by encrypting C and the current time $t_{C,Sreq}$ on C's system, given by the external process $Clock_C$, under the session key $SKey$) on the network and stores the relevant information about this request in the role state predicate L. C's second rule, $\alpha_{5.2}$, may be fired when the network contains a KRB_AP_REP message consisting of $t_{C,Sreq}$ encrypted under $SKey$. This rule reads the message from the network and stores the server name S and the session key $SKey$ in the $DoneMut_C$ predicate. Although not modelled in the abstract level formalization, this information is intended to be used in additional communications with S.

We omit the formal statement of the server's MSR rule, which is essentially reconstructible from the client's rules. If a KRB_AP_REQ message for a server S appears on the network, S may fire a rule that reads it off of the network and replies with a KRB_AP_REP message. Paralleling the TGS rule, this is constrained by a validity check on the KRB_AP_REQ message. S stores the data from the request in a memory predicate; while we do not make use of this predicate here, the session key now known to both S and the client may be used for future communication.

B   A Level Intruder Formalization

In this section, we present some of the rules specifying the Dolev-Yao intruder model for Kerberos 5; the full set of intruder rules is given in [5]. We ask the reader to ignore for the moment the grayed-out text as it describes additions needed for the more detailed (C level) intruder. We will come back to them in App. D.

We divide the actions available to the intruder into three categories:

- the fairly standard operations of interception/transmission of a message over the network, decomposition/composition of a pair, and decryption/encryption of a message given a known key (App. B.1);
- the often overlooked action of generating new data (App. B.2);
- and the use of accessible data (App. B.3).

B.1   Network, Pairing and Encryption Rules

We have the following rules describing how the Dolev-Yao intruder can intercept/transmit messages, decompose/compose pairs, and decrypt/encrypt messages under the various types of known keys. We have also some administrative rules that permit the duplication and deletion of deleted data.

The intruder is allowed to read messages from the network (removing them from the network in the process) and put messages that she knows onto the network. She may also break compound messages (*e.g.*, m_1, m_2) into their constituent parts and combine separate messages into a single message via concatenation.

The following two rules are samples of the intruder rules; these model decryption (SDC$'$) and encryption (SEC$'$) with a shared key. The type *ts* is one of the auxiliary types mentioned in Sect. 3 and includes both TGS and server.

$$\left(\begin{matrix} \forall C : \text{client} & . \\ \forall A : ts & \\ \forall e : \text{etype} & \cdot \frac{\mathsf{I}(\{m\}_k^e)}{\mathsf{I}(k)} \xrightarrow{\text{SDC}'} \mathsf{I}(m) \\ \forall k : \text{shK}^e\, C\, A. & \\ \forall m : \text{msg} & . \end{matrix}\right)^{\mathsf{I}} \qquad \left(\begin{matrix} \forall C : \text{client} & . \\ \forall A : ts & \\ \forall e : \text{etype} & \cdot \frac{\mathsf{I}(m)}{\mathsf{I}(k)} \xrightarrow{\text{SEC}'} \mathsf{I}(\{m\}_k^e) \\ \forall k : \text{shK}^e\, C\, A. & \\ \forall m : \text{msg} & . \end{matrix}\right)^{\mathsf{I}}$$

Similar rules allow the intruder to decrypt and encrypt using a long-term key that she knows.

Finally, the intruder is allowed to duplicate or delete any information that she knows; the ability to delete data might be dropped from the intruder specification without adverse effects.

B.2   Data Generation Rules

In general, the intruder should be able to generate everything an honest principal can generate—*i.e.*, nonces and session keys—and no more. In the case of Kerberos, we must admit an exception to this rule: because principals forward uninterpreted data, we must allow the intruder to create garbage, modelled as objects of the generic type msg.

We omit the intruder rules for generating nonces and session keys, but include the following rule for generating generic messages because this merits some discussion.

$$\left(\cdot \xrightarrow{\text{MG}} \exists m : \text{msg } \mathsf{I}(m) \right)^{\mathsf{I}}$$

Rule MG does not allow I to generate the long-term key of a principal because dbK A is never a subtype of msg. Note also that although the intruder may generate fresh messages, she may not type these as anything other than msg. The intruder is not allowed to generate any other kind of data, not principal names of any kind (the introduction of new agents happens out-of-band), not long-term keys (they are distributed out-of-band), and not timestamps (they are generated by an external clock, not by any principal). Allowing the intruder to generate data of these forms is incorrect since it would open the doors to countless false attacks.

B.3   Data Access Rules

The intruder is entitled to look up the same data as any other principal. She therefore has access to the names of all entities of type principal, to her keys (long-term and session), and to timestamps. Note that in this respect timestamps differ from nonces; we do not allow an intruder to guess the latter. We note that the ability to guess timestamps may give unreasonable strength to the intruder.

No other piece of information is accessible out of thin air by the intruder: unless she has intercepted this information otherwise, she should not be able to guess the nonces generated by other principals, or keys that do not belong to her, or clearly generic messages.

C   C Level Protocol Formalization

Our C level formalization extends the A level formalization by adding additional elements of the full protocol specification. In particular, we now include options in messages sent by a client (allowing her to request particular encryption methods and ANONYMOUS tickets and to specify whether a server should provide mutual authentication); the replies to these messages now include flag fields specifying which options were actually granted. Message digests now appear as specified by the protocol. We have also added error messages, and the authenticator in the KRB_TGS_REQ message now includes a timestamp which may be sent back to the client in an error message. We do not add any temporal checks, however.

The grayed-out portions of Fig. 1 and Figs. 3—6 are the details which are being added to the A level formalization to obtain the C level. When we refer to a

C level rule by name we will now use δ with an appropriate subscript as given in the various figures; this will mean the entire rule depicted in the figure, including the grayed-out portions. While fields specifying encryption type appear in several messages in this level, and should technically appear for every encrypted message that occurs (according to Sect. 3), we adopt the convention that we will omit the etype in this capacity unless we are explicitly discussing it. As for the A level formalization, the complete set of MSR rules is given in [5].

C.1   Authentication Service Exchange

We return to Fig. 3 to see the client's actions in the Authentication Service Exchange, now looking at both the black and the gray type. Rule $\delta_{1.1}$ allows C to send a KRB_AS_REQ message, and extends rule $\alpha_{1.1}$ by adding the options field $KOpts$ and the field e containing the requested encryption type(s) for the response. Rule $\delta_{1.2}$ allows the client to process the response; this now includes the $TFlags$ field indicating which options were granted by the KAS.

Rule $\delta_{1.2'}$ shows C's error processing of a generic error message, formalized by C storing relevant information in the memory predicate $ASError_C$. The $ErrorCode$ describes the reason why the KRB_AS_REQ failed.

The actions of the KAS K are formalized in Fig. 4, including both the black and gray type. Rule $\delta_{2.1}$ is similar to rule $\alpha_{2.1}$, except the validity check performed by K also covers the added message fields $KOpts$ and e. The external process $SetAuthFlags$ is used to determine which of the options requested in $TOpts$ should be approved; those granted are described by the flags $TFlags$.

If C's request is not valid for any reason (as determined by the external process $Invalid$, which we assume to hold iff the $Valid$ check fails), then K reads the current time $t_{K,err}$ from the local clock via the external process $Clock_K$. When rule $\delta_{2.1'}$ is fired, K sends an error message consisting of the time the error occurred ($t_{K,err}$) and the appropriate $ErrorCode$, along with the names C and K.

C.2   The Ticket-Granting Exchange

Considering both colors of type in Fig. 5 gives the C level client rules for the Ticket-Granting Exchange. Rule $\delta_{3.1}$ allows the client to send a KRB_TGS_REQ message and updates rule $\alpha_{3.1}$. This message now includes: the current time $t_{C,Treq}$ on the client's local clock, obtained via the external process $Clock_C$; a message digest, keyed by $AKey$, of the unencrypted portion of the KRB_TGS_REQ; the options field $TOpts$; and the requested encryption type(s) e. $TOpts$ may be used by the client to request an ANONYMOUS ticket-granting ticket.

Rule $\delta_{3.2}$ extends rule $\alpha_{3.2}$ and again allows the client to read from the network a KRB_TGS_REP that corresponds to her previous KRB_TGS_REQ message. The added details here are the flags in the response and the options, timestamp, and encryption type stored in the role state predicate. Note that if ANONYMOUS is one of the set flags in the KRB_TGS_REP message, then instead of the name C the dummy identifier USER will appear in the ticket Y in rule $\delta_{3.2}$.

The C level formalization adds error messages; rule $\delta_{3.2'}$ allows C to process these in the same manner as rule $\delta_{1.2'}$ did in the Authentication Service Exchange. Note that the names C and T in the error message must match those in the role state predicate L.

We again omit the formal MSR rules for a TGS as these are essentially reconstructible from the client rules for the Ticket-Granting Exchange. A TGS T now sets flags in response to the options requested by a client and also verifies the checksum included in the KRB_TGS_REQ message. The other notable difference from the A level TGS behavior is the addition of a rule to send error messages. This is essentially the same as rule $\delta_{2.1'}$ in the Authentication Service Exchange.

C.3   The Client/Server Exchange

Figure 6, including both colors of type, shows the role of the client C in this exchange. Rule $\delta_{5.1}$ is the obvious extension of rule $\alpha_{5.1}$; here we use the constraint $Mutual$ to indicate that the MUTUAL_REQUIRED option is being requested by C. Note that if the ticket Y stored in the $Service_C(-)$ predicate is ANONYMOUS (indicated by the presence of ANONYMOUS in the $SFlags$ field, also stored in $Service_C(-)$), then C will send the generic identifier USER in place of her name in the authenticator sent in rule $\delta_{5.1}$. We denote the message digest here by $[\ldots]_{SKey}$ because [3] specifies that this optional checksum is "application specific."

Rule $\delta_{5.2}$ is virtually identical to rule $\alpha_{5.2}$, the only difference being the presence of $SOpts$ in the role state predicate L. Rule $\delta_{5.2'}$ models C's handling of error messages in exactly the same way as in the previous exchanges with KAS and TGS, with C storing relevant information sent in the error message in the $APError$ memory predicate.

As for the first two exchanges, we omit the rules for processing the client's request. The server's response to a KRB_AP_REQ message requesting mutual authentication is constrained by a check of this option and a verification of the checksum (in addition to the general validity check used in the A level). There is no change in the KRB_AP_REP message, although the server is now allowed to send error messages in case of an invalid request from the client; these are essentially the same as in the other exchanges.

Our C level formalization allows for the client to request no mutual authentication from the application server S. In this case, C views the exchange as finished as soon as she sends her KRB_AP_REQ message, although she may still process error messages from S. Similarly, S does not send a reply to a valid request from C, although he may send error messages if needed.

D   C Level Intruder

The C level intruder rules update those of the A level to reflect the added detail of this formalization. The rules for interception/transmission, decomposition/composition, and decryption/encryption with a known key change only to the extent that we must take encryption types into account in the rules that involve cryptographic primitives. There is no disassembling rule for message digests because (cryptographic) hashing does not permit recovering a message. However, the intruder can construct a message digest as long as she knows the proper key; this is captured by a rule similar to SEC' above.

The updates to the generation rules are limited to allowing the intruder to choose the encryption type of any session key he may generate. None of the new data types introduced at this level of detail can be generated by the intruder (or any other principal). Therefore there are no additional data generation rules beyond those we presented in App. B.2.

Data access rules are subject to similar changes. However, the new data types, encryption types, options and flags, are treated similarly to timestamps: each of them range over a limited number of legal values, each being public knowledge. As for timestamps, we assume that encryption types, options and flags are guessable using rules parallel to TA. Other information that was inaccessible in the A level specification of the intruder remains inaccessible in the C level. Again, we leave the formal statement of the MSR rules to the detailed report [5] of our work.

A Cost Estimation Calculus for Analyzing the Resistance to Denial-of-Service Attack

Daigo Tomioka[1], Shin-ya Nishizaki[2], and Ritsuya Ikeda[2]

[1] NS Solutions Corporation
[2] Department of Computer Science, Tokyo Institute of Technology

Abstract. In order to describe and analyze cryptographic protocols, several researchers have proposed formal frameworks and have studied the security properties of communication protocols, such as authenticity. Abadi and Gordon used Milner's pi-calculus for their research into security properties. The resistance to denial-of-service (DoS) attacks is one of the most important properties of communication protocols. This paper proposes a new calculus for analyzing the resistance to DoS. One crucial point that the analysis considers is the estimation of the resource consumption in each CPU. In the proposed calculus, the time and space costs for each CPU are determined by referring to its type and application data.

1   Introduction

A denial-of-service (DoS) attack is one of the traditional concerns of computer security. It can make the normal services of a computer or network inaccessible to authorized users. A typical example of a DoS attack is a SYN flooding attack[SKK+97] on a transmission control protocol (TCP).

Before sending data from a source host S to a destination host D, they have to establish a connection between S and D, which is called *three-way handshake*. First, S sends a SYN packet including an initial sequence number x. Second, D replies to S with a message in which the SYN and ACK flags are set, indicating that D acknowledges the SYN. The message includes D's sequence number y and incremented S's sequence number $x+1$ as an ACK number. Third, S sends a message with an ACK bit, $x+1$, and $y+1$.

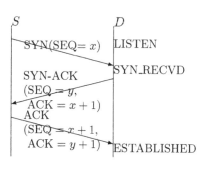

Consider a situation that lasts for a short period during which an attacker, A, sends several connection requests with spoofed source IP-addresses to a victim machine, D. The number of actual implementations of half-opened connections per port is limited since the memory allocation of data structures for such connections is limited.

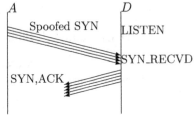

When the maximum number is reached, D refuses all successive connection establishment attempts until the timer expires. Actually, several solutions against TCP SYN-flooding attack are proposed ([SKK$^+$97]; for example, *SYN-cookie*.

Researchers have studied DoS attacks from various viewpoints, such as protection from DoS attacks using resource monitoring[Mil93] and the development of DoS resistance[AN97, ANL01]. Meadows studied a formal framework for DoS resistance analysis[Mea99, Mea01]. She extended the Alice and Bob notation by attaching a primitive procedure annotation to each communication. For example, consider a station-to-station (STS) protocol[Mea99] that is a three-pass variation of the basic Diffie-Hellman protocol. It allows the establishment of a shared secret key between two parties:

1. $A \rightarrow B$: α^{X_A}
2. $B \rightarrow A$: $\alpha^{X_B}, E_K(S_B(\alpha^{X_B}, \alpha^{X_A}))$
3. $A \rightarrow B$: $E_K(S_A(\alpha^{X_A}, \alpha^{X_B}))$,

where α signifies a primitive root of a shared prime number p, X_A and X_B are the secret values of A and B respectively, K is a Diffie-Hellman's key $\alpha^{X_A X_B}$, $E_K(-)$ is an encryption with the shared key K, and S_A and S_B are the signatures of A and B, respectively. For this protocol, the concrete operations in each stage are annotated as:

1. $A \rightarrow B$: $preexp_1, storename_1 \parallel$
   $\alpha^{X_A} \parallel$
   $storenonce_1, storename_2, accept_1$
2. $B \rightarrow A$: $preexp_2, sign_1, exp_1, encrypt_1 \parallel$
   $\alpha^{X_B}, E_K(S_B(\alpha^{X_B}, \alpha^{X_A}))$
   $checkname_1, retrievenonce_1, exp_2, decrypt_1, checksig_1, accept_2$
3. $A \rightarrow B$: $sign_2, encrypt_2 \parallel$
   $E_K(S_A(\alpha^{X_A}, \alpha^{X_B}))$
   $checkname_2, retrievenonce_2, decrypt_2, checksig_2, accept_4$.

The operation *preexp* is an exponential with a static base. The operation *exp* is an exponential with a dynamic base. The operations *storename* and *storenonce* are used to store a name and a nonce, respectively. By tracking the operations that are carried out during the processing of a protocol, we can calculate the total cost of each process in this framework. For example, if an attacker, I, sends a random message to B, then we know that B will execute the following processes:

$storenonce_1, storename_2, accept_1, preexp_2, sign_1, exp_1, and encrypt_1$.

A cost is assigned to each operation that is carried out during a process. In this case, operations *sign* and *exp* are *expensive*; *preexp* and *encrypt* are *intermediate*; and *storenonce* and *storename* are *cheap*. By calculating the total cost, we can determine that the processing cost of a simple challenge from an attacker can be prohibitive.

Cost price is assigned to each cost. In this case, Operations *sign* and *exp* are *expensive*; *preexp* and *encrypt* are *medium*; *storenonce* and *storename* are *cheap*.

By calculating the total cost, The total cost are counted as

$$2expensive + 2medium + 2cheap,$$

we can determine that the processing cost of a simple challenge from an attacker can be prohibitive.

We consider their approach an original formal framework for the analysis of DoS resistance. Furthermore, it is easy to understand, since it is based on the Alice and Bob notation. However, their cost estimation is based on an annotation that uses a description of the protocol that is dependent on the user's knowledge of the protocol's implementation. Although the cost of protocol processing is closely related to the protocol specification, the cost annotation is independent of the protocol specification. Protocol designers must be responsible for consistency between these two kinds of descriptions. If the primitive procedures of a protocol are not well understood or the amount of memory that is required for protocol processing is incorrect, the resulting cost estimation will be flawed.

Therefore, we decided to develop a protocol specification language in which the cost estimation is based on the operational semantics. The spi-calculus proposed by Abadi and Gordon [AG97a, AG97b] is one example of a formal calculus that is used to describe and analyze cryptographic protocols. In their calculus, they state their security properties in terms of coarse-grained notions of protocol equivalence. Gordon and Jeffrey [AA01a, AA01b, AA02] have developed type theoretic methods for proving authenticity properties.

In this paper, we present Spice calculus (secure pi-calculus for cost estimation), which is an extension of spi-calculus designed to describe and analyze DoS attack resistance.

In Section 2, we describe our Spice calculus, including its syntax, typing rules, and operational semantics with explicit cost estimation. In Section 3, we give an example of the use of Spice calculus by considering a typical DoS TCP SYN-flood attack, and its method of defense using SYN-cookies. The cost estimation is compared in the framework of Spice calculus. Section 4 summarizes our work and gives our conclusions.

2   Secure pi-Calculus for Cost-Estimation: Spice-Calculus

This section defines Spice calculus. First, the syntax of Spice calculus is presented, including its expressions, types, and typing rules. Then, the operational semantics with explicit cost estimation are described.

Definition 1 (Term). *We have assumed an infinite set of* names *and an infinite set of* variables. *The* terms *of our Spice calculus are defined using the following grammar:*

$L, M, N :=$		terms
	n	name
	x	variable
	0	zero
	$\mathsf{succ}(M)$	successor
	$\mathsf{pred}(M)$	predecessor
	$(M_1, \ldots, M_n)$	pair
	$\mathsf{hash}(M)$	hash expression
	$H(M)$	hash value
	$\mathsf{enc}(M, N)$	shared-key encryption expression
	$\{M\}_N$	shared-key encryption value
	$\mathsf{pubenc}(M, N)$	public-key encryption expression
	$\{\!\![M]\!\!\}_N$	public-key encryption value
	$\mathsf{sign}(M, N)$	signature expression
	$\{\![M]\!\}_N$	signature value
	$\mathsf{pubkey}(M)$	public key expression
	$pubkey_M$	public key value
	$\mathsf{privkey}(M)$	private key expression
	$privkey_M$	private key value

The variables, zero symbol, and successor function symbol are similar to those found in pi-calculus. Natural numbers are represented by the zero symbol and the successor function symbol. However, the encryption operators differ from those found in pi-calculus. Our calculus provides two kinds of operator for each encryption mechanism. Expression operators are used for procedure identifiers before computation. Value operators are used for computation results. For example, $\mathsf{enc}(M, N)$ signifies an encryption function call of message M by shared-key N. $\{M\}_N$ is the encrypted message obtained by the function call. Since we estimate several kinds of cost while processing a protocol, we distinguish pre-evaluated expressions from post-evaluated ones.

Definition 2 (Process). *The* processes *of our Spice calculus are defined using the following grammar:*

$P, Q, R ::=$	process
$\mathsf{out}\ M_{port}\ \langle N_{msg} \rangle; P$	output
$\mathsf{inp}\ M_{port}\ (x); P$	input
$(P \mid Q)$	composition
$\mathsf{new}(n); P$	restriction
$\mathsf{repeat}\ P$	replication
stop	nil
$\mathsf{match}\ M\ \mathsf{is}\ N\ \mathsf{err}\{P\}; Q$	matching
$\mathsf{split}\ (x_1, \ldots, x_n)\ \mathsf{is}\ M\ \mathsf{err}\{R\}; P$	pair splitting

decrypt M is enc(x, N) err$\{R\}; P$	shared-key decryption
decrypt M is pubenc(x, N) err$\{R\}; P$	public-key decryption
verify M is sign(x, N) err$\{R\}; P$	signature verification
store $x = M; P$	memory allocation
free $x; P$	memory deallocation

An output process, out M_{port} $\langle N_{msg}\rangle; P$, sends a message, N_{msg}, through a port, M_{port}, and then runs process P. An input process, inp M_{port} $(x); P$, receives the message through port M_{port}, binds a variable x to the message, and then runs process P. Composition $(P \mid Q)$ is used to invoke processes P and Q and running in parallel. Restriction new$(n); P$ coreates a new name, n, and then runs process P. The replication repeat P invokes an unspecified number of parallel executions of P. The nil process stop specifies the terminal form of processes.

The pair splitting split $(x_1, \ldots, x_n)$ is M err$\{R\}; P$ means that if M is computed and we obtain a pair, P is executed under the binding of x_1 for the first component of the pair, the binding of x_2 for the second component, ..., and the binding of x_n for the n-th component.

The shared-key decryption decrypt M is enc(x, N) err$\{R\}; P$ omeans that if M is computed and we obtain encrypted data with shared-key N, then we execute P under the binding of x to the decrypted message; otherwise, R is executed. The public-key decryption decrypt M is pubenc(x, N) err$\{R\}; P$ and signature verification verify M is sign(x, N) err$\{R\}; P$ have a similar meaning to the shared key description.

We use the a *agents* defined below to express operational semantics. These agents are intermediate expressions that occur during computation.

Definition 3 (Abstraction, Concretion, Agent). *An expression $(x)P$ is called an* abstraction *where x is a variable and P is a process. An expression $(\nu \overrightarrow{n})\langle M\rangle Q$ is called a* concretion, *where P is a process and M is a term. An* agent *is an abstraction, process, or concretion. We use $A, B, \ldots$ as metavariables on agents.*

$A, B :=$	*agent*
P	*process*
$(x)P$	*abstraction*
$(\nu \overrightarrow{n})\langle M\rangle Q$	*concretion*

A concretion $(\nu)\langle M\rangle Q$ stands for $(\nu \overrightarrow{n})\langle M\rangle Q$ where $\overrightarrow{n}$ is empty.

Definition 4 (Free Names and Free Variables). A set $fv(P)$ of *free variables* in a process P is defined inductively by the following equations.

$$fv(\text{out } M_{port} \ \langle N_{msg}\rangle; P) = fv(M) \cup fv(N) \cup fv(P),$$
$$fv(\text{inp } M_{port} \ (x); P) = fv(M) \cup fv(P) \setminus \{x\},$$
$$fv(P \mid Q) = fv(P) \cup fv(Q),$$

$$fv(\mathsf{new}(n); P) = fv(P), \quad fv(\mathsf{repeat}\, P) = fv(P), \quad fv(\mathsf{stop}) = \emptyset,$$

$$fv(\mathsf{match}\ M\ \mathsf{is}\ N\ \mathsf{err}\{P\}; Q) = fv(M) \cup fv(N) \cup fv(P) \cup fv(Q),$$
$$fv(\mathsf{split}\ (x_1, \ldots, x_n)\ \mathsf{is}\ M\ \mathsf{err}\{R\}; P) = fv(M) \cup (fv(P) \setminus \{x_1, \ldots, x_n\}) \cup fv(R),$$

$$fv(\mathsf{decrypt}\ M\ \mathsf{is}\ \mathsf{enc}(x, N)\ \mathsf{err}\{R\}; P)$$
$$= fv(\mathsf{decrypt}\ M\ \mathsf{is}\ \mathsf{pubenc}(x, N)\ \mathsf{err}\{R\}; P)$$
$$= fv(\mathsf{verify}\ M\ \mathsf{is}\ \mathsf{sign}(x, N)\ \mathsf{err}\{R\}; P)$$
$$= fv(M) \cup fv(N) \cup (fv(P) \setminus \{x\}) \cup fv(R),$$

$$fv(\mathsf{store}\ x = M; P) = fv(P) \setminus \{x\}, \quad fv(\mathsf{free}\ x; P) = fv(P),$$

where a set $fv(M)$ of free variables in a term M is defined as the set of variables occurring in a term M. In this definition, it is assumed that the binders of variables are input, pair splitting, shared-key and public-key decryption, signature verification, and memory allocation.

A set $fn(P)$ of *free names* in a process P is defined inductively by the following equations.

$$fn(\mathsf{new}(n); P) = fn(P) \setminus \{n\}$$

and for the other kinds of process, the equations are similar each other,

$$fn(\mathsf{out}\ M_{port}\ \langle N_{msg}\rangle; P) = fn(M) \cup fn(N) \cup fn(P),$$
$$fn(P \mid Q) = fn(P) \cup fn(Q),$$
$$fn(\mathsf{split}\ (x_1, \ldots, x_n)\ \mathsf{is}\ M\ \mathsf{err}\{R\}; P) = fn(M) \cup fn(P) \cup fn(R),$$

where a set $fn(M)$ of free names in a term M is defined as the set of names occurring in M. It is assumed that the restriction operator $\mathsf{new}(n)$ is only a binder of names in our calculus, in this definition.

We extend the restriction and composition operators for processes to agents by

$$\mathsf{new}(n); (x)P \equiv (x)\mathsf{new}(n); P$$
$$R \mid (x)P \equiv (x)(R \mid P) \quad \text{where } x \notin fv(R)$$
$$\mathsf{new}(m); (\nu\overrightarrow{n})\langle M\rangle Q \equiv (\nu m, \overrightarrow{n})\langle M\rangle Q \quad \text{if } m \in fn(M)$$
$$\equiv (\nu\overrightarrow{n})\langle M\rangle\mathsf{new}(m); Q \quad \text{otherwise}$$

where $m \notin \{\overrightarrow{n}\}$ and $\{\overrightarrow{n}\} \cap fn(R) = \emptyset$. The symmetric case $A|R$ is defined in a similar manner to that described above.

Definition 5 (Configuration Type). *The* configuration type *is defined using the following grammar:*

$$\mathcal{A}, \mathcal{B}, \mathcal{C} :=$$
$$a, b, c, \ldots \ \textit{machine name type}$$
$$(\mathcal{A} \mid \mathcal{B}) \quad \textit{composition type}$$

Each machine name type represents a computer connected to a network. The composition type constructs a distributed system connected by a network. For example, **a** | **b** means a "virtual" computer consisting of computers **a** and **b** and connected by a network. Composition type (**a** | **b**) | **c** means a "virtual" computer composed by virtual computer **a** | **b** and computer **c**.

Definition 6 (Typing Rules). *The typing of agents is specified using the following typing rules. Typing judgment* $A : \mathcal{A}$ *means that agent A is of type $\mathcal{A}$.*

$$\frac{P : \mathcal{A}}{(x)P : \mathcal{A}} \qquad \frac{Q : \mathcal{A}}{(\nu \overrightarrow{n})\langle M \rangle Q : \mathcal{A}} \qquad \frac{P : \mathcal{A}}{\mathsf{new}(n); P : \mathcal{A}} \qquad \frac{P : \mathcal{A} \quad Q : \mathcal{B}}{(P \mid Q) : (\mathcal{A} \mid \mathcal{B})}$$

$$\frac{P : a}{\mathsf{out}\ M\ \langle N \rangle; P : a} \qquad \frac{P : a}{\mathsf{inp}\ M\ (x); P : a} \qquad \frac{P : a}{\mathsf{repeat}\ P : a} \qquad \overline{\mathsf{stop} : a}$$

$$\frac{P : a \quad R : a}{\mathsf{split}\ (x_1, \ldots, x_n)\ \mathsf{is}\ M\ \mathsf{err}\{R\}; P : a}$$

$$\frac{P : a \quad R : a}{\mathsf{decrypt}\ M\ \mathsf{is}\ \mathsf{enc}(x, N)\ \mathsf{err}\{R\}; P} \qquad \frac{P : a \quad R : a}{\mathsf{decrypt}\ M\ \mathsf{is}\ \mathsf{pubenc}(x, N)\ \mathsf{err}\{R\}; P}$$

$$\frac{P : a \quad R : a}{\mathsf{verify}\ M\ \mathsf{is}\ \mathsf{sign}(x, N)\ \mathsf{err}\{R\}; P}$$

$$\frac{P : a}{\mathsf{store}\ x = M; P : a} \qquad \frac{P : a}{\mathsf{free}\ x; P : a}$$

This typing can also be extended to restriction and composition on agents under their syntactic definitions.

Definition 7 (Cost Values and Cost Assignment). *We assume a set whose element is called a* cost value kind. *A* cost value space *is a free Abelian group generated from the set of cost value kinds. Elements of a cost value space are called* cost values. *Symbols $c, d, \ldots$ are used for metavariables on cost values. In this paper, we use cost kinds such as store, hash, match, etc.*

A cost assignment *is a labeled product of cost vectors whose labels are machine names. We use $\sigma, \tau, \ldots$ for metavariables on cost assignments. For example, $\{\boldsymbol{a} :: (4store + 3match), \boldsymbol{b} :: (4store + match + 2hash)\}$ is a cost assignment.*

For a cost assignment $\sigma = \{\boldsymbol{a}_1 :: c_1, \ldots, \boldsymbol{a}_n :: c_n\}$, $\sigma(\boldsymbol{a}_i)$ stands for c_i. If $\boldsymbol{a}$ does not appear in σ, $\sigma(\boldsymbol{a})$ is defined as 0.

The addition of cost values is extended to cost assignments as an entry-wise addition: $(\sigma_1 + \sigma_2)(\boldsymbol{a}_i) = \sigma_1(\boldsymbol{a}_i) + \sigma_2(\boldsymbol{a}_i)$ for each $\boldsymbol{a}_i$.

Actually, such an Abelian group of cost assignment is isomorphic to a free Abelian group generated from the pairs of cost value kinds and machine names. Therefore, we sometimes write $\{\boldsymbol{a} :: 4store, \boldsymbol{a} :: 3match, \boldsymbol{b} :: 4store, \boldsymbol{b} :: match, \boldsymbol{b} :: 2hash\}$ instead of $\{\boldsymbol{a} :: (4store + 3match), \boldsymbol{b} :: (4store + match + 2hash)\}$.

Next, we describe the reduction of terms for cost estimation.

Definition 8 (Reduction with Cost Estimation on Terms). *The ternary relation $M > N : c$ among terms M, N and cost value c is defined inductively using the following rules:*

$$\frac{}{0 > 0 : 0} \qquad \frac{M > V : c}{\mathsf{succ}(M) > \mathsf{succ}(V) : c} \qquad \frac{M > \mathsf{succ}(V) : c}{\mathsf{pred}(M) > V : c}$$

$$\frac{M_1 > V_1 : c_1 \quad \cdots \quad M_n > V_n : c_n}{(M_1, \ldots, M_n) > (V_1, \ldots, V_n) : c_1 + \cdots + c_n + pair}$$

$$\frac{M > V : c \quad N > W : d}{\mathsf{enc}(M, N) > \{V\}_W : c + d + enc} \qquad \frac{M > V : c \quad N > pubkey_W : d}{\mathsf{pubenc}(M, N) > \{V\}_W : c + d + pubenc}$$

$$\frac{M > V : c}{\mathsf{pubkey}(M) > pubkey_V : c} \qquad \frac{M > V : c}{\mathsf{privkey}(M) > privkey_V : c}$$

$$\frac{M > V : c \quad N > privkey_W : d}{\mathsf{sign}(M, N) > \{V\}_W : c + d + sign} \qquad \frac{M > V : c}{\mathsf{hash}(M) > H(V) : c + hash}$$

The relation $M > N : c$ is read "M is reduced to N with cost value (or simply, cost) c".

Definition 9 (Reduction with Cost Estimation on Processes). *The ternary relation $P > Q : c$ among processes P, Q and cost value c is defined inductively using the following rules:*

$$\frac{}{\mathsf{repeat}\, P > P \mid (\mathsf{repeat}\, P) : repeat}$$

$$\frac{M > V : c}{\mathsf{store}\ x = M; P > P[V/x] : c + store}$$

$$\frac{}{\mathsf{free}\ x; P > P : -store}$$

$$\frac{M > V : c \quad N > V : d}{\mathsf{match}\ M\ \mathsf{is}\ N\ \mathsf{err}\{P\}; Q > Q :: c + d + match}$$

$$\frac{M > V : c \quad N > W : d \quad V \not\equiv W}{\mathsf{match}\ M\ \mathsf{is}\ N\ \mathsf{err}\{P\}; Q > P :: c + d + match}$$

$$\frac{M > (V_1, \ldots, V_n) : c}{\mathsf{split}\ (x_1, \ldots, x_n)\ \mathsf{is}\ M\ \mathsf{err}\{R\}; P > P[V_1/x_1, \ldots, V_n/x_n] : c + n \times store}$$

$$\frac{M > V : c \quad V \text{ is not a pair.}}{\mathsf{split}\ (x, y)\ \mathsf{is}\ M\ \mathsf{err}\{R\}; P > R : c}$$

$$\frac{M > \{L\}_V : c \quad N > V : d}{\mathsf{decrypt}\ M\ \mathsf{is}\ \mathsf{enc}(x, N)\ \mathsf{err}\{R\}; P > P[L/x] : c + enc + store}$$

$$\frac{M > W : c \quad N > V : d \quad \neg \exists L(W = \{L\}_V)}{\mathsf{decrypt}\ M\ \mathsf{is}\ \mathsf{enc}(x, N)\ \mathsf{err}\{R\}; R > R : c + d + enc}$$

$$\frac{M > \{\![L]\!\}_U : c \quad N > privkey_U : d}{\text{decrypt } M \text{ is pubenc}(x, N) \text{ err}\{R\}; P > P[L/x] : c + d + pubenc + store}$$

$$\frac{N > V : d \quad \neg \exists U (V = privkey_U)}{\text{decrypt } M \text{ is pubenc}(x, N) \text{ err}\{R\}; R > R : d}$$

$$\frac{N > privkey_U : d \quad M > W : c \quad \neg \exists L (W = \{\![L]\!\}_U)}{\text{decrypt } M \text{ is pubenc}(x, N) \text{ err}\{R\}; R > R : c + d + pubenc}$$

$$\frac{M > \{[L]\}_U : c \quad N > pubkey_U : d}{\text{verify } M \text{ is sign}(x, N) \text{ err}\{R\}; P > P[L/x] : c + d + sign + store}$$

$$\frac{N > V : d \quad \neg \exists U (V = pubkey_U)}{\text{verify } M \text{ is sign}(x, N) \text{ err}\{R\}; R > R : d}$$

$$\frac{M > W : c \quad N > pubkey_U : d \quad \neg \exists L (W = \{[L]\}_U)}{\text{verify } M \text{ is sign}(x, N) \text{ err}\{R\}; R > R : c + d + sign}$$

The reduction relation on processes represents an inner-process computation. The commitment relation introduced below represents an inter-process communication. Before defining the commitment relation, we must first introduce the notions of substitution and interaction. A substitution is similar to that found in spi-calculus, except for the memory deallocation free $x; P$. The memory deallocation expression free $x; P$ serves to hide the scope of a variable x in the succeeding process P. Later, we consider the memory deallocation expression in relation to the cost estimation of memory consumption.

Definition 10 (Substitution). The *substitution* $P[L/x]$ of term L for variable x in process P is defined inductively as follows:

(out $M \langle N \rangle; P)[L/x] = $ out $M[L/x] \langle N[L/x] \rangle; P[L/x]$

(inp $M (x); P)[L/x] = $ inp $M[L/x] (N); P$

(inp $M (y); P)[L/x] = $ inp $M[L/x] (y); P[L/x]$

$(P \mid Q)[L/x] = P[L/x] \mid Q[L/x]$

(new$(n); P)[L/x] = $ new$(n); P[L/x]$

(repeat $P)[L/x] = $ repeat $P[L/x]$

stop$[L/x] = $ stop

(match M is N err$\{P\}; Q)[L/x] = $ match $M[L/x]$ is $N[L/x]$ err$\{P[L/x]\}; Q[L/x]$

(split (x', y') is M err$\{R\}; P)[L/x] = $ split (x', y') is $M[L/x]$ err$\{R[L/x]\}; P[L/x]$

(decrypt M is enc(x', N) err$\{R\}; P)[L/x] = $
    decrypt $M[L/x]$ is enc$(x', N[L/x])$ err$\{R[L/x]\}; P[L/x]$

(decrypt M is pubenc(x', N) err$\{R\}; P)[L/x] = $
    decrypt $M[L/x]$ is pubenc$(x', N[L/x])$ err$\{R[L/x]\}; P[L/x]$

(verify M is sign(x', N) err$\{R\}; P)[L/x] = $
    verify $M[L/x]$ is sign$(x', N[L/x])$ err$\{R[L/x]\}; P[L/x]$

$$\text{(store } y = M; P)[L/x] = (\text{store } y = M[L/x]; P[L/x])$$
$$\text{(free } x; P)[L/x] = (\text{free } x; P)$$
$$\text{(free } x'; P)[L/x] = \text{free } x'; (P[L/x])$$

Renaming of names and variables is appropriately done in substitution, in order to avoide name clashes.

We assume a notational convention where $F, F', \ldots$ stand for abstractions, such as $(x)P$, and for $C, C', \ldots$ concretions, such as $(\nu \overrightarrow{n})\langle M \rangle Q$.

Definition 11 (Interaction). *Let F and C be $(x)P$ and $(\nu n_1, \ldots, n_k)\langle M \rangle Q$, respectively. We define* interactions *and $F @ C$ to be closed processes as*

$$(x)P @ (\nu n_1, \ldots, n_k)\langle M \rangle Q \equiv \mathsf{new}(n_1) \cdots \mathsf{new}(n_k)(P[M/x] \mid Q)$$
$$((\nu n_1, \ldots, n_k)\langle M \rangle Q) @ (x)P \equiv \mathsf{new}(n_1) \cdots \mathsf{new}(n_k)(Q \mid P[M/x])$$

An *action* is defined as a name m, a co-name $\overline{m}$, or the *silent action* τ. Metavariables such as $\alpha, \beta, \ldots$ are used for actions.

Definition 12 (Commitment Relation with Cost Estimation). The commitment relation with cost estimation $\mathcal{A} \vdash P \overset{\alpha}{\to} A : \sigma$ is a quinary relation among configuration type $\mathcal{A}$, process P, action α, agent A, and cost assignment σ, defined by the following rules:

$$\frac{}{\boldsymbol{a} \vdash \mathsf{inp}\ n\ (x); P \overset{n}{\to} (x)P : \{\boldsymbol{a} :: \mathrm{store}\}} \quad Comm\ In$$

$$\frac{}{\boldsymbol{a} \vdash \mathsf{out}\ n\ \langle N \rangle; P \overset{\overline{n}}{\to} (\nu)\langle N \rangle P : \{\}} \quad Comm\ Out$$

$$\frac{\mathcal{A} \vdash P \overset{n}{\to} F : \sigma_1 \quad \mathcal{B} \vdash Q \overset{\overline{n}}{\to} C : \sigma_2}{(\mathcal{A} \mid \mathcal{B}) \vdash (P \mid Q) \overset{\tau}{\to} F @ C : \sigma_1 + \sigma_2} \quad Comm\ Inter\ 1$$

$$\frac{\mathcal{A} \vdash P \overset{\overline{n}}{\to} C : \sigma_1 \quad \mathcal{B} \vdash Q \overset{n}{\to} F : \sigma_2}{(\mathcal{A} \mid \mathcal{B}) \vdash (P \mid Q) \overset{\tau}{\to} C @ F : \sigma_1 + \sigma_2} \quad Comm\ Inter\ 2$$

$$\frac{\mathcal{A} \vdash P \overset{\alpha}{\to} A : \sigma}{(\mathcal{A} \mid \mathcal{B}) \vdash (P \mid Q) \overset{\alpha}{\to} (A \mid Q) : \sigma} \quad Comm\ Par\ 1$$

$$\frac{\mathcal{A} \vdash Q \overset{\alpha}{\to} A : \sigma}{(\mathcal{A} \mid \mathcal{B}) \vdash (P \mid Q) \overset{\alpha}{\to} (P \mid A) : \sigma} \quad Comm\ Par\ 2$$

$$\frac{\mathcal{A} \vdash P \overset{\alpha}{\to} A : \sigma \quad \alpha \notin \{n, \overline{n}\}}{\mathcal{A} \vdash \mathsf{new}(n); P \overset{\alpha}{\to} \mathsf{new}(n); A : \sigma} \quad Comm\ Res$$

$$\frac{P > Q : c \quad \boldsymbol{a} \vdash Q \overset{\alpha}{\to} A : \sigma}{\boldsymbol{a} \vdash P \overset{\alpha}{\to} A : \{\boldsymbol{a} :: c\} + \sigma} \quad Comm\ Red$$

We assume that communication among processes is not charged as defined in rule *Comm In* and *Comm Out*.

Commitment relation $\mathcal{A} \vdash P \xrightarrow{\alpha} A$ means that process P makes an inner-process computation on system $\mathcal{A}$, emits a communication "signal," and then becomes agent A.

Next, we develop a subject reduction theorem for the typing system. To formulate the subject reduction theorem for the reduction relation on processes, we must introduce equivalence between configuration types. For example, consider a replication repeat P that is executed on machine $\mathbf{a}$. This process is reduced to $(P \mid \text{repeat } P)$ and is of type $(\mathbf{a} \mid \mathbf{a})..$ Actually, we may identify as $(\mathbf{a} \mid \mathbf{a})$, since we want to estimate the cost for each machine.

Definition 13 (Type Equivalence). *The equivalence between configuration types $\mathcal{A} \simeq \mathcal{B}$ is defined by the following rules:*

$$\frac{}{a \mid a \simeq a} \quad \frac{}{\mathcal{A} \simeq \mathcal{A}} \quad \frac{\mathcal{A} \simeq \mathcal{A}'}{(\mathcal{A} \mid \mathcal{B}) \simeq (\mathcal{A}' \mid \mathcal{B})} \quad \frac{\mathcal{B} \simeq \mathcal{B}'}{(\mathcal{A} \mid \mathcal{B}) \simeq (\mathcal{A} \mid \mathcal{B}')} \quad \frac{\mathcal{A} \simeq \mathcal{B} \quad \mathcal{B} \simeq \mathcal{C}}{\mathcal{A} \simeq \mathcal{C}}$$

The following lemma is used as a proof of the subject reduction theorem.

Lemma 1. *Let F and C be $(x)P$ and $(\nu \overrightarrow{n})\langle M \rangle Q$, respectively. If $F : \mathcal{A}$ and $F : \mathcal{B}$, then $(F \,@\, C) : (\mathcal{A} \mid \mathcal{B})$ and $(C \,@\, F) : (\mathcal{B} \mid \mathcal{A})$.*

Proof. Suppose that $F : \mathcal{A}$ and $F : \mathcal{B}$. Then, we know $P : \mathcal{A}$; therefore, $P[M/x] : \mathcal{A}$, by a typing rule. We also know $Q : \mathcal{B}$ by the supposition. Hence, we have $(P[M/x] \mid Q) : (\mathcal{A} \mid \mathcal{B})$. Using the definition of interaction, $F \,@\, C \equiv (\nu \overrightarrow{n})\langle [M/x]P \mid Q \rangle$, we obtain $F \,@\, C : (\mathcal{A} \mid \mathcal{B})$. $(C \,@\, F) : (\mathcal{B} \mid \mathcal{A})$ can be proven in a similar manner.

The following property is proven in a straightforward case-analysis of reduction.

Proposition 1 (Subject Reduction Theorem of Reduction on Processes). *If $P : \mathcal{A}$ and $P > P' : c$, then $P' : \mathcal{A}'$ holds for some $\mathcal{A}'$ satisfying that $\mathcal{A} \simeq \mathcal{A}'$.*

Then, we have a subject reduction theorem for commitment relations on agents.

Theorem 1 (Subject Reduction Theorem of Commitment Relation on Agents). *If $P : \mathcal{A}$ and $\mathcal{A} \vdash P \xrightarrow{\alpha} A : \sigma$, then $A : \mathcal{A}'$ holds for some $\mathcal{A}'$ satisfying that $\mathcal{A} \simeq \mathcal{A}'$.*

Proof. This theorem can be proven by induction on the structure of the commitment relation $\mathcal{A} \vdash P \xrightarrow{\alpha} A : \sigma$.

Case of *Comm In*: suppose that inp n $(x); P : \mathbf{a}$ and $\mathbf{a} \vdash$ inp n $(x); P \xrightarrow{n} (x)P$. By the first supposition, we have $P : \mathbf{a}$, and therefore, $(x)P : \mathbf{a}$.

Case of *Comm Out*: proven similarly to the above case.

Case of *Comm Inter 1*: suppose that $(\mathcal{A} \mid \mathcal{B}) \vdash (P \mid Q) \xrightarrow{\tau} F \,@\, C : \sigma_1 + \sigma_2$ and $(P \mid Q) : (\mathcal{A} \mid \mathcal{B})$. By the first supposition, we know $\mathcal{A} \vdash P \xrightarrow{n} F : \sigma_1$ and

$\mathcal{B} \vdash Q \xrightarrow{\overline{n}} C : \sigma_2$. By the second supposition, $P : \mathcal{A}$ and $P : \mathcal{B}$. By the induction hypothesis, we have $F : \mathcal{A}'$ and $C : \mathcal{B}'$ for some $\mathcal{A}'$ and $\mathcal{B}'$ satisfying that $\mathcal{A} \simeq \mathcal{A}'$ and $\mathcal{B} \simeq \mathcal{B}'$. Then, by Lemma 1, we obtailn $(F @ C) : (\mathcal{A}' \mid \mathcal{B}')$. By the definition of type equivalece, we have $\mathcal{A} \mid \mathcal{B} \simeq \mathcal{A}' \mid \mathcal{B}'$.

Case of *Comm Inter 2*: proven in a similar manner to the case of *Comm Inter 1*.

Case of *Comm Par 1*: suppose that $(P \mid Q) : (\mathcal{A} \mid \mathcal{B})$ and $(\mathcal{A} \mid \mathcal{B}) \vdash (P \mid Q) \xrightarrow{\alpha} (A \mid Q) : \sigma$. By the second supposition, we have $\mathcal{A} \vdash P \xrightarrow{\alpha} A : \sigma$. By the first supposition, we have $P : \mathcal{A}$. Then, by the induction hypothesis, we know that $A : \mathcal{A}'$ for some $\mathcal{A}'$ satisfying $\mathcal{A}' \simeq \mathcal{A}$. Then, we have $(A \mid Q) : (\mathcal{A}' \mid \mathcal{B})$ by typing rules, and $(\mathcal{A}' \mid \mathcal{B}) \simeq (\mathcal{A} \mid \mathcal{B})$ by type equivalence rules.

Case of *Comm Par 2*: proven in a similar manner to the case for *Comm Par 1*.

Case of *Comm Res*: suppose that $\mathsf{new}(n); P : \mathbf{a}$ and $\mathcal{A} \vdash \mathsf{new}(n); P \xrightarrow{\alpha} \mathsf{new}(n); A : \sigma$. By the first supposition, we know $P : \mathcal{A}$. By the second supposition, we have $\mathcal{A} \vdash P \xrightarrow{\alpha} A : \sigma$. By the induction hypothesis, it can be derived that $A : \mathcal{A}'$ exists for some $\mathcal{A}'$ satisfying $\mathcal{A}' \simeq \mathcal{A}$. By typing rules, we have $\mathsf{new}(n); A : \mathcal{A}'$.

Case of *Comm Red*: suppose that $P : \mathbf{a}$, $P > Q : c$ and $\mathbf{a} \vdash Q \xrightarrow{\alpha} A : \sigma$. From Proposition 1, it can be derived that $Q : \mathcal{A}$ for some $\mathcal{A}$ satisfying $\mathbf{a} \simeq \mathcal{A}$. Then, by the induction hypothesis, we have $A : \mathcal{A}'$ for some $\mathcal{A}'$ satisfying $\mathcal{A}' \simeq \mathcal{A}''$. By transitivity of type equivalence, we have $\mathbf{a} \simeq \mathcal{A}''$.   □

We will often use transitive closures of reduction and commitment relations with the silent action τ. Costs are counted cumulatively in the sequences of such relations. Moreover, the reduction relation is not defined for either composition $(P \mid Q)$ or restriction $\mathsf{new}(n)P$. Therefore, we extend the reduction to a relation satisfying reflexivity and transitivity that is also defined for compositions and restriction.

Definition 14 (Multi-reduction Relation). Multi-reduction relation $\mathcal{A} \vdash P \gg Q$ *is a binary relation between processes defined by the following rules:*

$$\frac{}{\mathcal{A} \vdash P \gg P : \{\}} \quad \frac{P > P' : c}{\mathbf{a} \vdash P \gg P' : \{\mathbf{a} :: c\}} \quad \frac{\mathcal{A} \vdash P \gg P' : \sigma_1 \quad \mathcal{A} \simeq \mathcal{A}' \quad \mathcal{A}' \vdash P' \gg P'' : \sigma_2}{\mathcal{A} \vdash P \gg P'' : \sigma_1 + \sigma_2}$$

$$\frac{\mathcal{A} \vdash P \gg P' : \sigma_1 \quad \mathcal{B} \vdash Q \gg Q' : \sigma_2}{(\mathcal{A} \mid \mathcal{B}) \vdash (P \mid Q) \gg (P' \mid Q') : \sigma_1 + \sigma_2} \quad \frac{\mathcal{A} \vdash P \gg P' : \sigma}{\mathcal{A} \vdash \mathsf{new}(n)P \gg \mathsf{new}(n)P' : \sigma}$$

The commitment is also extended to a relation satisfying reflexivity and transitivity that is also based on multi-reduction.

Definition 15 (Multi-commitment Relation). *The* multi-commitment relation $P \xrightarrow{\tau} Q$ *is a binary relation between processes defined by the following rules:*

$$\frac{\mathcal{A} \vdash P \xrightarrow{\tau} P' : \sigma}{\mathcal{A} \vdash P \xrightarrow{\tau}\!\!\!\!\!\twoheadrightarrow P' : \sigma} \quad \frac{\mathcal{A} \vdash P \xrightarrow{\tau} P' : \sigma_1 \quad \mathcal{A} \simeq \mathcal{A}' \quad \mathcal{A}' \vdash P' \xrightarrow{\tau} P'' : \sigma_2}{\mathcal{A} \vdash P \xrightarrow{\tau}\!\!\!\!\!\twoheadrightarrow P'' : \sigma_1 + \sigma_2}$$

$$\frac{\mathcal{A} \vdash P \xrightarrow{\tau}\!\!\!\!\!\twoheadrightarrow P' : \sigma_1 \quad \mathcal{A} \simeq \mathcal{A}' \quad \mathcal{A}' \vdash P' \gg P'' : \sigma_2}{\mathcal{A} \vdash P \xrightarrow{\tau}\!\!\!\!\!\twoheadrightarrow P'' : \sigma_1 + \sigma_2}$$

3 An Example of Spice-Calculus

This section presents an example of Spice-calculus.
  Abbreviations below are used for readability.

   match M_1 is N_1 and M_2 is N_2 and $\cdots$ and M_n is N_n err$\{R\}; P$
 $\equiv$ match M_1 is N_1 err$\{R\}$; match M_2 is N_2 err$\{R\}$; $\cdots$ match M_n is N_n err$\{R\}; P$
   free $x_1, x_2, \ldots, x_n$
 $\equiv$ free x_1; free x_2; $\ldots$ free x_n; stop

3.1 A TCP SYN-Flood Attack

The Alice and Bob notation formulates the three-way handshake for establishing
a TCP connection as follows:

$$A \rightarrow B : A, B, S_A$$
$$B \rightarrow A : B, A, S_B, S_A + 1$$
$$A \rightarrow B : A, B, S_A + 1, S_B + 1.$$

A and B in the messages stands for IP-addresses and port numbers. S_A and
S_B are the initial sequence numbers of A and B, respectively.
  The first through fourth fields of each message correspond to the IP address
of the source, the IP address of the destination, the SEQ number of the message,
and its ACK number. Data transmission obeys the three-way handshake. Hosts
A and B are formulated in our calculus as follows:

$P_A \overset{def}{=}$ new(S_A);
    store $x_{sa} = S_A$;
    out $\bar{c} \langle (A, B, x_{sa}) \rangle$;
    inp $c\ (p)$; split $(x'_b, x'_a, x'_{sb}, x'_{sa1})$ is p err$\{$free $x_{sa}, p\}$; free p;
    match x'_a is A and x'_b is B and x'_{sa1} is succ(x_{sa})
     err$\{$free $x_{sa}, x'_b, x'_a, x'_{sb}, x'_{sa1}, p\}$
    free x'_b, x'_a, x'_{sa1};
    out $\bar{c} \langle (A, B, \text{succ}(x_{sa}), \text{succ}(x'_{sb})) \rangle$;
    P'_A,

where A and B are numbers representing the identities (i.e., IP-addresses and port numbers) of hosts A and B, respectively.

$$P_B \stackrel{def}{=} \mathsf{new}(S_B);$$

$\qquad$ $\mathsf{inp}\ c\ (q_1); \mathsf{split}\ (y_a, y_b, y_{sa})\ \mathsf{is}\ q_1\ \mathsf{err}\{\mathsf{free}\ q_1\}; \mathsf{free}\ q_1;$

$\qquad$ $\mathsf{match}\ y_b\ \mathsf{is}\ B\ \mathsf{err}\{\mathsf{free}\ y_a, y_b, y_{sa}\}; \mathsf{free}\ y_b;$

$\qquad$ $\mathsf{store}\ y_{sb} = S_B; \mathsf{out}\ \bar{c}\ \langle (B, y_a, y_{sb}, \mathsf{succ}(y_{sa})) \rangle;$

$\qquad$ $\mathsf{inp}\ c\ (q_2); \mathsf{split}\ (y_a', y_b', y_{sa1}', y_{sb1}')\ \mathsf{is}\ q_2\ \mathsf{err}\{\mathsf{free}\ y_a, y_{sa}, y_{sb}, q_1, q_2\}; \mathsf{free}\ q_2;$

$\qquad$ $\mathsf{match}\ y_b'\ \mathsf{is}\ B\ \mathsf{and}\ y_a'\ \mathsf{is}\ y_a\ \mathsf{and}\ y_{sa1}'\ \mathsf{is}\ \mathsf{succ}(y_{sa})\ \mathsf{and}\ y_{sb1}'\ \mathsf{is}\ \mathsf{succ}(y_{sb})$

$\qquad$ $\mathsf{err}\{\mathsf{free}\ y_a, y_{sa}, y_{sb}, y_b', y_a', y_{sa1}', y_{sb1}', q_1, q_2\}$

$\qquad$ $\mathsf{free}\ y_b', y_a', y_{sa1}', y_{sb1}';$

$\qquad$ P_B'

The normal configuration

$$NormalConfig \stackrel{def}{=} (\mathsf{repeat}\ P_A \mid \mathsf{repeat}\ P_B).$$

is determined by assuming two machine names **a** and **b** for host A and B respectively, then the process is typed as $NormalConfig : (\mathbf{a} \mid \mathbf{b})$.

Then, the normal progress of the protocol is expressed as the following commitment and reduction sequence. (For readability, we have omitted the configuration type annotation.)

$NormalConfig \equiv (\mathsf{repeat}\ P_A \mid \mathsf{repeat}\ P_B)$

$\qquad$ $\stackrel{\tau}{\rightarrow} \mathsf{new}(S_A); \mathsf{new}(S_B);$

$\qquad\qquad$ $(\mathsf{inp}\ c\ (p); \cdots) \mid \mathsf{repeat}\ P_A$

$\qquad\qquad$ $\mid (\mathsf{split}\ (y_a, y_b, y_c)\ \mathsf{is}\ q_1; \cdots) \mid \mathsf{repeat}\ P_B$

$\qquad\qquad$ $: \{\mathbf{a} :: store, \mathbf{b} :: store\}$

$\qquad$ $\gg \mathsf{new}(S_A); \mathsf{new}(S_B);$

$\qquad\qquad$ $(\mathsf{inp}\ c\ (p); \cdots) \mid \mathsf{repeat}\ P_A$

$\qquad\qquad$ $\mid (\mathsf{out}\ \bar{c}\ \langle (y_b, y_a, y_{sb}, \mathsf{succ}(y_{sa})) \rangle; \cdots) \mid \mathsf{repeat}\ P_B$

$\qquad\qquad$ $: \{\mathbf{b} :: 3store\} - \{\mathbf{b} :: store\} + \{\mathbf{b} :: match\} + \{\mathbf{b} :: -store\} + \{\mathbf{b} :: store\}$

$\qquad\qquad$ $= \{\mathbf{b} :: 2store, \mathbf{b} :: match\}$

$\qquad$ $\stackrel{\tau}{\rightarrow} \mathsf{new}(S_A); \mathsf{new}(S_B);$

$\qquad\qquad$ $(\mathsf{split}\ (x_b', x_a', x_{sb}', x_{sa1}')\ \mathsf{is}\ p \cdots) \mid \mathsf{repeat}\ P_A$

$\qquad\qquad$ $\mid (\mathsf{inp}\ c\ (q_2); \cdots) \mid \mathsf{repeat}\ P_B$

$\qquad\qquad$ $: \{\mathbf{a} :: store\}$

$\qquad$ $\gg \mathsf{new}(S_A); \mathsf{new}(S_B);$

$\qquad\qquad$ $(\mathsf{out}\ \bar{c}\ \langle (x_a, x_b, \mathsf{succ}(x_{sa}), \mathsf{succ}(x_{sb})) \rangle; \cdots) \mid \mathsf{repeat}\ P_A$

$\qquad\qquad$ $\mid (\mathsf{inp}\ c\ (q_2); \cdots) \mid \mathsf{repeat}\ P_B$

$$: \{\mathbf{a} :: 4store\} + \{\mathbf{a} :: -store\} + \{\mathbf{a} :: 3match\} - \{\mathbf{a} :: 3store\}$$
$$= \{\mathbf{a} :: 3match\}$$
$$\xrightarrow{\tau} \mathsf{new}(S_A); \mathsf{new}(S_B);$$
$$P_A \mid \mathsf{repeat}\, P_A \mid (\mathsf{split}\ (y'_a, y'_b, y'_{sa1}, y'_{sb1})\ \mathsf{is}\ q_2 \cdots) \mid \mathsf{repeat}\, P_B$$
$$: \{\mathbf{b} :: store\}$$
$$\gg \mathsf{new}(S_A); \mathsf{new}(S_B);$$
$$P'_A \mid \mathsf{repeat}\, P_A \mid P'_B \mid \mathsf{repeat}\, P_B$$
$$: \{\mathbf{b} :: 4store\} + \{\mathbf{b} :: -store\} + \{\mathbf{b} :: 4match\} + \{\mathbf{b} :: -4store\}$$
$$= \{\mathbf{b} :: -store, \mathbf{b} :: 4match\}$$

Altogether, we know the following cost estimation in the normal configuration.

$$NormalConfig \xrightarrow{\tau} (\mathsf{new}(S_A); P'_A) \mid \mathsf{repeat}\, P_A \mid (\mathsf{new}(S_B); P'_B) \mid \mathsf{repeat}\, P_B$$
$$: \{\mathbf{a} :: 2store, \mathbf{a} :: 3match, \mathbf{b} :: 4store, \mathbf{b} :: 5match\}$$

From this result, we know that the difference in the costs of A and B is negligible.

In place of host A, consider the following attacker I, which is the so-called SYN-flood attack.

$$I \to B : I_i, B, S_{I_i},$$
$$B \to I : B, I_i, S_B, S_{I_i} + 1,$$
$$(i = 1, 2, \ldots)$$

Attacker I is formulated in our calculus as follows:

$$P_I \overset{def}{=} \mathsf{new}(i); \mathsf{new}(s); \mathsf{out}\ \bar{c}\ \langle\langle(i, B, s)\rangle\rangle; \mathsf{stop}.$$

Messages that the attacker sends are lost in the network, since the destination IP-addresses are false. In order to formalize these message losses, we assume a process N representing the network.

$$P_N \overset{def}{=} \mathsf{inp}\ c\ (r); \mathsf{stop}.$$

The complete configuration for this case is defined by adding a machine type $\mathbf{i}$ for the attacker I and a machine type $\mathbf{n}$ for the network, in addition to machine types $\mathbf{a}$ and $\mathbf{b}$.

$$AttackConfig \overset{def}{=} (\mathsf{repeat}\, P_I \mid \mathsf{repeat}\, P_B \mid \mathsf{repeat}\, P_N).$$

We now have a commitment and reduction sequence for the configuration as:

$AttackConfig \equiv ($repeat $P_I \mid$ repeat $P_B \mid$ repeat $P_N)$

$\xrightarrow{\tau}$ new$(S_B);$ (stop $\mid$ repeat $P_I \mid$ (split (y_a, y_b, y_c) is $q_1; \cdots) \mid$ repeat P_B
$\mid$ inp c (r); stop $\mid$ repeat $P_N)$
$: \{\mathbf{b} :: store\}$

$\gg$ new$(S_B);$
(stop $\mid$ repeat $P_I \mid$ out $\overline{c}$ $\langle(y_b, y_a, y_{sb}, \mathsf{succ}(y_{sa}))\rangle; \cdots \mid$ repeat P_B
$\mid$ inp c (r); stop $\mid$ repeat $P_N)$
$: \{\mathbf{b} :: 3store\} + \{\mathbf{b} :: -store\} + \{\mathbf{b} :: store\} + \{\mathbf{b} :: -store\}$
$+\{\mathbf{b} :: match\} + \{\mathbf{b} :: store\}$
$= \{\mathbf{b} :: 3store, \mathbf{b} :: match\}$

$\gg$ new$(S_B);$
(stop $\mid$ repeat $P_I \mid$ inp c $(q_2); \cdots \mid$ repeat $P_B \mid$ stop $\mid$ repeat $P_N)$
$: \{\mathbf{n} :: store\}$

Therefore, the cost of the complete configuration for this attacking case is:

$AttackConfig \xrightarrow{\tau} $ new$(S_B);$
(stop $\mid$ repeat $P_I \mid$ inp c $(q_2); \cdots \mid$ repeat $P_B \mid$ stop $\mid$ repeat $P_N)$
$: \{\mathbf{b} :: 4store, \mathbf{b} :: match, \mathbf{n} :: store\}$

From this result, we know that the attacker's cost is negligible. However, B must incur some amount of memory cost for each challenge from the attacker. Since the total memory cost that B bears is proportional to the number of challenges from the attacker, it can be expensive.

3.2   Defense by SYN Cookie Against SYN-Flood Attack

Using a SYN cookie can foil SYN-flood attacks. Generally, in a SYN cookie, the initial sequence number of a source host is used for storage.

$$A \to B : A, B, S_A$$
$$B \to A : B, A, H(A, B, S_A, secret, count)$$
$$A \to B : A, B, S_A + 1, H(A, B, S_A, secret, count) + 1$$

Expression $H(A, B, S_A, secret, count)$ means a hash value consisting of the sequence $A, B, S_A, secret,$ and $count$. The constant $secret$ is a fixed number that is secret from the others, including B. The constant $count$ is a number that is incremented every minute.

Hosts A and B are formulated in our calculus as follows:

$A \overset{def}{=}$ (Same as the original case.)

$B \overset{def}{=}$ new($count$);

    inp c (q_1); split (y_a, y_b, y_{sa}) is q_1 err{free q_1}; free q_1;

    match y_b is B err{free y_a, y_b, y_{sa}}; free y_b;

    store $y_h = $ hash$((y_a, B, y_{sa}, secret, count))$;

    out $\bar{c}$ $\langle(B, y_a, y_h, \mathsf{succ}(y_{sa}))\rangle$; free y_a, y_{sa}, y_h;

    inp c (q_2); split $(y'_a, y'_b, y'_{sa1}, y'_{h1})$ is q_2 err{free y_a, y_{sa}, y_h, q_2}; free q_2;

    match y'_b is B err{free $y_a, y_{sa}, y_h, y'_a, y'_b, y'_{sa1}, y'_{h1}$}; free y'_b;

    store $y'_h = $ hash$((y'_a, y'_b, \mathsf{pred}(y'_{sa1}), secret, count))$;

    match y'_{h1} is $\mathsf{succ}(y'_h)$;

    P_B

The complete configuration of this case is represented as:

$$SYNcookieConfig \overset{def}{=} (\text{repeat } A \mid \text{repeat } B).$$

Then, the commitment and reduction sequences for a normal situation is as follows:

$SYNcookieConfig \equiv (\text{repeat } A \mid \text{repeat } B)$

    $\overset{\tau}{\rightarrow}$ new(S_A); new($count$);

      (inp c (p); $\cdots$) $\mid$ repeat A

      $\mid$ (split (y_a, y_b, y_c) is q_1; $\cdots$) $\mid$ repeat B

      : $\{\mathbf{a} :: store, \mathbf{b} :: store\}$

    $\gg$ new(S_A); new($count$);

      (inp c (p); $\cdots$) $\mid$ repeat A

      $\mid$ (out $\bar{c}$ $\langle(y_b, y_a, y_h, \mathsf{succ}(y_{sa}))\rangle$; $\cdots$) $\mid$ repeat B

      : $\{\mathbf{b} :: 3store\} + \{\mathbf{b} :: -store\} + \{\mathbf{b} :: match\} + \{\mathbf{b} :: -store\}$

      $+\{\mathbf{b} :: store\} + \{\mathbf{b} :: hash\}$

      $= \{\mathbf{b} :: 2store, \mathbf{b} :: match, \mathbf{b} :: hash\}$

    $\overset{\tau}{\rightarrow}$ new(S_A); new($count$);

      (split $(x'_b, x'_a, x'_{sb}, x'_{sa1})$ is $p \cdots$) $\mid$ repeat A

      $\mid$ (free y_a, y_{sa}, y_h; $\cdots$) $\mid$ repeat B

      : $\{\mathbf{a} :: store\}$

    $\gg$ new(S_A); new($count$);

      (out $\bar{c}$ $\langle(x_a, x_b, \mathsf{succ}(x_{sa}), \mathsf{succ}(x_{sb}))\rangle$; $\cdots$) $\mid$ repeat A

      $\mid$ (free y_a, y_{sa}, y_h; $\cdots$) $\mid$ repeat B

      : $\{\mathbf{a} :: 4store\} + \{\mathbf{a} :: -store\} + \{\mathbf{a} :: 3match\} - \{\mathbf{a} :: 3store\}$

      $= \{\mathbf{a} :: 3match\}$

$\xrightarrow{\tau}$ new(S_A); new($count$);

P_A | repeat A | split $(y'_a, y'_b, y'_{sa1}, y'_{h1})$ is $q_2 \cdots$ | repeat B

: $\{\mathbf{b} :: -3store\} + \{\mathbf{b} :: store\}\}$

= $\{\mathbf{b} :: -2store\}$

$\gg$ new(S_A); P_A | repeat A | P_B | repeat B

: $\{\mathbf{b} :: 4store\} + \{\mathbf{b} :: -store\} + \{\mathbf{b} :: match\} + \{\mathbf{b} :: -store\}$

$+ \{\mathbf{b} :: store\} + \{\mathbf{b} :: hash\} + \{\mathbf{b} :: match\}$

= $\{\mathbf{b} :: 3store, \mathbf{b} :: hash, \mathbf{b} :: match\}$

The total cost is determine as follows:

$SYNcookieConfig \xrightarrow{\tau} $ new(S_A); new($cookie$); $(P_A$ | repeat A | P_B | repeat $B)$

: $\{\mathbf{a} :: 2store, \mathbf{a} :: 3match, \mathbf{b} :: 4store, \mathbf{b} :: 2match, \mathbf{b} :: 2hash\}$

By using a SYN cookie, the losses incurred by victim B are reduced as follows.

$$DefendedConfig \stackrel{def}{=} (\text{repeat } I \mid \text{repeat } B \mid \text{repeat } N).$$

$DefendedConfig \equiv (\text{repeat } I \mid \text{repeat } B \mid \text{repeat } N)$

$\xrightarrow{\tau}$ new(S_B); (stop | repeat A | (split (y_a, y_b, y_c) is $q_1; \cdots$) | repeat B

| inp c (r); stop | repeat N)

: $\{\mathbf{b} :: store\}$

$\gg$ new(S_B);

(stop | repeat A | out $\overline{c}$ $\langle (y_b, y_a, y_{sb}, \mathsf{succ}(y_{sa})) \rangle; \cdots$ | repeat B

| inp c (r); stop | repeat N)

: $\{\mathbf{b} :: 3store\} + \{\mathbf{b} :: -store\} + \{\mathbf{b} :: match\}$

$+\{\mathbf{b} :: -store\} + \{\mathbf{b} :: store\} + \{\mathbf{b} :: hash\}$

= $\{\mathbf{b} :: 2store, \mathbf{b} :: match, \mathbf{b} :: hash\}$

$\gg$ new(S_B);

(stop | repeat A | inp c $(q_2); \cdots$ | repeat B | stop | repeat N)

: $\{\mathbf{b} :: -3store, \mathbf{n} :: store\}$

Therefore, the cost of the complete configuration for the case using a SYN cookie is:

$DefendedConfig \xrightarrow{\tau} $ new(S_B);

(stop | repeat A | inp c $(q_2); \cdots$ | repeat B | stop | repeat N)new(S_B);

: $\{\mathbf{b} :: hash, \mathbf{b} :: match, \mathbf{n} :: store\}$.

We confirmed that the memory cost of for a SYN-flood attack was reduced considerably by using a SYN cookie.

4   Summary and Discussion

This paper proposes a formal framework for describing and analyzing the resistance to DoS attack that is based on pi- and spi-calculi. The syntax of the terms and processes is based on spi-calculus. We introduced configuration types that represent computers distributed in a network. Then, we defined the operational semantics respecting typing based on pi-calculus and spi-calculus. We give an example of a description and analysis of DoS attack using a TCP SYN-flood attack and its defense using a SYN cookie. In comparison with Meadows' formal framework [Mea99, Mea01] for the analysis of DoS resistance, the cost estimation and operational semantics are closer in our framework, especially the memory costs. As we explained, protocol designers must be responsible for consistency between protocol behavior and the cost-estimation specification of their framework. Our framework incorporates this consistency.

References

[AA01a]   A.D.Gordon and A.Jeffrey. Authenticity by typing for security protocols. In *14th IEEE Computer Security Foundations Workshop*, pages 145–159, 2001.

[AA01b]   A.D.Gordon and A.Jeffrey. Typing correspondence assertions for communication protocols. *Electronic Notes in Theoretical Computer Science*, 45(17), 2001.

[AA02]   A.D.Gordon and A.Jeffrey. Types and effects for asymmetric cryptographic protocols. In *15th IEEE Computer Security Foundations Workshop*, pages 77–91, 2002.

[AG97a]   M. Abadi and A. D. Gordon. A calculus for cryptographic protocols: The spi calculus. In *Fourth ACM Conference on Computer and Communications Security*, pages 36–47. ACM Press, 1997.

[AG97b]   M. Abadi and A. D. Gordon. Reasoning about cryptographic protocols in the spi calculus. In *CONCUR'97: Concurrency Theory*, number 1243, pages 59–73. Springer-Verlag, Berlin Germany, 1997.

[AN97]   Tuomas Aura and Pekka Nikander. Stateless connections. In *International Conference on Information and Communications Security ICICS'97*, volume 1334 of *Lecture Notes in Computer Science*, pages 87–97. Springer-Verlag, 1997.

[ANL01]   Tuomas Aura, Pekka Nikander, and Jussipekka Leiwo. DOS-resistant authentication with client puzzles. In Christianson, Malcolm, Crispo, and Roe, editors, *Security Protocols, 8th International Workshop*, volume 2133 of *Lecture Notes in Computer Science*, pages 170–177. Springer-Verlag, 2001.

[Mea99]   Catherine Meadows. A formal framework and evaluation method for network denial of service. In *Proceeding of the 12th IEEE Computer Security Foundations Workshop*, pages 4–13, 1999.

[Mea01]   Catherine Meadows. A cost-based framework for analysis of denial of service networks. *Journal of Computer Security*, 9(1/2):143–164, 2001.

[Mil93]   Jonathan K. Millen. A resource allocation model for denial of service pro-
            tection. *Journal of Computer Security*, 2(2/3):89–106, 1993.
[SKK⁺97]   Christoph L. Schuba, Ivan V. Krsul, Markus G. Kuhn, Eugene H. Spafford,
            Aurobindo Sundaram, and Diego Zamboni. Analysis of a denial of service
            attack on TCP. In *Proceedings of the 1997 IEEE Symposium on Security
            and Privacy*, pages 208–223. IEEE Computer Society, IEEE Computer So-
            ciety Press, May 1997.

Formal Analysis of the NetBill
Electronic Commerce Protocol

Kazuhiro Ogata[1,2] and Kokichi Futatsugi[2]

[1] NEC Software Hokuriku, Ltd.
ogatak@acm.org
[2] Japan Advanced Institute of Science and Technology (JAIST)
kokichi@jaist.ac.jp

Abstract. NetBill is an electronic commerce protocol, which allows customers to purchase information goods from merchants over the Internet. It supports goods delivery as well as payment, while many other electronic commerce protocols do not take care of goods delivery. In this paper, we describe the case study in which NetBill has been analyzed with the OTS/CafeOBJ method.

Keywords: algebraic specification, CafeOBJ, electronic commerce, NetBill, OTS, security protocol, verification

1 Introduction

Security protocols deserve to be analyzed formally because they are one of the most important infrastructures in the Internet era and also subject to subtle errors[1, 2]. Therefore, there have been many attempts to apply formal methods to analyses of security protocols, especially authentication ones[3–7]. Electronic commerce protocols are security protocols that allows customers and merchants to conduct their business electronically over the Internet. Among them are SET[8] and NetBill[9]. We have been analyzing electronic commerce protocols with the OTS/CafeOBJ method[10, 11]. In this paper, we describe the case study in which the OTS/CafeOBJ method has been applied to the analysis of NetBill.

NetBill is designed for the purpose of making it possible for customers to purchase information goods, which can be transferred electronically, from merchants over the Internet. It supports goods delivery as well as payment, while many other electronic commerce protocols do not take care of goods delivery. Therefore, NetBill has many properties worth analyzing such as properties on the linkage between goods delivery and payment.

Security protocols are analyzed with the OTS/CafeOBJ method as follows. A security protocol is modeled as an OTS[6], which is a transition system that is suited for being described in terms of equations. The OTS is described in CafeOBJ[12, 13], an algebraic specification language. Properties to analyze are expressed as CafeOBJ terms, and proof scores showing that the OTS has the

K. Futatsugi et al. (Eds.): ISSS 2003, LNCS 3233, pp. 45–64, 2004.

properties are also written in CafeOBJ. Then the proof scores are executed with the CafeOBJ system.

The rest of the paper is organized as follows. Section 2 mentions CafeOBJ and OTSs. Section 3 presents NetBill, actually a simplified and altered NetBill. The ways of modeling the protocol, formalizing its properties and verifying that the protocol has the properties are described in Sect. 4, Sect. 5 and Sect. 6, respectively. Section 7 discusses some related work, and we conclude the paper in Sect. 8.

2 Preliminaries

2.1 CafeOBJ in a Nutshell

CafeOBJ[12, 13] can be used to specify abstract machines as well as abstract data types. A visible sort denotes an abstract data type, while a hidden sort the state space of an abstract machine. There are two kinds of operations to hidden sorts: action and observation operations. An action operation can change a state of an abstract machine. Only observation operations can be used to observe the inside of an abstract machine. An action operation is basically specified with equations by describing how the value of each observation operation changes. Declarations of observation and action operations start with bop or bops, and those of other operations with op or ops. Declarations of equations start with eq, and those of conditional ones with ceq. The CafeOBJ system rewrites a given term by regarding equations as left-to-right rewrite rules.

2.2 Observational Transition Systems

We assume that there exists a universal state space called Υ. We also suppose that each data type used has been defined beforehand, including the equivalence between two data values v_1, v_2 denoted by $v_1 = v_2$. A system is modeled by observing only quantities that are relevant to the system and how to change the quantities by state transition from the outside of each state of Υ. An OTS (observational transition system) can be used to model a system in this way. An OTS $\mathcal{S} = \langle \mathcal{O}, \mathcal{I}, \mathcal{T} \rangle$ consists of:

- $\mathcal{O}$: A set of observers. Each $o \in \mathcal{O}$ is a function $o : \Upsilon \to D$, where D is a data type and may be different for each observer. Given an OTS $\mathcal{S}$ and two states $v_1, v_2 \in \Upsilon$, the equivalence between two states, denoted by $v_1 =_{\mathcal{S}} v_2$, w.r.t. $\mathcal{S}$ is defined as $\forall o \in \mathcal{O}.o(v_1) = o(v_2)$.
- $\mathcal{I}$: The set of initial states such that $\mathcal{I} \subset \Upsilon$.
- $\mathcal{T}$: A set of conditional transitions. Each $\tau \in \mathcal{T}$ is a function $\tau : \Upsilon/=_{\mathcal{S}} \to \Upsilon/=_{\mathcal{S}}$ on equivalence classes of Υ w.r.t. $=_{\mathcal{S}}$. Let $\tau(v)$ be the representative element of $\tau([v])$ for each $v \in \Upsilon$ and it is called *the successor state* of v w.r.t. τ. The condition c_τ for a transition $\tau \in \mathcal{T}$ is called *the effective condition*. The effective condition is supposed to satisfy the following requirement: given a state $v \in \Upsilon$, if c_τ is false in v, then $v =_{\mathcal{S}} \tau(v)$.

1. $C \longrightarrow M$: Request, $\mathcal{H}(Goods)$
2. $M \longrightarrow C$: EncGoods, $\mathcal{E}_K(Goods), \mathcal{E}_{CM}(EPOID)$
3. $C \longrightarrow M$: Payment, $\mathcal{E}_{CM}(EPO, \mathcal{S}_C(EPO))$
4. $M \longrightarrow N$: Endorse, $\mathcal{E}_{MN}(EPO, \mathcal{S}_C(EPO), Goods, K,$
$\mathcal{S}_M(\mathcal{E}_{MN}(EPO), \mathcal{S}_C(EPO), Goods, K))$
5. $N \longrightarrow M$: Result, $\mathcal{E}_{MN}(Receipt, \mathcal{S}_N(Receipt), \mathcal{E}_{CN}(EPOID, CAcct))$
6. $M \longrightarrow C$: Forward, $\mathcal{E}_{CM}(Receipt, \mathcal{S}_N(Receipt), \mathcal{E}_{CN}(EPOID, CAcct))$

Fig. 1. The simplified and altered NetBill

An OTS is described in CafeOBJ. Observers are denoted by CafeOBJ observation operators, and transitions by CafeOBJ action operators.

An execution of $\mathcal{S}$ is an infinite sequence $\upsilon_0, \upsilon_1, \ldots$ of states satisfying:

- *Initiation*: $\upsilon_0 \in \mathcal{I}$.
- *Consecution*: For each $i \in \{0, 1, \ldots\}$, $\upsilon_{i+1} =_\mathcal{S} \tau(\upsilon_i)$ for some $\tau \in \mathcal{T}$.

A state is called *reachable* w.r.t. $\mathcal{S}$ iff it appears in an execution of $\mathcal{S}$. Let $\mathcal{R}_\mathcal{S}$ be the set of all the reachable states w.r.t. $\mathcal{S}$.

All properties considered in this paper are invariants, which are defined as follows:

$$\text{invariant } p \stackrel{\text{def}}{=} \forall \upsilon \in \mathcal{R}_\mathcal{S}.p(\upsilon).$$

Let $\boldsymbol{x}$ be all free variables except for one for states in p. We suppose that invariant p is interpreted as $\forall \boldsymbol{x}.(\text{invariant } p)$ in this paper.

3 NetBill

NetBill involves three parties - customers, merchants and NetBill servers. In this paper, we assume that principals know each other's identities, each principal is given a private/public key-pair; the private counterpart is only available to the owner, while the public one is available to every principal, and each pair of principals shares a symmetric key that is only available to the two principals.

NetBill transactions consist of three phases - the price request phase, the goods delivery phase and the payment phase. Since the last two phases are more important than the first one with respect to security, we only describe the last two phases. We also hide unnecessary quantities that are supposed to be irrelevant to properties we are interested in. Besides we alter NetBill so that NetBill can have more desired properties.

We show the simplified and altered NetBill in Fig. 1. C, M and N stand for a customer, a merchant and a NetBill serves, respectively. Request, EncGoods, Payment, Endorse, and Forward are tags of messages.

Cryptographic primitives used in the protocol are as follows:

- $\mathcal{H}(\cdot)$: A one-way hash function.
- $\mathcal{E}_K(\cdot)$: Encryption with symmetric key K. K may be denoted as XY, meaning the symmetric key shared by principals X and Y.
- $\mathcal{S}_X(\cdot)$: Signature computed with principal X's private key.

Quantities occurring in the protocols are as follows:

- K : Symmetric key generated by M to encrypt *Goods*.
- *Goods* : Information goods C purchases.
- *EPOID* : Transaction ID that is globally unique.
- *CAcct* : C's NetBill account number.

Composite fields used in the protocols are as follows:

- $EPO : C, M, \mathcal{H}(Goods), \mathcal{E}_K(Goods), EPOID, \mathcal{E}_{CN}(CAcct)$
- $Receipt : C, M, K, EPOID$

The first alteration of NetBill is to add *Goods* and $\mathcal{E}_K(Goods)$ in Endorse, although $\mathcal{E}_K(Goods)$ is put in *EPO*. Otherwise the NetBill server cannot check that K is genuine if she/he receives Endorse. Only this alteration does not allow the NetBill server to confirm that *Goods* is what the customer wants to purchase. Therefore we assume that the NetBill server computes hash values of goods merchants sell and singes the hash values, and the hash values and signatures are available to customers. When a customer send Request to a merchant, she/he obtains the hash value of the goods she/he wants to purchase and the corresponding signature, and verifies the signature and specifies the hash value in the message. The hash value of the goods is also put in *EPO*.

We are about to describe how the simplified and altered NetBill works.

- Request: C obtains the hash value of the goods she/he wants to purchase and the corresponding signature, verifies the signature and sends the hash value to M.
- EncGoods: On receipt of Request, M generates a fresh symmetric key K to encrypt the goods C orders and a unique ID *EPOID* to identify this transaction. M sends the encrypted goods to C, together with the transaction ID that is encrypted with the symmetric key shared by C and M.
- Payment: On receipt of EncGoods, C decrypts the cipher text to get *EPOID*, builds *EPO* and sends it and the C's signature on it to M, encrypted with the symmetric key shared by C and M.
- Endorse: On receipt of Payment, M decrypts the cipher text and verifies the signature in the message. M sends *EPO*, the C's signature on it, the goods ordered by C and K to N, together with the M's signature on the four items, encrypted with the symmetric key shared by M and N.
- Result: On receipt of Endorse, N decrypts the cipher text, verifies the two signatures in the message and checks that *CAcct* is C's account number, the account balance is enough to pay, etc. and *EPOID* is fresh and unique. If so, N credits some amount to M and debits the amount against C. Then N builds *Receipt* and sends it and the N's signature on it to M, together

with the cipher text of *EPOID* and *CAcct* encrypted with the symmetric key shared by C and N, entirely encrypted with the symmetric key shared by M and C,

- Forward: On receipt of Result, M decrypts the cipher text, verifies the signature in the message and forwards the three items in the message to C, encrypted with the symmetric key shared by C and M.

4 Modeling NetBill

4.1 Assumptions

We suppose that there exists one and only legitimate NetBill server, which is known by every principal. We also suppose that there not only exist multiple trustable customers and merchants but also multiple malicious (untrustable) principals. Trustable customers and merchants exactly follow the protocol, while malicious principals may do something against the protocol as well, namely eavesdropping and/or faking messages so as to attack the protocol. Instead of describing each malicious principal, the combination and cooperation of the malicious principals is modeled as the most general intruder à la Dolev and Yao[14]. The intruder may behave as a NetBill server as well as a customer and a merchant. The intruder can do the following:

- Eavesdrop any message flowing in the network.
- Glean any quantity from the message; however the intruder can decrypt a cipher text only if she/he knows the key to decrypt, and cannot compute preimages of a hash value if she/he does not know the preimages.
- Fake and send messages based on the gleaned information; however the intruder can encrypt and/or sign something only if she/he knows the key to encrypt and/or sign, and cannot guess unknown secret values.

Accordingly we can regard the network as part of the intruder or the storage that the intruder can use.

4.2 Formalization of Messages

Before formalizing messages exchanged in the protocol, we formalize quantities that constitute messages by means of initial algebra. We declare the following visible sorts and the corresponding data constructors for those quantities:

- Customer and Merchant denotes customers and merchants, respectively.
- Account denotes customers' NetBill account numbers. Given a customer c, her/his account number is denoted by term $\mathbf{a}(c)$.
- Server denotes NetBill servers. The NetBill server is denoted by constant netbill.
- SKey denotes symmetric keys shared by two principals. Given a customer c, a merchant m and a server s, the symmetric key shared by c and m is denoted by $\mathbf{k}(c,m)$, the one shared by c and s denoted by $\mathbf{k}(c,s)$ and the one shared by m and s denoted by $\mathbf{k}(m,s)$.

- Rand denotes unguessable random numbers.
- Epoid denotes EPOIDs. The EPOID that identifies the transaction where a customer c purchases goods from a merchant m is denoted by $\text{epoid}(m, c, r)$, where r is a random number that makes the EPOID globally unique.
- Key denotes symmetric keys to encrypt goods. The key generated by a merchant m to encrypt goods a customer c purchases is denoted by $\text{k}(m, c, r)$, where r is a random number that links the key to the EPOID denoted by $\text{epoid}(m, c, r)$ and makes the key fresh.
- Goods denotes goods. The goods a customer c purchases from a merchant m are denoted by $\text{g}(m, c, r)$, where r is a random number that links the goods to the EPOID denoted by $\text{epoid}(m, c, r)$.
- EncGoods denotes encrypted goods. Given a symmetric key k and goods g, the goods encrypted with the key are denoted by $\text{enc}(k, g)$
- Hash denotes hash values of goods. Given goods g, the hash value is denoted by $\text{h}(g)$.
- Cipher1 denotes EPOIDs encrypted by symmetric keys shared by two principals. Given a symmetric key sk shared by two principals and an EPOID epi, the EPOID encrypted with the key is denoted by $\text{enc1}(sk, epi)$.
- Cipher2 denotes NetBill account numbers encrypted by symmetric keys shared by two principals. Given a symmetric key sk shared by two principals and an account number a, the account number encrypted with the key is denoted by $\text{enc2}(sk, a)$.
- Epo denotes EPOs. Given a customer c, a merchant m, a hash value of goods h, encrypted goods eg, an EPOID epi and an encrypted account $c2$, the corresponding EPO is denoted by $\text{epo}(c, m, h, eg, epi, c2)$.
- Sig1 denotes signatures on EPOs computed by customers. Given a customer c and an EPO ep, the corresponding signature is denoted by $\text{sig1}(c, ep)$.
- Cipher3 denotes cipher texts appearing in Payment messages. Given a symmetric key sk shared by two principals, an EPO ep and a Sig1 $g1$, the corresponding cipher text is denoted by $\text{enc3}(sk, ep, g1)$.
- Sig2 denotes signatures computed by merchants on EPOs, Sig1s, goods and symmetric keys generated by merchants. Given a merchant m, an EPO ep, a Sig1 $g1$, goods g and a symmetric key k generated by a merchant, the corresponding signature is denoted by $\text{sig2}(m, ep, g1, g, k)$.
- Cipher4 denotes cipher texts appearing in Endorse messages. Given a symmetric key sk shared by two principals, an EPO ep, a Sig1 $g1$, goods g, a symmetric key k generated by a merchant and a Sig2 $g2$, the corresponding cipher text is denoted by $\text{enc4}(sk, ep, g1, g, k, g2)$.
- Receipt denotes receipts. Given a customer c, a merchant m, a symmetric key k generated by a merchant and an EPOID epi, the corresponding receipt is denoted by $\text{rec}(c, m, k, epi)$.
- Sig3 denotes signatures computed by NetBill servers on receipts. Given a NetBill server s and a receipt rc, the corresponding signature is denoted by $\text{sig3}(s, rc)$.
- Cipher5 denotes cipher texts of EPOIDs and NetBill account numbers. Given a symmetric key sk shared by two principals, an EPOID epi and

a NetBill account number a, the corresponding cipher text is denoted by
enc5(sk, epi, a).

- Cipher6 denotes cipher texts appearing in Result messages. Given a symmetric key sk shared by two principals, a receipt rc, a Sig3 $g3$ and a Cipher5 $c5$, the corresponding cipher text is denoted by enc6$(sk, rc, g3, c5)$.
- Cipher7 denotes cipher texts appearing in Forward messages. Given a symmetric key sk shared by two principals, a receipt rc, a Sig3 $g3$ and a Cipher5 $c5$, the corresponding cipher text is denoted by enc7$(sk, rc, g3, c5)$.

For each data constructor such as enc7 described above, projection operators such as sk and rc that return arguments are also defined. For example, sk(enc7$(sk, rc, g3, c5)$) = sk and rc(enc7$(sk, rc, g3, c5)$) = rc.

In addition to those visible sorts, we use visible sort Bool that denotes truth values, declared in built-in module BOOL. In the module, two constants true and false, and operators not_ for negation, _and_ for conjunction, _or_ for disjunction, _implies_ for implication and _iff_ for equivalence are also declared. An underscore '_' shows the place where an argument is put.

The six operators (data constructors) to denote the six kinds of messages are declared as follows:

```
op qm : Customer Customer Merchant Hash              -> Msg
op gm : Merchant Merchant Customer EncGoods Cipher1 -> Msg
op pm : Customer Customer Merchant Cipher3            -> Msg
op em : Merchant Merchant Server   Cipher4            -> Msg
op rm : Server   Server   Merchant Cipher6            -> Msg
op fm : Merchant Merchant Customer Cipher7            -> Msg
```

Msg is the visible sort denoting messages. qm stands for Request messages, gm for EncGoods messages, pm for Payment messages, em for Endorse messages, rm for Result messages and fm for Forward messages. For data constructor xm ($x =$ q, g, p, e, r, f), projection operators xc, xs and xd return the first, second and third arguments of terms of which top is xm respectively. Projection operators h, eg, c1, c3, c4, c6 and c7 are also defined. Moreover predicate xm? is defined, which checks if a given message is xm message, where $x =$ q, g, p, e, r, f.

The first, second and third arguments of each constructor mean the actual generator or sender, the source and the destination of the corresponding message. The first argument is meta-information that is only available to the outside observer and the principal that has sent the corresponding message, and that cannot be forged by the intruder, while the remaining arguments may be forged by the intruder. Therefore suppose that there exists a message in the network. It is true that the principal denoted by the first argument has sent the message. If the principal is trustable, we can also deduce that the second argument is the principal and the principal has sent the message to a principal denoted by the third argument. On the other hand, if the principal denoted by the first argument is the intruder, the second argument may not be the principal, which means that the intruder has faked the message.

4.3   Formalization of the Network

The network is modeled as a bag (multiset) of messages, which is used as the storage that the intruder can use. The network is also used as each principal's private memory that reminds the principal to send messages, of which first argument is the principal. Any message that has been sent or put once into the network is supposed to be never deleted from the network because the intruder can replay the message repeatedly, although the intruder cannot forge the first argument. Consequently, the emptiness of the network means that no messages have been sent.

The intruder tries to glean 17 kinds of quantities from the network as much as possible. The 17 kinds of quantities are symmetric keys shared by two principals, symmetric keys generated by merchants, customers' NetBill account numbers, goods, EPOIDs, hash values of goods, encrypted goods, seven kinds of cipher texts and three kinds of signatures.

The collections of those quantities gleaned by the intruder from the network are denoted by the following operators respectively:

```
op cskey  : Network -> ColSKey        op ckey   : Network -> ColKey
op cacct  : Network -> ColAccount     op cgoods : Network -> ColGoods
op cepoid : Network -> ColEpoid       op chash  : Network -> ColHash
op cencg  : Network -> ColEncGoods    op cci1   : Network -> ColCipher1
op cci2   : Network -> ColCipher2     op cci3   : Network -> ColCipher3
op cci4   : Network -> ColCipher4     op cci5   : Network -> ColCipher5
op cci6   : Network -> ColCipher6     op cci7   : Network -> ColCipher7
op csig1  : Network -> ColSig1        op csig2  : Network -> ColSig2
op csig3  : Network -> ColSig3
```

Network is the visible sort denoting the network. Col$X$ is the visible sort denoting collections of quantities denoted by visible sort X.

Those operators are defined with equations. In the rest of the paper, let MG, MG1, MG2, NW, C, M, G, R, SK, K, EPI, C2 and G2 be CafeOBJ variables for Msg, Msg, Msg, Network, Customer, Merchant, Goods, Rand, SKey, Key, Epoid, Cipher2 and Sig2, respectively.

Since any symmetric key shared by two principals does not appear in any message, cskey is defined as follows:

```
eq k(C,M) \in cskey(void) = (C = ic or M = im) .
eq k(C,S) \in cskey(void) = (C = ic and S = netbill) .
eq k(M,S) \in cskey(void) = (M = im and S = netbill) .
eq cskey(MG,NW) = cskey(NW) .
```

Constant void denotes the empty bag. Both constants ic and im denote the intruder acting as a customer and a merchant. Operator _\in_ is the membership predicate of collections. Operator _,_ of MG,NW is the data constructor of bags. The equations say that the symmetric keys the intruder initially knows are only available to the intruder.

ckey is defined as follows:

```
eq  ckey(void) = empk .
ceq ckey(MG,NW) = ckey(NW) if qm?(MG) or gm?(MG) or pm?(MG) or
                           (em?(MG) and not(sk(c4(MG)) \in cskey(NW))) or
                           (rm?(MG) and not(sk(c6(MG)) \in cskey(NW))) or
                           (fm?(MG) and not(sk(c7(MG)) \in cskey(NW))) .
ceq ckey(MG,NW) = k(c4(MG))     ; ckey(NW) if em?(MG) and sk(c4(MG)) \in cskey(NW) .
ceq ckey(MG,NW) = k(rc(c6(MG))) ; ckey(NW) if rm?(MG) and sk(c6(MG)) \in cskey(NW) .
ceq ckey(MG,NW) = k(rc(c7(MG))) ; ckey(NW) if fm?(MG) and sk(c7(MG)) \in cskey(NW) .
```

Constant empk denotes the empty collection and operator _;_ the data constructor of collections. The definition makes use of the fact that cskey(MG,NW) = cskey(NW).

As shown, two definition styles are used for the collections of quantities gleaned by the intruder from the network. The first one is called the observational style and the second one the constructor style. If `cskey` were defined in the constructor style, the following equation would be declared:

```
eq cskey(void) = k(ic,M) ; k(C,im) ; k(ic,netbill) ; k(im,netbill) .
```

However the equation cannot be used as a rewrite rule because the right-hand side has variables M and C that do not appear in the left-hand side. Such equations tend to be hard to use for verification because the reduction command does not use them automatically. `ckey` could be defined in the observational style. For verification, however, we want to express a collection of keys that includes a key k, which can be conveniently denoted by k ; ks in the constructor style, where ks is the collection from which k is excluded. In the observational style, such a collection cannot be conveniently expressed. If the collection of some quantities gleaned by the intruder from the network can be defined in either style, it may be a matter of taste. In this case study, only `ckey` is defined in the constructor style.

One more definition is shown. `cgoods` is defined as follows:

```
eq  G \in cgoods(NW) = G \in cgoods(NW) with ckey(NW) .
eq  G \in cgoods(void) with Ks = false .
ceq G \in cgoods(MG,NW) with Ks = true
    if gm?(MG) and k(eg(MG)) \in Ks and G = g(eg(MG)) .
ceq G \in cgoods(MG,NW) with Ks = true
    if pm?(MG) and k(c3(MG)) \in cskey(NW) and k(eg(ep(c3(MG)))) \in Ks and
       G = g(eg(ep(c3(MG)))) .
ceq G \in cgoods(MG,NW) with Ks = true
    if em?(MG) and k(c4(MG)) \in cskey(NW) and k(eg(ep(c4(MG)))) \in Ks and
       G = g(eg(ep(c4(MG)))) .
ceq G \in cgoods(MG,NW) with Ks = true
    if em?(MG) and k(c4(MG)) \in cskey(NW) and G = g(c4(MG)) .
ceq G \in cgoods(MG,NW) with Ks = G \in cgoods(NW) with Ks
    if not(gm?(MG) and k(eg(MG)) \in Ks and G = g(eg(MG))) and
       not(pm?(MG) and k(c3(MG)) \in cskey(NW) and k(eg(ep(c3(MG)))) \in Ks and
          G = g(eg(ep(c3(MG))))) and
       not(em?(MG) and k(c4(MG)) \in cskey(NW) and k(eg(ep(c4(MG)))) \in Ks and
          G = g(eg(ep(c4(MG))))) and
       not(em?(MG) and k(c4(MG)) \in cskey(NW) and G = g(c4(MG))) .
```

Suppose that nw denotes the network at some time, cgoods(nw) depends on ckey(nw), which is used as the third argument of operator `_\in_with_`.

The remaining operators can be defined in a similar way.

4.4   Formalization of Trustable Principals

Before modeling the behavior of trustable principals, we describe the values observable from the outside of the protocol. We suppose that the set of used random numbers and the network are observable. The observers that return the observable values are denoted by CafeOBJ observation operators `ur` and `nw`, respectively, which are declared as follows:

```
bop ur : Protocol -> URand
bop nw : Protocol -> Network
```

`URand` is the visible sort denoting sets of random numbers.

The behavior of trustable principals is modeled by six kinds of transitions that correspond to sending the six kinds of messages. The six kinds of transitions are denoted by CafeOBJ action operators sdqm, sdgm, sdpm, sdem, sdrm and sdfm. sdqm stands for s̲end R̲equest m̲essages, sdgm for s̲end Enc̲G̲oods m̲essages, sdpm for s̲end P̲ayment m̲essages, sdem for s̲end E̲ndorse m̲essages, sdrm for s̲end R̲esult m̲essages and sdfm for s̲end F̲orward m̲essages. The operators are declared as follows:

```
bop sdqm : Protocol Customer Merchant Hash        -> Protocol
bop sdgm : Protocol Merchant Goods     Rand Msg   -> Protocol
bop sdpm : Protocol Customer           Msg Msg    -> Protocol
bop sdem : Protocol Merchant           Rand Msg Msg -> Protocol
bop sdrm : Protocol                    Msg        -> Protocol
bop sdfm : Protocol Merchant           Rand Msg Msg -> Protocol
```

Protocol is the hidden sort denoting the state space. In the rest of the paper, let P be a CafeOBJ variable for Protocol.

The effective condition of any transition corresponding to sdpm is denoted by operator c-sdpm that is declared and defined as follows:

```
op c-sdpm : Protocol Customer Msg Msg -> Bool
eq c-sdpm(P,C,MG1,MG2)
  = (MG1 \in nw(P) and MG2 \in nw(P) and qm?(MG1) and gm?(MG2) and
     qc(MG1) = C and qs(MG1) = C and gd(MG2) = C and qd(MG1) = gs(MG2) and
     sk(c1(MG2)) = k(C,qd(MG1))) .
```

Operator _\in_ is the membership predicate of bags. Given a state p, a customer c and two messages mg_1 and mg_2, c-sdpm(p, c, mg_1, mg_2) means that the customer c has sent the Request message mg_1 to the merchant denoted by the third argument qd(mg_1) and there exists the EncGoods message mg_2 that seems to have been sent by the merchant in response to mg_1 in the network. Note that the customer cannot check who has actually sent mg_2.

Then sdpm is defined as follows:

```
eq  ur(sdpm(P,C,MG1,MG2)) = ur(P) .
ceq nw(sdpm(P,C,MG1,MG2))
  = pm(C,C,qd(MG1),enc3(k(C,qd(MG1)),
       epo(C,qd(MG1),h(MG1),eg(MG2),epi(c1(MG2)),enc2(k(C,netbill),a(C))),
       sig1(C,epo(C,qd(MG1),h(MG1),eg(MG2),epi(c1(MG2)),enc2(k(C,netbill),a(C))))))
    , nw(P)
    if c-sdpm(P,C,MG1,MG2) .
ceq sdpm(P,C,MG1,MG2)     = P if not c-sdpm(P,C,MG1,MG2) .
```

Operator _,_ of "pm(...) , nw(P)" is the data constructor for bags.

The effective condition of any transition corresponding to sdem is denoted by operator c-sdem that is declared and defined as follows:

```
op c-sdem : Protocol Merchant Rand Msg Msg -> Bool
eq c-sdem(P,M,R,MG1,MG2)
  = (MG1 \in nw(P) and MG2 \in nw(P) and gm?(MG1) and pm?(MG2) and
     gc(MG1) = M and gs(MG1) = M and pd(MG2) = M and gd(MG1) = ps(MG2) and
     sk(c3(MG2)) = k(gd(MG1),M) and sk(c1(MG1)) = k(gd(MG1),M) and
     c(ep(c3(MG2))) = ps(MG2) and m(ep(c3(MG2))) = M and
     h(ep(c3(MG2))) = h(g(eg(MG1))) and eg(ep(c3(MG2))) = eg(MG1) and
     epi(ep(c3(MG2))) = eoi(c1(MG1)) and g1(c3(MG2)) = sig1(gd(MG1),ep(c3(MG2))) and
     k(eg(MG1)) = k(M,ps(MG2),R) and epi(c1(MG1)) = epoid(M,ps(MG2),R) and
     g(eg(MG1)) = g(M,ps(MG2),R)) .
```

Given a state p, a merchant m, a random number r and two messages mg_1 and mg_2, c-sdem(p, m, r, mg_1, mg_2) means that the merchant m has sent the

EncGoods message mg_1 to the customer denoted by the third argument $\mathsf{gd}(mg_1)$, where m uses the random number r to generate the key to encrypt the goods, and there exists the Payment message mg_2 that seems to have been sent by the customer in response to mg_1 in the network.

The sdem is defined as follows:

```
eq  ur(sdem(P,M,R,MG1,MG2)) = ur(P) .
ceq nw(sdem(P,M,R,MG1,MG2))
    = em(M,M,netbill,enc4(k(M,netbill),ep(c3(MG2)),g1(c3(MG2)),g(eg(MG1)),k(eg(MG1)),
        sig2(M,ep(c3(MG2)),g1(c3(MG2)),g(eg(MG1)),k(eg(MG1))))) , nw(P)
    if c-sdem(P,M,R,MG1,MG2) .
ceq sdem(P,M,R,MG1,MG2)      = P if not c-sdem(P,M,R,MG1,MG2) .
```

The remaining operators can be defined in a similar way.

4.5   Formalization of the Intruder

Part of the intruder has been modeled as the network. We have defined what information the intruder can glean from the network. We next describe what messages the intruder fakes based on the gleaned information.

The transitions corresponding to the intruder's faking messages are divided into six classes, each of which fakes each type of messages. The effective condition of these transitions are that the intruder can take advantage of the necessary information to fake messages.

We suppose that the intruder can fake any message if the message can be made from the quantities gleaned by the intruder. However we do not have the intruder fake meaningless messages because such messages do not attack the protocol.

Transitions faking messages are denoted by CafeOBJ action operators. In this paper, we show the CafeOBJ action operators corresponding to transitions faking Endorse messages, which are declared as follows:

```
bop fkem1 : Protocol Merchant Cipher4                             -> Protocol
bop fkem2 : Protocol Merchant Customer SKey Goods Key Epoid Cipher2 Sig1
                                              Sig2 -> Protocol
bop fkem3 : Protocol Merchant Customer SKey Goods Key Epoid SKey Account
                                         Sig1 Sig2 -> Protocol
bop fkem4 : Protocol Merchant Customer SKey Goods Key Epoid Cipher2 Sig2 -> Protocol

bop fkem5 : Protocol Merchant Customer SKey Goods Key Epoid SKey Account
                                              Sig2 -> Protocol
bop fkem6 : Protocol Merchant Customer SKey Goods Key Epoid Cipher2 Sig1 -> Protocol
bop fkem7 : Protocol Merchant Customer SKey Goods Key Epoid SKey Account
                                              Sig1 -> Protocol
bop fkem8 : Protocol Merchant Customer SKey Goods Key Epoid Cipher2      -> Protocol
bop fkem9 : Protocol Merchant Customer SKey Goods Key Epoid SKey Account -> Protocol
```

fkem stands for <u>f</u>a<u>k</u>e <u>E</u>ndorse <u>m</u>essages.

The effective condition of any transition corresponding to fkem4 is denoted by operator c-fkem4 that is declared and defined as follows:

```
op c-fkem4 : Protocol Merchant Customer SKey Goods Key Epoid Cipher2 Sig2 -> Bool
eq c-fkem4(P,M,C,SK,G,K,EPI,C2,G2)
    = (SK \in cskey(nw(P)) and G \in cgoods(nw(P)) and K \in ckey(nw(P)) and
        EPI \in cepoid(nw(P)) and C2 \in cci2(nw(P)) and G2 \in csig2(nw(P))) .
```

Then `fkem4` is defined as follows:

```
eq  ur(fkem4(P,M,C,SK,G,K,EPI,C2,G2)) = ur(P) .
ceq nw(fkem4(P,M,C,SK,G,K,EPI,C2,G2))
    = em(im,M,netbill,enc4(SK,epo(C,M,h(G),enc(K,G),EPI,C2),
                           sig1(ic,epo(C,M,h(G),enc(K,G),EPI,C2)),G,K,G2)) , nw(P)
    if c-fkem4(P,M,C,SK,G,K,EPI,C2,G2) .
ceq fkem4(P,M,C,SK,G,K,EPI,C2,G2)    = P if not c-fkem4(P,M,C,SK,G,K,EPI,C2,G2) .
```

The remaining operators and those for other classes can be defined in a similar way.

5   Properties of NetBill

5.1   Formalization of Properties

In our way of modeling security protocols, their properties are expressed in terms of the existence of messages in the network and the existence of quantities in the collections gleaned by the intruder from the network. All properties to analyze for security properties in our method are invariants.

Given a state p, let $nw(p)$ denote the network in the state, let $cval(nw(p))$, $cval_1(nw(p))$ and $cval_2(nw(p))$ be collections of some quantities gleaned by the intruder from the network, and let $pred$ be a predicate. Moreover let msg be the data constructor for some message, let p_1, p_2 and q denote principals, and let b be a message body. Then properties of security protocols are expressed using the following six kinds of invariants:

1. invariant $(x \in cval(nw(p)) \Rightarrow pred(x))$.
   Secrecy properties can be expressed using this kind of invariant. For example, suppose that $pred(x)$ means that x is generated by the intruder, this invariant is to claim that quantities related to $cval$ are never leaked.
2. invariant $(x_1 \in cval_1(nw(p)) \Rightarrow x_2 \in cval_2(nw(p)))$.
   This kind of invariant makes it possible to express properties of $cval_1(nw(p))$ in terms of those of $cval_2(nw(p))$. If we know that quantities related to $cval_2$ are never leaked, then we can deduce that those related to $cval_1$ are never leaked as well from this invariant.
3. invariant $(x \in cval(nw(p)) \Rightarrow m \in nw(p))$.
   This kind of invariant means that x is never obtained unless m is sent. This can be used to express a property that quantities related to $cval$ cannot be illegally gleaned from the network.
4. invariant $(m \in nw(p) \Rightarrow x \in cval(nw(p)))$.
   This kind of invariant means that x can be gleaned from m.
5. invariant $(msg(p_2, p_1, q, b) \in nw(p) \Rightarrow msg(p_1, p_1, q, b) \in nw(p))$.
   This kind of invariant assures that the message originates from the right principal, namely that the intruder cannot fake this message unless the principal sends it. This is a special case of the following one.
6. invariant $(m_1 \in nw(p) \Rightarrow m_2 \in nw(p))$.
   One-to-many correspondences can be expressed using this kind of invariant. This invariant claims that if there exists m_1 in the network, then there also

exists m_2 in the network, although it does not claim that there exists one and only m_2 in the network. Let m_1 and m_2 be $msg_1(p_2, p_1, q_1, b_1)$ and $msg_2(p_3, p_3, q_2, b_2)$. Then this invariant claims that if q_1 receives m_1, no matter where m_1 originates from, then p_3 has always sent m_2 to q_2.

5.2   Properties to Verify

The informal description of some desired properties for the simplified and altered NetBill is first given.

1. Customers' NetBill account numbers are never leaked.
2. Keys generated by merchants are never leaked.
3. Keys generated by merchants cannot be obtained unless they are received legally.
4. Keys received by customers are proper.
5. If a customer is charged for the goods she/he purchases, then the customer always possesses the encrypted goods and the NetBill server always possesses the appropriate key to decrypt the encrypted goods.
6. Keys generated by merchants are obtained if and only if the corresponding goods are obtained.
7. If a customer receives the goods she/he purchases, then the customer is always charged for the goods.

There are two kinds of keys generated by merchants that the intruder can obtain legally. One is generated by the intruder as a merchant, and the other generated for the intruder as a customer. The second property claims that the keys generated by merchants that are available to the intruder are only these two kinds of keys. On the other hand, the third property claims that if the intruder has a key of the latter kind, then she/he has always received it legally.

Those properties are defined formally in the way described in the previous subsection. They are expressed as CafeOBJ terms. Before that, however, the following are defined:

$$\text{mkepo}(c, m, k, g, epi) \stackrel{\text{def}}{=}$$
$$\text{epo}(c, m, \mathbf{h}(g), \text{enc}(k, g), epi, \text{enc2}(\mathbf{k}(c, \mathbf{netbill}), \mathbf{a}(c))).$$
$$\text{mkc3}(c, m, k, g, epi) \stackrel{\text{def}}{=}$$
$$\text{enc3}(\mathbf{k}(c, m), \text{mkepo}(c, m, k, g, epi), \text{sig1}(c, \text{mkepo}(c, m, k, g, epi))).$$
$$\text{mkc4}(c, m, k, g, epi) \stackrel{\text{def}}{=}$$
$$\text{enc4}(\mathbf{k}(m, \mathbf{netbill}),$$
$$\quad \text{mkepo}(c, m, k, g, epi), \text{sig1}(c, \text{mkepo}(c, m, k, g, epi)), g, k,$$
$$\quad \text{sig2}(m, \text{mkepo}(c, m, k, g, epi), \text{sig1}(c, \text{mkepo}(c, m, k, g, epi)), g, k))).$$
$$\text{mkc6}(c, m, k, epi) \stackrel{\text{def}}{=}$$
$$\text{enc6}(\mathbf{k}(m, \mathbf{netbill}), \text{rec}(c, m, k, epi),$$
$$\quad \text{sig3}(\mathbf{netbill}, \text{rec}(c, m, k, epi)), \text{enc5}(\mathbf{k}(c, \mathbf{netbill}), epi, \mathbf{a}(c))).$$
$$\text{mkc7}(c, m, k, epi) \stackrel{\text{def}}{=}$$
$$\text{enc7}(\mathbf{k}(c, m), \text{rec}(c, m, k, epi),$$
$$\quad \text{sig3}(\mathbf{netbill}, \text{rec}(c, m, k, epi)), \text{enc5}(\mathbf{k}(c, \mathbf{netbill}), epi, \mathbf{a}(c))).$$

$\mathrm{mkepo}(c, m, k, g, epi)$, $\mathrm{mkc3}(c, m, k, g, epi)$, $\mathrm{mkc4}(c, m, k, g, epi)$, $\mathrm{mkc6}(c, m, k,$
$epi)$ and $\mathrm{mkc7}(c, m, k, epi)$ denote an EPO, a `Cipher3`, a `Cipher4`, a `Cipher6`
and a `Cipher7`, respectively, that are constructed according to the protocol.

The formal definitions of those properties are given.

invariant $(\mathrm{a}(c) \setminus \mathrm{in}\ \mathrm{cacct}(\mathrm{nw}(p))\ \mathtt{implies}\ c = \mathrm{ic})$.   (1)

invariant $(\mathrm{k}(m, c, r) \setminus \mathrm{in}\ \mathrm{ckey}(\mathrm{nw(p)})\ \mathtt{implies}\ m = \mathrm{im}\ \mathtt{or}\ c = \mathrm{ic})$.   (2)

invariant $((\mathtt{not}(m = \mathrm{im})\ \mathtt{and}\ \mathrm{k}(m, c, r) \setminus \mathrm{in}\ \mathrm{ckey}(\mathrm{nw}(p)))$
$\qquad$ `implies`   (3)
$\qquad \mathrm{fm}(m, m, c, \mathrm{mkc7}(c, m, \mathrm{k}(m, c, r), \mathrm{epoid}(m, c, r)))) \setminus \mathrm{in}\ \mathrm{nw}(p)$.

Invariant (3), together with invariant (2), claims that if the intruder as a
customer purchases goods from a merchant who is not the intruder, then the
intruder cannot obtain the key for the goods unless the key is legally sent by the
merchant.

invariant $(\mathrm{fm}(m', m, c, \mathrm{mkc7}(c, m, k, epi)) \setminus \mathrm{in}\ \mathrm{nw}(p)$
$\qquad$ `implies`   (4)
$\qquad (\mathrm{fm}(m, m, c, \mathrm{mkc7}(c, m, k, epi)) \setminus \mathrm{in}\ \mathrm{nw}(p)\ \mathtt{and}$
$\qquad\quad \mathrm{rm}(\mathtt{netbill}, \mathtt{netbill}, m, \mathrm{mkc6}(c, m, k, epi)) \setminus \mathrm{in}\ \mathrm{nw}(p)))$.

Invariant (4) claims that if a customer receives a Forward message that is built
according to the protocol and that seems to be sent by the intended merchant,
then the Forward message originates from the merchant and the NetBill server
has sent the corresponding Result message to the merchant. Since the NetBill
server is trustable, we can conclude that the key received is proper.

invariant $((\mathtt{not}(m = \mathrm{im}\ \mathtt{and}\ c = \mathrm{ic})\ \mathtt{and}$
$\qquad \mathrm{em}(m', m, \mathtt{netbill}, \mathrm{mkc4}(c, m, k, g, epi)) \setminus \mathrm{in}\ \mathrm{nw}(p))$
$\qquad$ `implies`   (5)
$\qquad (\mathrm{em}(m, m, \mathtt{netbill}, \mathrm{mkc4}(c, m, k, g, epi)) \setminus \mathrm{in}\ \mathrm{nw}(p)\ \mathtt{and}$
$\qquad\quad \mathrm{pm}(c, c, m, \mathrm{mkc3}(c, m, k, g, epi)) \setminus \mathrm{in}\ \mathrm{nw}(p)))$.

Before the NetBill server charges customers for goods, she/he should receive
Endorse messages that are built according to the protocol. Therefore invariant (5)
claims that if either a customer or a merchant is not the intruder and the NetBill
server receives an Endorse message that conforms to the protocol and says that
the customer intends to pay the merchant for the goods purchased, although
the message has been sent by another merchant, namely the intruder, then both
the merchant and the customer agree on the transaction. This invariant implies
that if a customer is charged for goods, then the goods are what the customer
wants to purchase, the customer possesses the encrypted goods and the NetBill
server possesses the key to decrypt the encrypted goods. Since the NetBill server
is trustable, the customer can expect to eventually receive the key.

invariant $(\mathrm{k}(m, c, r) \setminus \mathrm{in}\ \mathrm{ckey}(\mathrm{nw}(p))\ \mathtt{iff}\ \mathrm{g}(m, c, r) \setminus \mathrm{in}\ \mathrm{cgoods}(\mathrm{nw}(p)))$.   (6)

Invariant (6) claims that the intruder obtains goods if and only if she/he obtains the corresponding key. Together with invariant (2), we conclude that goods are never obtained illegally.

$$\text{invariant}\,((\texttt{not}(m = \texttt{im})\ \texttt{and}\ \texttt{g}(m,c,r)\ \texttt{\textbackslash in}\ \texttt{cgoods}(\texttt{nw}(p)))$$
$$\texttt{implies}\ \texttt{rm}(\texttt{netbill}, \texttt{netbill}, m, \qquad\qquad (7)$$
$$\texttt{mkc6}(c, m, \texttt{k}(m, c, r), \texttt{epoid}(m, c, r)))\ \texttt{\textbackslash in}\ \texttt{nw}(p)).$$

Invariant (7), together with invariants (2) and (6), claims that if the intruder as a customer purchases goods from a merchant who is not the intruder, then the intruder cannot obtain the goods unless the NetBill server charges the intruder for the goods.

Since the intruder has more ability to collect keys and goods, invariants (3), (6) and (7) can be applied to every customer, namely that every customer can obtain neither keys nor goods unless the NetBill server charges her/him for the goods.

6   Verification of NetBill

6.1   Verification Outline

To prove the seven invariants, we need 29 more invariants. Four of the invariants (including invariants (4), (5) and (7)) have been proved by reduction only, and the remaining by induction on the number of transitions applied. In any case, proof scores are written in CafeOBJ. We outline how to write proof scores if invariants are proved by induction on the number of transitions applied[15].

Suppose that we prove that the protocol has "invariant $pred(p, \boldsymbol{x})$" by induction on the number of transitions applied, where p is a free variable for states and $\boldsymbol{x}$ denotes other free variables of $pred$. In this subsection, let H be the hidden sort denoting the state space, instead of $\texttt{Protocol}$. We first write a module, say INV, where $pred(p, \boldsymbol{x})$ is expressed as a CafeOBJ term as follows:

```
op inv : H V -> Bool
eq inv(P, X) = pred(P, X) .
```

$\boldsymbol{V}$ is the list of visible sorts corresponding to $\boldsymbol{x}$, P is a CafeOBJ variable for H and $\boldsymbol{X}$ is a list of CafeOBJ variables for $\boldsymbol{V}$. Term $pred(P, \boldsymbol{X})$ denotes $pred(p, \boldsymbol{x})$.

In the module, we also declare constants $\mathbf{x}$ for $\boldsymbol{V}$. In proof scores, a constant that is not constrained is used for denoting any object for the intended sort. In a proof score, if we declare a constant k for $\texttt{Key}$, k can be used to denote any key generated by merchants. Such constants are constrained with equations, which makes it possible to split the state space. In addition to k, suppose that another constant eg for $\texttt{EncGoods}$ is declared. Let us split the state space into two: one where $\texttt{k}(eg)$ equals k, and the other where $\texttt{k}(eg)$ does not equal k. The former is expressed by declaring the equation $\texttt{eq}\ \texttt{k}(eg)\ \texttt{=}\ k$. The latter is expressed by declaring the equation $\texttt{eq}\ (\texttt{k}(eg)\ \texttt{=}\ k)\ \texttt{=}\ \texttt{false}$.

Let $init$ denote any initial state of the protocol. To show that $pred(p, \boldsymbol{x})$ holds in any initial state, the following proof score is written:

```
open INV
  red inv(init, x) .
close
```

CafeOBJ command red reduces a given term by regarding declared equations as left-to-right rewrite rules.

We next write a module, say ISTEP, where two constants p, p' denoting any state and the successor state after applying a transition in the state, and the predicate to prove in each inductive case is expressed as a CafeOBJ term as follows:

```
op istep : V -> Bool
eq istep(X) = inv(p, X) implies inv(p', X) .
```

In each inductive case, the state space is usually split into multiple subspaces with basic predicates declared in the specification such as those denoted by _\in_ in this case study as clues. Each case is expressed with equations as described. In each case where we prove that any transition denoted by CafeOBJ action operator a preserves $pred(p, x)$, we write a proof score that looks like the following:

```
open ISTEP
  Declare constants denoting arbitrary objects.
  Declare equations denoting the case.
  Declare equations denoting facts if necessary.
  eq p' = a(p, y) .
  red istep(x) .
close
```

y is a list of constants that are used as the arguments of CafeOBJ action operator a, which are declared in this proof score and denote arbitrary objects for the intended sorts. In addition to y, other constants may be declared in the proof score for the state split. As describe above, equations are used to express the case. If necessary, equations denoting facts about data types used, etc. may be declared as well. The equation with p' as its left-hand side specifies that p' denotes the successor state after applying the transition denoted by a in the state denoted by p. If $istep(x)$ is reduced to true, it is shown that the transition preserves $pred(p, x)$ in this case. Otherwise, we may have to split the case again, may need some invariants, or it may show some suggestions that $pred(p, x)$ is not invariant to the protocol.

Suppose that we need an invariant to make progress on the proof. Let the invariant be invariant $pred_1(p, x_1)$, which may be another invariant than one being currently proved, the same one, or one constructed by connecting multiple invariants with conjunction, and let operator inv_1 denote $pred_1$. Then, instead of $istep(x)$, we reduce $inv_1(p, x_1)$ implies $istep(x)$, where x_1 is a list of terms corresponding to x_1. If invariant $pred_1(p, x_1)$ has been proved independent of one being currently proved, we may reduce $inv_1(p', x_1)$ implies $istep(x)$.

6.2   Proof Scores

We partly show the proof of invariant (6). In module `INV`, the following operator is declared and defined:

```
op inv6 : Protocol Merchant Customer Rand -> Bool
eq inv6(P,M,C,R)
   = (k(M,C,R) \in ckey(nw(P)) iff g(M,C,R) \in cgoods(nw(P))) .
```

In module `ISTEP`, the following operator denoting the predicate to prove in each inductive case is declared and defined:

```
op istep6 : Merchant Customer Rand -> Bool
eq istep6(M,C,R) = claim6(p,M,C,R) implies claim6(p',M,C,R) .
```

Let us consider the inductive case where we show that any transition denoted by CafeOBJ action operator `sdem` preserves the predicate of invariant (6). We use constants `m1`, `r1`, `mg1` and `mg2` that denote any merchant, any random number, any message and any message, respectively, which are used as the arguments of `sdem`. In this inductive case, the state space is split into seven sub-spaces based on the following predicates:

BP1 $\stackrel{\text{def}}{=}$ `c-sdem(p,m1,r1,mg1,mg2)`.

BP2 $\stackrel{\text{def}}{=}$ `k(m1,netbill) \in cskey(nw(p))`.

BP3 $\stackrel{\text{def}}{=}$ `(m = m1 and c = ps(mg2) and r = r1)`.

BP4 $\stackrel{\text{def}}{=}$ `g(m,c,r) \in cgoods(nw(p))`.

BP5 $\stackrel{\text{def}}{=}$ `k(m,c,r) \in ckey(nw(p))`.

BP6 $\stackrel{\text{def}}{=}$ `g(m,c,r) \in cgoods(nw(p))`
         `with (k(m1,ps(mg2),r1) ; ckey(nw(p)))`.

Then the state space is split as follows:

1		¬BP2				
2			BP3			
3	BP1			BP4		
4		BP2	¬BP3		BP5	
5				¬BP4	¬BP5	¬BP6
6						BP6
7	¬BP1					

Each case is denoted by the predicate obtained by connecting the ones appearing in the row with conjunction. For example, case 6 means any state satisfying BP1 ∧ BP2 ∧ ¬BP3 ∧ ¬BP4 ∧ ¬BP5 ∧ BP6.

In this paper, the proof score for case 6 is shown. We need another invariant for this case, which is shown as follows:

$$\text{invariant}\,(\mathbf{g}(m_1,c_1,r_1) \text{ \in cgoods}(\text{nw}(p)) \text{ with } (\mathbf{k}(m_2,c_2,r_2) \text{ ; ckey}(\text{nw}(p)))$$
$$\text{implies } (\mathbf{g}(m_1,c_1,r_1) \text{ \in cgoods}(\text{nw}(p)) \text{ or} \qquad (8)$$
$$(\mathbf{k}(m_1,c_1,r_1) = \mathbf{k}(m_2,c_2,r_2) \text{ and}$$
$$\text{enc}(\mathbf{k}(m_1,c_1,r_1),\mathbf{g}(m_1,c_1,r_1)))) \text{ \in cencg}(\text{nw}(p))).$$

Invariant (8) tells us the condition on which the intruder cannot obtain new goods even if a key is added to her/his collection of keys generated by merchants.

The proof score for case 6 is written as follows:

```
open ISTEP
-- arbitrary objects
  op m1 : -> Merchant .  op r1 : -> Rand .
  ops mg1 mg2 : -> Msg .  op nw1 : -> Network .
-- assumptions
  -- eq c-sdem(p,m1,r1,mg1,mg2) = true .
  eq nw(p) = mg1 , mg2 , nw1 .  eq gm?(mg1) = true .  eq pm?(mg2) = true .
  eq gc(mg1) = m1 .    eq gs(mg1) = m1 .  eq pd(mg2) = m1 .  eq gd(mg1) = ps(mg2) .
  eq sk(c3(mg2)) = k(gd(mg1),m1) .       eq sk(c1(mg1)) = k(gd(mg1),m1) .
  eq c(ep(c3(mg2))) = ps(mg2) .          eq m(ep(c3(mg2))) = m1 .
  eq h(ep(c3(mg2))) = h(g(eg(mg1))) .    eq eg(ep(c3(mg2))) = eg(mg1) .
  eq epi(ep(c3(mg2))) = epi(c1(mg1)) .   eq g1(c3(mg2)) = sig1(gd(mg1),ep(c3(mg2))) .
  eq k(eg(mg1)) = k(m1,ps(mg2),r1) .     eq epi(c1(mg1)) = epoid(m1,ps(mg2),r1) .
  eq g(eg(mg1)) = g(m1,ps(mg2),r1) .
  --
  eq k(m1,netbill) \in cskey(nw1) = true .
  eq (m = m1 and c = ps(mg2) and r = r1) = false .
  eq g(m,c,r) \in cgoods(mg1,mg2,nw1) with ckey(nw1) = false .
  eq k(m,c,r) \in ckey(nw1) = false .
  eq g(m,c,r) \in cgoods(mg1,mg2,nw1) with (k(m1,ps(mg2),r1) ; ckey(nw1)) = true .
-- successor state
  eq p' = sdem(p,m1,r1,mg1,mg2) .
-- check if the predicate is true.
  red inv8(p,m,c,r,m1,ps(mg2),r1) implies istep6(m,c,r) .
close
```

The condition on which there exist two messages denoted by mg1 and mg2 in the network denoted by nw(p) is expressed by declaring the following equation: eq nw(p) = mg1 , mg2 , nw1 . Except for the two conjuncts corresponding to this condition, each conjunct in BP1 is expressed by declaring one equation. Basically normal forms should be written on the left-hand sides of equations so that the reduction command can use the equations as rewrite rules automatically because the CafeOBJ rewrite strategy is basically eager. The left-hand sides of all the equations in the proof score are in normal form.

7   Discussion

NetBill[9] as it is does not have the fifth property described in Subsect. 5.2 because the NetBill server is not given enough information to check if the received key is appropriate to decrypt the encrypted goods the customer is supposed to possess when the NetBill server receives an Endorse message. Therefore the Net-Bill server may charge the customer for the goods even if the received key is bogus. That is why we have altered NetBill. We noticed it while we were modeling NetBill, although you could find it without formal methods. We believe, however, that this is also one example showing that formal methods are useful to let us understand targets more profoundly and precisely.

We are not the first to analyze NetBill formally. Heintze, et al.[16] analyze NetBill with the FDR model checker. They make a finite model consisting of one customer, one merchant and one NetBill server and consider one protocol run. They check with FDR that the finite model has the property that goods must be paid before they are received. Untrustable principals are never taken into account.

In our case study, we make a possibly infinite model consisting of unbounded number of customers, unbounded number of merchants, one NetBill server and also the intruder. We prove, not model-check, that the model has several desired properties. Although our method is general because it can be applied to infinite as well as finite models, both methods should be complementary, for it is easier to model-check finite models.

Paulson's inductive method[7] is used to analyze TLS (Transport Layer Security)[17], Cardholder Registration phase of SET[18, 19] and the SET purchase protocols[20] (the simplified and combined Payment Authorization with Purchase Request). The proof assistant Isabelle/HOL is used to support verification in the inductive method.

The OTS/CafeOBJ method is similar to Paulson's inductive method. Paulson's inductive method automates verification process more than the OTS/ CafeOBJ method because the basic functionality for verification in Isabelle/HOL is resolution using higher-order unification, while that in CafeOBJ is equational reasoning using rewriting. We believe, on the other hand, that proof scores in the OTS/CafeOBJ method are easier to read, write and understand because equational reasoning is a way of reasoning used in everyday life and therefore easier to understand than resolution using higher-order unification.

8   Conclusion

We have shown the case study in which we prove that the simplified and altered NetBill has several desired properties.

The CafeOBJ specification has 32 modules and is approximately of 1,300 lines. The main module in which the OTS modeling the protocol is written is approximately of 400 lines. All the proof scores for the 36 invariants are approximately of 79,000 lines. It took about 37 minutes to have the CafeOBJ system load the CafeOBJ specification and execute all the proof scores on a laptop with 850MHz Pentium III processor and 512MB memory. It took about three weeks to complete the case study; about one week for modeling the protocol and writing the CafeOBJ specification and the remaining for writing the proof scores.

Some of the lessons learned through the case study are as follows:

- The reason why we were able to write such long proof scores in about two weeks is that the structures of all the proof scores are similar and the proof score for some invariant can be reused for other invariants. Therefore we could built a tool supporting automatic generation of outline of proof scores.
- The proposed way of modeling security protocols makes it possible to express many interesting properties of electronic commerce protocols, although the properties are all invariants.
- Formal analyses of targets, even formally modeling them, let us understand them more profoundly and precisely.

References

1. Lowe, G.: An attack on the Needham-Schroeder public-key authentication protocol. Information Processing Letters **56** (1995) 131–133
2. Ogata, K., Futatsugi, K.: Flaw and modification of the iKP electronic payment protocols. Information Processing Letters **86** (2003) 57–62
3. Abadi, M., Burrows, M., Needham, R.: A logic of authentication. ACM Transactions on Computer Systems **8** (1990) 18–36
4. Fábrega, F.J.T., Herzog, J.C., Guttman, J.D.: Strand spaces: Proving security protocols correct. Journal of Computer Security **7** (1999) 191–230
5. Lowe, G.: Breaking and fixing the Needham-Schroeder public-key protocol using FDR. In: TACAS '96. LNCS 1055, Springer (1996) 147–166
6. Ogata, K., Futatsugi, K.: Rewriting-based verification of authentication protocols. In: WRLA 2002. Volume 71 of ENTCS., Elsevier Science Publishers (2002)
7. Paulson, L.C.: The inductive approach to verifying cryptographic protocols. Journal of Computer Security **6** (1998) 85–128
8. MasterCard/Visa: SET secure electronic transactions protocol. Book One: Business Specifications, Book Two: Technical Specification, Book Three: Formal Protocol Definition (http://www.setco.org/set_specifications.html) (1997)
9. Cox, B., Tygar, J.D., Sirbu, M.: NetBill security and transaction protocol. In: First USENIX Workshop on Electronic Commerce. (1995) 77–88
10. Ogata, K., Futatsugi, K.: Formal analysis of the iKP electronic payment protocols. In: ISSS 2002. Volume 2609 of LNCS., Springer (2003)
11. Ogata, K., Futatsugi, K.: Formal verification of the Horn-Preneel micropayment protocol. In: VMCAI 2003. Volume 2575 of LNCS., Springer (2003) 238–252
12. CafeOBJ: CafeOBJ homepage. http://www.ldl.jaist.ac.jp/cafeobj/ (2001)
13. Diaconescu, R., Futatsugi, K.: CafeOBJ report. AMAST Series in Computing, 6. World Scientific, Singapore (1998)
14. Dolev, D., Yao, A.C.: On the security of public key protocols. IEEE Transactions on Information Theory **IT-29** (1983) 198–208
15. Ogata, K., Futatsugi, K.: Proof scores in the OTS/CafeOBJ method. In: FMOODS 2003. Volume 2884 of LNCS., Springer (2003) 170–184
16. Heintze, N., Tygar, J., Wing, J., Wong, H.C.: Model checking electronic commerce protocols. In: Second USENIX Workshop on Electronic Commerce. (1996) 147–164
17. Paulson, L.C.: Inductive analysis of the internet protocol TLS. ACM Transactions on Information and System Security **2** (1999) 332–351
18. Bella, G., Massacci, F., Paulson, L.C., Tramontano, P.: Formal verification of Cardholder Registration in SET. In: ESORICS 2000. LNCS 1709, Springer (1997) 159–174
19. Bella, G., Massacci, F., Paulson, L.C.: Verifying the SET registration protocols. IEEE Journal on Selected Area in Communications **21** (2003) 77–87
20. Bella, G., Massacci, F., Paulson, L.C.: The verification of an industrial payment protocol: The SET purchase phase. In: 9th ACM CCS, ACM Press (2002) 12–20

Inferences on Honesty in Compositional Logic for Protocol Analysis

Koji Hasebe and Mitsuhiro Okada*

Department of Philosophy, Keio University,
2-15-45 Mita, Minato-ku, Tokyo 108-8345, Japan
{hasebe,mitsu}@abelard.flet.keio.ac.jp

Abstract. We present an explicit treatment of assumptions on a principal's honesty in compositional logic. Our central idea is to divide an honest principal's role into its components, and these components are composed during the proving steps of a property useful to prove a protocol correctness. We distinguish the monotonic properties and the non-monotonic ones, and give a core inference system for the monotonic properties, which can be extended for non-monotonic ones.

1 Introduction

The main purpose of this paper is to make explicit compositionality of assumptions on honesty in the style of *compositional logic*, which was originally introduced by Durgin-Mitchell-Pavlovic [11] and Datta-Derek-Mitchell-Pavlovic [6, 7]. Especially this paper is aimed at introducing a core inference system of our framework as a first step. An extension is made by the subsequent paper [15] of ours.

Compositional logic is a proof system based on Floyd-Hoare style logical framework for proving protocol correctness. In this framework, a protocol is considered as a program, and a statement "from a principal P's viewpoint, a general property φ holds at the end of his/her protocol action $\vec{\alpha}$" can be represented as a formula of the form $[\vec{\alpha}]_P \ \varphi$ (or of the form $\theta[\vec{\alpha}]_P \ \varphi$ in [7]). One of the most advantageous points of this framework is its compositional approach for reasoning about a compound protocol: for proving a property about a compound protocol we can reuse already established properties about its components.

In the framework of compositional logic, statements are derived not only by means of some axioms about protocol actions but also by means of as-

---

* This work was partly supported by Grants-in-Aid for Scientific Research of MEXT, Center of Excellence of MEXT on Humanity Sciences (Keio University), the Japan-US collaborative research program of JSPS-NSF, Oogata-kenkyu-jyosei grant (Keio University) and Global Security Research Center grant (Keio University). The first author was also supported by Fellowship for Japan Young Scientists from Japan Society for the Promotion of Science.

K. Futatsugi et al. (Eds.): ISSS 2003, LNCS 3233, pp. 65–86, 2004.
© Springer-Verlag Berlin Heidelberg 2004

sumptions about the other principals' honesty. For formalizing such assumptions about honesty (called *honesty assumptions*), in [11, 6, 7] they use conditional statements of the form $Honest(Q) \supset \varphi$, which means "if a principal Q is honest, then φ holds in any run of the protocol in question". On the other hand, we propose a way to make more explicit the composing steps of the honesty assumptions during a proving process of a property. For that purpose we use the form of expression $Honest(\vec{\alpha}^Q) \supset \varphi$, instead of $Honest(Q) \supset \varphi$, where $\vec{\alpha}^Q$ represents a sequence of *primitive actions* (i.e., sending, receiving or generating actions) in a role performed by Q. Using this framework, an (often minimal) requirement of Q's honesty to derive a property φ from P's viewpoint is expressed by explicitly mentioning the part $\vec{\alpha}^Q$ of Q's role in a protocol.

The basic form of assertion in our inference system is as follows.

$$Honest(\vec{\alpha}_1^{Q_1}), \ldots, Honest(\vec{\alpha}_n^{Q_n}), \Gamma \vdash [\vec{\beta}]_P \, \varphi,$$

where each $\vec{\alpha}_i^{Q_i}$ represents a component part of role performed by a principal Q_i (for each $i = 1, \ldots, n$). The intended meaning of the above sequent is "if each Q_i honestly performs a part of his/her role $\vec{\alpha}_i^{Q_i}$, and if some properties Γ hold, then after P performs a sequence of actions $\vec{\beta}$, φ holds from P's viewpoint". (Here Q_i may be the same as Q_j for some $i, j = 1, \ldots, n$.)

In our framework during a proving process, such honesty assumptions are derived not only by some special inferences, called *honesty inferences*, but also by the following *weakening rule* which is an analogy to the weakening rule of the traditional logic.

$$\frac{Hon(\vec{\alpha}^Q; \vec{\alpha}'^Q), \Gamma \vdash [\vec{\beta}; \vec{\beta}']_P \, \varphi}{Hon(\vec{\alpha}^Q; \alpha''^Q; \vec{\alpha}'^Q), \Gamma \vdash [\vec{\beta}; \beta''; \vec{\beta}']_P \, \varphi} \quad \textbf{Weakening}$$

This means "from P's view, if a property φ is derived from Γ with Q's honesty on $\vec{\alpha}; \vec{\alpha}'$ after P's performance of $\vec{\beta}; \vec{\beta}'$, then φ is also derived from Γ with Q's honesty on $\vec{\alpha}; \alpha''; \vec{\alpha}'$ after P's performance of $\vec{\beta}; \beta''; \vec{\beta}'$, for any addition α'' and β'' in the roles". Here $\vec{\alpha}; \vec{\alpha}'$ ($\vec{\beta}; \vec{\beta}'$, resp.) is the sequential concatenation of two sequences of actions $\vec{\alpha}$ and $\vec{\alpha}'$ ($\vec{\beta}$ and $\vec{\beta}'$, resp.).

Moreover, by means of the weakening rule, honesty assumptions are composed by the following reasoning from P's view.

$$\frac{\dfrac{Hon(\vec{\alpha}^Q) \vdash [\vec{\beta}]_P \, x = t \quad Hon(\vec{\alpha}'^Q) \vdash [\vec{\beta}]_P \, \varphi}{Hon(\vec{\alpha}^Q), Hon(\vec{\alpha}'^Q) \vdash [\vec{\beta}]_P \, \varphi[t/x]} \, \textbf{Eq}}{Hon(\vec{\alpha}^Q \circ \vec{\alpha}'^Q) \vdash [\vec{\beta}]_P \, \varphi[t/x]} \, \textbf{Comp(Hon)}$$

The intended meaning of this reasoning is as follows. First assume the two assertions from P's view: "if Q follows a part of his/her role $\vec{\alpha}^Q$ honestly, then $x = t$ holds after P performs his/her role $\vec{\beta}$", and "if Q follows another part of his/her role $\vec{\alpha}'^Q$ honestly, then a property φ holds". Then by an equality inference, "if Q follows $\vec{\alpha}^Q$ as well as $\vec{\alpha}'^Q$, then $\varphi[t/x]$" holds from P's view.

Then by combining the two separated assumptions on Q's honesty into one assumption on Q's honesty (following his/her combined role $\vec{\alpha}^Q \circ \vec{\alpha}'^Q$), "if Q follows his/her combined role $\vec{\alpha}^Q \circ \vec{\alpha}'^Q$, then $\varphi[t/x]$" holds from P's view. Here $\vec{\alpha}^Q \circ \vec{\alpha}'^Q$ is a sequence of actions which includes all actions in the components $\vec{\alpha}^Q$ and $\vec{\alpha}'^Q$ and preserving order. This composition is formalized as a derived rule **Comp(Hon)**, which is actually obtained by combining basic and natural logical (structural) inferences (i.e., weakening rule as shown above and usual contraction rule of left hand side of a sequent). Another example of a composition of honesty assumptions using cut rule is as follows.

$$
\cfrac{\cfrac{Hon(\vec{\alpha}^Q) \vdash [\vec{\beta}]_P \, \varphi \qquad \varphi, Hon(\vec{\alpha}'^Q) \vdash [\vec{\beta}]_P \, \psi}{Hon(\vec{\alpha}^Q), Hon(\vec{\alpha}^Q) \vdash [\vec{\beta}]_P \, \psi} \text{ Cut}}{Hon(\vec{\alpha}^Q \circ \vec{\alpha}'^Q) \vdash [\vec{\beta}]_P \, \psi} \text{ Comp(Hon)}
$$

By using such composing steps, for proving a property about a compound protocol we can directly reuse assertions about its components to construct a proof of the property.

Here we remark a difference on the standpoints between our approach and that of [11, 6, 7]. In order to realize the compositionality on the honesty assumptions, our approach needs to restrict the forms of honesty inferences to a Horn-clause. Therefore, the following kind of inferences, which is considered in [11, 6, 7], is not considered in our system: "if a principal (say P) honestly follows a role $\vec{\alpha} = \alpha_1; \alpha_2; \alpha_3$ of a protocol, then one concludes $Honest(P) \wedge (P \text{ performs } \beta) \supset (\beta = \alpha_1) \vee (\beta = \alpha_2) \vee (\beta = \alpha_3)$" (i.e., if P is honest and he/she performs an primitive action β then it is α_1 or α_2 or α_3). This kind of inferences is not in harmony with the compositionality because our weakening rules may add other possibilities of disjunctions. As a result, our framework is simplified to be the Horn-clause basis while [11, 6, 7] uses more general language including disjunctions and negations.

In our framework if one can freely apply the weakening rule to φ, we call φ a *monotonic* property. Freshness, receiving-fact, which are used in BAN logic [1], are examples of monotonic properties. On the other hand, for example, property $HasAlone(P, m)$ (introduced in [6, 7]), which means that "a message m is possessed only by P", is *non-monotonic*, because if a receiving action of m is added into the component of Q's role, then $HasAlone(P, m)$ does not hold anymore. (Another example of non-monotonic property is *Source* introduced in [11].) The notion of monotonicity is essentially the same as the notion of *persistency* in the sense of [11, 6, 7]. However, while persistency is related only to the weakening rule for protocol actions (which are described in the square bracket "[ ]"), the notion of monotonicity is related to both weakening rules, for honesty assumptions and for protocol actions.

If we use such non-monotonic properties in our framework, we have to restrict the use of weakening rule by imposing appropriate conditions to preserve the properties, or to introduce a kind of temporal notion. However, so long as the monotonic properties are concerned, we do not need any restriction on the weakening rule nor any introduction of temporal notions. One of our aim in this paper is to explain our framework by restricting our attention within the core part of our inference system which is made up of only some monotonic properties. As an example, we take a set of properties which are useful for proving *agreement property* (in the sense of Woo-Lam [19]) of a protocol.[1] These properties are mainly chosen from the BAN logic predicates such as "*sends*", "*receives*", "*fresh*"[2], and so on. All of our chosen properties are monotonic except "*sends*".[3] However, if we want to prove a property stronger than the agreement property, we need to introduce some non-monotonic properties, and then to restrict the free use of the weakening rules. In the subsequent work [15] of ours, we show how to extend our framework by introducing some non-monotonic properties. As an example, in [15] we introduce a non-monotonic property, simply called *firstly sends*, means "a principal sends a message m containing n as a subterm, and he/she does not send any other message m' containing n before the sending of m". Moreover, we demonstrate that this property is useful to derive the *matching conversations* of *Challenge Response protocol* [9] (cf. also [6,7]), which is stronger than the agreement property.

In this paper, we use the following notations. (The complete definition of the language of our system is presented in Appendix A.1.) The letters A, B, $C,\ldots$ (P, Q, $R,\ldots$, resp.) are constants (variables , resp.) of principals' names. The capital letters $K, K',\ldots, K_1, K_2,\ldots$ and $N, N',\ldots, N_1, N_2,\ldots$ are constants of keys and of nonces, respectively, while the small letters $k, k',\ldots, k_1, k_2,\ldots$ and $n, n',\ldots, n_1, n_2,\ldots$ are variables of the same sorts as above. The letters $m, m',\ldots, m_1, m_2,\ldots$ are used to denote messages, and $\{m\}_K$ is the encryption of m with key K, and $\langle m_1,\ldots, m_n\rangle$ is the concatenation of messages $m_1,\ldots, m_n$. We also use the notation $m \sqsubseteq m'$ to represent the subterm relation as a meta symbol.

The rest of this paper is organized as follows. In Chapter 2 we give the definition of our inference system. In Chapter 3 we explain our proving method for a composed protocol by using the same example as [6,7]. In Chapter 4 we give a semantics of the system by means of the notion of trace. Finally, in Chapter 5 we present our conclusions and some further issues.

2   Inference System

In this section, we give the definition of our inference system. The complete list of the formal definitions is presented in Appendix A.

---

[1] We do not go into the secrecy issue in this paper.

[2] In [6,7], they use "t is *fresh*" differently from ours, namely as "no one else has seen any term containing t as a subterm". On the other hand, our use of freshness is the same as BAN logic [1].

[3] the property "*sends*" is non-monotonic with respect to the weakening rule for honesty assumptions. The details shall be explained in Section 2.

2.1   The Language

Predicates of our inference system are as follows: *P generates n*, *P receives m*[4], *P sends m*, $PK(P, k)$, $P \overset{k}{\leftrightarrow} Q$, *fresh(n)* and $t = t'$. The first three predicates are called *action predicates (performed by P)*. On the other hand, the last four predicates are called *non-action predicates*. All those predicates except equality are chosen from the BAN logic predicates [1]. Equality is used for explicit treatment of substitutions. As we have mentioned in Section 1, all those predicates except *sends* have *monotonic* properties (i.e., properties independent of the weakening rules for principal's actions and for honesty assumptions).[5] Here we introduce the following meta-symbols. The letters $\varphi, \psi, \ldots, \varphi', \ldots$ are used to denote *atomic formula* (or simply called *atoms*). The letters $\alpha, \beta, \gamma, \delta, \ldots, \alpha', \alpha'', \ldots, \alpha_1, \alpha_2, \ldots$ are used to denote atoms made of an action predicate (called *atomic action formulas*), and also $\alpha^P, \beta^P, \gamma^P, \delta^P, \ldots$ to denote atomic action formulas performed by P. The letters $\theta, \theta', \ldots, \theta_1, \theta_2, \ldots$ are atoms made of an non-action predicate (called *atomic non-action formulas*).

As logical connectives, we introduce only usual conjunction (denoted by ",") and non-commutative conjunction (denoted by ";"). Our intention is to use non-commutative conjunction to represent a sequence of principals' actions. While in [6, 7], they use some temporal operators to reason about the ordering of actions, we do not use any temporal operators: in our system orderings are directly expressed by non-commutative conjunction. We introduce the vector notation such as $\vec{\alpha}$ to denote a sequence (i.e., non-commutative conjunct) of atomic action formulas.

Our inference system uses a sequent calculus style assertion. The basic form of assertion is as follows (where Q_i may be the same as Q_j for some $i, j = 1, \ldots, n$).

$$Honest(\vec{\alpha}_1^{Q_1}), \ldots, Honest(\vec{\alpha}_n^{Q_n}), \Delta \vdash [\vec{\beta}]_A \, \varphi$$

Here $\vec{\alpha}_i^{Q_i}$ is a sequence of atomic action formulas performed by Q_i (for each $i = 1, \ldots, n$), which represents a part of his/her role. $\vec{\beta}$ is a sequence of actions performed by A.[6] φ is an atomic formula (made of an action or non-action predicate). Δ is of the form $\theta_1, \ldots, \theta_m, \vec{\gamma}_1, \ldots, \vec{\gamma}_k$. Each predicate of the form

---

[4] We distinguish two kinds of *"receives"*: the simple receiving and the receiving with decryptions. *P receives* $m(\{m'\}_k^*)$ means that "*P* receives a message m and decrypts the indicated subterm $\{m'\}_k$ of m. For a more formal description, instead of using *, we could introduce a new predicate *decrypts* and describe it by (*P receives m*) $\wedge$ (*P decrypts* $\{m'\}_k$).

[5] As we shall see in the explanation of Matching rule of the honesty inferences in Section 2.2 (III), predicate *"sends"* is monotonic w.r.t. the weakening for concrete actions, however it is non-monotonic w.r.t. the weakening for honesty assumptions. In other words, this predicate is non-monotonic in the sense of our terminology, whereas it is "persistent" in the sense of [11, 6, 7].

[6] For describing a sequence of action, while compositional logic of [11, 6, 7] uses the *cord calculus*, we describe it by a sequence (i.e., non-commutative conjunct) of action predicates.

$Honest(\vec{\alpha}_i^{Q_i})$ represents "principal Q_i honestly follows a part of his/her role $\vec{\alpha}_i^{Q_i}$". We call it Q_i's *honesty assumption*. Here, if $\vec{\alpha}_i^{Q_i}$ is $\alpha_{i_1}^{Q_i}; \cdots ; \alpha_{i_m}^{Q_i}$, we can consider the predicate $Honest(\vec{\alpha}_i^{Q_i})$ as an abbreviation of $Honest(\alpha_{i_1}^{Q_i}); \cdots ;$ $Honest(\alpha_{i_m}^{Q_i})$, which is a conjunct of non-commutative conjunction.

Therefore, the intuitive meaning of the sequent style assertion previously introduced is "if each principal Q_i honestly follows the parts of his/her role $\vec{\alpha}_i^{Q_i}$, and if some properties Δ hold, then after A performs a sequence of actions $\vec{\beta}$, φ holds from A's viewpoint". (Here $\vec{\beta}$ may be empty. In such case we often use the expression $\Gamma \vdash \varphi$, instead of $\Gamma \vdash [\ ]\varphi$.)

Finally, we introduce the postfix notation $[\vec{P}, \vec{n}, \vec{k}]$ in order to denote the lists of principal names $\vec{P}$ (list of variables $P_1, \ldots, P_m$), and the lists of variables of nonces and session keys $\vec{n}, \vec{k}$ (as variables). Substitutions are represented in terms of this notation.

2.2   Axioms and Inference Rules

Our inference system consists of the following four classes of axioms and inference rules. The complete list of the axioms and inference rules is presented in Appendix A.2.

(I)   Logical inferences with equality

(II)   Action properties axioms

(III)   Inferences related to the honesty assumption (which are called *honesty inferences*)

(IV)   Weakening rules for actions and honesty assumptions

(I) Logical Inferences with Equality

As logical inferences, we use some structural rules (weakening, contraction, exchange rules of the left hand side, and cut rule) and the equality inference rules. For example, the following inference rules are cut rule (in right below) and a typical equality inference rule which we often use (in left below). (Here t is any term and x is a variable.)

$$\frac{\Gamma \vdash [\vec{\alpha}]\varphi \quad \varphi, \Delta \vdash [\vec{\alpha}]\psi}{\Gamma, \Delta \vdash [\vec{\alpha}]\psi} \ \textbf{Cut} \qquad \frac{\Gamma \vdash [\vec{\alpha}]x = t \quad \Delta \vdash [\vec{\alpha}]\varphi}{\Gamma, \Delta \vdash [\vec{\alpha}]\varphi[t/x]} \ \textbf{Eq}$$

We also introduce the following inference (*substitution rule*) as a logical inference rule.

$$\frac{\Gamma \vdash [\vec{\alpha}]\varphi}{\Gamma[t/x] \vdash [\vec{\alpha}[t/x]]\varphi[t/x]} \ \textbf{Subst}$$

(II) Action Properties Axioms

Action properties axioms are the *axioms about actions* and the *axioms for relationship between properties* in the sense of [11]. Our proposed axioms are listed in

Appendix A.2. However, our framework does not depend on a specific set of axioms in this category. The followings are some examples of our action properties axioms.

Axioms About Primitive Actions:

$$\vdash [\alpha_1^P; \cdots; \alpha_n^P]\alpha_i^P \qquad \text{(for any principal } P \text{ and for any } i = 1, \ldots, n.)$$

Nonce Verification (Public Key):

$$(PK(k, Q)), (fresh(m)), (P \text{ receives } m'(\{m\}_{k^{-1}}^{*})) \vdash (Q \text{ sends } m'')$$

(Here $\{m\}_{K^{-1}} \sqsubseteq m', m''$.)

Note that Nonce Verification is a formalization of the *Incoming tests* of *Authentication tests* based *Strand space* method introduced by [13] (cf. also [12]). On the other hand, we need a non-monotonic property equivalent to the notion of "*uniquely originate*" (in the sense of [13]) to formalize *Outgoing tests*. This formalization is given by using the property "*firstly sends*" in [15].

(III) Honesty Inferences

In terms of the classes (I) and (II) of axioms introduced above, we can derive some actions performed by Q from another principal P's viewpoint. For example, we can derive "P knows that Q actually performed a sending action in a current run" from information about encrypted keys or fresh nonces, etc. included in the received message. However, to derive Q's other actions, P may assume Q's honesty and may use P's knowledge about Q's role in the protocol. For example, if P assumes that Q is honest and that P knows that Q sends the message m in the current run, then P can derive that Q also performed a previous action defined by Q's role. That is because Q should not send message m if Q does not perform all previous actions of his/her role.

For formalizing such an inference, compositional logic in [11, 6, 7] uses a special inference aimed at a conclusion of the form $Honest(Q) \supset \varphi$. On the other hand, in our system, inferences on honesty are formalized by the following inference rules, called *honesty inferences*. The central idea of ours is to separate Q's role into his/her primitive actions, and use a predicate of the form $Honest(\vec{\alpha}^Q)$ as an assumption where $\vec{\alpha}^Q$ is a part of his/her role. In this framework, Q's actions are derived directly from a corresponding (often minimal) part of his/her role.

Our honesty inferences are as follows.

Substitution (Receives):

$$\frac{\Gamma \vdash [\vec{\alpha}]_P \ Q \text{ receives } m[t/x]}{\Gamma, Honest(Q \text{ receives } m) \vdash [\vec{\alpha}]_P \ x = t} \ \textbf{Hon(Subst)}$$

(Here t is a constant, and x is a variable which has the same sort as t.)

We also admit an inference rule obtained from the above rule replacing "*receives*" with "*sends*".

The intended meaning of the inference rules is that if "Q knows that a principal P receives (or sends, resp.) a message m with some concrete values t (i.e., $m[t/x]$)", and if "P assumes that Q is honest and follows a receiving (or sending, resp.) action of message m", then we can conclude "P knows that x should be t".

Matching:

$$\frac{\Gamma \vdash [\vec{\alpha}]_P \ (Q \ sends \ m)}{\Gamma, Honest(Q \ sends \ m', m) \vdash [\vec{\alpha}]_P \ (Q \ sends \ m')} \ \textbf{Hon(Match)}$$

(Here $m \sqsubseteq m'$.)

The intended meaning of this inference rule is that if "P knows that Q sends a message m" and if "P assumes that Q is honest and follows the sending action $Q \ sends \ m'$ containing m", then we can conclude "P knows that Q has sent m'". This inference holds whenever the following additional condition is satisfied: "the set of honesty assumptions does not include any other Q's sending action of a message containing m as a subterm". This means that the formula "$Q \ sends \ m'$" appearing in the lower sequent is non-monotonic. Thus, to keep this formula monotonic, we restrict all applications of honesty inferences and of weakening rule for honesty assumptions (explained in the next item (IV)) so as to preserve this condition. More formally, we extend the language by introducing a new predicate $Honest(\alpha, m)$ (here the usual honesty assumption of the form $Honest(\alpha)$ previously introduced can be regarded as a special case that m is empty), and all applications of honesty inferences and the weakening rule for honesty assumptions are restricted by the following condition (denoted by ($\sharp$)).

($\sharp$) Both honesty assumptions $Honest(Q \ sends \ m', m)$ and $Honest(Q \ sends \ m'')$ (with $m \sqsubseteq m''$) do not appear in the left hand side of the lower sequent.

Note that we do not admit a rule obtained from the Matching rule above by replacing "*sends*" with "*receives*", because even if we assume principal Q is honest and follows a part of role $\vec{\alpha}^Q$, we cannot derive that Q receives only the messages following $\vec{\alpha}^Q$.

Deriving Another Action (Sends):

$$\frac{\Gamma \vdash [\vec{\alpha}]_P \ Q \ sends \ m}{\Gamma, Honest(Q \ receives \ m'; Q \ sends \ m) \vdash [\vec{\alpha}]_P \ Q \ receives \ m'} \ \textbf{Hon(Role)}$$

We also admit an inference rule obtained from the above rule by replacing "*receives*" with "*sends*" or "*generates*".

The intended meaning of this inference rule is that if "P knows that Q actually sends (or receives) a message m and Q follows a sequence of primitive actions $Q \ receives \ m'; Q \ sends \ m$", then "$Q$ actually performs action $Q \ receives \ m'$".

(IV) Weakening Rules for Honesty Assumptions and for Actions

The following inferences are *weakening rules* for *honesty assumptions* (in left below) and for *performed actions* (in right below).

$$\frac{\Gamma, Honest(\vec{\alpha}^Q; \vec{\alpha}'^Q) \vdash [\vec{\beta}]_P \, \varphi}{\Gamma, Honest(\vec{\alpha}^Q; \alpha''^Q; \vec{\alpha}'^Q) \vdash [\vec{\beta}]_P \, \varphi} \; \mathbf{W(Hon)} \qquad \frac{\Gamma \vdash [\vec{\alpha}; \vec{\alpha}']_P \, \varphi}{\Gamma \vdash [\vec{\alpha}; \alpha''; \vec{\alpha}']_P \, \varphi} \; \mathbf{W(Act)}$$

As we have mentioned in the explanation of Matching rule of honesty inferences, weakening rule for honesty assumptions should satisfy the ($\sharp$) condition so as to keep the correctness of Matching rule already applied in a proof.

In our system, free applications of the weakening rules are restricted by only ($\sharp$) to keep the monotonicity of predicate *sends*. Of course, if we eliminate the predicate *sends*, all of our predicates are completely monotonic and then we should restrict no application of the weakening rules. However, this property is indispensable to prove protocol correctness. In other words, our choice of predicates is one of the simplest formalism to prove the aimed property in this paper. However, as we have mentioned in Section 1, if some non-monotonic predicates such as "*Source*" in [11] or "*Fresh*" or "*HasAlone*" in [6,7] are used in our framework, some additional conditions for weakening and honesty inferences should be required. In the subsequent paper [15] of ours, we discuss what kind of additional conditions are required to introduce such non-monotonic properties.

In this paper, we restrict our attention to the protocol which does not include any *duplication of atomic actions*. We assume that each principal in a protocol does not send nor receive the same message twice. This assumption seems to be reasonable because in a protocol including such a duplication, a receiver of the same messages cannot distinguish one from another. Our inference system is sound under this assumption. See Section 4 for a more formal discussion of soundness.

Composing Steps in Our System:

By using the contraction rule for commutative conjunction (",") in (I) and weakening rules in (IV), operations for composition of honesty assumptions are interpreted by the following derived rule (called **Comp(Hon)**).

$$\frac{\dfrac{\Gamma, Hon(\vec{\alpha}^Q), Hon(\vec{\beta}^Q) \vdash [\vec{\gamma}]\varphi}{\Gamma, Hon(\vec{\alpha}^Q \circ \vec{\beta}^Q), Hon(\vec{\alpha}^Q \circ \vec{\beta}^Q) \vdash [\vec{\gamma}]\varphi}}{\Gamma, Hon(\vec{\alpha}^Q \circ \vec{\beta}^Q) \vdash [\vec{\gamma}]\varphi} \begin{array}{l} \mathbf{Weak(\; ; \;)} \\[6pt] \mathbf{Cont(\; , \;)} \end{array}$$

Here the notation $\vec{\alpha}^Q \circ \vec{\beta}^Q$ is a result of *order preserving merge* of sequence $\vec{\alpha}^Q$ and $\vec{\beta}^Q$. That is, $\vec{\alpha}^Q \circ \vec{\beta}^Q$ is a sequence of actions which includes all actions both in $\vec{\alpha}^Q$ and $\vec{\beta}^Q$, and preserving the order. (For example, $\alpha_3; \alpha_1; \alpha_2; \alpha_4; \alpha_3$ and $\alpha_1; \alpha_2; \alpha_3; \alpha_4$ are order preserving merges of two lists $\alpha_1; \alpha_2; \alpha_3$ and $\alpha_3; \alpha_4$.)

This derived rule is useful to prove properties of a composed protocol by reusing proofs of its components as follows. Assume that there are two proofs π_1 and π_2, whose end sequents are $\Gamma_1, Hon(\vec{\alpha}^Q) \vdash [\vec{\gamma}]\varphi_1$ and $\Gamma_2, Hon(\vec{\beta}^Q) \vdash [\vec{\gamma}']\varphi_2$, respectively. From these proofs, in our inference system we can get a composed proof by adding some inferences as follows.

$$\pi_1 \qquad\qquad\qquad \pi_2$$

$$\cfrac{\cfrac{\Gamma_1, Hon(\vec{\alpha}^Q) \vdash [\vec{\gamma}]\varphi_1}{\Gamma_1', Hon(\vec{\alpha}'^Q) \vdash [\vec{\delta}]\varphi_1'} \textbf{ S, W(A)} \qquad \cfrac{\cfrac{\Gamma_2, Hon(\vec{\beta}^Q) \vdash [\vec{\gamma}']\varphi_2}{\Gamma_2', Hon(\vec{\beta}'^Q) \vdash [\vec{\delta}]\varphi_2'} \textbf{ S, W(A)}}{} \textbf{Eq}}{\cfrac{\Gamma_1', \Gamma_2', Hon(\vec{\alpha}'^Q), Hon(\vec{\beta}'^Q) \vdash [\vec{\delta}']\varphi}{\Gamma_1', \Gamma_2', Hon(\vec{\alpha}'^Q \circ \vec{\beta}'^Q) \vdash [\vec{\delta}']\varphi} \textbf{Comp(Hon)}}$$

Step 1 (Substitutions): For the end sequents of π_1 and π_2, we apply some substitution rules and weakening rules so that each $\vec{\gamma}$ and $\vec{\gamma}'$ becomes the same action $\vec{\delta}$, where $\vec{\delta} = \vec{\gamma} \circ \vec{\gamma}'$. Here Γ_i', $\vec{\alpha}'$ ($\vec{\beta}'$, resp.) and φ_i' (for each $i = 1, 2$) are results of the substitutions, respectively.

Then, we apply an equality inference or cut rule (the above derivation is a case of equality inference). Here $[\vec{\delta}']\varphi$ is a result of $[\vec{\delta}']\varphi_1'$ and $[\vec{\delta}']\varphi_2'$ by equality inference.

Step 2 (Order Preserving Merge): We apply the composition rule for honesty assumptions (**Comp(Hon)**) to get the proof of a property φ about a composed protocol $\vec{\alpha}' \circ \vec{\beta}'$ which is an order preserving merge of $\vec{\alpha}$ and $\vec{\beta}$.

In the next section, we show a concrete example of this process.

3 An Example of Correctness Proof

In this section, we provide a case study of our compositional treatment of honesty assumptions. As an example we show a proof of the agreement property (in the sense of Woo-Lam [19]) of the *ISO-9798-3 protocol* [16]. This property is proved by the composition of freshness proof for *Diffie-Hellman protocol* [8] and authentication proof for *Challenge Response protocol*, which is already proved in [6, 7].

First, we show our interpretation of composing steps of the ISO 9798-3 protocol by using an informal description. (The notations are also used in the formal proof shown below.)

An Informal Description of Composition of the Protocols:
The following two protocols are informal descriptions of *the Diffie-Hellman Protocol* (denoted by Π) and *the Challenge Response Protocol* (denoted by Π'). Here we omit principals' names appearing in each message for readability. In this example, we suppose that in the Challenge Response protocol principals P and Q do not generate m and n as fresh values, respectively (cf. [6, 7]).

The Diffie-Hellman protocol: Π	The challenge response protocol Π'
1 $(\alpha_1^P; \alpha_2^P, \beta_1^Q).\ P \to Q\colon g^P$	1' $(\alpha_1'^P, \beta_1'^Q).\ P \to Q\colon m$
2 $(\beta_2^Q; \beta_3^Q, \alpha_3^P).\ Q \to P\colon g^Q$	2' $(\beta_2'^Q, \alpha_2'^P).\ Q \to P\colon n, \{n, m\}_{K_Q^{-1}}$
	3' $(\alpha_3'^P, \beta_3'^Q).\ P \to Q\colon \{m, n\}_{K_P^{-1}}$

In our interpretation, these protocols are composed by the following two steps. (These steps correspond to Composing steps in Section 2.2.)

Step 1. Substitutions: by replacing g^Q with $\langle g^Q, \{g^Q, g^P\}_{K_Q^{-1}}\rangle$ in the Diffie-Hellman protocol, and by replacing g^P with m and g^Q with n in the Challenge Response protocol, we get new protocols Π'' and Π''' as follows.

$$\Pi'' = \Pi[\langle g^Q, \{g^Q, g^P\}_{K_Q^{-1}}\rangle / g^Q] \quad \Pi''' = \Pi'[g^P/m, g^Q/n]$$

$1''\ (\alpha_1''^P; \alpha_2''^P, \beta_1''^Q).\ P \to Q{:}\ g^P$ $\quad$ $1'''\ (\alpha_1'''^P, \beta_1'''^Q).\ P \to Q{:}\ g^P$

$2''\ (\beta_2''^Q; \beta_3''^Q, \alpha_3''^P).$ $\qquad\qquad$ $2'''\ (\beta_2'''^Q, \alpha_2'''^P).\ Q \to P{:}\ g^Q, \{g^Q, g^P\}_{K_Q^{-1}}$

$\qquad Q \to P{:}\ g^Q, \{g^Q, g^P\}_{K_Q^{-1}}$ $\quad$ $3'''\ (\alpha_3'''^P, \beta_3'''^Q).\ P \to Q{:}\ \{g^P, g^Q\}_{K_P^{-1}}$

Here $\alpha_2''^P = \alpha_1'''^P$, $\alpha_3''^P = \alpha_2'''^P$, $\beta_1''^Q = \beta_1'''^Q$ and $\beta_3''^Q = \beta_2'''^Q$.

Step 2. Order Preserving Merge: by the composition of protocols Π'' and Π''', we get the ISO-9798-3 protocol as follows.

$$\text{protocol } (\Pi'' \circ \Pi''')$$

$1''\ (\alpha_1''^P; \alpha_1'''^P, \beta_1''^Q).\ P \to Q{:}\ g^P$

$2''\ (\beta_2''^Q; \beta_3''^Q, \alpha_2'''^P).\ Q \to P{:}\ g^Q, \{g^Q, g^P\}_{K_Q^{-1}}$

$3'''\ (\alpha_3'''^P, \beta_3'''^Q).\qquad P \to Q{:}\ \{g^P, g^Q\}_{K_P^{-1}}$

The notation $\Pi \circ \Pi'$ denotes a result of an *order-preserving merge* of lists Π and Π'.

From now, we give a formal proof of the agreement property for the ISO 9798-3 protocol. This property is stated informally as follows.

Agreement Property from A's View: Assume that a principal A follows the initiator's role of the protocol communicating with B, and that the responder, say Q, honestly follows his/her role. If A completes a run of the protocol using values N_1 and N_2, then A knows that B actually performs as the responder Q's role communicating with A using the same values N_1 and N_2.

In the following example, we omit the subscriptions of names P and Q from each meta-symbols $\alpha_i^P, \alpha_i'^P, \ldots$ and $\beta_j^Q, \beta_j'^Q, \ldots$, respectively.

Proving Process of the Agreement Property from Initiator's View for the ISO 9798-3 Protocol:

First for the Diffie-Hellman protocol, the following sequent is provable by using Axiom about primitive actions.

$$\vdash [\alpha_1; \alpha_2]_A fresh(g^A) \tag{1}$$

On the other hand, for the Challenge Response protocol, the following sequents are also provable. (The proving process of these sequent are shown in [15].)

$$fresh(N_1), Honest((\beta_1'; \beta_2'; \beta_3')) \vdash [\alpha_1'; \alpha_2'; \alpha_3']_A B \text{ receives } \langle a, b, N_1 \rangle \qquad (2)$$

$$fresh(N_1), Honest((\beta_1'; \beta_2'; \beta_3'))$$
$$\vdash [\alpha_1'; \alpha_2'; \alpha_3']_A B \text{ sends } \langle b, a, N_2, \{N_2, N_1, a\}_{K_B^{-1}} \rangle \qquad (3)$$

From (2) and (3) we prove the agreement property of the Challenge Response protocol. However, in our logic, a non-commutative conjunct appears only in the left hand side of a sequent, then we cannot express directly the agreement property. That is, we cannot state that "B performs the following actions in order: receiving $\langle a, b, N_1 \rangle$ and then sending $\langle b, a, N_2, \{N_2, N_1, a\}_{K_B^{-1}} \rangle$" from A's view. Nevertheless, if we assume Q honestly follows his/her role (i.e., Q follows the sequence of parameterized actions in order: he/she first receives $\langle p, q, m \rangle$ and then sends $\langle q, p, n, \{n, m, p\}_{K_Q^{-1}} \rangle$), and if A knows B actually performs the actions corresponding his/her role, then A can know the order of B's actual actions by matching. In other words, information about ordering of actions performed by an honest principal is implicitly contained in the honesty assumptions. Therefore, if we must formalize a derivation of the agreement property, we can formalize it by introducing the following inference rule.

$$\frac{\Gamma, Hon(\vec{\alpha}^Q) \vdash [\vec{\beta}]_A \, B \, act_1 \, \sigma m_1 \qquad}{\Gamma, Hon(\vec{\alpha}^Q) \vdash [\vec{\beta}]_A \, B \, act_2 \, \sigma m_2 \qquad \Gamma, Hon(\vec{\alpha}^Q) \vdash [\vec{\beta}]_A \, \vec{x} = \vec{t}}{\Gamma, Hon(\vec{\alpha}^Q) \vdash [\vec{\beta}]_A \, (B \, act_1 \, \sigma m_1; B \, act_2 \, \sigma m_2)}$$

where each act_1 and act_2 is a primitive action of receiving, sending, or generating, and σ is $[\vec{t}/\vec{x}]$, and these satisfy the following conditions:

- $\vec{\alpha}^Q$ includes primitive actions α_1^Q and α_2^Q, where α_1^Q precedes α_2^Q.
- If $act_i \, \sigma m_i$ (for each $i = 1, 2$) is a sending action, then α_i^Q is also "Q sends m_i". (The case of receiving is the same as sending.)
- If $act_i \, \sigma m_i$ is a generating action, then α_i^Q is also "P generates x" with $\sigma x = m_i$.

Therefore, from the above results of (2) and (3), it is clear that the agreement property from A's view is provable in the extended system. Then, the following sequent is provable.

$$fresh(N_1), Honest((\alpha_1'; \alpha_2'; \alpha_3')) \vdash [\beta_1'; \beta_2'; \beta_3']_A \, Agree_B \qquad (4)$$

(Here the statement $Agree_B$ is the abbreviation of "B receives $\langle a, b, N_1 \rangle$; B sends $\langle b, a, N_2, \{N_2, N_1, a\}_{K_B^{-1}} \rangle$", which represents B's actions guaranteeing the agreement for B.)

From now, by composing proofs of (1) and (4), we prove our aimed property. First, following the procedure of Step 1, we substitute g^P for m and g^Q for n, respectively, in the proofs of (1), and also substitute $\langle g^Q, \{g^Q, g^P\}_{K_Q^{-1}} \rangle$ for g^Q in the proofs of (4) to get the following sequents.

$$\vdash [\beta_1''; \beta_2'']_A \ fresh(g^A) \qquad (5)$$

$$fresh(g^A), Honest((\alpha_1'''; \alpha_2'''; \alpha_3'''))$$
$$\vdash [\beta_1'''; \beta_2'''; \beta_3''']_A \ Agree_B[g^A/N_1, g^B/N_2] \qquad (6)$$

Then, by applying weakening rules for actions to (5) and (6), respectively, we get the following sequents.

$$\vdash [\beta_1''; \beta_2''; \beta_3''; \beta_3''']fresh(g^A) \qquad (7)$$

$$fresh(g^A), Honest((\alpha_1'''; \alpha_2'''; \alpha_3'''))$$
$$\vdash [\beta_1''; \beta_1'''; \beta_2'''; \beta_3''']_A \ Agree_B[g^A/N_1, g^B/N_2] \qquad (8)$$

Since $\beta_2'' = \beta_1'''$ and $\beta_3'' = \beta_2'''$, $\beta_1''; \beta_2''; \beta_3''; \beta_3'''$ in (7) and $\beta_1''; \beta_1'''; \beta_2'''; \beta_3'''$ in (8) are the same action. Then by applying the cut rule to (7) and (8), we get a new proof of the following sequent.

$$Honest((\alpha_1'''; \alpha_2'''; \alpha_3'''))$$
$$\vdash [\beta_1''; \beta_1'''; \beta_2'''; \beta_3''']_A \ Agree_B[g^A/N_1, g^B/N_2] \qquad (9)$$

This is a proof of agreement property for the ISO-9798-3 protocol from P's view.

4   Trace Semantics and Soundness of the System

In this section we give a semantics for our inference system. We give the definition of our semantics (in Section 4.1) and a sketch of soundness proof for our system (in Section 4.2).

4.1   Trace Semantics

The basic notion of our semantics is *primitive state* of the form "principal P has information m", and denoted by $P(m), Q(m), \ldots$. We also introduce a special kind of primitive state "message m sent by P is currently transmitted through the network", and denoted by $Net(m, P)$. A *state* is a multiset of primitive states and a *trace* is a finite sequence of states. We use the following notations. The letters $\mathbf{s}, \mathbf{s}', \ldots$ are used to denote traces, and $s_i, s_i', \ldots$ to denote the i-th elements of $\mathbf{s}, \mathbf{s}', \ldots$, respectively. The number i is called the *position* of s_i in $\mathbf{s}$. We also introduce some notions related to traces. We say $s_i \in \mathbf{s}'$ (where $\mathbf{s}' = s_1', \ldots, s_n'$) if $s_i = s_j'$ for some $j = 1, \ldots, n$. For a sequence $\mathbf{s} = s_1, \ldots, s_n$ and for $s_i, s_j \in \mathbf{s}$, we denote $s_i \leq_{\mathbf{s}} s_j$ if $i \leq j$. For traces $\mathbf{s}$ and $\mathbf{s}'$, if $s_i \in \mathbf{s}'$ for all $s_i \in \mathbf{s}$ and if $\forall s_i, s_j \in \mathbf{s}.(s_i \leq_{\mathbf{s}} s_j \Rightarrow s_i \leq_{\mathbf{s}'} s_j)$, we say $\mathbf{s}'$ is an *extension* of $\mathbf{s}$ and denote it by $\mathbf{s} \subseteq \mathbf{s}'$.

Here we only consider the traces satisfying the following condition: for any $s_i, s_j \in \mathbf{s}$, if $s_i <_{\mathbf{s}} s_j$ and $P(m) \in s_i$ then $P(m) \in s_j$. In other words, we consider only traces where, once information is possessed by a principal, it does not disappear in his/her memory.

We denote the number of occurrence of primitive state $P(m)$ in a state s_i by $\| s_i \|_{P(m)}$ (e.g. if $s_i = \{P(m), P(m), Q(m)\}$, then $\| s_i \|_{P(m)} = 2$). $Key(P, s_i)$ is used to denote the set of key possessed by principal P at position s_i. For messages m, m' and a set of keys $\{k_1, \ldots, k_l\}$, "m is *accessible* in m' with keys $\{k_1, \ldots, k_l\}$" (denoted by $m \in_{\{k_1, \ldots, k_l\}} m'$) is the reflexive-transitive closure satisfying the following conditions: (i) $m_i \in_{\{k_1, \ldots, k_l\}} \langle m_1, \ldots, m_n \rangle$ for some $i = 1, \ldots, n$, (ii) $m \in_{\{k_1, \ldots, k_l\}} \{m\}_{k_j}$ for some $j = 1, \ldots, l$.

By means of the notion of trace, truth conditions for predicates of our syntax are defined as follows. We denote the basic semantic relation "φ is true at state s_i in $\mathbf{s}$" by "$\models_{\langle \mathbf{s}, i \rangle} \varphi$".

Truth Condition for Predicates:

- $\models_{\langle \mathbf{s}, i \rangle} PK(P, k)$ iff $P(k'), KeyPair(k, k') \in s_i$ and $\forall X \neq P.(X(k') \notin s_i)$.

- $\models_{\langle \mathbf{s}, i \rangle} P \overset{k}{\leftrightarrow} Q$ iff $P(k), Q(k) \in s_i$ and $\forall X \neq P, Q.(X(k) \notin s_i)$.

- $\models_{\langle \mathbf{s}, i \rangle} t = t'$ (for any terms t and t')   iff $s_i[t/x] = s_i[t'/x]$.

- $\models_{\langle \mathbf{s}, i \rangle} P$ *sends* m iff $P(m) \in s_{i-1}$, $Net(m, P) \notin s_{i-1}$ and $Net(m, P) \in s_i$.

- $\models_{\langle \mathbf{s}, i \rangle} P$ *receives* $m(\{m_1\}_{k_1}^*, \ldots, \{m_n\}_{k_n}^*)$ iff $\exists X. (Net(m, X) \in s_{i-1}$ and $Net(m, X) \notin s_i)$ and $\| s_{i-1} \|_{P(m)} + 1 = \| s_i \|_{P(m)}$, and $\{m_j\}_{k_j} \in_{Key(P, s_i)} m$ and $\| s_{i-1} \|_{P(m_j)} + 1 = \| s_i \|_{P(m_j)}$ for each $j = 1, \ldots, n$.

- $\models_{\langle \mathbf{s}, i \rangle} P$ *generates* m iff $P(m) \notin s_{i-1}$ and $P(m) \in s_i$.

- $\models_{\langle \mathbf{s}, i \rangle} fresh(m)$ iff $\exists X \exists n.(X(n) \notin s_{i-1}$ and $X(n) \in s_i)$ and $n \sqsubseteq m$.

- $\models_{\langle \mathbf{s}, i \rangle} \alpha_1; \cdots; \alpha_n$ iff $\models_{\langle \mathbf{s}, i_1 \rangle} \alpha_1$ and $\cdots$ and $\models_{\langle \mathbf{s}, i_n \rangle} \alpha_n$, and $i_1 \leq \cdots \leq i_n \leq s_i$.

Next, the definition "φ is true for trace $\mathbf{s}$" (denoted by $\models_{\mathbf{s}} \varphi$) is as follows.

- $\models_{\mathbf{s}} \beta$ iff $\forall s_i \in \mathbf{s}.(\models_{\langle \mathbf{s}, i \rangle} \beta)$ (where $\beta = PK(P, k)$ or $P \overset{k}{\leftrightarrow} Q$, or $t = t'$.)

- $\models_{\mathbf{s}} fresh(m)$ iff $\exists s_i \in \mathbf{s}.(\models_{\langle \mathbf{s}, i \rangle} fresh(m))$.

- $\models_{\mathbf{s}} \alpha_1; \cdots; \alpha_n$ iff $\exists s_i \in \mathbf{s}.(\models_{\langle \mathbf{s}, i \rangle} \alpha_1; \cdots; \alpha_n)$ (where each α_i is an action predicate.)

We define that $\models_{\mathbf{s}} \Gamma$ iff "$\models_{\mathbf{s}} \vec{\alpha}$ and ... and $\models_{\mathbf{s}} \vec{\beta}$, and $\models_{\mathbf{s}} \theta_i$ for each $i = 1, \ldots, n$" (where $\Gamma = \vec{\alpha}, \ldots, \vec{\beta}, \theta_1, \ldots, \theta_n$). By the above definition, it is clear that for any φ if $\models_{\mathbf{s}} \varphi$ then $\models_{\mathbf{s}'} \varphi$ for any $\mathbf{s} \subseteq \mathbf{s}'$.

In terms of the above definitions, we define the basic form of assertion as true under $\mathbf{s}$, that is to say:

$$Honest(\alpha_1^P); \cdots; Honest(\alpha_n^P), \ldots Honest(\alpha_1^Q); \cdots; Honest(\alpha_k^Q), \ldots, \Gamma \models_{\mathbf{s}} [\vec{\alpha}]\varphi$$

if and only if the following is satisfied (where φ is a single action or non-action predicate).

If

C1 $\forall i \leq n. \forall i' < i.(\models_{\mathbf{s}} \alpha_i^P \Rightarrow \models_{\mathbf{s}} \alpha_{i'}^P)$, and
      $\forall j \leq k. \forall j' < j.(\models_{\mathbf{s}} \alpha_j^Q \Rightarrow \models_{\mathbf{s}} \alpha_{j'}^Q)$,
C2 $\exists \mathbf{s}'.(\mathbf{s} \subseteq \mathbf{s}' \wedge \forall i \leq n.(\models_{\mathbf{s}'} \alpha_i) \wedge \forall j \leq k.(\models_{\mathbf{s}'} \alpha_j))$,
C3 $\models_{\mathbf{s}} \Gamma$,
C4 $\models_{\mathbf{s}} \vec{\alpha}$,

then $\models_{\mathbf{s}} \varphi$.

Here for each predicate $Honest(\alpha_i^X)$, if it is of the form $Honest(\alpha_i^X, m_i^X)$ for $X = P, Q$ and for $i = 1, \ldots, n$ or $1, \ldots, k$ (i.e., m_i^X is not empty), then the following condition is also satisfied:

C5 $\forall m'.((m' \sqsupseteq m_i^X) \wedge (m' \neq m'') \wedge (\alpha_i^X = X \text{ sends } m''))$
      $\Rightarrow \forall \mathbf{s}' \sqsupseteq \mathbf{s}.(\not\models_{\mathbf{s}'} X \text{ sends } m'))$.

We need this additional condition for the following reason: first recall that $Honest(\alpha_i^X, m_i^X)$ (where m_i^X is not empty term) means "X honestly follows the sending action α_i^X (say, X sends m'') and he/she does not follow any other sending actions of the message m' including m_i^X". Therefore, to satisfy this restriction, we assume X sends m'' is false for any extension $\mathbf{s}'$ of $\mathbf{s}$.

If the above form of assertion is true for any trace $\mathbf{s}$, then this assertion is called *valid* and we omit the subscription $\mathbf{s}$.

Finally, to prove the soundness of our system, we introduce the notion of *duplication of atomic actions in trace* $\mathbf{s}$ as follows. We say "two atomic action formulas α and β are duplicated in trace $\mathbf{s}$", when the following condition is satisfied: "for some $s_i, s_j \in \mathbf{s}$ with $i \neq j$, there exists a substitution σ such that $\sigma\alpha = \sigma\beta$ and that $\models_{\langle \mathbf{s}, i \rangle} \alpha$ and $\models_{\langle \mathbf{s}, j \rangle} \beta$". As we mentioned in Section 2, our inference system is sound under the assumption that no trace includes atomic actions which are duplicated.

Therefore, our soundness theorem proved in the next subsection is stated as follows.

Theorem (Soundness). If a sequent (i.e., a basic form of assertion) S is provable in our inference system, then S is true for any trace $\mathbf{s}$ which includes no duplicated atomic actions.

4.2   Soundness of the System

In this subsection we sketch out a proof of the soundness.

(I) Logical Inference Rules
Here we give a soundness proof only for **Cut** rule as follows. Proofs for the other rules in this class are similar.

$$\frac{\Gamma \vdash [\vec{\alpha}]\varphi \quad \varphi, \Delta \vdash [\vec{\alpha}]\psi}{\Gamma, \Delta \vdash [\vec{\alpha}]\psi} \textbf{ Cut}$$

Assume that the upper sequents are both valid. That is, for any s and s', (i) if $\models_s \Gamma$ and $\models_s \vec{\alpha}$, then $\models_s \varphi$, and (ii) if $\models_{s'} \varphi$ and $\models_{s'} \Delta$ and $\models_{s'} \vec{\alpha}$, then $\models_{s'} \psi$ hold. Assume that for any s", $\models_{s''} \Gamma$ and $\models_{s''} \Delta$ and $\models_{s''} \vec{\alpha}$. Then by (i), $\models_{s''} \varphi$ holds. Then by (ii), $\models_{s''} \psi$ holds. Therefore the lower sequent is also valid.

(II-1) Axioms About Primitive Actions:

$$\vdash [\alpha_1^P; \cdots; \alpha_n^P]\alpha_i^P \qquad \text{(for } i = 1, \ldots, n.)$$

This sequent is valid if, for any s, if $\models_s \alpha_1^P, \ldots, \models_s \alpha_n^P$ then $\models_s \alpha_i^P$ for any $i = 1, \ldots, n$. This condition immediately holds by the definition.

(II-2) Axioms for Relationship Between Properties:
Here we show only the case of Freshness 1 and 2, and Nonce Verification. Proofs for the other axioms are similar.

Freshness 1:

$$P \text{ generates } m \vdash fresh(m)$$

Assume that $\models_s P \text{ generates } m$ for any s. That is, $\exists s_i \in s.((P(m) \notin s_{i-1}) \wedge (P(m) \in s_i))$ holds. Then, $\exists X \exists n.((X(n) \notin s_{i-1}) \wedge (X(n) \in s_i))$ with $n \sqsubseteq m$ holds. This is the truth condition for $fresh(m)$.

Freshness 2:

$$fresh(m) \vdash fresh(m') \qquad \text{(where } m \sqsubseteq m')$$

Assume that $\models_s fresh(m)$ for any s. That is, $\exists s_i \in s \exists X \exists m''.((X(m'') \notin s_{i-1}) \wedge (X(m'') \in s_i))$ with $m'' \sqsubseteq m$. By assumption of $m \sqsubseteq m'$, $m'' \sqsubseteq m'$ also holds. Therefore is the truth condition for $fresh(m')$ is satisfied.

Nonce Verification:

$$(PK(k, Q)), (fresh(m)), (P \text{ receives } m'(\{m\}_{k-1}^*)) \vdash Q \text{ sends } m''$$

$$(\text{where } \{m\}_{k-1} \sqsubseteq m', m''.)$$

Assume that all atoms in the left hand side of this axiom are valid. That is, for any s, (i) $\forall s_i \in s.((Q(k^{-1}) \in s_i) \wedge \forall X \neq Q.(X(k^{-1}) \notin s_i))$, (ii) $\exists s_i \in s \exists X \exists n.((X(n) \notin s_{i-1}) \wedge (X(n) \in s_i))$, and (iii) $\exists s_i \in s \exists X.((Net(m', X) \in s_{i-1}) \wedge (\|s_{i-1}\|_{P(m')} + 1 = \|s_i\|_{P(m')}) \wedge (\|s_{i-1}\|_{P(m)} + 1 = \|s_i\|_{P(m)}))$. Informally, by (i) and (iii), $\exists s_i \in s.(Net(m'', Q) \in s_{i-1})$ with $\{m\}_{k-1} \sqsubseteq m''$ holds. That is, $\exists s_j <_s s_i.((Net(m', Q) \notin s_j) \wedge (Q(m') \in s_j))$. Then, by (ii) $\exists s_k \in s.((s_k <_s s_i) \wedge (Net(m', Q)) \wedge (Q(m') \in s_k))$. This is the truth condition for $Q \text{ sends } m''$.

(III) Honesty Inferences:

(1) Substitution:

$$\frac{\Gamma \vdash [\vec{\alpha}]Q \text{ sends } m[t/x]}{\Gamma, Honest(Q \text{ sends } m) \vdash [\vec{\alpha}]x = t}$$

(where t is a constant and x is a variable which has the same sort as t.)

Assume that the upper sequent is valid. That is, for any s, "if $\models_s \Gamma$ and if $\models_s \vec{\alpha}$, then $\models_s Q \; sends \; m[t/x]$" holds. Here we also assume that, for any s', (i) $\models_{s'} \Gamma$ and $\models_s \vec{\alpha}$, and (ii) conditions C1 and C2 for $Honest(Q \; sends \; m)$ hold. By assumption (i), $\models_{s'} Q \; sends \; m[t/x]$ holds. By assumption (ii), because the condition C2 for the honesty assumption holds, there exists a trace $s'' \supseteq s'$ such that $\models_{s''} Q \; sends \; m$ holds, and under such s'', $\models_{s''} Q \; sends \; m[t/x]$ also holds. Therefore for some $s_i, s_j \in s$, $\models_{\langle s'', i \rangle} Q \; sends \; m$ and $\models_{\langle s'', j \rangle} Q \; sends \; m[t/x]$. Here by the assumption such that s'' does not include any duplicated atomic actions, for some $s_i \in s''$, $s_i = s_i[t/x]$ and $\models_{\langle s'', i \rangle} Q \; sends \; m$ and $\models_{\langle s'', i \rangle} Q \; sends \; m[t/x]$ hold. Here, it is easy to show that $\forall s_j \in s''.(s_j = s_j[t/x])$ by the definition of traces. (Remind that each trace satisfies the condition that for any primitive state of the form $P(m)$, $\forall s_i, s_j \in s.(s_i < s_j$ and $P(m) \in s_i$ then $P(m) \in s_j).$) That is, $\models_{s''} x = t$ holds, and then by $s' \subseteq s''$, $\models_{s'} x = t$ holds. This is the truth condition for the lower sequent.

(2) Matching:

$$\frac{\Gamma \vdash [\vec{\alpha}]Q \; sends \; m}{\Gamma, Honest(Q \; sends \; m', m) \vdash [\vec{\alpha}]Q \; sends \; m'}$$

Assume that the upper sequent is valid. That is, for any s, "if $\models_s \Gamma$ and if $\models_s \vec{\alpha}$, then $\models_s Q \; sends \; m$". Here we also assume that, for any s', (i) $\models_{s'} \Gamma$ and $\models_{s'} \vec{\alpha}$ hold, and (ii) conditions C1, C2 and C5 for $Honest(Q \; sends \; m', m)$ hold. By assumption (i) and the validity of the upper sequent, $\models_s Q \; sends \; m$ holds. By condition C2 of (ii), $\exists s'' \supseteq s'.(\models_{s''} Q \; sends \; m')$ holds. Moreover, by C5 of (ii), $\forall m''.((m'' \sqsupseteq m) \wedge (m'' \neq m') \Rightarrow \forall s'' \supseteq s.(\not\models_{s''} Q \; sends \; m''))$. That is, $\forall m''.((m'' \sqsupseteq m) \wedge (m'' \neq m') \Rightarrow \neg \exists s'' \supseteq s'.(\not\models_{s''} Q \; sends \; m''))$. Therefore, $\models_{s'} Q \; sends \; m'$. This is the truth condition for the lower sequent.

(3) Deriving Another Actions:

$$\frac{\Gamma \vdash [\vec{\alpha}]Q \; sends \; m}{\Gamma, Honest(Q \; sends \; m'; Q \; sends \; m), \vdash [\vec{\alpha}]Q \; sends \; m'}$$

Assume that the upper sequent is valid. That is, for any s, $\models_s \Gamma$ and $\models_s \vec{\alpha}$, then $\models_s Q \; sends \; m$ holds. Here we also assume that, for any s', (i) $\models_{s'} \Gamma$ and $\models_{s'} \vec{\alpha}$, and (ii) conditions C1 and C2 for $Honest(Q \; sends \; m'; Q \; sends \; m)$ hold. By assumption (i) and the validity of upper sequent, $\models_{s'} Q \; sends \; m$ holds. By condition C1 of (ii), $\models_{s'} Q \; sends \; m'$ also holds. This is the truth condition for the lower sequent.

(IV) Weakening Rules:

$$\frac{\Gamma, Honest(\vec{\alpha}^P; \vec{\alpha}'^P) \vdash [\vec{\beta}]\varphi}{\Gamma, Honest(\vec{\alpha}^P; \alpha''^P; \vec{\alpha}'^P) \vdash [\vec{\beta}]\varphi} \; \mathbf{W(Hon)} \qquad \frac{\Gamma \vdash [\vec{\alpha}^P; \vec{\alpha}'^P]\varphi}{\Gamma \vdash [\vec{\alpha}^P; \alpha''^P; \vec{\alpha}'^P]\varphi} \; \mathbf{W(Act)}$$

(1) Weakening (Honesty): We should only show that, for any s, if s satisfies the conditions C1 and C2 for $Honest(\vec{\alpha}^P; \alpha''^P; \vec{\alpha}'^P)$, s also satisfies the conditions C1 and C2 for $Honest(\vec{\alpha}^P; \vec{\alpha}'^P)$. C1 is satisfied, because for any sequence $\vec{\beta}$, if $\forall \alpha_i, \alpha_j \in \vec{\beta}.((j \le i) \Rightarrow (\models_s \alpha_i \Rightarrow \models_s \alpha_j))$, then this property also holds for any $\vec{\beta}'$ such that $\vec{\beta}' \subseteq \vec{\beta}$. C2 is also satisfied, because for any $s' \supseteq s$ and for any $\vec{\beta}, \forall \alpha_i \in \vec{\beta}(\models_{s'} \alpha_i)$ holds, then, for the same s' at least, this condition also holds for any $\vec{\beta}'$ such that $\vec{\beta}' \subseteq \vec{\beta}$.

(2) Weakening (Actions): We should only show that for any s, if $\models_s \vec{\alpha}; \alpha''; \vec{\alpha}'$ then $\models_s \vec{\alpha}; \vec{\alpha}'$. This immediately follows from the definition of $\models_s \vec{\alpha}; \alpha''; \vec{\alpha}'$.

5   Conclusions

We presented an inference system based on a framework of compositional logic originally introduced by [11, 6, 7]. The main difference between the compositional logic of [11, 6, 7] and ours was the way to formalize inferences on a principal's honesty: while in [11, 6, 7] assumptions on a principal's honesty were represented by the implication of the form $Honest(P) \supset \varphi$, in our framework we divided each honest principal's role into its components (i.e., his/her primitive actions) and introduced some special kinds of inference rules, called *honesty inferences*, to derive a minimal requirement on principal's honesty to conclude a property. Such honesty assumptions were composed during a proving process by using *weakening rules* analogous to the structural rules of traditional logic. For this formalization, the language of our system is restricted to Horn-clauses, in other words we do not use logical negations nor nested implications (nor disjunctions appearing in the right hand side of a sequent) which were used in [11, 6, 7].

We also introduced the distinction between the *monotonic* properties and *non-monotonic* ones. In this paper, by restricting our attention to the monotonic properties, we gave a core inference system and showed a proof of the *agreement property* of the ISO 9798-3 protocol. Such restriction leads to a simplification of the system, because we do not need any restriction on a free application of weakening rules and honesty inferences. However, the use of non-monotonic properties provides us more powerful derivations. In the subsequent work [15] of ours, we show the way to extend our system by introducing non-monotonic properties. As an example, in [15] we introduce the non-monotonic property "P firstly_sends (m,n)" (which means "P sends a message m containing n as a subterm, and P does not send any other message m' containing n before the sending of m"). This property is useful to derive information about ordering of actions performed by different principals, which cannot be proved in the system of this paper, and by this information we prove *matching conversation* of the *Challenge Response protocol* (cf. [9]), which was originally proved in [6, 7].

Acknowledgments

We would like to express our sincere thanks to Drs. Andre Scedrov and Iliano Cervesato for their invaluable comments and discussions. We also would like to express our sincere thanks to Mrs. Lam Ta-Minh and Pierre Grialou for their helpful comments. Finally, helpful comments from the anonymous reviewers results in improvements to this paper.

References

1. M. Burrows, M. Abadi and R. Needham. A Logic of Authentication. *Technical Report 39*, Digital System Research Center, 1989.
2. I. Cervesato, N.A. Durgin, P.D. Lincoln, J.C. Mitchell and A. Scedrov. A meta-notation for protocol analysis. *12th IEEE Computer Security Foundations Workshop*, 1999.
3. I. Cervesato, N.A. Durgin, P.D. Lincoln, J.C. Mitchell and A. Scedrov. A Comparison between Strand Spaces and Multiset Rewriting for Security Protocol Analysis. M. Okada, B. Pierce, A. Scedrov, H. Tokuda and A. Yonezawa (eds.), *Software Security — Theories and Systems*, Lecture Notes in Computer Science, Hot Topics, vol.2609, Springer-Verlag, pp.356-382, 2003.
4. I. Cervesato, N.A. Durgin, P.D. Lincoln, J.C. Mitchell and A. Scedrov. Multiset rewriting and the complexity of bounded security protocols. *Journal of Computer Security*, vol.12, no.1, pp.677-722, 2004.
5. J. Clark and J. Jacob. A Survey of Authentication Protocol Literature: Version 1.0 (web draft), 1997.
6. A. Datta, A. Derek, J. C. Mitchell and D. Pavlovic. A Derivation System for Security Protocols and its Logical Formalization. *Journal of Computer Security, Special Issue of Selected Papers from CSFW-16*, 2004.
7. A. Datta, A. Derek, J. C. Mitchell and D. Pavlovic. Secure Protocol Composition. *Proceedings of 19th Annual Conference on Mathematical Foundations of Programming Semantics, ENTCS Vol. 83*, 2004.
8. W. Diffie and M. E. Hellman. New directions in cryptography. *IEEE Transactions on Information Theory*, IT-22(6), pp.644-654, 1976.
9. W. Diffie, P. C. van Oorschot and M. J. Wiener. Authentication and authenticated key exchange *Designs, Codes and Cryptography*, vol.2, pp.107-125, 1992.
10. N.A. Durgin, P.D. Lincoln, J.C. Mitchell and A. Scedrov. Undecidability of bounded security protocol. *The 1999 Federated Logic Conference (FLoC '99)*, 11 pages, 1999.
11. N. Durgin, J. Mitchell, and D. Pavlovic. A compositional logic for proving security properties of protocols. *Journal of Computer Security*, vol.11, no.4, pp.677-721, 2003.
12. F. J. T. Fábrega, J. C. Herzog and J. D. Guttman. Strand spaces: Why is a security protocol correct? *Proceedings of the 1998 IEEE Symposium on Security and Privacy*, pp.160-171, 1998.
13. J. D. Guttman and F. J. T. Fábrega. Authentication tests and the structure of bundles. *Theoretical Computer Science*, vol. 283(2), pp.333-380, 2002.
14. K. Hasebe and M. Okada. A Logical Verification Method for Security Protocols Based on Linear Logic and BAN Logic. M. Okada, B. Pierce, A. Scedrov, H. Tokuda and A. Yonezawa (eds.), *Software Security — Theories and Systems*, Lecture Notes in Computer Science, Hot Topics, vol.2609, Springer-Verlag, pp.417-440, 2003.

15. K. Hasebe and M. Okada. Non-monotonic Properties for Proving Correctness in a Framework of Compositional Logic. to appear in the *proceedings of the workshop on Foundations of Computer Security '04 (LICS and ICALP affiliated workshop)*, Turku, Finland, 12 pages, 2004.
16. IEEE. Entity Authentication Mechanisms - part 3: Entity Authentication Using Asymmetric Techniques. Technical report ISO/IEC IS 9798-3, ISO/IEC, 1993.
17. A. J. Menezes, P. C. van Oorschot and S. A. Vanstone. *Handbook of Applied Cryptography*. CRS press, 1996 (fifth printing, 2001).
18. P. Syverson and I. Cervesato. The Logic of Authentication Protocols. *Lecture notes in Computer Science*, Vol. 2171, pp. 63-136, 2001.
19. T. Y. C. Woo and S. S. Lam. Verifying authentication protocols: Methodology and example. *Proceedings of the International Conference on Network Protocols*, 1993.

Appendix

A   Inference System

A.1   The Language

(I) Sorts and Terms

The language is many sorted. (However sorts are not explicitly indicated in the language.) Name, PublicKey, SecretKey, SharedKey and Nonce are primitive sorts. (Key is used to denote PublicKey or SecretKey or SharedKey.) Message is also sort defined below.

The letters A, B, C,... are constants of sort Name (i.e., specific principal's names), while the letters P, Q, R,... are variables of sort Name (i.e., parameterized principal's names). The capital letters $K, K', \ldots, K_1, K_2, \ldots$ and $N, N', \ldots, N_1, N_2, \ldots$ are constants of sort Key and of sort Nonce, respectively, while the small letters $k, k', \ldots, k_1, k_2, \ldots$ and $n, n', \ldots, n_1, n_2, \ldots$ are variables of the same sorts as above. All constants and variables of sort Name or Key or Nonce are terms of sort Message, and the letters $m, m', \ldots, m_1, m_2, \ldots$ are used to denote terms of the sort Message. $\{m\}_K$ (the encryption of m with key K) and $\langle m_1, \ldots, m_n \rangle$ (the concatenation of messages $m_1, \ldots, m_n$) are also terms of sort Message, where $\{*\}_K$ and $\langle *, \ldots, * \rangle$ are functions of sort Message $\times$ Key $\rightarrow$ Message and of sort Message^n $\rightarrow$ Message, respectively.

We use the following binary relations as meta-symbols. $m \sqsubseteq m'$ represents that m is subterm of m'.

(II) Basic Form of Assertion

$Honest(\alpha_{1_1}^{Q_1}); \cdots; Honest(\alpha_{1_m}^{Q_1}), \ldots,$
$\qquad Honest(\alpha_{n_1}^{Q_n}); \ldots; Honest(\alpha_{n_m}^{Q_n}), \Gamma \vdash [\vec{\beta}]_P \varphi$

(where Q_i may be the same as Q_j for some $i, j = 1, \ldots, n$.)

- *Action predicates* (performed by P) are as follows.

    - *P generates m*: P generates a nonce or session key m.

- P *receives* m: P receives a message m.
- P *sends* m: P sends a message m.
- *Non-action predicates* are as follows.
  - $fresh(n)$: n is a fresh value.
  - $PK(P, k)$: k is a public key of P. (Here k^{-1} denotes the secret key of k.)
  - $P \overset{K}{\leftrightarrow} Q$: k is a shared key for P and Q.
  - $t = t'$: (usual equality)
- Each $\alpha_{i_j}^{Q_i}$ (for $i = 1, \ldots, n$) is an atomic formula made of an action predicate.
- $\vec{\beta}$ is a sequence of action predicates performed by P.
- φ is a single atomic formula (made of an action or non-action predicate).
- $Honest(\alpha_{i_j}^{Q_i})$: a principal Q_i honestly follows a primitive action $\alpha_{i_j}^{Q_i}$.
- $Honest(\alpha_{i_1}^{Q_i}); \cdots; Honest(\alpha_{i_m}^{Q_i})$: a principal Q_i honestly follows a sequence of primitive actions $\alpha_{i_1}^{Q_i}; \cdots; \alpha_{i_m}^{Q_i}$. (We also use the abbreviation $Honest(\alpha_{i_1}^{Q_i}; \cdots; \alpha_{i_m}^{Q_i})$.)

A.2   Axioms and Inference Rules

Here each Γ, Δ represents a set of atoms or a sequence of atomic formulas, which may includes honesty assumptions.

(I) Logical Inference Rules

(1) Structural rules: weakening, contraction and exchange rules in the left hand side, and cut rule (**Cut**) (2) Inference rules for equality (**Eq**) (a typical rule which we often use is presented below), (3) Substitution rule (**Subst**).

$$\frac{\Gamma \vdash [\vec{\alpha}]\varphi \quad \varphi, \Delta \vdash [\vec{\alpha}]\psi}{\Gamma, \Delta \vdash [\vec{\alpha}]\psi} \textbf{ Cut} \qquad \frac{\Gamma \vdash [\vec{\alpha}]x = t \quad \Delta \vdash [\vec{\alpha}]\varphi}{\Gamma, \Delta \vdash [\vec{\alpha}]\varphi[t/x]} \textbf{ Eq}$$

$$\frac{\Gamma \vdash [\vec{\alpha}]\varphi}{\Gamma[t/x] \vdash [\vec{\alpha}[t/x]]\varphi[t/x]} \textbf{ Subst}$$

(II-1) Axioms About Primitive Actions

$\vdash [\alpha_1^P; \cdots; \alpha_n^P]\alpha_i^P$ (for any $i = 1, \ldots, n$ and for any principal P.)

(II-2) Axioms for Relationships Between Properties

Freshness 1:   **Freshness 2:** (where $m \sqsubseteq m'$.)
　　P *generates* $n \vdash fresh(n)$ $fresh(m) \vdash fresh(m')$

Nonce Verification: (where $\{m\}_{k^{-1}} \sqsubseteq m', m''$.)
　　$(PK(k, Q)), (fresh(m)), (P$ *receives* $m'(\{m\}_{k^{-1}}^*)) \vdash (Q$ *sends* $m'')$

We also admit the axiom obtained by replacing $PK(k,Q)$ with $P \overset{k}{\leftrightarrow} Q$.

Shared Secret: (where $K' \sqsubseteq m_1, m_2$.)

$$(P \text{ sends } \{m_1\}_{K_1}), (P \text{ sends } \{m_2\}_{K_2}), (P \text{ generates } K'),$$
$$(P \overset{K_1}{\leftrightarrow} Q), (P \overset{K_2}{\leftrightarrow} R) \vdash (Q \overset{K'}{\leftrightarrow} R)$$

(III) Honesty Inferences

For (1) Substitution and for (3) Deriving another action, we also admit the inference rules obtained by replacing *"receives"* with *"generates"* or *"sends"*, respectively. These rules satisfy the ($\sharp$) condition. (See Section 2.2.)

(1) Substitution:

$$\frac{\Gamma \vdash [\vec{\alpha}](Q \text{ receives } m[t/x])}{\Gamma, Honest(Q \text{ receives } m) \vdash [\vec{\alpha}]x = t} \text{ Hon(Subst)}$$

(where t is a constant and x is a variable which has the same sort of t.)

(2) Matching:

$$\frac{\Gamma \vdash [\vec{\alpha}](Q \text{ sends } m)}{\Gamma, Honest(Q \text{ sends } m', m) \vdash [\vec{\alpha}](Q \text{ sends } m')} \text{ Hon(Match)}$$

(3) Deriving Another Action in a Role:

$$\frac{\Gamma \vdash [\vec{\alpha}](Q \text{ sends } m)}{\Gamma, Honest(Q \text{ receives } m'; Q \text{ sends } m) \vdash [\vec{\alpha}](Q \text{ receives } m')} \text{ Hon(Role)}$$

(IV) Weakening Rules for Actions and Honesty Assumptions

Weakening rule for honesty assumptions (left below) satisfies ($\sharp$) condition.

$$\frac{\Gamma, Honest(\vec{\alpha}^P; \vec{\alpha}'^P) \vdash [\vec{\beta}]\varphi}{\Gamma, Honest(\vec{\alpha}^P; \alpha''^P; \vec{\alpha}'^P) \vdash [\vec{\beta}]\varphi} \text{ W(Hon)} \qquad \frac{\Gamma \vdash [\vec{\alpha}^P; \vec{\alpha}'^P]\varphi}{\Gamma \vdash [\vec{\alpha}^P; \alpha''^P; \vec{\alpha}'^P]\varphi} \text{ W(Act)}$$

A Formal System for Analysis of Cryptographic Encryption and Their Security Properties

Ashraf Bhery, Shigeki Hagihara, and Naoki Yonezaki

Department of Computer Science,
Graduate School of Information Science and Engineering,
Tokyo Institute of Technology,
2-12-1 Ookayama, Meguro-ku, Tokyo 152-8552, Japan
Tel (Fax): +81-3-5734-2772
{ashraf, hagihara, yonezaki}@fmx.cs.titech.ac.jp

Abstract. Providing a way to achieve the privacy and authenticity of information transmitted over or stored in an unreliable medium is a prime necessity in the world of computing and communication. In this paper, we propose a new deduction system called *judgment deduction system*(or JD-System), which can be used to formalize an idealized asymmetric (and symmetric) encryption scheme. In our system, deductive reasoning is used to identify the security properties of asymmetric and symmetric encryption. New notions are introduced for describing several security properties. For example, we use the notion of "judgment" in our system. Conversely, we also introduce the notion of "unjudgment" as a property of JD-system. By using these notions, we can express and prove the security properties *content-indistinguishability*, *key-indistinguishability*, *content-non-malleability*, *content-length-indistinguishability*, *key-length-indistinguishability*, *content-length-non-malleability*, and *key-length-non-malleability* of asymmetric (and symmetric) encryption schemes and the security property *key-non-malleability* of asymmetric encryption. Formal proofs are given showing the sufficient conditions for these security properties and showing formally the difference between asymmetric encryption and symmetric encryption scheme. Some security properties can be achieved in case of asymmetric encryption and cannot be achieved in case of symmetric encryption.

Keywords: encryption, judgment, unjudgment, deduction systems, symmetric-content-non-malleability, symmetric-content-indistinguishability, symmetric-key-indistinguishablity, symmetric-content-length-indistinguishability.

1 Introduction

There are two different mechanisms for formalizing cryptographic primitive [13]. The first mechanism is simple and relies on the use of functions over the symbol space. For example, $\{T\}_k$ represents the formal encryption of the message T with the key k. Its security relies on the assumption that "in order to recover

K. Futatsugi et al. (Eds.): ISSS 2003, LNCS 3233, pp. 87–112, 2004.
© Springer-Verlag Berlin Heidelberg 2004

message T from $\{T\}_k$, one must know the corresponding (i.e., correct) secret key k^{-1}". The second mechanism is *modern cryptography* or *provable secure*. It is based upon computational *complexity theory*, and relies on the use of functions on strings of bits. Its security relies on assumptions about the computational limitations of an attacker together with assumptions about the computational hardness of some problems. In modern cryptography, several notions for secure asymmetric encryption schemes and symmetric encryption schemes have been proposed. For example, the essential security notion for defining a secure asymmetric (or symmetric) encryption scheme is *indistinguishability*, which captures the strong notion of *privacy* that was introduced by Goldwasser and Micali[25]. This notion formalizes an attacker's inability to learn any useful information about a message just from seeing its ciphertext. *Non-malleability*, another security notion for an asymmetric (or symmetric) encryption scheme, was proposed by Dolev, Dwork and Naor [7]. The non-malleability notion for an asymmetric (or symmetric) encryption scheme formalizes an attacker who has been given an example ciphertext to output a different ciphertext such that their plaintexts are related. Most of these notions are characterized and proven by using the notions of probability and complexity theory [7, 11, 16–19, 21, 25–28]. In this paper, we propose a new deduction system called the Judgment Deduction System (or the *JD-system*). JD-system is considered as an extension to JDE-system [1, 2] to include symmetric encryption. Another extension can be found in [3, 4] to include keyless hash function. Using the JD-system, we can analyze the security properties of both asymmetric encryption scheme and symmetric encryption scheme as a security properties of the system. To accomplish this, we use the notion *judgment* in our JD-system. Conversely, we also use the notion of *unjudgment*[1–4]. With these two notions, a proof is given showing that the sufficient conditions for the *asymmetric-(or symmetric-) content-indistinguishability, key-indistinguishability, content-non-malleability, content-length-indistinguishability, key-length-indistinguishability, content-length-non-malleability,* and *key-length-non-malleability* of encryption schemes. A proof is given to clarify their relationships. Also a proof is given showing some security properties can be achieved in case of asymmetric encryption and cannot be achieved in case of symmetric encryption. For example, the security property *key-non-malleability* that introduced by Bhery, Hagihara, and Yonezaki [1–4] can be achieved for an asymmetric encryption scheme but not in case of symmetric encryption.

Related Work. Many formal approaches have been proposed for the analysis of security protocols including the BAN logic of authentication by Burrows, Abadi, and Needham[20], the CSP with a model checking FDR approach[10, 23, 29], equation rewriting tools [24], and the inductive approach for the analysis of security protocols by Paulson [12] which provides automated support using his Isabelle proof assistant. Another approach for modeling and reasoning about security protocols is the spi-calculus, introduced by Abadi and Gordon in [14, 15]. Most of these approaches focused on proving the authentication and secrecy properties of security protocols, however, in these formal methods there are a common set of rules, which defines the analysis of an attacker's knowledge. For examples, in Paulson approach [12], attacker's knowledge is defined as a set of terms S and the attacker's analysis of his knowledge S are defined by the fundamental operations $parts(S)$, $analz(S)$, and $synth(S)$. With this analysis some useful properties are obtained such as $synth(analz(S))$ which represents the set of terms which the attacker can be obtained and generated from the set of knowledge S. A similar set of inference rules is found in the Schneider approach [29]. In [6], Bolignano describes the basic attacker's operations (encrypt, decrypt, pairing, decomposition of a pair) as a transformation relation from a set of terms S to a set S'. Multiple application of these basic operations to a set of terms S provides a new terms (set or single) S'. Such analysis is used to define the relations S' *known-in* S and S' *comp-of* S. Then some impossibility properties like $\neg(b$ *comp-of* $S) \Rightarrow \neg(b$ *known-in* $S)$ are proved. As we have seen, there is a common set of rules for the analysis of an attacker's knowledge. With this common relation Abadi and Rogaway[13] give a formal treatment of symmetric encryption and then they prove formally that equivalent expressions have computational indistinguishable ensembles, as long as the expressions are acyclic. In this paper, we also use this common set of rules as basic rule in the construction of our system (see Section 2.1). In this paper we extend the formal system introduced in [1, 2] for asymmetric encryption scheme to include symmetric encryption. Another extension can be found in [3, 4] to include keyless hash function. By using our JD-system, We can express and prove many security properties of asymmetric and symmetric encryption by giving sufficient conditions for them. A formal proof is given showing formally that some security properties can be achieved in case of asymmetric encryption and cannot be achieved in case of symmetric encryption.

This paper is organized as follows: section 2 presents a common symmetric and asymmetric encryption scheme. We consider this to be a basic semantic of encryption. It is used to construct the JD-system. The JD-system is defined in section 3. In section 4, we state various facts about the JD-system for symmetric and asymmetric encryption schemes. Using these facts, various syntactic security notions of an asymmetric and symmetric encryption scheme are stated in section 5. Finally in section 6, we give our conclusions and suggestions for future work.

2   A Basic Encryption Scheme

In this section, we explain a basic encryption scheme based on the current literature for the formal analysis of security protocols [5, 6, 10, 12, 20, 23, 24, 29, 30]. We start by defining the primitive data types (sorts) that are used in this paper. **Public-Data, P-Keys**, and **S-Keys** are disjoint sets of atomic terms. **Public-Data** is the set of symbols 0 and 1. **P-Keys** is a nonempty set denoting the set of long-term keys. It consists of the set of public keys **Public-Key** and the set of corresponding private keys **Private-Key**. There is a one-to-one relationship between public keys and their corresponding private keys. We will denote the public keys by $k_1, k_2, ...$ and their corresponding private keys by $k_1^{-1}, k_2^{-1}, ...$

respectively. **S-Keys** is a nonempty set of symmetric keys. We will denote the elements of this set by $sk_1, sk_2, ...$ If we use only one key, then we will remove the subscript. Compound terms can be constructed by either asymmetric, symmetric encryption, digital signature, or concatenation. We will write **Terms** as a set of terms that is defined as follows:

Definition 1 (Term). *A term T is a well formed expression defined as*

$$\langle Primitive \rangle \begin{cases} i & \text{for each } i \text{ in } \textbf{Public-Data;} \\ sk & \text{for each } sk \text{ in } \textbf{S-Keys;} \\ k & \text{for each } k \text{ in } \textbf{Public-Key} \\ k^{-1} & \text{for each } k^{-1} \text{ in } \textbf{Private-Key} \end{cases}$$

$$\langle Compound \rangle \begin{cases} \{T\}_{sk} & \text{for symmetric encryption} \\ \{T\}_k & \text{for asymmetric encryption} \\ \{T\}_{k^{-1}} & \text{for signature} \\ T_1, T_2 & \text{for concatenation} \end{cases}$$

Informally, $\{T\}_{sk}$ represents the symmetric encryption of term T using a secret key sk. $\{T\}_k$ represents the asymmetric encryption of term T using a public key k. $\{T\}_{k^{-1}}$ represents the digital signature of term T using a private key k^{-1}. T_1, T_2 represents the concatenation of the two terms T_1 and T_2. For concatenation, we use parentheses when it is deemed necessary to ensure that only one interpretation can be inferred. We consider that each term T is associated with a natural number $len(T)$ that represents its length. For the encryption scheme, we assume the following conditions:

1. Encryption and signature are *perfect*, i.e. it satisfies the following:
    (a) It is impossible to produce $\{T\}_k$ without knowing T and k.
    (b) It is impossible to produce $\{T\}_{k^{-1}}$ without knowing T and k^{-1}.
    (c) It is impossible to produce $\{T\}_{sk}$ without knowing T and sk.
    (d) In order to recover T from $\{T\}_k$, one must know k^{-1}.
    (e) In order to verify $\{T\}_{k^{-1}}$, one must know k.
    (f) In order to recover T from $\{T\}_{sk}$, one must know sk.
    (g) Given $\{T\}_k$, it is impossible to recover k.
    (h) Given $\{T\}_{k^{-1}}$, it is impossible to recover k^{-1}.
    (i) Given $\{T\}_{sk}$, it is impossible to recover sk.
2. Only by seeing T, the attacker can determine the length of T.
3. If T_1 and T_2 are syntactically different, then the values of T_1 and T_2 are different.
4. An attacker always distinguishes encrypted terms from non-encrypted terms.
5. An attacker always distinguishes the concatenation of terms from terms of different constructions.
6. An attacker always distinguishes the signature of terms from terms of different constructions.
7. An attacker distinguishes the symmetric encryption from asymmetric encryption.

In the above sense, we consider that our JD-system is ideal for asymmetric and symmetric encryption.

2.1   An Attacker's Composition and Decomposition Relationship

In this section, we give the basic attacker's composition and decomposition relationship for an asymmetric and a symmetric encryption. The basic definition was given by Dolev and Yao [8] and has been used in the formal analysis of security protocols [5, 6, 12, 20, 23, 24, 29, 30]. Also with this basic relation Abadi and Rogaway[13] give a formal treatment of symmetric encryption and then they prove formally that equivalent expressions give computational indistinguishable ensembles, as long as the expressions does not contains encryption cycle. In this paper, we also use this relation as basic relation in constructing JD-system.

Definition 2 (Basic-Rules). *Let T_1 and T_2 be two terms. The relation $\models$ over T_1, T_2, denoted by $T_1 \models T_2$, is defined as the least relation that satisfies the following rules:*

1. $\models_i$ (for each $i \in$ **Public-Data**),

2. $\models_k$ (for each $k \in$ **Public-Key**),

3. $\dfrac{\models T_1}{T \models T_1}$,

4. $\dfrac{}{T \models T}$,

5. $\dfrac{T \models T_1, T_2}{T \models T_1}$, $\dfrac{T \models T_1, T_2}{T \models T_2}$,

6. $\dfrac{T \models T_1, T \models T_2}{T \models T_1, T_2}$,

7. $\dfrac{T \models T_1, T \models sk}{T \models \{T_1\}_{sk}}$,

8. $\dfrac{T \models T_1, T \models k}{T \models \{T_1\}_k}$,

9. $\dfrac{T \models T_1, T \models k^{-1}}{T \models \{T_1\}_{k^{-1}}}$,

10. $\dfrac{T \models \{T_1\}_k, T \models k^{-1}}{T \models T_1}$,

11. $\dfrac{T \models \{T_1\}_{sk}, T \models sk}{T \models T_1}$,

12. $\dfrac{T \models \{T_1\}_{k^{-1}}, T \models k}{T \models T_1}$.

Intuitively $T_1 \models T_2$ infers not only what an attacker can obtain from T_1 but also which terms an attacker can generate from T_1 with the knowledge of public keys and public data. For example, an attacker can generate terms such as $\models \{0\}_k$, and $\models \{1, k_1\}_k$ from the above rules.

3   The JD-System

In this section, we extend the inference system (JDE-system) for an asymmetric encryption schemes [1, 2] to include symmetric encryption. The extension sys-

tem is called Judgment Deduction system (or JD-system). Another extension
to include keyless hash function can be found in [3, 4]. The JD-system can be
used for reasoning about the security properties of cryptographic primitives. It
consists of a triple $(\sum, JD, \vdash_{JD})$, where:

1. $\sum$ is the set of judgment.
2. JD is the set of JD-inference rules. Each JD-inference rule has zero or more
   premises and a conclusion. A conclusion is called an *evidence* and is said to
   be *derivable* if it can be deduced using the given JD-inference rules.
3. $\vdash_{JD}$ is the JD-derivation relation, which is defined using a sequence of applications of JD-inference. It is also defined inductively.

3.1   Judgment

In order to define judgment [1, 2, 3, 4], we must first extend the set **Terms** to the
set **Ex-Terms** by using the following constructors. Then we can define *propositions* over the new set **Ex-Terms**.

Definition 3 (Ex-Terms). *Let f be a meta variable of the sort {content-of,
key-of, key-for}. The set of extended terms denoted by **Ex-Terms** is defined as
follows:*

1. *If $T \in$ **Terms**, then $T \in$ **Ex-Terms**,*
2. *If $\{T_1\}_k \in$ **Terms**, then $f(\{T_1\}_k) \in$ **Ex-Terms**,*
3. *If $\{T_1\}_{sk} \in$ **Terms**, then content-of$(\{T_1\}_{sk}) \in$ **Ex-Terms**,*
4. *If $\{T_1\}_{sk} \in$ **Terms**, then key-of$(\{T_1\}_{sk}) \in$ **Ex-Terms**,*
5. *If $\{T_1\}_{k^{-1}} \in$ **Terms**, then $f(\{T_1\}_{k^{-1}}) \in$ **Ex-Terms**,*

The constructors *key-of*, *key-for*, and *content-of* are intended to have the
following meaning.

$$- \text{ The value of } \text{``}key\text{-}of(\text{T})\text{''} = \begin{cases} k & \text{if } T = \{T_1\}_k; \\ sk & \text{if } T = \{T_1\}_{sk}; \\ k^{-1} & \text{if } T = \{T_1\}_{k^{-1}}. \end{cases}$$

$$- \text{ The value of } \text{``}key\text{-}for(\text{T})\text{''} = \begin{cases} k^{-1} & \text{if } T = \{T_1\}_k; \\ k & \text{if } T = \{T_1\}_{k^{-1}}. \end{cases}$$

- The value of "*content-of*(T)"$= T_1$, where $T = \{T_1\}_k$ or $T = \{T_1\}_{k^{-1}}$ or
  $T = \{T_1\}_{sk}$.

The constructor *key-for* is needed only for asymmetric encryption since we
have two different keys. One for encryption and the other for decryption. But in
case of symmetric encryption we only need the constructor of *key-of* since the
key used in encryption is also used for decryption. With the constructor *key-of*,
we are able to analyze whether the attacker can determine that two ciphertexts
are encrypted with the same key without knowing the decryption keys in case
of asymmetric encryption. The constructor *key-for* can be used to analyze the
fact that attacker has opportunity to see whether two different digital signature

terms request the same key for verification. The constructor *content-of* is used to analyze whether the attacker has the opportunity to see that two different ciphertexts have the same content without seeing the contents of the actual ciphertexts.

Next, we define *propositions* over **Ex-Terms** as follows:

Definition 4 (Proposition). *Let T_i and T_j be meta variables that range over the set **Ex-Terms**. $T_i = T_j$ and $len(T_i) = len(T_j)$ are propositions. If P is a proposition, then $\neg P$ is also a proposition.*

The proposition $\neg(T_i = T_j)$ is abbreviated as $T_i \neq T_j$. Similarly, the proposition $\neg(len(T_i) = len(T_j))$ is abbreviated as $len(T_i) \neq len(T_j)$.

Definition 5 (Judgment). *Judgment is expressed as $T \models P$, which means that by knowing T, an attacker can see the fact P that is represented by a proposition.*

3.2 JD-Inference Rules

In this section we extend the set of inference rules defined in [1, 2] to include symmetric encryption. Each inference rule has the form $\frac{premises}{conclusion}$, where the premises are a set of statements and a conclusion is a statement. This means that from the premises, we can arrive at a conclusion. In the following JD-inference rules, we use $T_1, T_2, ...$ to denote meta-variables of sort **Terms**, $T_1', T_2', ...$ to denote meta-variables of sort **Ex-Terms**, and $T_1'', T_2'', ...$ to denote meta-variables of sort **Ex-Terms** $\cup \{len(T)|T \in$ **Ex-Terms**$\}$. Let f be meta variable ranging over the set $\{content\text{-}of, key\text{-}of, key\text{-}for\}$, and g be meta variable ranging over the set $\{content\text{-}of, key\text{-}of\}$.

1. Basic-rules in Definition 2.

2. $$\frac{T \models T_1}{T \models len(T_1)}$$

   If an attacker obtains term T_1 from T, then he can determine its length.

3. $$\frac{T \models T_1}{T \models T_1 = T_1}$$

   If an attacker obtains term T_1 from term T, then he can determine that the values of these terms are equal.

4. $$\frac{T \models T_1, T \models T_2}{T \models T_1 \neq T_2} \text{ (where T_1 is not syntactically equal to T_2)}$$

   With the knowledge of term T, if an attacker obtains the two terms T_1 and T_2 with the condition that T_1 and T_2 are syntactically different, then he can determine that these terms have different values.

5. $$\frac{T \models \{T_1\}_{k_i} = \{T_2\}_{k_j}}{T \models f(\{T_1\}_{k_i}) = f(\{T_2\}_{k_j})}$$

With the knowledge of T, if an attacker can deduce that the values of two encrypted terms are equal then he can determine that these two encrypted terms have the same content and the same encrypted keys, and that they need the same key for decryption.

6. $$\frac{T \models \{T_1\}_{sk_i} = \{T_2\}_{sk_j}}{T \models g(\{T_1\}_{sk_i}) = g(\{T_2\}_{sk_j})}$$

This rule is similar to the above but in case of symmetric encryption.

7. $$\frac{T \models \{T_1\}_{k_i^{-1}} = \{T_2\}_{k_j^{-1}}}{T \models f(\{T_1\}_{k_i^{-1}}) = f(\{T_2\}_{k_j^{-1}})}$$

With the knowledge of T, if an attacker can deduce that the values of two digital signature terms are equal then he can determine that these two terms have the same content and the same signed keys, and that they need the same key for verification.

8. $$\frac{T \models T_1'' = T_2''}{T \models T_2'' = T_1''}$$

9. $$\frac{T \models T_1'' \neq T_2''}{T \models T_2'' \neq T_1''}$$

These two rules represent the symmetry of judgment.

10. $$\frac{T \models T_1'' = T_2'', T \models T_2'' = T_3''}{T \models T_1'' = T_3''}$$

11. $$\frac{T \models T_1'' = T_2'', T \models T_2'' \neq T_3''}{T \models T_1'' \neq T_3''}$$

12. $$\frac{T \models T_1}{T \models \textit{content-of}(\{T_1\}_k) = T_1}$$

This rule must be valid, because even if an attacker does not know the private key k^{-1}, if he knows T_1 and if the public key k is available, he can generate $\{T_1\}_k$. Then, he can determine that the values of the two encrypted terms are equal. Otherwise, if he knows the private key, then this rule is trivially valid.

13. $$\frac{T \models \{T_1\}_{sk}, T \models sk}{T \models \textit{content-of}(\{T_1\}_{sk}) = T_1}$$

This rule must be valid, because the attacker knows the decryption key.

14.
$$\frac{T \models \{T_1\}_{k^{-1}}}{T \models \text{content-of}(\{T_1\}_{k^{-1}}) = T_1}$$

This rule is valid because an attacker knows the public key k. He can verify the signature using the public key K.

15.
$$\frac{T \models T_1}{T \models \text{key-of}(\{T_1\}_k) = k}$$

This rule is similar to the rule 12 and it summarizes two rules for asymmetric encryption. If the attacker knows the decryption key, then this rule trivially holds; otherwise the attacker knows all the public keys and knows T_1. Hence he can generate $\{T_1\}_k$ and compare between the terms. Then, he can determine that the values of the two encrypted terms are equal.

16.
$$\frac{T \models \{T_1\}_{sk}, T \models sk}{T \models \text{key-of}(\{T_1\}_{sk}) = sk}$$

This rule must be valid, because the attacker knows the decryption key.

17.
$$\frac{T \models \{T_1\}_{sk_j}, T \models sk_i \quad (sk_i \text{ is not syntactically equal } sk_j)}{T \models \text{key-of}(\{T_1\}_{sk_j}) \neq sk_i}$$

This rule must be valid, because the attacker knows the decryption key sk_i and this key cannot decrypt the ciphertext $\{T_1\}_{sk_j}$. Hence he can determine that the value of encrypted key of the term $\{T_1\}_{sk_j}$ is different from the value of the key sk_i.

18.
$$\frac{T \models \{T_1\}_{k^{-1}} \quad (k \text{ is the inverse key of } k^{-1})}{T \models \text{key-for}(\{T_1\}_{k^{-1}}) = k}$$

This rule is valid because an attacker knows all of the public keys and there is a one-to-one relationship between the public and private keys.

19.
$$\frac{T \models \{T_1\}_{k_i}, T \models k_j^{-1}}{T \models \text{key-of}(\{T_1\}_{k_i}) \neq k_j} \quad \begin{array}{l}(\text{where } k_i \text{ is not syntactically equal to } k_j \text{ and } k_i \text{ is} \\ \text{the inverse of } k_i^{-1})\end{array},$$

This rule must be valid, because the attacker knows the decryption key k_j^{-1} and this key cannot decrypt the ciphertext $\{T_1\}_{k_i}$. Hence he can determine that the value of encrypted key of the term $\{T_1\}_{k_i}$ is different from the value of the public key k_j.

20.
$$\frac{T \models \text{key-of}(\{T_1\}_{k_i}) = \text{key-of}(\{T_2\}_{k_j})}{T \models \text{key-for}(\{T_1\}_{k_i}) = \text{key-for}(\{T_2\}_{k_j})}$$

This rule is valid because if the attacker knows two encryption terms are encrypted by the same key, then he knows that these two encrypted terms are needs the same key for decryption.

21. $$\dfrac{T \models key\text{-}of(\{T_1\}_{k_i}) \neq key\text{-}of(\{T_2\}_{k_j})}{T \models key\text{-}for(\{T_1\}_{k_i}) \neq key\text{-}for(\{T_2\}_{k_j})}$$

This rule is valid because if the attacker knows two encryption terms are encrypted by different key, then he knows that these two encrypted terms are needs the different key for decryption.

22. $$\dfrac{T \models key\text{-}for(\{T_1\}_{k_i^{-1}}) = key\text{-}for(\{T_2\}_{k_j^{-1}})}{T \models key\text{-}of(\{T_1\}_{k_i^{-1}}) = key\text{-}of(\{T_2\}_{k_j^{-1}})}$$

This rule is valid because if the attacker knows two digital signature terms are needs the same public key for verification, then he knows that these two digital signatures are signed by the same key.

23. $$\dfrac{T \models key\text{-}for(\{T_1\}_{k_i^{-1}}) \neq key\text{-}for(\{T_2\}_{k_j^{-1}})}{T \models key\text{-}of(\{T_1\}_{k_i^{-1}}) \neq key\text{-}of(\{T_2\}_{k_j^{-1}})}$$

This rule is valid because if the attacker knows two digital signature terms are needs different keys for verification, then he knows that these two digital signature terms are signed by different keys.

24. $$\dfrac{T \models T_1' = T_2'}{T \models len(T_1') = len(T_2')}$$

If an attacker knows about the equality of the values of two terms, then he can determine the equality of their length.

25. $$\dfrac{T \models len(T_1), T \models len(T_2)}{T \models len(T_1) = len(T_2)} \text{ (where } len(T_1) = len(T_2))$$

26. $$\dfrac{T \models len(T_1), T \models len(T_2)}{T \models len(T_1) \neq len(T_2)} \text{ (where } len(T_1) \neq len(T_2))$$

With the above two rules, we means that from the knowledge of T, if an attacker can obtain $len(T_1)$ and $len(T_2)$ from T, then he can determine whether they have the same length or they have different length.

3.3   JD-Derivation and Unjudgment

In the preceding subsections we have defined judgment and JD-inference rules. In this section, we give an inductive definition of JD-derivation. With this notion we give the notion of unjudgment, which represents the situation where no knowledge about equality and non-equality of pair of terms can be derived in any JD-derivation.

Definition 6 (Statement). *A statement is defined as an expression of the form $T \models T_1$ or of the form $T \models P$. We use meta variables $S_1, S_2, \dots$ to range over statements.*

Definition 7 ($\vdash_{JD}$). *Consider S_1, S_2 and S_3 are meta variables range over statement, $\vdash_{JD}$ is defined inductively as follows.*

1. *Base case. If the JD-inference rule of the form $\overline{S_1}$, then $\vdash_{JD} S_1$ is a JD-derivation.*
2. *Induction case. If we have JD-derivation $\vdash_{JD} S_1, \vdash_{JD} S_2$, and there is a JD-inference rule of the form $\frac{S_1, S_2}{S_3}$ (or of the form $\frac{S_1}{S_3}$), then $\vdash_{JD} S_3$ is a JD-derivation.*

For our JD-system, we propose a set of JD-inference rules that are sufficient for defining all of the possible actions that can be taken by an attacker. An attacker can decompose, compose, encrypt, and decrypt. In some cases, an attacker can determine the contents of asymmetric encrypted terms without knowing the secret key, determine the encrypted key from examining the ciphertext, see whether the terms have the same length, and compare between terms. These rules are sufficient for formalizing all of an attacker's abilities. For instance, consider the following rule:

$$\frac{T \models \{T_1\}_{k_i} \neq \{T_2\}_{k_j}, T \models \textit{content-of}(\{T_1\}_{k_i}) = \textit{content-of}(\{T_2\}_{k_j})}{T \models \textit{key-of}(\{T_1\}_{k_i}) \neq \textit{key-of}(\{T_2\}_{k_j})}$$

This rule states that if two terms are syntactically different and have the same content, then these two terms must use different keys for asymmetric encryption. However, we do not have to add this rule to the JD-inference rules because the judgment

$$T \models \textit{key-of}(\{T_1\}_{k_i}) \neq \textit{key-of}(\{T_2\}_{k_j})$$

can be deduced in the JD-scheme if an attacker can deduce the judgments

$$T \models \{T_1\}_{k_i} \neq \{T_2\}_{k_j} \text{ and } T \models \textit{content-of}(\{T_1\}_{k_i}) = \textit{content-of}(\{T_2\}_{k_j})^1.$$

For the same reason, we do not have to add the following inference rule.

$$\frac{T \models \{T_1\}_{k_i} \neq \{T_2\}_{k_j}, T \models \textit{key-of}(\{T_1\}_{k_i}) = \textit{key-of}(\{T_2\}_{k_j})}{T \models \textit{content-of}(\{T_1\}_{k_i}) \neq \textit{content-of}(\{T_2\}_{k_j})}.$$

As another example to support our premise that we have a sufficient set of JD-inference rules, it is not necessary to add the following inference rules

1. $\dfrac{T \models k^{-1}, T \models \{T_1\}_{k^{-1}}}{T \models \textit{key-of}(\{T_1\}_{k^{-1}}) = k^{-1}}$

2. $\dfrac{T \models k_i^{-1}, T \models \{T_1\}_{k_j^{-1}}}{T \models \textit{key-of}(\{T_1\}_{k_j^{-1}}) \neq k_i^{-1}}$ (k_i^{-1} is not syntactically equal to k_j^{-1})

---

[1] In order to the attacker deduce these judgments, he must deduce first the statements $T \models T_1$ and $T \models T_2$. By using these statements and the JD-inference rules 4, 8,9,11, and 15 we can get the conclusion.

3. $$\frac{T \models k^{-1}, T \models \{T_1\}_k}{T \models \textit{key-for}(\{T_1\}_k) = k^{-1}}$$

4. $$\frac{T \models k_i^{-1}, T \models \{T_1\}_{k_j}}{T \models \textit{key-for}(\{T_1\}_{k_j}) \neq k_i^{-1}} \quad (k_i^{-1} \text{ is not inverse key of } k_j)$$

to deduce either the judgment

$$T \models f(T_1') = f(T_2') \text{ or the judgment } T \models f(T_1') \neq f(T_2'),$$

where $f \in \{\textit{key-of}, \textit{key-for}\}$ and T_1', T_2' are either of the form $\{T_1\}_k$ or $\{T_1\}_{k^{-1}}$. For example, the judgment $T \models \textit{key-of}(\{T_1\}_{k^{-1}}) = \textit{key-of}(\{T_2\}_{k^{-1}})$ can be proven by using the following JD-derivation tree:

$$\cfrac{\cfrac{T \models \{T_1\}_{k^{-1}}}{T \models \textit{key-for}(\{T_1\}_{k^{-1}}) = k} \quad , \quad \cfrac{\cfrac{T \models \{T_2\}_{k^{-1}}}{T \models \textit{key-for}(\{T_2\}_{k^{-1}}) = k}}{T \models k = \textit{key-for}(\{T_2\}_{k^{-1}})}}{\cfrac{T \models \textit{key-for}(\{T_1\}_{k^{-1}}) = \textit{key-for}(\{T_2\}_{k^{-1}})}{T \models \textit{key-of}(\{T_1\}_{k^{-1}}) = \textit{key-of}(\{T_2\}_{k^{-1}})}}$$

Definition 8 (Unjudgment). $\dashv_{JD} T \models^? P \overset{def}{\Leftrightarrow} (\nvdash_{JD} T \models P \wedge \nvdash_{JD} T \models \neg P)$.

Definition 8 gives a formal description of the Unjudgment relation [1, 2, 3, 4], which means that from the term T, the attacker has no evidence in any JD-derivation to allow him to determine whether the statement $T \models P$ or the statement $T \models \neg P$ holds. The definition of an Unjudgment relation can be considered as the heart of our formalization for the security notions of an encryption scheme.

4   Facts About the JD-System

In this section, we describe various important facts about the JD-system. This facts are divided into two classes of facts. One is for symmetric encryption and the other is for asymmetric encryption. These facts can be used in several ways to express several security notions of asymmetric and a symmetric encryption scheme.

4.1   Facts About Symmetric Encryption

In this section, we state various JD-properties about symmetric encryption and give their proofs.

Theorem 1. *Even if the attacker knows one of the keys used in two symmetric encrypted terms, he cannot get any information about relations between their contents.*

If $(\nvdash_{JD} T \models \{T_1\}_{sk_i} \text{ or } \nvdash_{JD} T \models \{T_2\}_{sk_j})$ or $(\{T_1\}_{sk_i} \neq \{T_2\}_{sk_j} \text{ and } (\nvdash_{JD} T \models sk_i \text{ or } \nvdash_{JD} T \models sk_j))$, then

$$\dashv_{JD} T \models^? \textit{content-of}(\{T_1\}_{sk_i}) = \textit{content-of}(\{T_2\}_{sk_j}).$$

Proof. Suppose $\{T_1\}_{sk_i} \neq \{T_2\}_{sk_j}$. From the symmetry of the assumption of the theorem 1, it is sufficient to prove that if $\nvdash_{JD} T \models sk_i$ or $\nvdash_{JD} T \models \{T_1\}_{sk_i}$, then

$$\dashv_{JD} T \models^? \text{content-of}(\{T_1\}_{sk_i}) = \text{content-of}(\{T_2\}_{sk_j}).$$

By assuming $\nvdash_{JD} T \models sk_i$ or $\nvdash_{JD} T \models \{T_1\}_{sk_i}$, and there exists a JD-derivation of either

$$\vdash_{JD} T \models \text{content-of}(\{T_1\}_{sk_i}) = \text{content-of}(\{T_2\}_{sk_j}) \tag{1}$$

or

$$\vdash_{JD} T \models \text{content-of}(\{T_1\}_{sk_i}) \neq \text{content-of}(\{T_2\}_{sk_j}), \tag{2}$$

we are going to prove the contradicting facts $\vdash_{JD} T \models sk_i$ and $\vdash_{JD} T \models \{T_1\}_{sk_i}$ by using proposition 1 (for the case (1)) and proposition 2 (for the case (2)).

Proposition 1. *If $\vdash_{JD} T \models T_x = T_y$ such that T_x or T_y is of the form content-of$(\{T_1\}_{sk_i})$, and $(T_x \neq \text{content-of}(\{T_1\}_{sk_i})$ or $T_y \neq \text{content-of}(\{T_1\}_{sk_i}))$, then $\vdash_{JD} T \models sk_i$ and $\vdash_{JD} T \models \{T_1\}_{sk_i}$.*

Proof. **Base Cases.**

1. Suppose the final JD-inference rule used in the derivation is the JD-inference rule 6 of the form
$$\frac{T \models \{T_z\}_{sk_i''} = \{T_u\}_{sk_j''}}{T \models g(\{T_z\}_{sk_i''}) = g(\{T_u\}_{sk_j''})}.$$
From the conditions of the proposition, the conclusion part should be of the form
$$T \models \text{content-of}(\{T_1\}_{sk_i}) = \text{content-of}(\{T_w\}_{sk_l})$$
such that $\{T_1\}_{sk_i} \neq \{T_w\}_{sk_l}$. Considering the general fact that $T \models T' = T''$ holds only for the case that T' and T'' are syntactically identical terms, we see $T_w = T_1$ and $sk_l = sk_i$. This contradicts the fact that $\{T_1\}_{sk_i} \neq \{T_w\}_{sk_l}$. Therefore, the proposition becomes trivially valid.

2. Suppose the final JD-inference rule used in the derivation is the JD-inference rule 13 of the form
$$\frac{T \models \{T_z\}_{sk_i''}, T \models sk_i''}{T \models \text{content-of}(\{T_z\}_{sk_i''}) = T_z}.$$
By the conditions of the proposition, we have that $\text{content-of}(\{T_z\}_{sk_i''}) = \text{content-of}(\{T_1\}_{sk_i})$, the premise should be $T \models \{T_1\}_{sk_i}, T \models sk_i$. Hence we have $\vdash_{JD} T \models sk_i$ and $\vdash_{JD} T \models \{T_1\}_{sk_i}$.

Induction Steps

1. Suppose the final JD-inference rule used in the derivation is the JD-inference rule 8 of the form
$$\frac{T \models T_y = T_x}{T \models T_x = T_y}.$$

By the similarity of the form of premise and conclusion of this rule, we have that if the conclusion satisfies the conditions of proposition 1, then the premise satisfies the same conditions. Hence by induction hypothesis we have derivations of $\vdash_{JD} T \models sk_i$ and $\vdash_{JD} T \models \{T_1\}_{sk_i}$ for the derivation $\vdash_{JD} T \models T_y = T_x$. Therefore, for the derivation $\vdash_{JD} T \models T_x = T_y$ we have derivations $\vdash_{JD} T \models sk_i$ and $\vdash_{JD} T \models \{T_1\}_{sk_i}$.

2. For the case that the final JD-inference rule used in the derivation is the JD-inference rule 10,

$$\frac{T \models T_x = T_z, T \models T_z = T_y}{T \models T_x = T_y}.$$

Suppose T_x or T_y satisfies the conditions of proposition 1, then we have the following cases.

(a) If $T_x = content\text{-}of(\{T_1\}_{sk_i})$, then $T_y \neq content\text{-}of(\{T_1\}_{sk_i})$.

 i. If $T_z \neq content\text{-}of(\{T_1\}_{sk_i})$, then $\vdash_{JD} T \models T_x = T_z$ satisfies the condition part of proposition 1. From the induction hypothesis, we have $(\vdash_{JD} T \models sk_i$ and $\vdash_{JD} T \models \{T_1\}_{sk_i})$ for the derivation $\vdash_{JD} T \models T_x = T_z$. Therefore, for the derivation $\vdash_{JD} T \models T_x = T_y$ we have derivations of $\vdash_{JD} T \models sk_i$ and $\vdash_{JD} T \models \{T_1\}_{sk_i}$.

 ii. If $T_z = content\text{-}of(\{T_1\}_{sk_i})$, then from $T_y \neq content\text{-}of(\{T_1\}_{sk_i})$ we have $T \models T_z = T_y$ satisfying the condition part of proposition 1. From the induction hypothesis, we have $(\vdash_{JD} T \models sk_i$ and $\vdash_{JD} T \models \{T_1\}_{sk_i})$ for the derivation $\vdash_{JD} T \models T_z = T_y$. Therefore, for the derivation $\vdash_{JD} T \models T_x = T_y$ we have derivations $\vdash_{JD} T \models sk_i$ and $\vdash_{JD} T \models \{T_1\}_{sk_i}$.

(b) If $T_y = content\text{-}of(\{T_1\}_{sk_i})$, by the same way as (a) or (b), we get derivations of $\vdash_{JD} T \models sk_i$ and $\vdash_{JD} T \models \{T_1\}_{sk_i}$.

If other JD-inference rule is used as the final JD-inference rule in derivation the derivation , then the form of conclusion does not match with the condition part of the proposition.   □

Proposition 2. *If $\vdash_{JD} T \models T_x \neq T_y$ such that T_x or T_y is of the following form $content\text{-}of(\{T_1\}_{sk_i})$, then $(\vdash_{JD} T \models sk_i$ and $\vdash_{JD} T \models \{T_1\}_{sk_i})$.*

Proof. 1. Suppose the final JD-inference rule used in the derivation is the JD-inference rule 9 of the form

$$\frac{T \models T_y \neq T_x}{T \models T_x \neq T_y}.$$

By the similarity of the forms in the conclusion part and the premise part, we have that if the conclusion part satisfies the conditions of proposition 2, then the premise part satisfies the same conditions. Hence by induction hypothesis, we have ($\vdash_{JD} T \models sk_i$ and $\vdash_{JD} T \models \{T_1\}_{sk_i}$) from a derivation of $\vdash_{JD} T \models T_y \neq T_x$. Therefore, we have the same conclusion from a derivation of $\vdash_{JD} T \models T_x \neq T_y$.

2. Suppose the final JD-inference rule used in the derivation is the JD-inference rule 11 of the form

$$\frac{T \models T_x = T_z, T \models T_z \neq T_y}{T \models T_x \neq T_y}.$$

From the conclusion we see either T_x or T_y takes the forms as in proposition 2, we consider the following case.

- If $T_x = content\text{-}of(\{T_1\}_{sk_i})$, then we consider the following cases.

  • If $T_z \neq content\text{-}of(\{T_1\}_{sk_i})$, then $T \models T_x = T_z$ satisfies the conditions of proposition 1. Hence from the proof of equality case, we have ($\vdash_{JD} T \models sk_i$ and $\vdash_{JD} T \models \{T_1\}_{sk_i}$) for the derivation $\vdash_{JD} T \models T_x = T_z$ (this is the base case). Therefore, for the derivation $\vdash_{JD} T \models T_x \neq T_y$ we also have derivations of $\vdash_{JD} T \models sk_i$ and $\vdash_{JD} T \models \{T_1\}_{sk_i}$.

  • If $T_z = content\text{-}of(\{T_1\}_{sk_i})$, then the derivation $\vdash_{JD} T \models T_z \neq T_y$ satisfies the conditions of proposition 2. Hence by the induction hypothesis, we have $\vdash_{JD} T \models sk_i$ and $\vdash_{JD} T \models \{T_1\}_{sk_i}$ for the derivation $\vdash_{JD} T \models T_z \neq T_y$. Therefore, for the derivation $\vdash_{JD} T \models T_x \neq T_y$ we have $\vdash_{JD} T \models sk_i$ and $\vdash_{JD} T \models \{T_1\}_{sk_i}$.

- If $T_y = content\text{-}of(\{T_1\}_{sk_i})$, then the derivation of right premise $T \models T_z \neq T_y$ satisfies the same conditions of proposition 2. Therefore, by the induction hypothesis, we have ($\vdash_{JD} T \models sk_i$ and $\vdash_{JD} T \models \{T_1\}_{sk_i}$) for the derivation $\vdash_{JD} T \models T_z \neq T_y$. Therefore, for the derivation $\vdash_{JD} T \models T_x \neq T_y$ we also have $\vdash_{JD} T \models sk_i$ and $\vdash_{JD} T \models \{T_1\}_{sk_i}$.

If other JD-inference rule is used as the final JD-inference rule in derivation the derivation, then the form of conclusion does not match with the condition part of proposition 2. $\square$

Suppose $\{T_1\}_{sk_i} = \{T_2\}_{sk_j}$. It is sufficient to prove that if $\nvdash_{JD} T \models \{T_1\}_{sk_i}$, then $\dashv_{JD} T \models^? content\text{-}of(\{T_1\}_{sk_i}) = content\text{-}of(\{T_2\}_{sk_j})$. By assuming $\nvdash_{JD} T \models \{T_1\}_{sk_i}$ and either $\vdash_{JD} T \models content\text{-}of(\{T_1\}_{sk_i}) = content\text{-}of(\{T_2\}_{sk_j})$ or $\vdash_{JD} T \models content\text{-}of(\{T_1\}_{sk_i}) \neq content\text{-}of(\{T_2\}_{sk_j})$, we are going to prove the contradicting fact $\vdash_{JD} T \models \{T_1\}_{sk_i}$. Since $\{T_1\}_{sk_i} = \{T_2\}_{sk_j}$, $\nvdash_{JD} T \models content\text{-}of(\{T_1\}_{sk_i}) \neq content\text{-}of(\{T_2\}_{sk_j})$, we just consider the following case.

Proposition 3. If $\{T_1\}_{sk_i} = \{T_2\}_{sk_j}$ and there exists a JD-derivation of $\vdash_{JD} T \models content\text{-}of(\{T_1\}_{sk_i}) = content\text{-}of(\{T_2\}_{sk_j})$, then $\vdash_{JD} T \models \{T_1\}_{sk_i}$.

Proof. **Base Cases.** Suppose the final JD-inference rule used in the derivation is the JD-inference rule 6 of the form

$$\frac{T \models \{T_z\}_{sk_i''} = \{T_u\}_{sk_j''}}{T \models g(\{T_z\}_{sk_i''}) = g(\{T_u\}_{sk_j''})}.$$

From the conditions of the proposition, the conclusion part should be of the form

$$T \models \text{content-of}(\{T_1\}_{sk_i}) = \text{content-of}(\{T_2\}_{sk_j}),$$

and the premise should be $T \models \{T_1\}_{sk_i} = \{T_2\}_{sk_j}$. By the fact that if $\vdash_{JD} T \models T_x = T_y$ and $T_x \in$ **Terms**, $T_y \in$ **Ex-Terms**, then $\vdash_{JD} T \models T_x$ (this fact can be simply proved by induction), we have $\vdash_{JD} T \models \{T_1\}_{sk_i}$.

Induction Steps

1. Suppose the final JD-inference rule used in the derivation is the JD-inference rule 8 of the form
$$\frac{T \models T_y = T_x}{T \models T_x = T_y}.$$

   From the conditions of the proposition, the conclusion part should be of the form
$$T \models \text{content-of}(\{T_1\}_{sk_i}) = \text{content-of}(\{T_2\}_{sk_j}),$$

   and the premise should be $T \models \text{content-of}(\{T_2\}_{sk_j}) = \text{content-of}(\{T_1\}_{sk_1})$. By the similarity of the form of premise and conclusion of this rule, we have that if the conclusion satisfies the conditions of proposition 3, then the premise satisfies the same conditions. Hence by induction hypothesis we have derivations of $\vdash_{JD} T \models \{T_1\}_{sk_i}$ for the derivation $T \models \text{content-of}(\{T_2\}_{sk_j}) = \text{content-of}(\{T_1\}_{sk_i})$. Therefore, for the derivation $T \models \text{content-of}(\{T_1\}_{sk_i}) = \text{content-of}(\{T_2\}_{sk_j})$ we have a derivation $\vdash_{JD} T \models \{T_1\}_{sk_i}$.

2. For the case that the final JD-inference rule used in the derivation is the JD-inference rule 10 of the form
$$\frac{T \models T_x = T_z, T \models T_z = T_y}{T \models T_x = T_y}.$$

   From the conditions of the proposition, the conclusion part should be of the form $T \models \text{content-of}(\{T_1\}_{sk_i}) = \text{content-of}(\{T_2\}_{sk_j})$ and the premise should be $T \models \text{content-of}(\{T_1\}_{sk_i}) = T_z, T \models T_z = \text{content-of}(\{T_2\}_{sk_j})$. Hence, we consider the following two cases.

   (a) If $T_z = \text{content-of}(\{T_2\}_{sk_j})$, then the premises $T \models \text{content-of}(\{T_1\}_{sk_i}) = T_z$ and $T \models T_z = \text{content-of}(\{T_2\}_{sk_j})$ are satisfying the conditions of the proposition 3. Hence by induction hypothesis we have derivations of $\vdash_{JD} T \models \{T_1\}_{sk_i}$ for the derivation $T \models \text{content-of}(\{T_1\}_{sk_i}) = T_z$ (or the derivation $T \models T_z = \text{content-of}(\{T_2\}_{sk_j})$). Therefore, for the derivation $T \models \text{content-of}(\{T_1\}_{sk_i}) = \text{content-of}(\{T_2\}_{sk_j})$ we have a derivation $\vdash_{JD} T \models \{T_1\}_{sk_i}$.

(b) If $T_z \neq$ content-of$(\{T_1\}_{sk_i})$, then the premises are satisfying the conditions of proposition 1. Hence by using proposition 1, we have $\vdash_{JD} T \models \{T_1\}_{sk_i}$ from the premises. Therefore, we have the same conclusion from the derivation $\vdash_{JD} T \models$ content-of$(\{T_1\}_{sk_i}) =$ content-of$(\{T_2\}_{sk_j})$.

□

Theorem 2. *If the attacker can see the encryption keys of two symmetric encrypted terms, then he can know whether these two encrypted terms have the same contents or not. Also if the attacker knows two symmetric encrypted terms and that the value of them are the same, then he can know that these two symmetric encrypted terms have the same contents.*

If $(\{T_1\}_{sk_i} = \{T_2\}_{sk_j}$ and $\vdash_{JD} T \models \{T_1\}_{sk_i})$ or $(\vdash_{JD} T \models \{T_1\}_{sk_i}$ and $\vdash_{JD} T \models \{T_2\}_{sk_j}$ and $\vdash_{JD} T \models sk_i$ and $\vdash_{JD} T \models sk_j)$, then either

$$\vdash_{JD} T \models \text{content-of}(\{T_1\}_{sk_i}) = \text{content-of}(\{T_2\}_{sk_j}) \tag{3}$$

or

$$\vdash_{JD} T \models \text{content-of}(\{T_1\}_{sk_i}) \neq \text{content-of}(\{T_2\}_{sk_j}). \tag{4}$$

holds.

Proof. For each assumption of the theorem, we can construct a JD-derivation, conclusion of which is about equality of contents.   □

Theorem 3. *Without knowing the encryption keys for two different encrypted terms, the attacker cannot get any information about the relation between the encryption keys of the two encrypted terms and vice versa.*

$(\nvdash_{JD} T \models \{T_1\}_{sk_i}$ or $\nvdash_{JD} T \models \{T_2\}_{sk_j})$ or $(\{T_1\}_{sk_i} \neq \{T_2\}_{sk_j}$ and $(\nvdash_{JD} T \models sk_i$ and $\nvdash_{JD} T \models sk_j)) \Leftrightarrow \dashv_{JD} T \models^? \text{key-of}(\{T_1\}_{sk_i}) = \text{key-of}(\{T_2\}_{sk_j})$.

Proof. By similar way as theorem 1 and theorem 2.   □

Theorem 4. *Even if an attacker knows one of the keys used in two symmetric encrypted terms, he cannot obtain any information about the relationship between the contents length of the two encrypted terms.*

If $(\nvdash_{JD} T \models \{T_1\}_{sk_i}$ or $\nvdash_{JD} T \models \{T_2\}_{sk_j})$ or $(\{T_1\}_{sk_i} \neq \{T_2\}_{sk_j}$ and $(\nvdash_{JD} T \models sk_i$ or $\nvdash_{JD} T \models sk_j))$, then

$$\dashv_{JD} T \models^? len(\text{content-of}(\{T_1\}_{sk_i})) = len(\text{content-of}(\{T_2\}_{sk_j})).$$

Proof. Suppose $\{T_1\}_{sk_i} \neq \{T_2\}_{sk_j}$. From the symmetry of the assumption of the theorem 4, it is sufficient to prove that if $\nvdash_{JD} T \models sk_i$ or $\nvdash_{JD} T \models \{T_1\}_{sk_i}$, then

$$\dashv_{JD} T \models^? len(\text{content-of}(\{T_1\}_{sk_i})) = len(\text{content-of}(\{T_2\}_{sk_j})).$$

By assuming $\nvdash_{JD} T \models sk_i$ or $\nvdash_{JD} T \models \{T_1\}_{sk_i}$, and there exists a JD-derivation of either

$$\vdash_{JD} T \models len(\text{content-of}(\{T_1\}_{sk_i})) = len(\text{content-of}(\{T_2\}_{sk_j})) \tag{5}$$

or

$$\vdash_{JD} T \models len(content\text{-}of(\{T_1\}_{sk_i})) \neq len(content\text{-}of(\{T_2\}_{sk_j})), \qquad (6)$$

we are going to prove the contradicting facts $\vdash_{JD} T \models sk_i$ and $\vdash_{JD} T \models \{T_1\}_{sk_i}$ by using proposition 4 (for the case (5)) and proposition 5 (for the case (6)).

Proposition 4. *If $\vdash_{JD} T \models T_x = T_y$ such that T_x or T_y is of the form len $(content\text{-}of(\{T_1\}_{sk_i}))$, and $(T_x \neq len(content\text{-}of(\{T_1\}_{sk_i}))$ or $T_y \neq len(content\text{-}of (\{T_1\}_{sk_i})))$, then $\vdash_{JD} T \models sk_i$ and $\vdash_{JD} T \models \{T_1\}_{sk_i}$.*

Proof. **Base Cases.** Suppose the final JD-inference rule used in the derivation is the JD-inference rule 24 of the form

$$\frac{T \models T_u = T_v}{T \models len(T_u) = len(T_v)},$$

where $T_u, T_v \in$ **Ex-Terms**. Suppose $len(T_u)$ or $len(T_v)$ satisfies the conditions of proposition 4, then we have the following cases.

1. If $T_u = content\text{-}of(\{T_1\}_{sk_i})$, then $T_v \neq content\text{-}of(\{T_1\}_{sk_i})$. Hence the premise $T \models content\text{-}of(\{T_1\}_{sk_i}) = T_v$ satisfies the conditions of proposition 1. By using proposition 1, we have $\vdash_{JD} T \models sk_i$ and $\vdash_{JD} T \models \{T_1\}_{sk_i}$ from the premise. Therefore, from the conclusion $T \models len(content\text{-}of(\{T_1\}_{sk_i})) = len(T_v)$ we have derivations of $\vdash_{JD} T \models sk_i$ and $\vdash_{JD} T \models \{T_1\}_{sk_i}$.
2. If $T_v = content\text{-}of(\{T_1\}_{sk_i})$, then $T_u \neq content\text{-}of(\{T_1\}_{sk_i})$. By the same way as above case, we have derivations of $\vdash_{JD} T \models sk_i$ and $\vdash_{JD} T \models \{T_1\}_{sk_i}$.

Induction Steps. If the final JD-inference rule used in the JD-derivation is either the JD-inference rule 8 or the JD-inference rule 10, then by similar way as the proof of induction step of proposition 1, we have derivations of $\vdash_{JD} T \models sk_i$ and $\vdash_{JD} T \models \{T_1\}_{sk_i}$. If other JD-inference rule is used as the final JD-inference rule in derivation the derivation, then the form of conclusion does not match with the condition part of proposition 4.

Proposition 5. *If $\vdash_{JD} T \models T_x \neq T_y$ such that T_x or T_y is of the following form $len(content\text{-}of(\{T_1\}_{sk_i}))$, then $\vdash_{JD} T \models sk_i$ and $\vdash_{JD} T \models \{T_1\}_{sk_i}$.*

Proof. By similar way as the proof of proposition 2.

Suppose $\{T_1\}_{sk_i} = \{T_2\}_{sk_j}$. It is sufficient to prove that if $\nvdash_{JD} T \models \{T_1\}_{sk_i}$, then $\dashv_{JD} T \models^? len(content\text{-}of(\{T_1\}_{sk_i})) = len(content\text{-}of(\{T_2\}_{sk_j}))$. By assuming $\nvdash_{JD} T \models \{T_1\}_{sk_i}$ and there is either a JD-derivation $\vdash_{JD} T \models len(content\text{-}of (\{T_1\}_{sk_i})) = len(content\text{-}of(\{T_2\}_{sk_j}))$ or a JD-derivation $\vdash_{JD} T \models len(content\text{-}of (\{T_1\}_{sk_i})) \neq len(content\text{-}of(\{T_2\}_{sk_j}))$, we are going to prove the contradicting fact $\vdash_{JD} T \models \{T_1\}_{sk_i}$. Since $\{T_1\}_{sk_i} = \{T_2\}_{sk_j}$, $\nvdash_{JD} T \models len(content\text{-}of(\{T_1\}_{sk_i}))$ $\neq len(content\text{-}of(\{T_2\}_{sk_j}))$, we just consider the following case.

Proposition 6. *If $\{T_1\}_{sk_i} = \{T_2\}_{sk_j}$ and there exists a JD-derivation of $\vdash_{JD}$ $T \models len(content\text{-}of(\{T_1\}_{sk_i})) = len(content\text{-}of(\{T_2\}_{sk_j}))$, then $\vdash_{JD} T \models \{T_1\}_{ski}$.*

Proof. **Base Cases.** Suppose the final JD-inference rule used in the derivation is the JD-inference rule 24 of the form

$$\frac{T \models T_u = T_v}{T \models len(T_u) = len(T_v)},$$

where $T_u, T_v \in$ **Ex-Terms.** Suppose the conclusion satisfies the conditions of proposition 6, then the conclusion takes the form $T \models len(content\text{-}of(\{T_1\}_{sk_i})) = len(content\text{-}of(\{T_2\}_{sk_j}))$ and the premise takes the form $T \models content\text{-}of(\{T_1\}_{sk_i}) = content\text{-}of(\{T_2\}_{sk_j})$. From the condition $\{T_1\}_{sk_i} = \{T_2\}_{sk_j}$, the premise satisfies the conditions of proposition 3. Hence by using proposition 3, we have a derivation $\vdash_{JD} T \models \{T_1\}_{ski}$ from the premise. Therefore, we have a derivation $\vdash_{JD} T \models \{T_1\}_{ski}$ from the conclusion $T \models len(content\text{-}of(\{T_1\}_{sk_i})) = len(content\text{-}of(\{T_2\}_{sk_j}))$.

Induction Steps. If the final JD-inference rule used in the JD-derivation is either the JD-inference rule 8 or the JD-inference rule 10, then by similar way as the proof of induction step of proposition 3, we can prove that there is a derivation of $\vdash_{JD} T \models \{T_1\}_{sk_i}$. If other JD-inference rule is used as the final JD-inference rule in derivation the derivation, then the form of conclusion does not match with the condition part of proposition 6.

Theorem 5. *Even if an attacker knows one of the keys used in two symmetric encrypted terms, he cannot obtain any information about the relationship between the encryption keys length of the two symmetric encrypted terms.*

If $(\nvdash_{JD} T \models \{T_1\}_{sk_i}$ or $\nvdash_{JD} T \models \{T_2\}_{sk_j})$ or $(\{T_1\}_{sk_i} \neq \{T_2\}_{sk_j}$ and $(\nvdash_{JD} T \models sk_i$ or $\nvdash_{JD} T \models sk_j))$, then

$$\dashv_{JD} T \models^? len(key\text{-}of(\{T_1\}_{sk_i})) = len(key\text{-}of(\{T_2\}_{sk_j})).$$

Proof. By same way as the proof of theorem 4. □

4.2   Facts About Symmetric Encryption

In this section, we recall the facts stated in [1, 2, 3, 4] for asymmetric encryption scheme.

Theorem 6. *Even if an attacker knows the content of one of the two encrypted terms, he cannot obtain any information about the relationship between the contents of the two encrypted terms.*

If $(\nvdash_{JD} T \models \{T_1\}_{k_i}$ or $\nvdash_{JD} T \models \{T_2\}_{k_j})$ or $(\{T_1\}_{k_i} \neq \{T_2\}_{k_j}$ and $(\nvdash_{JD} T \models T_1$ or $\nvdash_{JD} T \models T_2))$, then

$$\dashv_{JD} T \models^? content\text{-}of(\{T_1\}_{k_i}) = content\text{-}of(\{T_2\}_{k_j}).$$

Proof. By same way as theorem 1. □

Theorem 7. *If* $(\{T_1\}_{k_i} = \{T_2\}_{k_j}$ *and* $\vdash_{JD} T \models \{T_1\}_{k_i})$ *or* $(\vdash_{JD} T \models T_1$ *and* $\vdash_{JD} T \models T_2)$, *then either:*

1. $\vdash_{JD} T \models$ *content-of*$(\{T_1\}_{k_i}) =$ *content-of*$(\{T_2\}_{k_j})$ *or:*
2. $\vdash_{JD} T \models$ *content-of*$(\{T_1\}_{k_i}) \neq$ *content-of*$(\{T_2\}_{k_j})$ *is valid.*

Proof. For each assumption of the theorem, we can construct a JD-derivation, conclusion of which is about equality of contents. □

Theorem 8. *Even if an attacker knows the content of one of the two encrypted terms, an attacker cannot obtain the relationship between the encryption keys of the two encrypted terms.*

If $(\nvdash_{JD} T \models \{T_1\}_{k_i}$ *or* $\nvdash_{JD} T \models \{T_2\}_{k_j})$ *or* $(\{T_1\}_{k_i} \neq \{T_2\}_{k_j}$ *and* $(\ (\nvdash_{JD} T \models T_1$ *and* $\nvdash_{JD} T \models k_j^{-1})$ *or* $(\nvdash_{JD} T \models T_2$ *and* $\nvdash_{JD} T \models k_i^{-1})))$, *then*

$$\dashv_{JD} T \models^? key\text{-}of(\{T_1\}_{k_i}) = key\text{-}of(\{T_2\}_{k_j}).$$

Proof. By the same way as theorem 1. □

Theorem 9. *If* $(\vdash_{JD} T \models \{T_1\}_{k_i}$ *and* $\vdash_{JD} T \models \{T_2\}_{k_j}$ *and* $(\{T_1\}_{k_i} = \{T_2\}_{k_j}$ *or* $(\vdash_{JD} T \models T_1$ *or* $\vdash_{JD} T \models k_j^{-1})$ *and* $(\vdash_{JD} T \models T_2$ *or* $\vdash_{JD} T \models k_i^{-1}))$, *then we have either:*

1. $\vdash_{JD} T \models key\text{-}of(\{T_1\}_{k_i}) = key\text{-}of(\{T_2\}_{k_j})$ *or:*
2. $\vdash_{JD} T \models key\text{-}of(\{T_1\}_{k_i}) \neq key\text{-}of(\{T_2\}_{k_j})$ *holds.*

Proof. For each assumption of the theorem, we can construct a JD-derivation, conclusion of which is about equality of the encryption keys of the two encrypted terms. □

Theorem 10. *If* $(\nvdash_{JD} T \models \{T_2\}_{k_j}$ *or* $\nvdash_{JD} T \models \{T_1\}_{k_i})$ *or* $(\{T_1\}_{k_i} \neq \{T_2\}_{k_j}$ *and* $(\nvdash_{JD} T \models T_1$ *or* $\nvdash_{JD} T \models T_2))$, *then*

$$\dashv_{JD} T \models^? len(content\text{-}of(\{T_1\}_{k_i})) = len(content\text{-}of(\{T_2\}_{k_j})).$$

Proof. By the same way as theorem 4. □

Theorem 11. *If* $(\nvdash_{JD} T \models \{T_2\}_{k_j}$ *or* $\nvdash_{JD} T \models \{T_1\}_{k_i})$ *or* $(\{T_1\}_{k_i} \neq \{T_2\}_{k_j}$ *and* $(\nvdash_{JD} T \models T_1$ *or* $\nvdash_{JD} T \models T_2))$, *then*

$$\dashv_{JD} T \models^? len(key\text{-}of(\{T_1\}_{k_i})) = len(key\text{-}of(\{T_2\}_{k_j})).$$

Proof. By the same way as theorem 4. □

5   Security Notions of Asymmetric and Symmetric Encryption Using JD-System

There are various notions of the security of asymmetric and symmetric encryption schemes and various mechanized proofs. Most of these proofs are based on the notion of probability and complexity theory. For example, in the case of public-key, the most basic one is the notion of *probabilistic indistinguishability* introduced by Goldwasser and Micali[25, 26, 27, 28], which captures the infeasibility of obtaining any information from a challenge ciphertext about the corresponding plaintext. Another notion is called *probabilistic non-malleability* introduced by Dolev, Dwork and Naor [17, 18], which captures the infeasibility of changing ciphertext. The *probabilistic non-malleability* is the property that given a challenge ciphertext, the adversary hardly generates a different ciphertext such that their contents are meaningfully related. The relation between these notions is defined in [17, 19]. In the symmetric encryption setting, the probabilistic characterization of indistinguishability and non-malleability can be found in [19]. Several various formulations of indistinguishability for symmetric encryption scheme are introduced, and they are proved equivalent under the consideration of complexity of reduction between algorithms which relate to these different notions.

In this section, we propose a new characterization for the security notions *asymmetric-* (or *symmetric-*) *content-non-malleability*, *content-indistinguishability*, *key-indistinguishability*, *key-length-indistinguishability*, *key-length-non-malleability*, and *content-length-indistinguishability* of encryption scheme. Our analysis formally states the conditions that are sufficient for these security properties. A similar characterization for asymmetric encryption scheme can be found in [1, 2]. Basic intuition security notion of *content-non-malleability* in this paper is similar to the security notion of *non-malleability* in [18], however, semantics are different. The security notion *asymmetric-*(or *symmetric-*)*content-indistinguishability* is the most natural security property to be satisfied and introduced in [14, 15, 22]. The security property *key-non-malleability* is introduced by Bhery, Hagihara, and Yonezaki [1, 2, 3, 4] as new security notions for asymmetric encryption scheme. Such security notion can not be verified for symmetric encryption but can be verified for asymmetric encryption. The security properties ,*symmetric-content-indistinguishability*, *symmetric-key-indistinguishability*, and *symmetric-content-length-indistinguishability* are combined into one notion called type-0 in the study of Abadi and Rogaway [13]. In contrast to the fact that the rules introduced in this paper are based on deterministic algorithms of attackers, in Abadi and Rogaway work, they assume probabilistic algorithms of attackers. This difference is reflected in the definition of indistinguishability. For instance in the case that $\{T_1\}_{sk_i} = \{T_2\}_{sk_j}$ they are said to be distinguishable in our case, however, according to Abadi and Rogaway, they are indistinguishabile. Also in our approach, we extend the security notion of *symmetric-key-indistinguishability* to that of *symmetric-key-length-indistinguishability* for a symmetric encryption.

Corollary 1 (Symmetric-Content-Non-malleability). *If* $(\vdash_{JD} T \models \{T_1\}_{sk_i}, \vdash_{JD} T \models T_2, \vdash_{JD} T \models sk_j, \not\vdash_{JD} T \models sk_i)$, *then* $\dashv_{JD} T \models^? content\text{-}of$ $(\{T_1\}_{sk_i}) = content\text{-}of(\{T_2\}_{sk_j})$.

Proof. Immediate from theorem 1. □

Corollary 2 (Asymmetric-Content-Non-malleability). *If* $(\vdash_{JD} T \models \{T_1\}_{k_i}, \vdash_{JD} T \models T_2, \not\vdash_{JD} T \models T_1)$, *then* $\dashv_{JD} T \models^? content\text{-}of(\{T_1\}_{k_i}) = content\text{-}of(\{T_2\}_{k_j})$.

Proof. Immediate from theorem 6. □

Corollary 3 (Symmetric-Content-Indistinguishability). *If* $(\vdash_{JD} T \models \{T_1\}_{sk_i}, \vdash_{JD} T \models \{T_2\}_{sk_j}, \{T_1\}_{sk_i} \neq \{T_2\}_{sk_j}, \not\vdash_{JD} T \models sk_i, \not\vdash_{JD} T \models sk_j)$, *then* $\dashv_{JD} T \models^? content\text{-}of(\{T_1\}_{sk_i}) = content\text{-}of(\{T_2\}_{sk_j})$.

Proof. Immediately from theorem 1. □

Corollary 4 (Asymmetric-Content-Indistinguishability). *If* $(\vdash_{JD} T \models \{T_1\}_{k_i}, \vdash_{JD} T \models \{T_2\}_{k_j}, \{T_1\}_{k_i} \neq \{T_2\}_{k_j}, \not\vdash_{JD} T \models T_1, \not\vdash_{JD} T \models T_2)$, *then* $\dashv_{JD} T \models^? content\text{-}of(\{T_1\}_{k_i}) = content\text{-}of(\{T_2\}_{k_j})$.

Proof. Immediate from theorem 6. □

Corollary 5 (Symmetric-Key-Indistinguishability). *If* $(\vdash_{JD} T \models \{T_1\}_{sk_i}, \vdash_{JD} T \models \{T_2\}_{sk_j}, \{T_1\}_{sk_i} \neq \{T_2\}_{sk_j}, \not\vdash_{JD} T \models sk_i, \not\vdash_{JD} T \models sk_j)$, *then* $\dashv_{JD} T \models^? key\text{-}of(\{T_1\}_{sk_i}) = key\text{-}of(\{T_2\}_{sk_j})$.

Proof. Immediately from Theorem 3. □

Corollary 6 (Asymmetric-Key-Indistinguishability). *If* $(\vdash_{JD} T \models \{T_1\}_{k_i}, \vdash_{JD} T \models \{T_2\}_{k_j}, \{T_1\}_{k_i} \neq \{T_2\}_{k_j}, \not\vdash_{JD} T \models T_1, \not\vdash_{JD} T \models T_2)$, *then* $\dashv_{JD} T \models^? key\text{-}of(\{T_1\}_{k_i}) = key\text{-}of(\{T_2\}_{k_j})$.

Proof. Immediate from theorem 8 □

Corollary 7 (Symmetric-Content-Length-Indistinguishability). *If* $(\vdash_{JD} T \models \{T_1\}_{sk_i}, \vdash_{JD} T \models \{T_2\}_{sk_j}, \{T_1\}_{sk_i} \neq \{T_2\}_{sk_j}, \not\vdash_{JD} T \models sk_i, \not\vdash_{JD} T \models sk_j)$, *then* $\dashv_{JD} T \models^? len(content\text{-}of(\{T_1\}_{sk_i})) = len(content\text{-}of(\{T_2\}_{sk_j}))$.

Proof. immediate from theorem 4. □

Corollary 8 (Asymmetric-Content-Length-Indistinguishability). *If* $(\vdash_{JD} T \models \{T_1\}_{k_i}, \vdash_{JD} T \models \{T_2\}_{k_j}, \{T_1\}_{k_i} \neq \{T_2\}_{k_j}, \not\vdash_{JD} T \models T_1, \not\vdash_{JD} T \models T_2)$, *then* $\dashv_{JD} T \models^? len(content\text{-}of(\{T_1\}_{k_i})) = len(content\text{-}of(\{T_2\}_{k_j}))$.

Proof. immediate from theorem 10. □

Corollary 9 (Symmetric-Key-Length-Indistinguishability). *If* $(\vdash_{JD} T \models \{T_1\}_{sk_i}, \vdash_{JD} T \models \{T_2\}_{sk_j}, \{T_1\}_{sk_i} \neq \{T_2\}_{sk_j}, \not\vdash_{JD} T \models sk_i, \not\vdash_{JD} T \models sk_j)$, *then* $\dashv_{JD} T \models^? len(key\text{-}of(\{T_1\}_{sk_i})) = len(key\text{-}of(\{T_2\}_{sk_j}))$.

Proof. Immediately from Theorem 5.   □

Corollary 10 (Asymmetric-Key-Length-Indistinguishability). *If* $(\vdash_{JD} T \models \{T_1\}_{k_i}, \vdash_{JD} T \models \{T_2\}_{k_j}, \{T_1\}_{k_i} \neq \{T_2\}_{k_j}, \not\vdash_{JD} T \models T_1, \not\vdash_{JD} T \models T_2)$ *then* $\dashv_{JD} T \models^? len(key\text{-}of(\{T_1\}_{k_i})) = len(key\text{-}of(\{T_2\}_{k_j})).$

Proof. Immediately from Theorem 11.   □

Corollary 11 (Asymmetric-Key-Non-malleability). *If* $(\vdash_{JD} T \models \{T_1\}_{k_i}, \vdash_{JD} T \models T_2, \not\vdash_{JD} T \models T_1, \not\vdash_{JD} T \models k_j^{-1})$, *then* $\dashv_{JD} T \models^? key\text{-}of(\{T_1\}_{k_i}) = key\text{-}of(\{T_2\}_{k_j}).$

Proof. Immediate from theorem 8.   □

For symmetric encryption, the security property of *symmetric-key-malleability* can be characterized as follows. If $(\vdash_{JD} T \models \{T_1\}_{sk_i}, \vdash_{JD} T \models T_2, \vdash_{JD} T \models sk_j, \not\vdash_{JD} T \models sk_i)$ then $\dashv_{JD} T \models^? key\text{-}of(\{T_1\}_{sk_i}) = key\text{-}of(\{T_2\}_{sk_j}).$

This security property cannot be verified for symmetric encryption. Since The attacker can be determine the judgment $T \models key\text{-}of(\{T_1\}_{sk_i}) \neq key\text{-}of(\{T_2\}_{k_j})$ by using the JD-inference rules.

Corollary 12 (Symmetric-Key-Length-Non-malleability). *If* $(\vdash_{JD} T \models \{T_1\}_{sk_i}, \vdash_{JD} T \models T_2, \vdash_{JD} T \models sk_j, \not\vdash_{JD} T \models sk_i)$, *then* $\dashv_{JD} T \models^? len(key\text{-}of(\{T_1\}_{sk_i})) = len(key\text{-}of(\{T_2\}_{sk_j})).$

Proof. Immediate from theorem 5.   □

Corollary 13 (Asymmetric-Key-Length-Non-malleability). *If* $(\vdash_{JD} T \models \{T_1\}_{k_i}, \vdash_{JD} T \models T_2, \not\vdash_{JD} T \models T_1)$, *then* $\dashv_{JD} T \models^? len(key\text{-}of(\{T_1\}_{k_i})) = len(key\text{-}of(\{T_2\}_{k_j})).$

Proof. Immediate from theorem 11.   □

Corollary 14 (Symmetric-Content-Length-Non-malleability). *If* $(\vdash_{JD} T \models \{T_1\}_{sk_i}, \vdash_{JD} T \models T_2, \vdash_{JD} T \models sk_j, \not\vdash_{JD} T \models sk_i)$, *then* $\dashv_{JD} T \models^? len(content\text{-}of(\{T_1\}_{sk_i})) = len(content\text{-}of(\{T_2\}_{sk_j})).$

Proof. Immediate from theorem 4.   □

Corollary 15 (Asymmetric-Content-Length-Non-malleability). *If* $(\vdash_{JD} T \models \{T_1\}_{k_i}, \vdash_{JD} T \models T_2, \not\vdash_{JD} T \models T_1)$, *then* $\dashv_{JD} T \models^? len(content\text{-}of(\{T_1\}_{k_i})) = len(content\text{-}of(\{T_2\}_{k_j})).$

Proof. Immediate from theorem 10.   □

6   Conclusion and Future Work

In this paper, we proposed a formal deduction system called JD-system. It
can be used to analyze cryptographic primitives of asymmetric and symmetric encryption schemes. The JD-system formalizes all of the attacker's abilities, which are summarized in the assumptions of an encryption scheme. As
a property of this system, we can prove that some security properties can be
satisfied in the case of asymmetric encryption and can not be satisfied in the
case of symmetric encryption. In JD-system, we use the notions of *judgment*
and *unjudgment*. With these notions, we have found several properties, from
which we deduce *asymmetric-(or symmetric-) content-indistinguishability*, *key-
indistinguishability*, *content-non-malleability*, *content-length-indistinguishability*,
key-length-indistinguishability, *content-length-non-malleability*, and *key-length-
non-malleability* of encryption schemes. In this work, keys are restricted to be
atomic. In general, keys might be compound terms. The extension of the syntax of keys to compound terms are straightforward. All the rules we introduced
are still valid in this extension. Another extension of our system is to consider
an encryption system with random number. For this kind of encryption system
we also can formalize the scheme in the same framework, however, we have to
modify some JD-inference rules such that the random number element in ciphertext cannot be seen when it is decrypted, and we also have to introduce a
meta rule such that for every encryption a fresh random number should be used.
This change is conservative in the sence that knowledge about the contents does
not increase. With this consideration we believe that security properties such
as theorem 1 hold in the extended framework. Our results can be directly extended to the encryption schemes including keyed hash function. Our work is
closely related to the ongoing efforts towards reducing the gap between formal
analysis and modern cryptographic analysis for cryptographic primitives. Our
future work will also include the extension of our JD-inference rules to reflect
the probabilistic behavior of an attacker as considered in modern cryptography.

References

1. A. Bhery, S. Hagihara, and N. Yonezaki. A new deduction system of cryptographic
   primitives and their security properties. *Information Processing Society of Japan
   (IPSJ 03)*, SIG technical reports Vol 2003 No. 74.
2. A. Bhery, S. Hagihara, and N. Yonezaki. Judgment deduction system of asymmetric
   encryption scheme(JDE-system). *The 4^{Th} International Workshop on Information
   Security Applications(WISA03), Korea*,WISA 03 proceeding.
3. A. Bhery, S. Hagihara, and N. Yonezaki. A formal system for analysis of cryptographic primitives and their security properties. *Japan Society for Software and
   Technology (JSST03)*, Japan. Proceeding of 20^{Th} annual conference, 2003.
4. A. Bhery, S. Hagihara, and N. Yonezaki. The characterization of cryptographic
   primitives and their security properties. *The 2003 International Workshop on
   Cryptography and Network Security (CANS03), USA*, DMS'03.

5. B. Pfitzmann, M. Schunter and M.Waidner. Cryptographic security of reactive systems (extended abstract). In *Electronic Notes in Theoretical Computer Science,32*, April 2000.
6. D. Bolignano. An approach to the formal verification of cryptographic protocols. In *Proceeding of the 3rd ACM Conference on Communications and Computer Security (CCS-96)*, pages 106-118, 1996.
7. D. Dolev, C. Dwork and M. Naor. Non-malleable cryptography. In *Proceeding of the 33rd Annual ACM Symposium on the Theory of Computing*, ACM 1991.
8. D. Dolev, C. Yao. On the security of public key protocols. In *IEEE Transactions and Information Theory*, IT-29(12):189-208,1983.
9. Douglas R. Stinson. Cryptography theory and practice. Second edition, Chapman&Hall/CRC, 2002.
10. G. Lowe. Breaking and fixing the Needham-Schroeder public-key protocol using FDR. In *proceedings of 10th IEEE Computer Security Foundations Workshop*, pages 45-58,1997.
11. J. Katz and M. Yung. Complete characterization of security notions for probabilistic private-key encryption. In *Proceedings of the thirty-second annual ACM symposium on Theory of computation*, may 1999.
12. L. C.Paulson. The inductive approach to verifying cryptographic protocols.*Journal of Computer Security,*6(1-2):85-128,1998.
13. M.Abadi and P.Rogaway. Reconciling two views of cryptography: The computational soundness of formal encryption. In *IFIP International Conference on Theoretical Computer Science*, August, 2000.
14. M. Abadi and A. D. Gordon. A calculus for cryptographic protocols: The Spi calculus. In *proceedings of the Forth ACM Conference on Computer and Communications Security*, pages 36-47, 1997.
15. M. Abadi and Andrew D. Gordon. A bisimulation method for cryptographic protocols: The Spi calculus. In *Nordic Journal of Computing*, 5(4):267-303, Winter 1998.
16. M. Bellare and P. Rogaway. Random oracles are practical: A paradigm for designing efficient protocols. In *Proceedings of the 1st ACM Conference on Computer and Communications Security*, pages 62-73,1993.
17. M. Bellare and P. Rogaway. Relations among notions of security for public-key encryption schemes. In *Advances in Cryptology-Lecture Notes in Computer Science*. No. 1462, Springer-Verlag, 1998, pages 26-45.
18. M. Bellare, A. Sahai. Non-malleability encryption: equivalence between two notions, and an indistinguishability-based characterization. In *Advances in Cryptology-Crypto '99 Proceedings, LNCS Vol. 1666, M.J. Wiener ed., Springer-Verlag*, 1999.
19. M. Bellare, A. Desai, E. Jokipii, and P. Rogaway. A concrete security treatment of symmetric encryption. In *38 Annual Symposium on Foundations of Computer Science*, pages 394-403,1997.
20. M. Burrows, M. Abadi and R. Needham. A logic of authentication. *Proceedings of the Royal Society of London A*, 426:233-271, 1989.
21. O. Goldreich. Foundations of cryptography: basic tool, *Cambridge University Press, New York, NY*, 2000.
22. P.Lincoln, J. Mitchell, M. Mitchell, and A.Scedrov. A probabilistic poly-time framework for protocol analysis. In *Proceedings of the Fifth ACM Conference on Computer and Communications Security*, pages 112-121,1998.
23. P. Ryan and S. Schneider. Modelling and analysis of security protocols. *Addison Wesley,*2001.

24. R. Kemmerer, C. Meadows, and J. Millen. Three systems for cryptographic protocol analysis. *Journal of Cryptography*, 7(2), 1994.
25. S. Goldwasser and S. Micali. Probabilistic encryption.*Journal of Computer and System Science,* 28:270-299,April 1984.
26. S. Goldwasser, S. Micali, and C. Rackoff. The Knowledge Complexity of Interactive Proof Systems. In *SIAM Journal on Computing*, 18(2):186-208, February 1989. Earlier version in *Proc. of the 17th STOC(1985)*,291-305.
27. S. Goldwasser, M. Bellare. Lecture notes on cryptography. August 1999. Available from http://www.cs.columbia.edu/ jkatz/crypto/readings.html.
28. S. Micali, C. Rackoff and B. Sloan. The notion of security for probabilistic cryptosystem. In*SIAM Journal of computing*, April 1988.
29. S. Schneider. Security Properties and CSP. IN *IEEE Symposium on Security and Privacy,*pages 174-187,1996.
30. T.Y.C.Woo and S.S.Lam. A semantic model for authentication protocols. In *Proceedings IEEE Symposium on Research in Security and Privacy*, Oakland, CA, May 1993.

Formal Specification and Verification of Resource Bound Security Using PVS*

Weijiang Yu and Aloysius K. Mok

Department of Computer Sciences,
University of Texas at Austin,
Austin, Texas 78712 USA
{wjyu, mok}@cs.utexas.edu

Abstract. Resource usage abuse is a major security concern for computer systems that run programs uploaded from other computers. In the absence of any guarantee on resource usage bounds, we cannot have any confidence that the external codes have been supplied by trustworthy computers or the codes have not been tempered with by a third party. In a previous report [1], we described the TINMAN security architecture and a tool set for enforcing resource safety of external C code. In this paper, we detail the formalization of resource specification and verification of the resource safety properties. This formal framework is based on an extended Hoare logic with resource usage variables. We formalize the construct (*tasks*) and resource safety assertions (*resource specifications*) in a proof system that is built on the PVS theorem prover. We also discuss the proof strategies for different types of resource usage verification tasks that are important for the mechanization of TINMAN.

1   Introduction

A common feature of open or extensible systems in the age of the Internet is to accept and execute programs from different sources. These "external" programs may be buggy or malicious and should in general be deemed to be untrustworthy. As such, a major concern is the lack of limitations on resource usage by external programs. Resource usage bound enforcement is a difficult issue for resource-critical host systems, particularly for mobile code which may run all over the Internet. Ideally, the security architecture of a host system should be able to properly delimit resource consumption such as CPU cycles, memory and network bandwidth by an external program.

To address this issue, we have designed and prototyped the TINMAN resource security architecture [1] whose goal is to efficiently and effectively perform resource usage bound checks on external code, whether it is from a trusted or

---

* This research is supported by a research gift from Microsoft Corporation and by a grant from the US Office of Naval Research under grant number N00014-99-1-0402 and N00014-03-1-0705.

K. Futatsugi et al. (Eds.): ISSS 2003, LNCS 3233, pp. 113–133, 2004.

untrusted source. TINMAN's tool set allows the programmer to predict an upper bound on resource consumption by a program. This is done by an off-line analysis, and the bounds are formally proven by TINMAN's verification tools that are built on top of a theorem prover, resulting in a proof of the bound. Upon receiving external code and a proof, called a *certificate*, the host system attempts to verify the certificate. On condition that the certificate passes verification, the host grants resources for the external code to run. TINMAN does not depend on a theorem prover's capability to fully automate the resource bound proof; this is in general beyond current capabilities for both theoretical and practical reasons. TINMAN allows human assistance by accepting hints (unproven assertions) from the programmer of the external program. To ensure safety, the programmer-provided hints or any other unproven assertions obtained off-line are automatically monitored on-line with relatively small overhead.

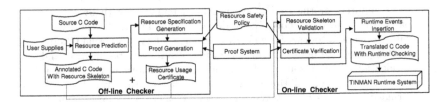

Fig. 1. The TINMAN Architecture

Figure 1 illustrates the overall architecture of TINMAN. The following describes the major steps in the typical flow of control of TINMAN users, where the first two steps pertain to the application of the off-line checker, and the last two steps are grouped into the on-line checker.

- **Step 1.** A programmer uses TINMAN tools to predict the resource bound of his C code. The programmer is allowed to enter assertions that help resource usage analysis. The output is annotated C code, where the annotations and assertions, called the *resource skeleton*, capture the resource usage behavior of the code. The annotated C code is then automatically translated into a specification consisting of a group of predicates in a formal logic of the PVS system.
- **Step 2.** Given a formal specification, the TINMAN proof generator attempts to prove it with the help of PVS. A set of proof strategies are developed to help automatic proof generation in this stage. In order to reduce its size, the proof, called the *resource usage certificate*, is further converted into a *certificate skeleton*. The certificate skeleton, together with the annotated code, is ready to be sent to or downloaded by a remote host.
- **Step 3.** Upon receiving the annotated code with the certificate skeleton, a remote host (code recipient) validates the annotations, checks for any inconsistency with respect to the imported code (annotations and assertions

should be inserted if and only if necessary). If no violation to the resource safety policy is detected, the full resource usage certificate is restored and then verified. The certificate verification tool verifies the resource specification within the PVS system. All user-input assertions are treated as axioms in this stage.

- **Step 4.** Assertions whose validity is not proven off-line are monitored on-line. This is done by having the program annotations automatically translated into event generator code that notifies the run-time system on the progress of the mobile code execution. The run-time resource usage monitor matches the events generated at run time with the behavior inferred from the resource skeleton.

The idea of proof carrying code is a well established idea through excellent work such as PCC (Proof Carrying Code) by Necula [2] and Typed Assembly Language (TAL) by Morrisett *et al.* [3]. The target programs are usually low-level machine codes, and the focus has been on logical rather than resource safety properties (e.g., memory usage upper bound and program termination). The TINMAN architecture, however, targets high-level programming languages, currently C, since many external programs are written in C and they lack security checks on resource bounds. For example, a user might try to extend system software by adding an external software component, or download and install open source software and applications that are often in the form of C source code, and the code can be from both trusted and untrusted sources.

More recently, some researchers have presented proposals for securing resource bounds of functional programs [4, 5]. In these approaches, including PCC and TAL, a formal system is constructed based on a specially designed type system, and security properties are ensured by type checking. It is in general a difficult task to apply this approach to assure the resource bound safety of a program written in an unsafe language such as C which is currently the language in daily use by industry. Also, the resource bounds are supplied by the programmers of these systems and this may not be a practical assumption.

By extending the classical Hoare logic and by using formal methods adopted from the real-time system community [6, 7], we have developed a formal framework in which resource bound properties are formalized and then verified. We do so by extending Hoare logic with resource variables. Resource usage properties obtained by either TINMAN's program analyzing tools or the user's input are transformed to assertions on the resource variables. The correctness of the resource safety properties of a program can be verified if the resource usage assertions are proven in the formal framework.

One of the main difficulties in theorem proving for assertional logic such as Hoare logic is the requirement for frequent user intervention. Inasmuch as we want to automate the enforcement of resource safety, we aim at formulating a proof system that supports automatic generation of resource bound assertions as well as exploiting powerful theorem proving capabilities. In our approach, the extended Hoare logic integrates compound programming constructs (called verification tasks or simply *tasks*) with resource assertions (called *resource specifications*) in a unified framework. For theorem proving, we have been using a general purpose theorem prover, the PVS Specification and Verification System[8] from SRI International. To check for compliance with a resource bound specification of a program, we have developed a *compositional* proof system such that for each verification task there is a rule for establishing the resource usage specifications without depending on knowledge of the internal structure of the task. Furthermore, to generate a proof as automatically as possible, we have developed a set of proof strategies by taking advantage of the support PVS provides.

Various aspects of the TINMAN architecture have been discussed in our previous papers. In this paper, we shall discuss the formal framework for formalizing resource bound prediction and reasoning about resource bound safety in TINMAN. With respect to figure 1, we shall focus on the modules of *Resource Specification Generation, Proof Generation* and the *Proof System*. In the next section, we define tasks and the concept of a resource skeleton. The formal framework on resource specification and verification is discussed in Section 3. Section 4 discusses the implementation of the formal framework in PVS. The proof of resource specifications using PVS strategies is presented in Section 5. Finally, we have the concluding remarks and future work in Section 6.

2   Tasks and Resource Skeleton

The current target programming language of TINMAN is a subset of C. This subset keeps most of programming constructs of C, but restricts some language features, similar to the type-safe subset of C described in PCC [9]. Specifically, no casts, pointer arithmetic and address operations are used. All variables must be declared with types, and variables including structure fields must be initialized before being used. All array subscripting operations are checked for bound violation. In addition, no recursive calls are allowed since it would be prohibitively expensive to perform resource-bound checking. Our main goal is to ensure resource safety for system management programs such as network management, resource discovery in grid computing, etc., and it is our contention that most of these programs can be written in C subject to the above mentioned restrictions.

In TINMAN, the execution time and the memory requirement at each point of a source program are determined by a resource usage bound prediction tool (the off-line checker). Detailed description of resource usage prediction is described in [1]. Keeping the bound information at the statement level, however, will generate many useless assertions in the succeeding stages of proof generation and make the verification unnecessarily complicated. Instead, we keep resource usage information for each verification task.

2.1   Task

In the following, we shall use the term *task* to denote a syntactic object in a program which may consume CPU cycles and/or memory. A task $t(texp, mexp)$ is a sequence of one or more simple statements, or a compound statement, and *texp* and *mexp* are the worst-case execution time and memory requirement of the task, respectively. A task is also an object for which we perform resource usage analysis. Thus, a task serves the dual role of a resource consumer with respect to program execution and also as a unit of work with respect to the theorem prover.

There are seven types of tasks, and they are divided into two groups. The definitions of these tasks are given below, where t_1 is execution time, and m_1 is memory requirement of a task.

Simple Tasks

- A basic block task BB (t_1) is one or more sequential simple statements that take at most t_1 abstract time ticks (also referred as to time units throughout this paper). There is no memory requirement for a basic block task BB.
- A service call task SRVC (t_1, m_1) is a system function call that takes at most t_1 abstract time ticks, and m_1 memory units.
- A conditional expression task COND (t_1, m_1) is a conditional expression statement in a compound task (see below). We define a COND task for the convenience of formalization and the derivation of the correctness proof of a program. The t_1 and m_1 are respectively maximum time and memory requirements to evaluate the corresponding condition.
- A loop bound operation task LBOP $(li = li + x;)$ is an assignment statement, where li and x are auxiliary variables with domain the real numbers, and are independent to program variables. A LBOP task is an internal task that is only used in loop invariant construction of a loop task (see below). It has no resource consumption requirements.

Compound Tasks

- A sequential task SEQ $(T1; T2)$ is the sequential composition of a task $T1$ and a task $T2$.
- A branch task BRANCH $(cond, T1, T2)$ is a branch statement **if** *cond* **then** $T1$ **else** $T2$, where *cond* is a COND task, and $T1$ $(T2)$ is either a simple task or a compound task.
- A loop task LOOP $(cond, T)$ denotes a loop construct where *cond* is a COND task, and loop body T is a simple task or a compound task. In practice, a loop construct such as **for**, **while** or {**do** ... **while**} will be identified and transformed into a unified **while** loop construct.

2.2   Resource Skeleton

As discussed above, the time and memory bound information for each task of a program is obtained by using an off-line checker. We call this resource usage

Resource Annotation:

⟨*ResourceAnnotation*⟩	→ /*@ ⟨*TaskID*⟩ ⟨*ResourceProperties*⟩⋆ */
⟨*TaskID*⟩	→ ⟨*TaskType*⟩ ⟨*Integer*⟩
⟨*TaskType*⟩	→ B | S | LB | C | BR | L | U | Entry
⟨*ResourceProperties*⟩	→ ⟨*TimeExp*⟩ | ⟨*MemExp*⟩
	| ⟨*LbExp*⟩ | ⟨*ArgRangeList*⟩
⟨*TimeExp*⟩	→ T[⟨*Exp*⟩] | TMAX[⟨*TimeExp*⟩, ⟨*TimeExp*⟩]
⟨*MemExp*⟩	→ M[⟨*Exp*⟩] | MMAX[⟨*MemExp*⟩, ⟨*MemExp*⟩]

Constraints:

⟨*LbExp*⟩	→ ⟨*TaskID*⟩lb=⟨*Exp*⟩
⟨*ArgRangeList*⟩	→ ⟨*ArgRange*⟩ {AND ⟨*ArgRangeList*⟩ }
⟨*ArgRange*⟩	→ ⟨*TaskID*⟩Arg⟨*Integer*⟩ ⟨*RangeOp*⟩ ⟨*Exp*⟩
⟨*RangeOp*⟩	→ > | >= | = | <= | <

Miscellaneous:

⟨*Exp*⟩	→ ⟨*Term*⟩ | ⟨*Exp*⟩ ⟨*Op*⟩ ⟨*Term*⟩
⟨*Op*⟩	→ + | - | *
⟨*Term*⟩	→ ⟨*Constant*⟩ | ⟨*Identifier*⟩ | ⟨*TaskID*⟩

Fig. 2. Syntax of Resource Skeleton

characterization of a program its *resource skeleton*. The goal of using a resource skeleton is to convey resource usage properties and program flow information to other components in the TINMAN suite of tools in a simple declarative manner in order to formally specify and prove the program's resource usage properties.

Figure 2 gives the syntax of the resource skeleton. The *Resource Annotation* for a task is enclosed in "/*@ ...*/" which is identified in TINMAN and ignored by a standard compiler. The *TaskID* for a task is labeled with its *TaskType* (e.g. L = LOOP task) followed by a global counter value. The task types in a resource skeleton are slightly different from those defined in the previous section. For example, a SEQ task is not identified since all of its constituent tasks must be identified in the first place. The SEQ tasks are introduced only in the formal framework to reduce the verification overhead. On the contrary, a user defined function call, labeled as U is only identified in a resource skeleton. A U task is used for simplicity of program analysis, and is replaced by the constituent (sequential) task(s).

The *ResourceProperties* represents the resource usage expressions or constraints on the variables appearing in the resource expressions. In the resource property of a task, T[*TimeExp*] and M[*MemExp*] represent its maximum time and memory requirements, respectively; and the *Constraints* give its loop bounds (*e.g.*, LBOP tasks) or value ranges for resource usage-related variables (*e.g.*, SRVC tasks). As a result, a program is annotated with its own resource skeleton that asserts its resource usage properties at the points of interest. An example segment of annotated C code is given below. The resource annotations are self-explanatory.

```
/*@ BO ...... */
if (x > y) {
  /*@ BR1 T[T[B0]+3] M[M[B0]]
  /*@ L3lb=100 */
  for (i = 0; i < length; i++)
      sum += i;
      /*@ B2 T[5] M[0]*/
  /*@ L3 T[T[BR1]+L3lb*(T[B2]+4)+5] M[M[BR1]+L3lb*M[B2]*/
}else {
 serv();
 /*@ S4 T[T[BR1]+tserv] M[M[BR1]+mserv]*/
}
/*@ C5 TMAX[T[L3], T[S4]] MMAX[M[L3], M[S4]]
```

3   Proof System

The resource skeleton of a program can be viewed as an abstraction of the program's resource consumption behavior. Specifically, the resource annotations can be viewed as assertions about resource usage properties of the corresponding tasks. In this section, we describe the formal framework in which a resource skeleton is translated into assertional logic. We also present a proof system in which the correctness of the resource assertions can be verified.

Our formal framework is based on an extended Hoare logic. By "extended" we mean that resource variables such as time, memory and computing termination are embedded in the classical Hoare logic. In section 3.1, we define the value domains of resources variables. The extended Hoare triple for the tasks, called *resource specification* is introduced in section 3.2. We formulate the proof system in section 3.3 and give some examples to show how the rules are used to reason about task resource specifications.

3.1   Time and Memory

The time domain TIME is the set of non-negative real numbers: TIME = $\{\, t \in R \mid t \geq 0 \,\}$. The memory domain MEM is the set of integers (*i.e.*, memory size in bytes): MEM = $\{\, m \mid m \in Z \,\}$. For our purpose, the value of a MEM variable may be negative since a task may deallocate any amount of memory.

The initial value of TIME and MEM of a program are denoted by t_0 and m_0, respectively. In practice, m_0 is replaced with the actual allocated memory size after a program is loaded. There are two TIME values of interest at the point immediately before a task, say $k(t_{k1}, m_{k1})$, starts. One is the time point, t_k, in the computation of the program (starting from t_0) up to the start of the task k. The other is the TIME expression t_{k1} which asserts that the task k must be finished within the time interval $(t_k, t_k + t_{k1}]$. Similarly, there are two MEM values: the total memory requirement of a program at that point, and a MEM expression m_{k1} denoting the upper bound of memory requirement of the task k.

The arithmetic operations "+", "−" (only for MEM variables) and "∗" are defined as having the usual meaning in the corresponding domains. In addition, we define $timemax$ $(t1, t2 : TIME)$ to be the bigger TIME value between $t1$ and $t2$. $memmax$ $(m1, m2 : MEM)$ is defined similarly.

Predicates on the TIME and MEM domains are defined to deal with assertions on resource properties:

PREDTIME = { $P \mid P : TIME \rightarrow boolean$ }
PREDMEM = { $P \mid P : MEM \rightarrow boolean$ }

Negation, conjunction, and disjunction are defined for these predicates. For example, a conjunction of two PREDMEM variables P_{m1} and P_{m2} is defined as follows: $(P_{m1} \wedge P_{m2})(m) \equiv P_{m1}(m) \wedge P_{m2}(m)$. A boolean variable **terminate** denotes the termination of the execution of a program.

3.2   Resource Specification

Given the common definitions on resources, we define task resource specifications.

Definition 1. *A resource specification for a task T is an extended Hoare triple* $\{P\}$ *T* $\{Q\}$, *where the assertion P on resource properties is the precondition, and the assertion Q is the postcondition which holds if P is true and T terminates.*

We can now introduce two special variables: TIME variable **t** and MEM variable **m**. The variables **t** (**m**) respectively denote the time point (the allocated memory) before, if they are in P, or after, if in Q, the execution of a task. P and Q are represented as first-order logic formulae which are conjunctions of predicates over the program variables (such as internal loop index), PREDTIME(**t**), PREDMEM(**m**), and termination variable **terminate**.

With this terminology, a resource skeleton can be formulated as a logical specification. For example, the resource annotation for a BB task B1(4) is mapped to a resource specification:

$\{\mathbf{t} = t0 \wedge \mathbf{m} = m0 \wedge \mathbf{terminate}\}$
    B1: BB (4)
$\{\mathbf{t} <= t0 + 4 \wedge \mathbf{m} = m0 \wedge \mathbf{terminate}\}$

And for a BRANCH task BR10(COND10, L11, B12), we have

$\{\mathbf{t} <= t0 + 4 + tx \wedge \mathbf{m} = m0 + mx \wedge \mathbf{terminate}\}$
    BR10: BRANCH (COND10, L11, B12)
$\{\mathbf{t} <= t0 + 4 + tx + 3 + timemax(T[L11], T[B12]) \wedge$
$\mathbf{m} <= m0 + mx + memmax(M[L11], M[B12]) \wedge \mathbf{terminate}\}$

where T$[t_k]$ (M$[t_k]$) extracts the $texp$ ($mexp$) of a task t_k.

It should be pointed out that a resource usage specification may contain predicates on loop bounds and ranges of parameters to library or system services that are derived from the *Constraints* part of a resource annotation.

3.3   Proof System

To verify a task resource specification, we construct a *compositional* proof system: for every type of task there is an axiom or proof rule with which the specification of the task can be verified without any information about the internal structure of the task. We first give a few general rules applicable to any task, then present the axioms and inference rules by formalizing all types of tasks.

Initially, a program starts from a state (t_0: TIME, m_0: MEM), and the **terminate** holds true.

Axiom 1. *(Init)* $\mathbf{t} = t_0 \wedge \mathbf{m} = m_0 \wedge$ **terminate**

Next we give a conjunction rule and a disjunction rule that are identical to the corresponding rules in Hoare logic.

Rule 1. *(Conjunction)* $\dfrac{\{P1\}\ T\ \{Q1\},\ \{P2\}\ T\ \{Q2\}}{\{P1 \wedge P2\}\ T\ \{Q1 \wedge Q2\}}$

Rule 2. *(Disjunction)* $\dfrac{\{P1\}\ T\ \{Q1\},\ \{P2\}\ T\ \{Q2\}}{\{P1 \vee P2\}\ T\ \{Q1 \vee Q2\}}$

The consequence rule strengthens preconditions and weaken postconditions.

Rule 3. *(Consequence)* $\dfrac{P \rightarrow P1,\ Q1 \rightarrow Q,\ \{P1\}\ T\ \{Q1\}}{\{P\}\ T\ \{Q\}}$

Now we give the axioms for simple tasks.

Axiom 2. *(BB task)*
$\forall$ *texp: TIME,*
$\{P\}$ BB *(texp)* $\{Q\}$, *where* $P = Q[(\mathbf{t} + texp\,)/\mathbf{t} \wedge$ **terminate**$]$

The axiom asserts that if P is true in the precondition of a BB task, then the value of P($\mathbf{t}$) in the postcondition is equal to the execution time for the task.

Axiom 3. *(SRVC task)*
$\forall$ *texp: TIME, mexp: MEM,*
$\{P\}$ SRVC *(texp, mexp)* $\{Q\}$, *where* $P = Q[(\mathbf{t} + texp)/\mathbf{t},\ (\mathbf{m} + mexp)/\mathbf{m} \wedge$
terminate$]$

For example, the specification

P1: $\{\mathbf{t} = t0 + 6 \wedge \mathbf{m} = m0 + 200 \wedge$ **terminate**$\}$
SRVC (7, 80)
P2: $\{\mathbf{t} = t0 + 13 \wedge \mathbf{m} = m0 + 280 \wedge$ **terminate**$\}$

can be verified by Axiom 3 (SRVC task), since the axiom leads to

P2": $\{\mathbf{t} + 7 = t0 + 13 \wedge \mathbf{m} + 80 = m0 + 280 \wedge$ **terminate**$\}$
SRVC (7, 80)
P2': $\{\mathbf{t} = t0 + 13 \wedge \mathbf{m} = m0 + 280\}$

Since P2 implies P2', and P2" is equivalent to P1, the consequence rule yields the specification {P1} SRVC(7, 80) {P2}.

Similarly, a conditional expression task and a loop bound operation task are axiomatized as below.

Axiom 4. *(COND task)*
$\forall$ *texp: TIME, mexp: MEM,*
{P} COND*(texp, mexp)* {Q}, *where* $P = Q[(t + texp)/t, (m + mexp)/m \wedge$ **terminate***]*

Axiom 5. *(LBOP task)*
$\exists\ x,\ li : real,$
{P} LBOP*(li = li + x)* {Q}, *where* $P = Q[(li + x\ /\ li) \wedge$ **terminate***]*

Axiom 5 does not refer to TIME and MEM predicates since a LBOP task is an internal task and has no resource requirements.

The inference rule for SEQ tasks is similar to the corresponding rule in Hoare logic.

Rule 4. *(SEQ task)* $\dfrac{\{P\}\ T1\ \{R\},\ \{R\}\ T2\ \{Q\}}{\{P\}\ \text{SEQ}\ (T1,\ T2)\ \{Q\}}$

The inference rule for BRANCH tasks considers the resource requirements for the related COND tasks.

Rule 5. *(BRANCH task)*
$\forall$ *texp: TIME, mexp: MEM, c : COND (texp, mexp)*
$\dfrac{\{P \wedge c\}\ \text{SEQ}(c,\ T1)\ \{Q\},\ \{P \wedge \neg\ c\}\ \text{SEQ}(c,\ T2)\ \{Q\}}{\{P\}\ \text{BRANCH}\ (c,\ T1,\ T2)\ \{Q\}}$

The inference rule for LOOP tasks is similar to the rule in Hoare logic.

Rule 6. *(LOOP task)*
$\forall$ *texp: TIME, mexp: MEM, c : COND (texp, mexp)*
$P \rightarrow Inv$,
$\dfrac{\begin{array}{l} \{Inv \wedge c \wedge \textbf{terminate}\}\ \text{SEQ}(c,\ T)\ \{Inv\}, \\ \{Inv \wedge \neg\ c \wedge \textbf{terminate}\}\ c\ \{R\}, \\ (R \vee (Inv \wedge \neg\textbf{terminate})) \rightarrow Q \end{array}}{\{P\}\ \text{LOOP}\ (c,\ T)\ \{Q\}}$

Here is a brief description of conditions in the loop rule.

(1) A resource predicate P implies a loop invariant Inv.
(2) Inv is true, and if the loop condition c is true, Inv holds after the sequential execution of c and the loop body T.
(3) Inv is true, and if c becomes false, then Inv with internal loop index substituted by the corresponding loop bound (*i.e.*, predicate R) holds after the execution of c.
(4) Either R is true, or Inv holds and the computation is nonterminating, which implies the resource predicate Q.

4   Implementation in PVS

In the previous section, we have described the approach by which the resource safety properties of a program are formalized. The difficulty with the formal verification of a resource skeleton is the formidable semantic gap between a program and the abstract high level resource skeleton. To address this problem, the formalization of program constructs (*i.e.*, tasks) and the resource specification are integrated into a unified framework in TINMAN. We use the verification system PVS for this purpose. The PVS system supports a specification language based on typed higher-order logic, and provides tools to allow mechanized checking on reasoning about expressions in the logic. We have extended and modified Hooman's [7] framework, which was introduced to formalize real-time systems.

4.1   More Definitions

The definitions of basic types are implemented using the PVS logic language. First, the TIME and MEM domains are defined as the identical built-in types in PVS.

```
Time : TYPE = { t : real | t >= 0 }
Mem : TYPE = { m : integer }
```

Next, the type of program variables concerning resource constraints is defined as a set type:

```
ProgVar : TYPE = { interlb1, interlb2, v1, v2 ... }
```

The elements in `ProgVar` for a concrete TINMAN program (in PVS specification) are the program variables of interest and relevant variables over branch tasks and loop tasks. Program variables not appearing in resource annotations are ignored.

Program tasks are identified with their operational semantics, *i.e.*, relations on states. A *state* contains the current time, allocated memory, and a mapping of program variables to values. A computation of a program is a sequence of states such that adjacent states are related by the program tasks. The PVS representation of a state is a record type with the fields program variables, Time, Mem and an termination indicator.

```
State: TYPE = [#t: Time, m: Mem, pv: [ProgVar -> real], terminate:
bool#]
```

A PVS operation `t(s)` extracts the time point `t` at a state `s`. Similarly, `m(s)` extracts the memory value `m` at a state `s`, and `pv(s)(x)` extracts the value of a variable `x` at a state `s` where `x` is an element of `ProgVar`.

Since a task is a binary relation between states, a PVS task is defined as a function mapping two states to a boolean value.

```
Task : TYPE = [ State , State -> bool ]
```

Given the definitions of basic types, some operators are defined for the valid operations over the relevant variables.

The addition '+', subtraction '-' and multiplication '*' operators on Time and Mem have the same meaning as in arithmetic. With respect to the *maximum* operation in a resource skeleton, we define the corresponding operators in PVS:

```
timemax(t1, t2: Time): Time = (IF t1 <= t2 THEN t2 ELSE t1 ENDIF)
memmax(m1, m2: Mem): Mem = (IF m1 <= m2 THEN m2 ELSE m1 ENDIF)
```

The PVS constructs IF, THEN *etc.* keep the semantics of the maximum operations.

Predicates on Time, Mem and State are defined as

```
PredTime : TYPE = [Time -> bool]
PredMem : TYPE = [Mem -> bool]
PredState : TYPE = [State -> bool]
```

All boolean operations over these predicate types in a resource specification, such as $\wedge$, $\vee$ and $\rightarrow$, are implemented using standard PVS operators. For example,

```
AND(Pm,Qm: PredMem):PredMem=((LAMBDA m: Mem): Pm(m) AND Qm(m));
```

defines the conjunction of two PredMem variables. Similarly, the disjunction over PredTime variables is defined as

```
OR(Pt,Qt: PredTime):PredTime=((LAMBDA t: Time): Pt(t) OR Qt(t));
```

And,

```
IMPLIES(Ps, Qs: PredState): PredState = ((LAMBDA s: State): Ps(s)
IMPLIES Qs(s));
```

defines the implication between two state predicates Ps and Qs on a state s.

Validity of a state predicate is defined by

```
VALID(Ps: PredState): PredState = ((LAMBDA s: State): (FORALL s:
Ps(s)));
```

The VALID operator is useful in the verification of the correctness of a resource specification. A resource safety assertion at a point in a program can be viewed as a predicate on a state. Therefore, a resource specification {P} t {Q} for a task t which relates the pre-state to the post-state is defined in PVS as

```
TaskSpec (t : Task, P : PredState, Q : PredState) : bool =
(FORALL(s0: State),(s1: State):(t(s0,s1) AND P(s0)) IMPLIES Q(s1));
```

A TaskSpec is usually a PVS theory that needs to be proven for the resource specification of the related task.

4.2   Task Construction

All the task types defined in Section 2 have been implemented in PVS using the basic types and operators defined in the previous subsection. We make the following assumptions on the types of variables appearing in the following PVS definitions for tasks.

```
texp: Time; mexp: Mem; pvar: ProgVar; s0, s1, s2 : State;
t1, t2: Task; cexp : [State -> bool]
```

It should be pointed out that `texp` and `mexp` have different meanings than `t(s)` and `m(s)` for a state `s`. `texp` is a time interval and `mexp` is an amount of memory, and negative `mexp` means the memory deallocation.

Simple Tasks

The BB tasks, SRVC tasks and COND tasks are represented in PVS by their definitions.

```
BB(texp) : Task = (LAMBDA s0, s1 : terminate(s0) IMPLIES
        t(s1) <= t(s0) + texp AND m(s1) = m(s0) AND
        pv(s1) = pv(s0) AND terminate(s1) )

SRVC(texp, mexp) : Task = (LAMBDA s0, s1 : terminate(s0) IMPLIES
        t(s1) <= t(s0) + texp AND m(s1) <= m(s0) + mexp AND
        pv(s1) = pv(s0) AND terminate(s1) )

COND(texp, mexp) : Task = (LAMBDA s0, s1 : terminate(s0) IMPLIES
        t(s1) <= t(s0) + texp AND m(s1) <= m(s0) + mexp AND
        pv(s1) = pv(s0) AND terminate(s1) )
```

A LBOP task, say $LBOP(x, e)$ (s_k, s_{k+1}), means that the the only variable that changes from s_k to s_{k+1} is the variable x whose value is e in s_{k+1}.

```
LBOP(pvar, exp:[State->real]): Task=(LAMBDA s0,s1: terminate(s0)
IMPLIES t(s1) = t(s0) AND m(s1) = m(s0) AND
        pv(s1) = pv(s0) WITH [(pvar) := exp(s0)] AND terminate(s1))
```

Compound Tasks

```
SEQ(t1, t2) : Task = (LAMBDA s0 , s1 : terminate(s0) IMPLIES
        (EXISTS s : t1(s0,s) AND t2(s,s1)) )
```

PVS keywords such as IF, THEN, ELSE and ENDIF are used to map a BRANCH task to a PVS specification in keeping with its semantics.

```
BRANCH(cexp, texp, mexp, t1, t2) : Task =
        (LAMBDA s0 , s1 : terminate(s0) IMPLIES
        IF cexp(s0)
          THEN (SEQ(COND(texp, mexp), t1)(s0,s1))
          ELSE (SEQ(COND(texp, mexp), t2)(s0,s1))
        ENDIF )
```

Based on the semantics description for a loop rule (see Rule 6) , we define
LOOP tasks by extending the iteration construction defined in [7].

```
LOOP(cexp, texp, mexp, t1) : Task =
  (LAMBDA s0 , s1 : terminate(s0) IMPLIES
  (EXISTS (ss :sequence[State]) : s0 = ss(0) AND
  ((EXISTS (k : nat) : (
    (terminate(ss(k)) AND NOT cexp(ss(k)) AND
      COND(texp, mexp)(ss(k),s1))
    OR (NOT terminate(ss(k)) AND s1 = ss(k)))
    AND (FORALL (j:nat): j<k IMPLIES cexp(ss(j)) AND terminate
        (ss(j)) AND SEQ(COND(texp, mexp), t1)(ss(j),ss(j+1))))
  OR (NOT terminate(s1) AND
      (FORALL (j : nat) : cexp(ss(j)) AND terminate(ss(j)) AND
      SEQ(COND(texp, mexp), t1)(ss(j),ss(j+1)))))))))
```

4.3   Proof System

As discussed in the previous sections, the program tasks and specifications on
resource safety properties are integrated into a unified framework using PVS.
This makes it possible to use automatic theorem proving on the resource specification. In this section, we present the PVS implementation of the proof system
described in Section 3.3. A complete implementation in PVS for the proof system is too lengthy to describe in this paper, and only a few non-trivial rules are
presented here.

For example, the Rule 1 (Conjunction) is rewritten in PVS as:

```
ConjunctionRule : THEOREM
  (TaskSpec( t, P0, Q0 )) AND ( TaskSpec( t, P1, Q1 ))
    IMPLIES (TaskSpec ( t, P0 AND P1 , Q0 AND Q1 ))
```

Rules for specifications of branch tasks and loop tasks are defined as

```
BranchRule : THEOREM
TaskSpec(t1, P AND cexp, Q) AND TaskSpec(t2, P AND NOT cexp, Q)
IMPLIES (TaskSpec (BRANCH(cexp, texp, mexp, t1, t2), P, Q ))
```

```
LoopRule : THEOREM
(EXISTS Inv, R :
VALID(P IMPLIES Inv) AND
TaskSpec(SEQ(COND(texp, mexp), t), (Inv AND cexp AND terminate),
Inv) AND
  TaskSpec(COND(texp,mexp),(Inv AND NOT cexp AND terminate),R) AND
  VALID( R OR (Inv AND NOT terminate) IMPLIES Q))
IMPLIES TaskSpec( LOOP(cexp, texp, mexp, t), P, Q)
```

4.4   Resource Specification Generation

We have defined resource specification for tasks and the related proof rules in PVS. In this section, we briefly present the translation of a program with its resource skeleton to a PVS specification.

A PVS specification of a program has four parts. The first part contains program variables including internal variables that are used to construct the set type `ProgVar`. It also has a list of constants representing user provided information (*e.g.* loop bound). Parameters used in the resource skeleton are declared as variables of appropriate types. For example, suppose a `SRVC` task foo() costs (at most) $tfoo$ time units and $mfoo$ bytes. Then $tfoo$ is declared as a `Time` variable and $mfoo$ is declared as a `Mem` variable. All the variables are used without any changes during the PVS specification generation and verification, and will be instantiated to concrete values that are defined in a resource safety policy by a code recipient.

The second part defines a set of axioms asserting that the value of a program variable is always within some given range. The axioms are used in proving task specifications. For example, the value of an internal loop index $interlb2$ is in the range $[0, lb2]$, where lb2 is the loop bound of the loop task $L2$. It is represented in PVS as

```
s : VAR State
axiomlb2 : AXIOM pv(s)(interlb2) <= lb2 AND pv(s)(interlb2) >=0
```

All the predicates on states are defined in the third part. The `PredTime` and `PredMem` predicates are typically generated based on the resource annotation and the type of the related task.

Two special predicates for loop tasks are also defined in this part. First, we define a loop invariant predicate. With respect to the example above, a loop invariant for $L2$ is

```
Inv2 : PredState = LAMBDA (s: State) :
    t(s) <= t0 + ... + pv(s)(interlb2) * (t2exp) AND
    m(s) <= m0 + ... + pv(s)(interlb2) * (m2exp) AND terminate(s)
```

The value of $interlb2$ is modified by an additional internal task (*i.e.*, a LBOP task), and is not modified by the program. Therefore, the predicate Inv maintains the program semantics, and is an invariant on the resource bounds.

The other special predicate, $loopR$ is defined similarly except that an internal loop index is replaced by the corresponding loop bound. $loopR$ usually is the postcondition of the corresponding loop task. In order to validate $loopR$, an internal PVS statement is added into the beginning of the loop body. This approach takes advantage of the fact that a loop bound is known. It makes it easy to define (rather than 'find') a loop invariant. We only need to monitor the value of the loop bound at run time if there is no other way to guarantee an upper bound for the loop.

All the tasks of a program and their corresponding resource specifications are defined in part four. For a simple task, its PVS representation is deduced from the PVS task definition framework, by replacing parameters with values in its resource annotations. Given a task definition, and the predicates in part three, the resource specification for a simple task is generated directly.

For a compound task, however, some other issues need to be considered. For example, two components of a sequential task or a branch task, and a loop body task may be either a simple task or compound task that requires careful handling. The construction of tasks are performed recursively from the bottom of a program task tree. On the other hand, the resource specification for a compound task may need auxiliary predicates for verification purposes. We demonstrate this with the following example of a branch task, say $brt1$,

> **if** $(i < j)$
> **then** { {R1} seqt2; {R2} }
> **else** { {R1} srvct3; {R3} }

where $seqt2$ is a SEQ task, $srvct3$ is a SRVC task, and $R1, R2$ and $R3$ are predicates. In order to verify the resource specification of $brt1$, say {P} $brt1$ {Q}, the Rule 5 (BRANCH task) must be applied, which in turn yields the following predicates to be verified.

> {P $\wedge$ c } SEQ(c, seqt2) {Q}
> {P $\wedge \neg$ c } SEQ(c, srvct3) {Q}

where c is the conditional task $(i < j)$. Furthermore, a set of PVS lemmas is generated in order to verify the validity of these predicates. These lemmas are also placed in part four. For example, the first predicate {P $\wedge$ c } SEQ(c, seqt2) {Q} yields the following PVS obligations (cor1t1~cor1t5).

```
c : [State -> bool] = (LAMBDA s: pv(s)(i)<pv(s)(j))
  cond1 : Task = COND(3,0)
  cor1cond : LEMMA TaskSpec(cond1, P, R1)
  cor2    : LEMMA TaskSpec(seqt2, R1, R2)
  cor1t1 : LEMMA VALID((P AND c) IMPLIES P)
  cor1t2 : LEMMA VALID(R2 IMPLIES Q)
  cor1t3 : LEMMA (FORALL (s0, s1 : State) : (P(s0) IMPLIES R2(s1))
IMPLIES
                  ((P(s0) AND c) IMPLIES Q(s1)))
  cor1t4 : LEMMA TaskSpec(SEQ(cond1, seqt2), P, R2)
  cor1t5 : LEMMA TaskSpec(SEQ(cond1, seqt2),(P AND c), Q)
```

The second predicate {P $\wedge \neg$ c } SEQ(c, srvct3) {Q} also yields a similar set of PVS lemmas. We shall go over the proof of these lemmas in the next section. We will also show how these lemmas are used to prove the resource specification for the branch task $brt1$.

5   Verification Using PVS

To verify a PVS specification, one would ordinarily construct proofs interactively using the PVS theorem prover. This requires the programmer to have significant knowledge of the PVS proof system. The goal of TINMAN system, however, is to perform the verification as automatically as possible. PVS provides a mechanism for automatic theorem proving by composing proof steps into proof strategies. Having gained some experience with using TINMAN on some real programs, we have now developed proof strategies for all types of tasks.

The proof strategy for a simple task consists of a sequence of built-in PVS proof. In this strategy, a theory definition of a simple task resource specification is expanded by automatic rewrite rules, and then skolemization and decision procedures are invoked repeatedly until the theory is proven. For example,

```
cor1 : THEOREM TaskSpec(srvct3, R1, R3)
```

is proven by using this strategy by first auto-rewriting `TaskSpec`, `R1`, `R3` and `srvcrt3`, expanding the PVS definitions of `FORALL`, `IMPLIES`, `SRVC` etc., and then repeatedly invoking PVS prover commands ASSERT and SKOSIMP∗ until the theorem `cor1` is proven.

We use the example task *brt1* from the previous section to explain the proof strategy for branch tasks. In order to prove {P} *brt1* {Q}, we apply the Rule 5 (BRANCH task) which yields two predicates that in turn yield a set of lemmas, `cor1t1`, `cor1t2`, *etc.*.

- Lemma `cor1t1` is proven by auto-rewriting PVS definitions of `VALID`, `AND` and `IMPLIES`, and invoking the PVS prover commands SKOSIMP and GROUND.
- Lemma `cor1t2` is proven similarly except that predicates `R2` and `Q` needs to be expanded which in turn expand `Timemax` and `Memmax`.
- Lemma `cor1t3` is proven by applying lemma `cor1t1`, `cor1t2` and the Rule 3(Consequence Rule).
- Lemma `cor1t4` is proven by applying lemma `cor1cond`, `cor2` and the Rule 4(SEQ task), and then repeatedly invoking the PVS prover commands INST? and GROUND until the theorem `cor1t4` is proven.
- Lemma `cor1t5` is proven by applying lemma `cor1t3` and `cor1t4`, and then invoking the PVS prover commands SKOSIMP, INST? and GROUND.

The lemmas for the "else" part are proven similarly. Finally, the specification {P} *brt1* {Q} is proven by applying `cor1t5`, `cor1e5` (the corresponding lemma for the "else" part) and the Rule 5 (BRANCH task), expanding the PVS definitions, and then invoking the PVS prover commands SKOSIMP, INST? and GROUND. The complete PVS representation of the proof for resource specification of task *brt1* is given in the appendix.

The proof strategy for a loop task involves the Rule 6 (LOOP task), a loop invariant and a predicate, say *loopR* on states that is satisfied if the loop terminates. We have discussed the construction of the loop invariant and *loopR*. A loop task specification is proven by applying the Rule 6 (LOOP task), instantiating variables of the rule with the loop invariant and *loopR*, applying the axioms on the loop bound, and invoking the PVS commands SPLIT, SKOSIMP and GRIND. We give the PVS proof for an example loop task in the appendix.

By using these proof strategies, a PVS proof for a specification can be automatically generated. Since the size of a complete proof is usually very large, we further simplify the usage certificate by only keeping the strategies and the related parameters for reconstructing a proof. More details can be found in [1].

6   Conclusion

The TINMAN architecture has been implemented and applied to some applications, such as active network and mobile SNMP agents [10]. The summary of the experimental results and our observations are given as follows:

- The certificates of all experimental programs are generated and verified completely automatically. The interpreted PVS prover and catch-all prover commands like GRIND involved in our proof strategies for loops and choice tasks are two major factors of the overhead in the certificate generation and validation.
- The programs with resource skeletons are usually between $15\% \sim 30\%$ larger than the original ones. The certificate size is significantly decreased by using a certificate skeleton; and the size of a certificate skeleton is usually 13% or less of total size of an annotated program.
- The overhead of on-line certificate check is comparable with off-line certificate validation. The reason comes from the fact that the PVS system we are using is not customized with only related modules being used.
- The overhead of running a mobile program with annotations comes from run-time monitoring of programmer-provided information and the communication between the annotated program and the on-line checker during the execution. All of them have small monitoring overheads.

We recently applied TINMAN system to practical mobile applications running in a Familiar-linux [11] PDA. The results will be reported in our another paper. The success of TINMAN ported to the handheld devices demonstrates the effectiveness and practicality of the TINMAN architecture.

There are two directions for future work. First, more programming constructs (such as pointers and recursive calls) can be incorporated in the framework. This will involve investigation on both resource prediction techniques and formalization in the extended Hoare logic. Second, we need to understand PVS well in order to reduce the size of the trusted computing base of TINMAN and improve the verification performance at a code receiver site (reported in [10]). One possible way is to modularize the PVS system, and put only the related PVS modules into the TINMAN suite of tools. In addition, by using the intermediate proof log that is generated during the proof generation stage we should be able to reduce significantly the verification overhead at the code receiver's site. This will involve modifying some PVS modules to reduce the size of the log which is usually too large to transfer.

It has been common wisdom that the greatest impediment in the deployment of formal method tools is the amount of training required of the programmer/user of the tool. While we agree that more lightweight techniques and tool sets need to be developed, our limited experience with the TINMAN architecture seems to indicate that for practical network management code, this is not necessarily the case. The logic of these application programs is generally not overly complicated and the resource usage analysis tasks can be mechanized largely by syntax-directed strategies as reported in this paper.

References

1. Mok, A.K., Yu, W.: TINMAN: A Resource Bound Security Checking System for Mobile Code. 7th European Symposium on Research in Computer Security. Lecture Notes in Computer Science 2502, Springer-Verlag (2002) 178–193
2. Necula, G.C.: Proof-Carrying Code. ACM Symposium on Principles of Programming Languages (1997) 106–119
3. Morrisett, G., Walker, D., Crary, K., Glew, N.: From System F to Typed Assembly Language. ACM Symposium on Principles of Programming Languages (1998) 85–97
4. Crary, K., Weirich, S.: Resource Bound Certification. The 27th Annual ACM Symposium on Principles of Programming Languages, (2000) 184–198
5. Hofmann, M.: A Type System for Bounded Space and Functional In-Place Update–Extended Abstract. Lecture Notes in Computer Science 1782, Springer-Verlag (2000) 165–179
6. Evans, N., Schneider, S.: Analysing Time Dependent Security Properties in CSP Using PVS. 6th European Symposium on Research in Computer Security (2000) 222–237
7. Hooman, J.: Correctness of Real Time Systems by Construction. Formal Techniques in Real-Time and Fault-Tolerant Systems. Lecture Notes in Computer Science 863, Springer-Verlag, (1994) 19–40
8. Owre, S., Rushby, J., Shankar, N.: PVS: A Prototype Verification System. 11th International Conference on Automated Deduction. Lecture Notes in Artificial Intelligence, Springer-Verlag (1992) 748–752
9. Necula, G.C., Lee, P.: The Design and Implementation of a Certifying Compiler. Proceedings of the ACM Conference on Programming Language Design and Implementation, (1998) 333–344
10. Yu, W. Mok, A.K.: Enforcing Resource Bound Safety for Mobile SNMP Agents. 18th Annual Computer Security Applications Conference (2002) 69–77
11. The Familiar Project. http://familiar.handhelds.org

Appendix: Example Proofs for Branch and Loop Tasks

• **Branch Task Example:** the branch task $brt1$ is taken from section 4.

the PVS proof for the $brt1$ task specification:

```
(|cor1cond|
  ""(expand "cond1") ((""(expand "c") (("" "(expand "P") (("" "(expand "R1")
  (("" "(expand "TaskSpec") (("" "(skosimp) (("" (ground) nil nil))nil))nil))
    nil)) nil)) nil)) nil)) nil)

(|cor1t1|
  ""  (expand "VALID") (("" (skosimp) (("" (expand "IMPLIES")
  (("" (expand "AND") (("" (ground) nil nil)) nil)) nil)) nil)) nil)

(|cor1t2|
  ""  (expand "VALID") (("" (expand "R2") (("" (expand "Q")
  (("" (expand "timemax") (("" (expand "memmax")
    (("" (skosimp) (("" (expand "IMPLIES")
      (("" (grind) nil nil)) nil)) nil)) nil)) nil)) nil)) nil)) nil)

(|cor1t3|
  ""  (lemma "cor1t1") (("" (lemma "cor1t2")
  (("" (rewrite "ConsequenceRule") nil nil)) nil)) nil)

(|cor1t4|
  ""  (lemma "cor1cond") (("" (expand "seqt2")
  (("" (lemma "cor2") (("" (lemma "SeqRule")
    (("" (inst?) (("" (ground) (("" (inst?)
      (("" (ground) nil nil)) nil)) nil)) nil)) nil)) nil)) nil)) nil)

(|cor1t5|
  ""  (lemma "cor1t4") (("" (lemma "cor1t3") (("" (expand "TaskSpec")
  (("" (skosimp) (("" (inst?) (("" (inst?)
    (("" (ground) nil  nil)) nil)) nil)) nil)) nil)) nil)) nil)

(|cor1e1|
  ... ...
(|cor1e5| ... ... (omitted)

(|cor1|
  ""(expand "brt1")
  (("" "(lemma "cor1t5") (("" "(lemma "cor1e5") (("" "(lemma "BranchRule")
  (("" "(inst - "P" "Q" "cond1" "0" "2")
    (("" "(expand "cond1") (("" "(expand "BRANCH") (("" "(expand "TaskSpec")
    (("" "(skosimp) (("" "(inst?) (("" "(inst?) (("" "(inst?)
      (("" "(expand  "SEQ") (("" "(expand  "c")
      (("" "(expand  "AND") (("" "(expand  "NOT")
        (("" "(ground) nil nil)) nil)) nil)) nil)) nil)) nil)) nil)) nil))
        nil)) nil)) nil)) nil)) nil)) nil)) nil)) nil)
```

- **Loop Task Example:** {P} loop2(loop2cond, 4, 0, SRVC(tfoo,mfoo)) {Q}

(1) the PVS specification for the *loop2* task:

```
....
% Loop2 init Task
loop2init  : Task = LBOP(interlb2, (LAMBDA s: 0))
cor2init   : LEMMA TaskSpec(loop2init, P, P1)

% Loop2 cond Task
loop2cond  : PredState  = (LAMBDA s : pv(s)(interlb2) < lb2 )
loop2body  : Task = SEQ(SRVC(7+tfoo, mfoo), LBOP(interlb2,
             (LAMBDA s: val(s)(inter_lb2) + 1)))

% Loop2 Task
loop2pre   : Task = LOOP(loop2cond, 4, 0, loop2body)
cor2loop   : LEMMA TaskSpec(loop2pre, P1, Q)
loop2      : Task = SEQ(loop2init, loop2pre)
cor2       : LEMMA TaskSpec(loop2, P, Q)
```

(2) the PVS proof for the *loop2* task resource specification:

```
(|cor2init|
  "" (expand "loop2init") (("" (expand "P") (("" (expand "P1")
  (("" (expand "TaskSpec") (("" (expand "LBOP") (("" (assert)
   (("" (skosimp*) (("" (assert) (("" (skosimp*) (("" (assert) nil nil))
     nil)) nil)) nil)) nil)) nil)) nil)) nil)) nil)) nil)

(|cor2loop|
  ""    (lemma "LoopRule") (("" (expand "loop2pre") (("" (inst?) (("" (ground)
  (("" (inst + "Inv2" "loop2R") (("" (hide 2) (("" (lemma "axiomlb2")
   (("" (split)
    (("1" (grind) nil nil)
     ("2" (expand "=>") (("2" skosimp) (("2" (grind) nil nil)) nil)) nil)
     ("3" (expand "=>") (("3" (skosimp) (("2" (grind) nil nil)) nil)) nil)
     ("4" (grind) nil nil)) nil)) nil)) nil)) nil)) nil)) nil)) nil)) nil)

(|cor2|
  "" (expand "loop2")
  (("" (lemma "cor2init") (("" (lemma "cor2loop") (("" (lemma "SeqRule")
   (("" (inst?) (("" (ground) (("" (inst?)
    (("" (ground) nil nil)) nil)) nil)) nil)) nil)) nil)) nil)) nil)
```

Java Program Verification at Nijmegen: Developments and Perspective

Bart Jacobs and Erik Poll

University of Nijmegen,
P.O. Box 9010, 6500 GL Nijmegen, The Netherlands
{bart,erikpoll}@cs.kun.nl

Abstract. This paper presents a historical overview of the work on Java program verification at the University of Nijmegen (the Netherlands) over the past six years (1997–2003). It describes the development and use of the LOOP tool that is central in this work. Also, it gives a perspective on the field.

1 Introduction

The LOOP project started out as an exploration of the semantics of object-oriented languages in general, and Java in particular. It has evolved to become what we believe is one of the largest attempts to date at formalising a real programming language and using this formalisation as a basis for program verification. It is probably also one of the largest attempts to date at using mechanical theorem provers. This paper attempts to give an overview of the whole project. It is unavoidable that we have to resort to a high level of abstraction to do this in the limited space here. Therefore, our main aim is to convey the general principles and we will frequently refer to other papers for much more of the technical details.

From the outset, a goal of the project has been to reason about a *real* programming language, and not just a toy object-oriented language. Apart from leaving out threads, all the complications of real Java are covered, including

- side-effects in expressions (something often omitted in the toy languages studied in theoretical computer science),
- exceptions and all other forms of abrupt control flow (including the more baroque constructs that Java offers, such as labeled breaks and continues),
- static and non-static field and methods,
- overloading,
- all the complications of Java's inheritance mechanism, including late binding for methods, early binding for fields, overriding of methods, and shadowing (or hiding) of fields.

Apart from threads, the only major feature of Java not supported is inner classes.

K. Futatsugi et al. (Eds.): ISSS 2003, LNCS 3233, pp. 134–153, 2004.

When using our formal semantics of sequential Java as a basis for program verification, the need for a convenient specification language, to specify the properties to be verified, became apparent. For this we adopted the Java Modeling Language (JML) [24], a specification language specifically designed for specifying properties of Java programs, and the semantics of Java was extended to also provide a semantics for the core of JML.

The LOOP Tool. What we call the LOOP tool is effectively a compiler, written in O'Caml. Fig. 1 illustrates roughly how it is used. As input, the LOOP tool takes sequential Java programs, and specifications written (as annotations in the Java source files) in the Java Modeling Language JML [24]. Fig. 2 gives an example of a Java class with a JML specification. As output, the LOOP tool generates several files which, in the syntax of the theorem prover PVS [32], describe the meaning of the Java program and its JML specification. These files can be loaded into PVS, and then one can try to prove that the Java program meets its JML specification.

In addition to the automatically generated PVS files, there are also several hand-written PVS files, the so-called prelude. These files define the basic building blocks for the Java and JML semantics, and define all the machinery needed, in the form of PVS theories and lemmas, to support the actual work of program verification.

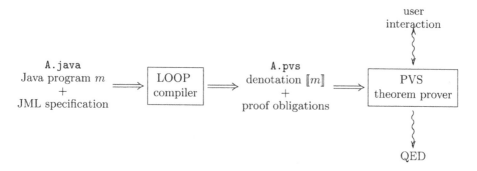

Fig. 1. The LOOP tool as pre-processor for PVS

Organisation of This Paper. The next section begins by giving an example of a Java program with JML specification to illustrate the kind of program verification we are doing. The organisation of the rest of this paper is then more or less chronological, and follows the bottom-up approach that we have taken over the years, starting at the detailed representation of the Java semantics at a low level, on top of which further abstractions are built. The LOOP project started with the definition of a formal semantics for Java in higher-order logic, by giving a so-called shallow embedding, and using coalgebras as a means of organising the semantics of objects. This is described in Sect. 3. The project then evolved to also provide a formal semantics of the Java specification language JML in PVS, as discussed in Sect. 4, and to provide techniques for the verification Java programs with JML specifications on the basis of these formal semantics, which we discuss in Sect. 5. Sect. 6 compares the LOOP projects with other work on providing theorem prover supported program verification for Java.

2   Specification and Verification Example

Fig. 2 gives an example of a simple Java method `arrayCopy` preceded by a specification written in JML. It illustrates some of the complications that may arise in actual specification and verification. Although the idea of copying part of one array into another is quite simple, an accurate specification turns out to be surprisingly subtle. The specification makes many possibilities explicit, and serves as a precise documentation that can help a programmer who wants to use this `arrayCopy` method.

This JML specification consists of

- a precondition, the **requires** clause;
- a so-called frame property, the **assignable** clause, that restricts the possible side effects of the method;
- a postcondition, the **ensures** clause;
- an "exceptional" postcondition, the **signals** clause.

The meaning of the specification is that if the precondition is met, then either the method terminates normally making the postcondition true, or the method terminates abnormally by throwing an `ArrayIndexOutOfBoundsException` making the associated exceptional postcondition true, and the method will not change any fields other than those listed in the **assignable** clause.

The use of \old in the postcondition allows us to refer to the value of an expression in the pre-state of the method invocation. We need to use \old here in the postcondition to allow for the possibility that the two arrays `src` and `dest` are aliases. This possibility is also reason for the case distinction in the implementation. Omitting \old in the postcondition is an easy mistake to make, as is not making the case distinction in the implementation. Either mistake, or both at the same time, would make it impossible to verify correctness of the implementation with respect to the specification.

A subtle point that has to be taken into account is overflow of the additions that are used. If `destOff+length` yields an overflow, the resulting value becomes negative. This is excluded in the precondition (and is needed for the **assignable** clause to make sense). However, the addition `srcOff+length` may also cause an overflow. This possibility is not excluded in the precondition, but handled explicitly in the (normal and exceptional) postconditions.

Fig. 2 gives only one possible spec for `arrayCopy`, but many variations are possible. E.g., we could strengthen the precondition to exclude the possibility of an `ArrayIndexOutOfBoundsException`, or we could weaken the precondition to include the possibility of a `NullPointerException`.

We have used the LOOP tool and PVS to prove that the Java code in Fig. 2 satisfies the JML specification given there. This verification can be done both

```
class ArrayCopy {

   /*@    requires src != null && dest != null &&
    @               destOff+length >= 0; // no overflow
    @
    @  assignable dest[destOff..destOff+length-1];
    @
    @    ensures (length > 0 ==>
    @        (srcOff >= 0  && srcOff+length <= src.length &&
    @            srcOff+length >= 0 &&
    @         destOff >= 0 && destOff+length <= dest.length))
    @        &&
    @        (\forall int i; 0 <= i && i < length ==>
    @            dest[destOff+i] == \old(\old(src)[\old(srcOff)+i]));
    @
    @    signals (ArrayIndexOutOfBoundsException)
    @        length > 0 &&
    @        (srcOff < 0  || srcOff+length > src.length ||
    @            srcOff+length < 0 // caused by overflow
    @         || destOff < 0 || destOff+length > dest.length);
    @*/
   public static void arrayCopy(byte[] src,    int srcOff,
                                byte[] dest,   int destOff,
                                int    length)
   {   if (length <= 0) return;
       if (srcOff > destOff) {
           for (int i = 0; i < length; i++)
               dest[destOff+i] = src[srcOff+i];
       }
       else {
           for (int i = length-1; i >= 0 ; i--)
               dest[destOff+i] = src[srcOff+i]; }
   }
}
```

Fig. 2. Example JML specification, proven correct

with Hoare logic, and with weakest precondition reasoning, see Section 4. In both cases it requires the specification of the loop invariants for the two for-loops, which we have omitted from Fig. 2 to save space.

Similar verification challenges may be found in [20].

3   Semantical Phase

This first phase of the project concentrated on the semantical set-up for the sequential part of Java. This grew out of earlier work on so-called coalgebraic specification. Important issues at this stage were the underlying memory model [1] and the semantics of inheritance [15]. This semantics is fairly stable since about the year 2000, and has undergone only relatively minor, modular changes such as the move from unbounded to bounded semantics for integral types [18], see Sect. 3.5.

We shall briefly review the main points. A more detailed description of the material presented in this section can be found in Chapter 2 of [14].

3.1   Coalgebraic Origins

During the mid-nineties Horst Reichel [34] was the first who clearly described the view that the semantics of objects and classes can be phrased in terms of coalgebras, soon followed by others [17, 26]. Coalgebras are the formal duals of algebras. Algebras describe data, but coalgebras describe dynamical systems. Coalgebras consist of a set S together a function acting on S. The elements of S are usually called states, and therefore S is often referred to as the state space. The function acting on S is typically of the form $S \to \boxed{\cdots}$ and gives more information about states. For instance, it may involve a map of the form $S \to$ int which represents an integer-valued field. In each state it tells the value of the field. But also the function may involve a transition function $S \to S$, or $S \to \{\bot\} \cup S$, or $S \to \mathcal{P}(S)$ describing ways to move to successor states. Hence the result type $\boxed{\cdots}$ tells us what kind of functions we have on our state space S^1.

A class in an object-oriented programming language (like Java) combines data (in its fields) with associated operations (in its methods). The key point is that such a class may be considered as a coalgebra, and an object of the class as a state of this coalgebra (i.e. as an element of the state space). Given such an object/state o, field access o.i yields the value of the field function i in the state (referred to by) o. Similarly, a method invocation o.m yields a successor state resulting from the application of the function m to the state o.

Suppose a method in Java is declared as boolean m(int j){...}. Such a method usually terminates normally, producing a Boolean result value, and implicitly, a new state. But also it may hang, if it gets into an infinite loop or recursion. There is a third option, since it may throw an exception of some sort, caused for instance by a division by zero. Semantically, we shall interpret such a method m as a function $[\![m]\!]$ of the coalgebraic form:

$$S \xrightarrow{\quad [\![m]\!] \quad} \left(\{\bot\} + (S \times \text{boolean}) + (S \times \text{Exception}) \right)^{\text{int}} \tag{1}$$

where $+$ describes disjoint union. This says that m takes a state/object $x \in S$ and an integer $j \in$ int and produces a result $[\![m]\!](x)(j)$ which is either:

- $\bot$, in case $[\![m]\!](x)(j)$ hangs;
- (s', b) in case $[\![m]\!](x)(j)$ terminates normally with successor state x' and boolean result value b;

---

[1] Formally, in categorical terminology, this box is an endofunctor acting on a suitable category of state spaces, see [22].

- (x', e) in case $[\![\mathtt{m}]\!](x)(j)$ terminates abruptly because of exception e, with successor state x'.

The modeling of a `void` method is similar. The normal termination case (the second one) is then without result value, and the abrupt termination case (the third one) involves besides exceptions also a possible return, break or continue.

The semantics of a Java method is defined by induction over the structure of the methods body. To do this we define the semantics of all Java statements and expression, by induction over their structure, which amounts to defining the semantics of all of Java's language constructs for statements and expressions. For example, $[\![s_1; s_2]\!]$ is defined as $[\![s_1]\!] ; [\![s_2]\!]$, where ; is the function that maps functions s_1 and s_2 of type $S \to (\{\bot\} + S + (S \times \mathtt{Exception}))$ to the function

$$\lambda x : S. \begin{cases} \bot, & \text{if } s_1(x) = in_1(\bot) & \text{i.e. if } s_1(x) \text{ hangs,} \\ s_2(x') & \text{if } s_1(x) = in_2(x') & \text{if } s_1(x) \text{ terminates normally} \\ & & \text{in state } x', \\ in_3(x', e), & \text{if } s_1(x) = in_3(x', e), & \text{i.e. if } s_1(x) \text{ terminates abruptly by} \\ & & \text{throwing exception } e \text{ in state } x' \end{cases}$$

of the same type.

The main point is that a class with fields $f_1 \colon A_1, \ldots, f_n \colon A_n$, and methods $m_1, \ldots, m_k$ is interpreted as a single coalgebra of the form:

$$S \xrightarrow{\quad c \quad} A_1 \times \cdots A_n \times M_1(S) \times \cdots M_k(S)$$

(2)

where M_j is the result type corresponding to method m_j, like in (1). Hence c combines data and operations in a single function. The individual fields and methods can be reconstructed from c via appropriate projections[2].

In work on coalgebraic specification [17, 13, 12, 35, 36] coalgebras are studied together with certain assertions that constrain the possible behaviour. A format has been defined, in a language called CCSL for Coalgebraic Class Specification Language, in which such specifications could be written. A special compiler translates these specifications to the language of the theorem prover PVS [32]. The compiler is called LOOP, for Logic of Object-Oriented Programs. Coalgebraic notions like invariance, bisimilarity and refinements can then be used to reason about models of class specifications.

Soon after the start of this work on coalgebraic class specifications it was realised that the assertions could also be used to bind method names to method bodies (implementations) and fields to particular access functions. This led to an extension of the LOOP compiler that works on Java programs and also produces output for PVS.

For some time the LOOP compiler was developed jointly for CCSL and for Java. Internally, a representation of an abstract formulation of higher-order logic

---

[2] For reasons of simplicity, we have omitted constructors. But they can be understood as special methods.

is used. A pretty printer is available for PVS, and also one for Isabelle/HOL [30]. For various practical and organisational reasons the two translations of the tools (for CCSL and for Java) were split. The version for CCSL is now publicly available[3]. It is maintained in Dresden and still supports output for both PVS and Isabelle, see [36]. The version of the LOOP tool for Java is maintained in Nijmegen. A comparison between its performance in PVS and Isabelle is given in [11, 14]. But currently, the translation to Isabelle is no longer supported.

When we talk about the LOOP tool in the remainder of this paper we refer to the one that translates Java (and JML) to PVS. It is described in [2].

The theory of coalgebras has gone through rapid development during the last few years. However, coalgebras are only used as convenient representational device for classes in the LOOP translation from Java to PVS. The associated theory is not really used in any depth, and is not needed to understand the translation.

3.2   Memory Model

The discussion above mentions a state space S that methods act on, without going into detail of what this state space consists of. The coalgebraic representation of classes (2) takes a functional view in which each class has its own state space and in which there is no object identity. Clearly, this does not work at all for an imperative language such as Java. Here the state space that programs act on is the entire memory of the computer, i.e. the heap and the stack. The heap records all the objects in existence, their states, i.e. values of all fields, and their run-time types. The representation of all this in PVS is what we call the memory model or object memory. For a more detailed description of the memory model we refer to [1]. Here we just explain the main idea.

The memory model is represented in PVS as a complicated type called OM, for Object Memory. It consists of three infinite series of memory cells, one for the heap, one for the stack, and one for static data. Each cell can store the data of an arbitrary object (including its run-time type, represented as a string). An object is represented as either the null-reference, or a reference to a particular cell on the heap. This reference consists simply of a natural number n, pointing to the n-th cell. Associated with the memory are various put and get operations. The LOOP compiler binds these to the variables occurring in the programs that are translated. For instance, for integer fields i,j, the translation of an assignment i=5 involves the put operation associated with i. It is a functional operation which maps the memory x: OM before the assignment to an entirely new memory $x' = \mathsf{put}(x,$ "position of i"$, 5)$: OM after the assignment. The value of j is obtained via its get operation. There are obvious put-get rules ensuring that the value of j in x' is the same as in x. During verifications these rules are loaded in PVS as so-called auto-rewrite rules and applied automatically. Hence the reader does not have to worry about these low-level memory issues, including references and aliasing.

---

[3] At wwwtcs.inf.tu-dresden.de/~tews/ccsl/.

One difficulty in defining a suitable type OM in PVS is the constraints imposed by the PVS type system. Intuitively, the state of an individual object can be seen as a record value—eg, the state of an object with a field x of type int and a field b of type boolean would be a record value of a record type {x:int, b:boolean}—and the heap can be regarded as a list of such record values. However, dealing with Java's hiding (or shadowing) of superclass fields will require some additional machinery in such an approach. Also, such a representation is not that convenient in PVS: it would require a heterogeneous list of record values, since objects on the heap have different types, and PVS doesn't support such heterogeneous lists. A way around this would be to have separate heap for each class, but then interpreting subtyping causes complications.

Despite the absence of the horrible pointer arithmetic à la C(++), references remain the main complication in reasoning about Java programs, as the basic "pointer spaghetti" difficulties associated with references, like aliasing and leakage of references, remain. One would really like Java to offer some notion of encapsulation or confinement and alias control, such as the universes [29], which could then be reflected in the memory model.

3.3   Inheritance

The way that inheritance is handled by the LOOP tool is fairly complicated—because inheritance itself is fairly complicated. Here we shall only describe the main ideas, and we refer to [15] for the details.

When Java class B inherits from class A, all the methods and field from A are in principle accessible in B. If the current object this belongs to class B, then (super)this belongs to A, and allows access to the fields and methods of A. Class B may thus add extra fields and methods to those of its superclass A. This is unproblematic. But B may also re-introduce methods and fields that already occur in A. In that case one speaks of *hiding* of fields and of *overriding* of methods. The terminology differs for fields and methods because the underlying mechanisms differ. Field selection o.i is based on the compile-time type of the the receiving object o, whereas method invocation o.m() uses the run-time type of o.

The basis for our handling of inheritance can be explained in terms of the coalgebraic representation. Suppose the class A is represented as a coalgebra $S \to \widehat{A}(S)$, like in (2). The representation of class B is then of the form $S \to [\cdots] \times \widehat{A}(S)$, where the part $[\cdots]$ corresponds to the fields and methods of B. In this the operations from A are accessible in B: the super operation involves a projection.

But there is also a second (semantical) mapping possible from B to A, namely the one which replaces in $\widehat{A}$ those methods that are overridden in B. These two different mappings allow us to model the difference between hiding and overriding.

The LOOP tool inserts the appropriate mapping from subclasses to superclasses. As a result, the selection of appropriate get and put operations for fields,

142   B. Jacobs and E. Poll

and of the appropriate method body for methods is not a concern for the user. It is handled automatically.

3.4   Executability of the Semantics

Although our Java semantics is denotational rather than operational, it is still executable in PVS to a degree, in the sense that PVS can try to rewrite $[\![s]\!]$ to some normal form using a given set of equalities. PVS will not always produce a readable result, or, indeed, any result at all, as the attempted evaluation might not terminate (notably, if the program diverges), but in many cases PVS can symbolically execute programs in this way.

In fact, one could use the LOOP tool as a normal Java compiler, which produces binaries that can be executed inside PVS instead of class files which can be executed on a virtual machine. Of course, this is not very practical, because such executions are extremely slow and use huge amounts of memory, and because we do not have an implementation of the entire Java API in PVS.

This possibility of symbolic execution has been extremely useful in testing and debugging our formal semantics. By comparing the results of the normal execution of a Java program, i.e. the result of executing its bytecode on a Java VM, and the symbolically execution of its semantics in PVS, we can check if there are no mistakes in our semantics.

It is somewhat ironic that we have to rely on the down-to-earth method of testing to ensure the correctness of our formal semantics, when this formal semantics is used as the basis for the more advanced method of program verification. But given there is nothing that we can formally verify our semantics against—this would presuppose another formal semantics—such testing is the only way to to ensure the absence of mistakes in our semantics, apart from careful, but informal, verification against the official Java Language Specification [10].

Symbolic execution is also extremely useful in the verification of Java programs as discussed later in Sect. 5: for relatively simple fragments of code, and relatively simple specifications, PVS can often fully automatically decide correctness by symbolic execution of the code.

3.5   Java Arithmetic

Initially, the Java semantics simply interpreted all of Java's numeric types—byte (8 bits), short (16 bits), int (32 bits) and long (64 bits)—as PVS integers. This was just done to keep things simple; our main interest was the semantics of Java features such as object-orientation, inheritance, exceptions, etc., and interpretation of the base types is orthogonal to the semantics of these. Later, when this became relevant for the Java Card smart card programs we wanted to verify, a correct formalisation of the semantics of Java numeric types, with all the peculiarities of the potential overflow during arithmetic operations, was included [18]. It is used in the verification example in Section 2.

4   Specification Phase

The semantics of sequential Java described in the previous section was developed with the aim to do program verification. This requires specification of properties that we want to verify. One option is to specify such properties directly in PVS, i.e. at the semantical level. This approach was used initially, for instance in [23]. However, this approach quickly becomes impractical, as specifications become very complicated and hard to read.

This is why we decided to adopt JML as our specification language, and extended the LOOP tool to provide not just a formal semantics of Java, but also a formal semantics of JML. The fact that JML is a relatively small extension of Java has the pleasant consequence that much of our Java semantics could be re-used—or extended—to provide a semantics for JML.

The LOOP tool provides the semantics of a JML specification for an individual method as a proof obligation in PVS. Taking some liberties with the syntax, and ignoring the exceptional postconditions expressed by signals clauses, the proof obligation corresponding with a JML specification of the form

```
/*@ requires    Pre;
  @ assignable Assign;
  @ ensures     Post;
  @*/
  public void m()   ...
```

is of the following form

$$\forall x : \mathsf{OM}. \ [\![Pre]\!] (x) \Rightarrow [\![Post]\!] (x, [\![m]\!] (x)) \tag{3}$$
$$\wedge \ \forall l \notin [\![Assign]\!] . \ x.l = [\![m]\!] (x).l$$

Here $[\![m]\!]$ is the semantics of the method involved, $[\![Pre]\!]$ the semantics of its precondition, a predicate on OM, $[\![Post]\!]$ the semantics of its postcondition, a relation on OM, and $[\![Assign]\!]$ the meaning of the assignable clause, a subset of locations in OM. Just like the LOOP tool generates a PVS file defining $[\![m]\!]$, it generates a file defining $[\![Pre]\!]$, $[\![Post]\!]$ and $[\![Assign]\!]$.

To produce such proof obligations, the LOOP tool translates any **assignable** clause to a set $[\![A]\!]$ of locations in the object memory OM, and translates any pre- and postconditions to a PVS predicates or relations on the object memory OM.

JML's syntax for preconditions, postconditions, and invariants extends Java's boolean expressions, for example with a logical operator for implication, ==>, as well as universal and existential quantification, \forall and \exists. So, to provide a formal semantics for JML, the LOOP semantics for Java had to be extended to support these additional operations.

One complicating factor here is that Java boolean expression may not terminate, or throw an exception, but we want our interpretations of pre- and postconditions to be proper two-valued PVS booleans. This is a drawback of using Java syntax in a specification language, as is discussed in [25]. We deal with this by interpreting any Java boolean expression that does not denote `true` or `false` by an unspecified boolean value in PVS.

Some PVS definitions are used to express the proof obligations in a more convenient form, which is closer to the original JML format and closer to the conventional notion of Hoare triple:

$$\forall z\colon \mathsf{OM}.\quad \mathsf{SB}\cdot(\ \mathsf{requires} = \lambda x\colon \mathsf{OM}.\ [\![Pre]\!]\,(x) \wedge x = z,$$
$$\mathsf{statement} = [\![m]\!]\,,$$
$$\mathsf{ensures} = \lambda x\colon \mathsf{OM}.\ [\![Post_{norm}]\!]\,(x,z)$$
$$\wedge\ \forall l \notin [\![Assign]\!]\,.\ x.l = z.l, \tag{4}$$
$$\mathsf{signals} = \lambda x\colon \mathsf{OM}.\ [\![Post_{excp}]\!]\,(x,z)$$
$$\wedge\ \forall l \notin [\![Assign]\!]\,.\ x.l = z.l\ )$$

Here SB, an abbreviation of statement behaviour, is a function acting on a labeled record with four fields. A so-called logical variable z is used to relate pre- and post-state and to give a meaning to uses of \old in postconditions.

If we omit the signals clause, we effectively have a traditional Hoare triple, consisting of a precondition, a statement, and a postcondition. But note that unlike in conventional Hoare logics, $[\![m]\!]$ is not a statement in Java syntax, but rather its denotation, so we have a Hoare logic at the semantic rather than the syntactic level. However, given that the semantics is compositional, $[\![m]\!]$ has the same structure as m in Java syntax, and reasoning with these 'semantic' Hoare tuples is essentially the same as reasoning with conventional 'syntactic' Hoare tuples.

We have omitted some further complications in the discussion above. Firstly, rather than having Hoare 4-tuples as in (4), giving a precondition, statement, postcondition, and exceptional postcondition, we actually have Hoare 8-tuples, to cope with the other forms of abrupt control flow in Java, by return, break, and continue statements, and to specify whether or not the statement is allowed to diverge, allowing us to specify both total and partial correctness. Secondly, in addition to have Hoare n-tuples for statements, we also have them for expressions.

The format for our proof obligations in (4) is convenient for several reasons. It is more readable, as it closely resembles the original JML specification. Moreover, it allows the formulation of suitable PVS theories, i.e. collections of PVS theorems, that can be used to prove proof obligations of this form in a convenient way. How we go about proving these Hoare n-tuples is the subject of the next section.

5   Verification Phase

Using the semantics of Java and JML discussed in the previous sections, the LOOP tool translates JML-annotated Java code to proof obligations in PVS. This is by no means the end of the story. A lot of PVS infrastructure, in the form of theories and PVS proof strategies, is needed to make proving these proof obligations feasible.

This section describes the three different techniques that we have developed for this. Each of these techniques involves a collection of PVS lemmas, in the hand-written prelude or the PVS theories generated by the LOOP tool, and associated PVS strategies, which can automate large parts of proofs.

5.1   Semantical Proofs by Symbolic Execution

In the early, semantical phase of the LOOP project—described in Sect. 3— the proofs were "semantical". What this means is that these proofs worked by using the underlying semantics: the method bodies involved are expanded (in a controlled fashion) until nothing remains but a series of put and get operations on the memory model, for which the required properties are established.

These semantical proofs can be very efficient, but they only work well for very small programs, without complicated control structures like (while or for) loops. To verify the correctness of larger programs we use the program logics described in the next sections, which provide Hoare logics and weakest precondition calculi for Java. These logics are used to break complicated method bodies iteratively into simple parts, for which semantical reasoning can be used. Hence semantical proofs are not abolished, but are postponed to the very end, namely to the leafs of the proof trees.

5.2   Hoare Logic

As we already emphasised, Java programs have various termination modes: they can hang, terminate normally, or terminate abruptly (typically because of an exception). An adaptation of Hoare logic for Java with different termination modes has been developed in [16]. It involves separate rules for the different termination modes. Although this logic has been used successfully for several examples, it is not very convenient to use because of the enormous number of rules involved.

With the establishment of JML as specification language, it became clear that the most efficient logic would not use Hoare triples, but the "JML n-tuples" already discussed Sect. 4. The proof obligation resulting from a JML specification for a Java method is expressed as a Hoare n-tuple, and for these n-tuples we can formulate and prove deduction rules like those used in conventional Hoare logic, one for every programming language construct. For example, for composition we have the deduction rule NB.

$$
\frac{
\begin{array}{ll}
\mathsf{SB} \cdot (\ \mathsf{requires} = Pre, & \mathsf{SB} \cdot (\ \mathsf{requires} = Q, \\
\quad \mathsf{statement} = m_1, & \quad \mathsf{statement} = m_2, \\
\quad \mathsf{ensures} = Q, & \quad \mathsf{ensures} = Post_{norm}, \\
\quad \mathsf{signals} = Post_{excp}\ ) & \quad \mathsf{signals} = Post_{excp}\ )
\end{array}
}{
\begin{array}{l}
\mathsf{SB} \cdot (\ \mathsf{requires} = Pre, \\
\quad \mathsf{statement} = m_1; m_2, \\
\quad \mathsf{ensures} = Post_{norm}, \\
\quad \mathsf{signals} = Post_{excp}\ )
\end{array}
}
$$

The rule above has been *proven* as a lemma inside PVS. Thus it is sound in our Java semantics. All the deduction rules have been proved correct in this way, establishing soundness of the Hoare logic. Because we have a shallow embedding rather than a deep embedding of Java in PVS, proving completeness of the rules is not really possible. For more details about this Hoare logic for for Java and JML, see [19].

The bottleneck in doing Hoare logic proofs is, as usual, providing the intermediate assertions, such as Q in the proof rule for composition above. This is aggravated by the fact that our Hoare logic works at the semantical level, which means that these intermediate assertions have to be expressed at semantical level and are therefore less readable that they would be in a Hoare logic at the syntactic level. One way to alleviate this is to specify intermediate assertions in the Java program; JML provides the `assert` keyword to do this, and the LOOP tool can parse these assertions to provide the (less readable) semantical counterparts, which can then serve as the intermediate predicate in the Hoare logic proof. Another way, discussed in the next subsection, is the use of a weakest precondition calculus.

5.3   Weakest Precondition

The latest stage in the development of PVS infrastructure for easing the job of verifying Java programs has been the development of a weakest precondition (wp) calculus. Here we just discuss the main ideas; for more details see [19].

The fact that JML distinguishes normal and exceptional postconditions means a wp-calculus for Java and JML is slightly different than usual. Where normally the wp function acts on a statement s and a postcondition $Post$ to provide the weakest precondition $\mathsf{wp}(s, Post)$, our wp function will act on a statement s and a pair of postconditions $(Post_{norm}, Post_{excp})$, the postcondition for normal termination and exceptional termination, respectively[4].

We can actually define the weakest precondition function inside PVS, as follows:

$$\mathsf{wp}(s, Post_{norm}, Post_{excp}) \stackrel{\mathrm{def}}{=} \lambda x.\ \exists P.\ P(x) \wedge \mathsf{SB} \cdot (\ \mathsf{requires} = P, \\ \mathsf{statement} = m, \\ \mathsf{ensures} = Post_{norm}, \\ \mathsf{signals} = Post_{excp}\ ) \tag{5}$$

The definition above is not useful in the sense that we can ask PVS to compute it. Instead, we prove suitable lemmas about the wp function as defined above, one for every language construct, and then use these lemmas as rewrite rules in PVS to compute the weakest preconditions. E.g., for the composition we prove that

---

[4] As before, we oversimplify here; instead of 2 postconditions, our wp function actually works on 5 postconditions, to cope not just with normal termination and exceptions, but also with (labeled) breaks and continues and with return statements.

$$\mathsf{wp}(m_1; m_2, Post_{norm}, Post_{excp})$$
$$= \mathsf{wp}(m_1, \mathsf{wp}(m_2, Post_{norm}, Post_{excp}), Post_{excp})$$

and we can use this lemma as a rewriting rule in PVS to compute (or rather, to let PVS compute) the weakest precondition.

The definition of wp in terms of the notion of Hoare n-tuple above in (5) allows us to prove the correctness of these lemma in PVS, thus establishing the correctness of our wp-calculus with respect to our Java semantics. So, as for soundness of our Hoare logic, for correctness of our wp-calculus with respect to the Java semantics we have a completely formal proof, inside PVS.

It turns out that there are several ways to go about computing weakest preconditions. The traditional, 'backward', approach is to peel of statements at the back,

$$\mathsf{wp}(m_1; m_2; \ldots; m_n, Post_{norm}, Post_{excp})$$
$$= \mathsf{wp}(m_1; \ldots; m_{n-1}, \mathsf{wp}(m_n, Post_{norm}, Post_{excp}), Post_{excp})$$

and then evaluate the inner call to wp, i.e. $\mathsf{wp}(m_n, Post_{norm}, Post_{excp})$, before peeling of the next statement m_{n-1}. But an alternative, 'forward', approach is to begin by peeling of statements at the front,

$$\mathsf{wp}(m_1; m_2; \ldots; m_n, Post_{norm}, Post_{excp})$$
$$= \mathsf{wp}(m_1, \mathsf{wp}(m_2; \ldots; m_n, Post_{norm}, Post_{excp}), Post_{excp})$$

and then to evaluate the outer call to wp. Of course, the approaches are logically equivalent, and will ultimately produce the same result. But computationally the approaches are different, and the costs of letting PVS compute the wp-function, measured in the time and memory PVS needs for the computation, turn out to be very different for the two approaches.

Two strategies for letting PVS computing weakest preconditions have been implemented in PVS, in a forward or backward style sketched above. Each of these implementation relies on its own collection of lemmas serving as rewrite rules and relies on a a different PVS proof tactic. For a discussion of these strategies we refer to [19].

Using the wp-calculi, program verification can be completely automated in PVS. However, there are limitations to the size of program fragment that one can verify using the wp-calculi. PVS can run for hours without completing the proof, or it can crash because the proof state becomes too big. The most effective approach for larger programs seems to a combination of Hoare logic to break up proof obligation for a large program into chunks that are small enough to handle with the wp-calculus.

6   Related Work

There are quite a number of groups working on the tool-supported verification of Java programs that use theorem provers, such as ESC/Java [9], Bali [31],

JACK [5], Krakatoa [27], Jive [28], and Key [8]. With more of such tools now appearing, comparing them and understanding their fundamental differences and similarities becomes more important.

In a way, ESC/Java is the odd one out in the list above, in that its developers have deliberately chosen an approach that is unsound and incomplete, as their aim was to maximise the number of (potential) bugs that the tool can spot fully automatically. Still, ESC/Java does use a theorem prover and a wp-calculus to find these potential bugs, and it probably the most impressive tool to date when it comes to showing the potential of program verification.

Of the tools listed above, ESC/Java, JACK, Krakatoa, and LOOP use JML as specification language. Jive will also start supporting JML in the near future. The KeY system uses OCL as specification language. The fact that several tools support JML has its advantages of course: it makes it easy to compare tools, to work on common case studies, to reuse each other's specifications (especially for APIs), or to use different tools on different parts of the same program. Recently, the ESC/Java approach has received new impetus, by the (open source) upgrade of the system [7]. Through its push-button nature and the quality of its feedback this ESC/Java 2 tool gives Java code developers good reasons to include JML assertions in their work. Theorem prover based approaches can then be reserved for the more difficult "left-overs".

The tools differ a lot in the fragment of Java that they support, and how complicated a specification language they support. Currently, the LOOP tool and ESC/Java 2 probably cover the largest subset of Java, and the LOOP tool probably supports the most complicated specification language.

One distinguishing feature of the LOOP project is that it uses a shallow embedding of Java in PVS. This has both advantages and disadvantages.

An advantage is that is has allowed us to give a completely formal proof of the soundness of all the programming logic we use, inside the theorem prover PVS. Of the projects listed above, only in Bali and LOOP has the soundness of the programming logic been formally proved using a theorem prover. In fact, in the Bali project, where a deep embedding is used, completeness has also been proved, which is hard for a shallow embedding.

A disadvantage of the use of a shallow embedding is that much of the reasoning takes places at the semantic level, rather than the syntactical level, which means that during the proof we have an uglier and, at least initially, less familiar syntax to deal with. Using the LOOP tool and PVS to verify programs requires a high level of expertise in the use of PVS, and an understanding of the way the semantics of Java and JML has been defined.

A difference between LOOP and many of the others approaches (with the possible exception of Bali, we suspect) is in the size of the proof obligations that are produced as input to the theorem prover. The LOOP tool produces a single, big, proof obligation in PVS for every method, and then relies on the capabilities of PVS to reduce this proof obligation into ever smaller ones which we can ultimately prove. Most of the other tools already split up the proof obligation for a single method into smaller chunks (verification conditions) before feeding them to the theorem prover, for instance by using wp-calculi. A drawback of the LOOP approach is that the capabilities of theorem prover become a bottleneck sooner than in the other approaches. After all, there is a limit to the size of proofs that PVS—or any other theorem prover for that matter—can handle before becoming painfully slow or simply crash. Note that this is in a way a consequence of the use of a shallow embedding, and of formalising and proving the correctness of the entire programming logic inside the theorem prover. A drawback of the "early-split" approach is that one may end up with very many separate proof obligations.

7   Perspective

Most of the case studies for which the LOOP tool has been used are so-called Java Card programs designed to run on smart cards. Java Card programs are an excellent target for trying out formal methods, because they are small, their correctness is of crucial importance, and they use only a very limited API (for much of which we have developed a formal specification in JML [33]). Many of the groups working on formal verification for Java are targeting Java Card. Indeed, the JACK tool discussed above has been developed by a commercial smartcard manufacturer.

For examples of such case studies see [3] or [21]. The largest case study to date that has been successfully verified using the LOOP tool and PVS is a Java Card applet of about several hundred lines of code provided by one of the industrial partners in the EU-sponsored VerifiCard project (www.verificard.com). What is interesting about this case study is that it is a real commercial application (so it might be running on your credit card . . .) and that it has gone through the internal evaluation process, but that verification has revealed bugs, albeit bugs that do not compromise the security.

Even if program verification for small programs such as smart card applets is becoming technically possible, this does not mean that it will become feasible to do it an industrial practice. Any industrial use of formal methods will have to be economically justified, by comparing the costs (the extra time and effort spent, not just for verification, but also for developing formal specifications) against the benefits (improvements in quality, number of bugs found). Here, one of the benefits of JML as a specification language is that there is a range of tools that support JML that can be used to develop and check specifications. For example, the JML runtime assertion checker [6] *tests* whether programs meet specifications. This clearly provides less assurance than program verification, but requires a lot less effort, and may provide a very cost-effective way of debugging of code and formal specifications. Similarly, ESC/Java 2 can be used to automatically check for bugs in code and annotations. We believe that having a range of tools, providing different levels of assurance at different costs, is important if one really wants to apply formal methods in practice. For an overview of the different tools for JML, see [4].

Despite the progress in the use of theorem-provers for program verification in the past years, there are still some deep, fundamental, open research problems in the field of program verification for Java or object-oriented programs in general.

Firstly, as already mentioned in Sect. 3.2, the problems caused by references, such as aliasing and the leakage of references, remains a bottleneck in formal verification. One would hope that these problems can be mitigated by introducing suitable notions of ownership or encapsulation.

Another, and somewhat related issue, is how to deal with class invariants. In the paper we have only mentioned pre- and postconditions, and we have ignored the notion of class invariant that JML provides. Class invariants are properties that have to be preserved by all the methods; in other words, all class invariants are implicitly included in the pre- and postcondition of every method. However, there is a lot more to class invariants than this, and class invariants are *not* just a useful abbreviation mechanism. For instance, for more complex object structures, ruling out that methods disturb invariants of other objects is a serious challenge.

Finally, even though security-sensitive smart cards programs provide an interesting application area for program verification, it is usually far from clear what it really means for an application to be 'secure', let alone how to specify this formally. How to specify relevant security properties in a language like JML remains a largely open research question.

Acknowledgements. Thanks to all the former and current members of the LOOP group—Joachim van den Berg, Cees-Bart Breunesse, Ulrich Hensel, Engelbert Hubbers, Marieke Huisman, Joe Kiniry, Hans Meijer, Martijn Oostdijk, Hendrik Tews, and Martijn Warnier—for their contributions.

References

1. J. van den Berg, M. Huisman, B. Jacobs, and E. Poll. A type-theoretic memory model for verification of sequential Java programs. In D. Bert, C. Choppy, and P. Mosses, editors, *Recent Trends in Algebraic Development Techniques*, number 1827 in Lect. Notes Comp. Sci., pages 1–21. Springer, Berlin, 2000.
2. J. van den Berg and B. Jacobs. The LOOP compiler for Java and JML. In T. Margaria and W. Yi, editors, *Tools and Algorithms for the Construction and Analysis of Systems*, number 2031 in Lect. Notes Comp. Sci., pages 299–312. Springer, Berlin, 2001.
3. C.-B. Breunesse, J. van den Berg, and B. Jacobs. Specifying and verifying a decimal representation in Java for smart cards. In H. Kirchner and C. Ringeissen, editors, *Algebraic Methodology and Software Technology*, number 2422 in Lect. Notes Comp. Sci., pages 304–318. Springer, Berlin, 2002.
4. L. Burdy, Y. Cheon, D. Cok, M. Ernst, J. Kiniry, G.T. Leavens, K.R.M. Leino, and E. Poll. An overview of JML tools and applications. In Th. Arts and W. Fokkink, editors, *Formal Methods for Industrial Critical Systems (FMICS 03)*, volume 80 of *Electronic Notes in Theoretical Computer Science (ENTCS)*, pages 73–89. Elsevier, 2003.

5. L. Burdy, A. Requet, and J.-L. Lanet. Java applet correctness: A developer-oriented approach. In K. Araki, S. Gnesi, and D. Mandrioli, editors, *Formal Methods Europe (FME 2003)*, number 2802 in Lect. Notes Comp. Sci., pages 422–439. Springer, Berlin, 2003.

6. Y. Cheon and G.T. Leavens. A runtime assertion checker for the Java Modeling Language (JML). In Hamid R. Arabnia and Youngsong Mun, editors, *the International Conference on Software Engineering Research and Practice (SERP '02)*, pages 322–328. CSREA Press, 2002.

7. ESC/Java2. Open source extended static checking for Java version 2 (ESC/Java 2) project. Security of Systems Group, Univ. of Nijmegen www.cs.kun.nl/ita/research/projects/sos/projects/escjava.html.

8. W. Ahrendt et al. The key tool. Technical report in computing science no. 2003-5, Dept. of Computing Science, Chalmers University and Göteborg University, Göteborg, Sweden, 2003.

9. C. Flanagan, K. R. M. Leino, M. Lillibridge, G. Nelson, J. B. Saxe, and R. Stata. Extended static checking for Java. In *ACM SIGPLAN 2002 Conference on Programming Language Design and Implementation (PLDI'2002)*, pages 234–245, 2002.

10. J. Gosling, B. Joy, G. Steele, and G. Bracha. *The Java Language Specification Second Edition*. The Java Series. Addison-Wesley, 2000. http://java.sun.com/docs/books/jls/second_edition/html/j.title.doc.html.

11. D. Griffioen and M. Huisman. A comparison of PVS and Isabelle/HOL. In J. Grundy and M. Newey, editors, *Theorem Proving in Higher Order Logics*, number 1479 in Lect. Notes Comp. Sci., pages 123–142. Springer, Berlin, 1998.

12. U. Hensel. *Definition and Proof Principles for Data and Processes*. PhD thesis, Techn. Univ. Dresden, Germany, 1999.

13. U. Hensel, M. Huisman, B. Jacobs, and H. Tews. Reasoning about classes in object-oriented languages: Logical models and tools. In Ch. Hankin, editor, *European Symposium on Programming*, number 1381 in Lect. Notes Comp. Sci., pages 105–121. Springer, Berlin, 1998.

14. M. Huisman. *Reasoning about JAVA Programs in higher order logic with PVS and Isabelle*. PhD thesis, Univ. Nijmegen, 2001.

15. M. Huisman and B. Jacobs. Inheritance in higher order logic: Modeling and reasoning. In M. Aagaard and J. Harrison, editors, *Theorem Proving in Higher Order Logics*, number 1869 in Lect. Notes Comp. Sci., pages 301–319. Springer, Berlin, 2000.

16. M. Huisman and B. Jacobs. Java program verification via a Hoare logic with abrupt termination. In T. Maibaum, editor, *Fundamental Approaches to Software Engineering*, number 1783 in Lect. Notes Comp. Sci., pages 284–303. Springer, Berlin, 2000.

17. B. Jacobs. Objects and classes, co-algebraically. In B. Freitag, C.B. Jones, C. Lengauer, and H.-J. Schek, editors, *Object-Orientation with Parallelism and Persistence*, pages 83–103. Kluwer Acad. Publ., 1996.

18. B. Jacobs. Java's integral types in PVS. In E. Najim, U. Nestmann, and P. Stevens, editors, *Formal Methods for Open Object-Based Distributed Systems (FMOODS 2003)*, number 2884 in Lect. Notes Comp. Sci., pages 1–15. Springer, Berlin, 2003.

19. B. Jacobs. Weakest precondition reasoning for Java programs with JML annotations. *Journ. of Logic and Algebraic Programming*, 58:61–88, 2004.

20. B. Jacobs, J. Kiniry, and M. Warnier. Java program verification challenges. In F. de Boer, M. Bonsangue, S. Graf, and W.-P. de Roever, editors, *Formal Methods for Components and Objects (FMCO 2002)*, number 2852 in Lect. Notes Comp. Sci., pages 202–219. Springer, Berlin, 2003.

21. B. Jacobs, M. Oostdijk, and M. Warnier. Source code verification of a secure payment applet. *Journ. of Logic and Algebraic Programming*, 58:107–120, 2004.

22. B. Jacobs and E. Poll. Coalgebras and monads in the semantics of Java. *Theor. Comp. Sci.*, 291(3):329–349, 2003.

23. B. Jacobs, J. van den Berg, M. Huisman, M. van Berkum, U. Hensel, and H. Tews. Reasoning about classes in Java (preliminary report). In *Object-Oriented Programming, Systems, Languages and Applications (OOPSLA)*, pages 329–340. ACM Press, 1998.

24. G.T. Leavens, A.L. Baker, and C. Ruby. JML: A notation for detailed design. In H. Kilov and B. Rumpe, editors, *Behavioral Specifications of Business and Systems*, pages 175–188. Kluwer, 1999.

25. G.T. Leavens, Y. Cheon, , C. Clifton, C. Ruby, and D.R. Cok. How the design of JML accommodates both runtime assertion checking and formal verification. In F. de Boer, M. Bonsangue, S. Graf, and W.-P. de Roever, editors, *Formal Methods for Components and Objects (FMCO 2002)*, number 2852 in Lect. Notes Comp. Sci., pages 262–284. Springer, Berlin, 2003.

26. G. Malcolm. Behavioural equivalence, bisimulation and minimal realisation. In M. Haveraaen, O. Owe, and O.J. Dahl, editors, *Recent Trends in Data Type Specification*, number 1130 in Lect. Notes Comp. Sci., pages 359–378. Springer, Berlin, 1996.

27. C. Marché, C. Paulin, and X. Urbain. The KRAKATOA tool for certification of JAVA/JAVACARD programs annotated in JML. *Journ. of Logic and Algebraic Programming*, 58:89–106, 2004.

28. J. Meyer and A. Poetzsch-Heffter. An architecture for interactive program provers. In S. Graf and M. Schwartzbach, editors, *Tools and Algorithms for the Construction and Analysis of Systems*, number 1785 in Lect. Notes Comp. Sci., pages 63–77. Springer, Berlin, 2000.

29. P. Müller, A. Poetzsch-Heffter, and G. T. Leavens. Modular specification of frame properties in JML. *Concurrency and Computation: Practice and Experience*, 15(2):117–154, 2003.

30. Tobias Nipkow, Lawrence C. Paulson, and Markus Wenzel. *Isabelle/HOL — A Proof Assistant for Higher-Order Logic*, volume 2283 of *LNCS*. Springer, 2002.

31. D. von Oheimb and T. Nipkow. Hoare logic for NanoJava: Auxiliary variables, side effects and virtual methods revisited. In L.-H. Eriksson and P. Lindsay, editors, *Formal Methods – Getting IT Right (FME'02)*, volume 2391 of *LNCS*, pages 89–105. Spinger Verlag, 2002.

32. S. Owre, S. Rajan, J.M. Rushby, N. Shankar, and M. Srivas. PVS: Combining specification, proof checking, and model checking. In R. Alur and T.A. Henzinger, editors, *Computer Aided Verification*, number 1102 in Lect. Notes Comp. Sci., pages 411–414. Springer, Berlin, 1996.

33. E. Poll, J. van den Berg, and B. Jacobs. Formal specification of the JavaCard API in JML: the APDU class. *Computer Networks*, 36(4):407–421, 2001.

34. H. Reichel. An approach to object semantics based on terminal co-algebras. *Math. Struct. in Comp. Sci.*, 5:129–152, 1995.
35. J. Rothe, H. Tews, and B. Jacobs. The coalgebraic class specification language CCSL. *Journ. of Universal Comp. Sci.*, 7(2), 2001.
36. H. Tews. *Coalgebraic Methods for Object-Oriented Specification.* PhD thesis, Techn. Univ. Dresden, Germany, 2002.

Decision Procedures for Several Properties of Reactive System Specifications

Noriaki Yoshiura

Computer Center, Gunma University,
1-5-1, Tenjin-cho, Kiryu City,
Gunma Prefecture, Japan
Tel:+81-277-30-1160, Fax:+81-277-30-1169
yoshiura@lab.cc.gunma-u.ac.jp
http://www.lab.cc.gunma-u.ac.jp/

Abstract. Reactive systems, such as operating systems or elevator control systems, are systems that ideally never terminate and are intended to maintain some interaction with their environment. Temporal logic is one of the methods for formal specification descriptions of reactive systems. By describing the formal specifications of reactive systems we can check the consistency of the specifications and whether they contain defects. By using a synthesis algorithm we also obtain reactive system programs from the formal specifications and prevent programming bugs. Therefore, it is important to describe reactive system formal specifications to secure reactive system programs. However, it is difficult to describe realizable reactive system specifications and it is important to revise unrealizable reactive system specifications into realizable reactive system specifications. In previous research, three properties have been introduced into unrealizable reactive system specifications. By using these properties, we can acquire more detailed information about the cause of the defects of unrealizable reactive system specifications in the specification description process. In this paper, we propose decision procedures that judge whether a reactive system specification has these properties. We also prove the soundness and completeness of these procedures.

Keywords: Reactive System, Temporal Logic, Specification Description.

1   Introduction

Since the publication of a landmark paper on the subject [1], numerous attempts have been made to apply temporal logic to computer science [2]. Among the many applications of temporal logic are the specification and synthesis of reactive systems[3, 4]. Reactive systems, such as operating systems or elevator control systems, are systems which ideally never terminate and are intended to maintain some interaction with their environment. Temporal logic is well suited for describing and reasoning reactive systems.

The realizability problem was first reported in references [5] and [6]. Both of these references, however, impose a restriction: objects are not allowed to interact with their environment. Systems with this restriction are called closed systems. In this case, realizability is equivalent to satisfiability. This restriction was removed in the descriptions of

K. Futatsugi et al. (Eds.): ISSS 2003, LNCS 3233, pp. 154–173, 2004.
© Springer-Verlag Berlin Heidelberg 2004

the problem in references [4] and [7], which consider open systems, which are allowed to interact with their environment. In this case, realizability is not simply equivalent to satisfiability, but stronger than it. For a reactive system specification to be satisfiable requires that there exists behavior which satisfies the specification. A behavior of a reactive system consists of an input event sequence from its environment and an output event sequence from the system. Since systems cannot control their environment, the realizability of a reactive system specification requires the existence of a system which satisfies the specification for every possible input event sequence. This condition is, of course, stronger than that of satisfiability.

A number of different studies into reactive systems have been undertaken. The study detailed in reference [8] focused on asynchronous systems and that in reference [3] introduced different concepts of realizability. Although the decision algorithm of these concepts were not given in reference [3], a decision algorithm for realizability under fairness has been given in references [9] and [10]. Reference [11] studies realizability in the circumstance where systems acquire incomplete information of the environment. The synthesis of reactive system has been studied in several frameworks. References [4] and [7] present a realizability checking algorithm based on an automata theoretic method. In this method, in order to examine the realizability of a reactive system specification, we construct a tree-automaton in the infinite trees language from the specifications, such that every infinite tree accepted by the automaton represents specified behavior for every possible input event sequence. Then, by checking whether there exists an infinite tree language accepted by the automaton, we can determine the realizability of the specification. This method also synthesizes programs of reactive systems.

Hence, several studies have been undertaken on the program synthesis problem. However, specifications from which programs cannot be synthesized, i.e. unrealizable specifications, have been little researched. The discovery and correction of defects in specifications is an important element of software processes like the program synthesis problem and describing a realizable program specification is necessary for program synthesis. However, it is difficult to describe realizable specifications. Describing realizable specifications requires finding the defects of the described specification and correcting them. In this process of revising a described unrealizable specification, it is important to clarify what properties the specification has or how much the specification is separated from realizability. For the classification of unrealizable specifications, three properties were introduced in reference [12], strong satisfiability, stepwise satisfiability, and stepwise strong satisfiability. Based on these classifications, we can analyze why specifications become unrealizable and classify specifications which are satisfiable but unrealizable into five classes.

In reference [12], judgment procedures of these properties were given, but they are not sound or complete. In this paper, we give procedures for judging whether a specification fills these three properties and prove that these procedures are sound and complete. The judgment procedures use the tableau method and graphs (deterministic tableau), which are obtained by making a tableau deterministic by a set of input event propositions or a set of input and output event propositions.

This paper is organized as follows: Section 2 presents a definition of reactive systems and Section 3 shows a method for specification descriptions of reactive systems.

Section 4 presents several properties of reactive system specifications. Section 5 presents decision procedures of these properties. Section 6 proves the soundness and completeness of these procedures. Section 7 concludes this paper.

2   Reactive System

This section provides a formal definition of a reactive system, based on references [4] and [12].

Let A be a finite set. A^+ and A^ω denote the set of *finite sequences* and the set of *infinite sequences* over A respectively. $A^\dagger$ denotes $A^+ \cup A^\omega$. Sequences in $A^\dagger$ are indicated by $\hat{a}, \hat{b}, \cdots$, sequences in A^+ by $\bar{a}, \bar{b}, \cdots$ and sequences in A^ω by $\tilde{a}, \tilde{b}, \cdots$. $|\hat{a}|$ denotes the *length* of $\hat{a}$ and $\hat{a}[i]$ denotes the *i-th element* of $\hat{a}$. If B is a set whose elements are also sets, '$\sqcup$' is defined over $B^\dagger \times B^\dagger$ by

$$\hat{a} \sqcup \hat{b} = \hat{a}[0] \cup \hat{b}[0], \hat{a}[1] \cup \hat{b}[1], \hat{a}[2] \cup \hat{b}[2], \cdots.$$

Finally, the *infinity set* of $\tilde{a} \in A^\omega$ is defined by

$$inf(\tilde{a}) = \{a \in A \mid a \text{ occurs infinitely often in } \tilde{a}\}.$$

Definition 1. *A reactive system RS is a triple $RS = \langle X, Y, r \rangle$, where*

- *X is a finite set of input events produced by the environment.*
- *Y ($X \cap Y = \emptyset$) is a finite set of output events produced by the system itself.*
- *$r : (2^X)^+ \to 2^Y$ is a reaction function.*

A subset of X is called an *input set* and a sequence of input sets is called an *input sequence*. Similarly, a subset of Y is called an *output set* and a sequence of output sets is called an *output sequence*. In this paper, a reaction function corresponds to a reactive system program.

Definition 2. *Let $RS = \langle X, Y, r \rangle$ be a reactive system and $\hat{a} = a_0, a_1, a_2, \cdots \in (2^X)^\dagger$ be an input sequence. The behavior of RS for $\hat{a}$, denoted $behav_{RS}(\hat{a})$, is the following sequence:*

$$behav_{RS}(\hat{a}) = \langle a_0, b_0 \rangle, \langle a_1, b_1 \rangle, \langle a_2, b_2 \rangle, \ldots,$$

where for each i ($0 \le i < |\hat{a}|$), $b_i = r(a_0, \ldots, a_i) \in 2^Y$.

3   Specification

We use propositional linear-time temporal logic (PLTL) as a specification language for reactive systems.

3.1   Syntax

A PLTL *formula* is defined as follows:

- An atomic proposition $p \in \mathscr{P}$ is a formula.
- If f_1 and f_2 are formulas, then $f_1 \wedge f_2$, $\neg f_1$ $f_1 U f_2$ are formulas.

We use $\Box f_1$ as the abbreviation of $f_1 U (f_2 \wedge \neg f_2)$. $\Box f_1$ means that f_1 always holds. We also use $\Diamond f_1$ as the abbreviation of $\neg \Box \neg f_1$. $\Diamond f_1$ means that f_1 eventually holds. $\vee$, $\rightarrow$ and $\leftrightarrow$ are the usual abbreviations.

3.2 Semantics

A *structure* for a PLTL formula is a triple $M = \langle S, R, \pi \rangle$, where

- S is a countable set of *states*.
- $R : S \rightarrow S$ is a *successor function* that gives a unique next state for each state.
- $\pi : S \rightarrow 2^{\mathscr{P}}$ is a *labeling function* that assigns truth values to the atomic propositions in each state.

The relation "f holds at s in M", denoted by $\langle M, s \rangle \models f$, is defined inductively as follows:

- $\langle M, s \rangle \models p$ **iff** $p \in \pi(s)$.
- $\langle M, s \rangle \models f_1 \wedge f_2$ **iff** $\langle M, s \rangle \models f_1$ and $\langle M, s \rangle \models f_2$.
- $\langle M, s \rangle \models \neg f$ **iff** not $\langle M, s \rangle \models f$.
- $\langle M, s \rangle \models f_1 U f_2$ **iff**
$$(\forall i \geq 0) \; \langle M, R^i(s) \rangle \models f_1 \text{ or}$$
$$(\exists i \geq 0) \; \big(\langle M, R^i(s) \rangle \models f_2 \text{ and}$$
$$\forall k \, (0 \leq k < i \text{ implies } \langle M, R^k(s) \rangle \models f_1) \big).$$

An *interpretation* is a pair $I = \langle M, s \rangle$, where $M = \langle S, R, \pi \rangle$ is a structure and s is a state in S. An interpretation I is a *model* for f if $I \models f$. We say that f is *satisfiable* if there exists a model for f.

3.3 Specification

A *PLTL-specification* for a reactive system is a triple $Spec = \langle \mathscr{X}, \mathscr{Y}, \varphi \rangle$, where

- $\mathscr{X}$ is a set of *input propositions* that are atomic propositions corresponding to the input events of the intended reactive system, i.e. the truth value of an input proposition represents the occurrence of the corresponding input event.
- $\mathscr{Y}$ is a set of *output propositions* that are atomic propositions corresponding to the output events of the intended reactive system, i.e. the truth value of an output proposition represents the occurrence of the corresponding output event.
- φ is a formula in which all the atomic propositions are elements of $\mathscr{X} \cup \mathscr{Y}$.

For simplicity, we write $Spec = \langle \mathscr{X}, \mathscr{Y}, \varphi \rangle$ just as φ if there is no confusion. We identify an infinite sequence of event sets $\tilde{e} \in (2^{X \cup Y})^{\omega}$ with the interpretation $I = \langle \langle S, R, \pi \rangle, s \rangle$ that satisfies the following condition:

$$\text{for every } i \geq 0, e \in \tilde{e}[i] \text{ iff } e' \in \pi(R^i(s)),$$

where e' is the atomic proposition that corresponds to event e. Accordingly, we extend the use of "$\models$" so that a sequence of event sets can be on the left of "$\models$". For example, $behav_{RS}(\tilde{a}) \models \varphi$ means that the interpretation represented by $behav_{RS}(\tilde{a})$ is a model of φ.

Finally, we define the realizability of reactive system specifications [4, 12].

Definition 3. *A reactive system RS is an implementation of a specification φ if for every input sequence ã, behav$_{RS}$(ã) ⊨ φ. A specification is realizable if it has an implementation.*

4   Classification of Reactive System Specification

In this section, we describe other properties of specifications, *strong satisfiability, stepwise satisfiability* and *stepwise strong satisfiability*. These properties are introduced in references [12] and [13]. We explain those properties by showing examples of simple specifications. Throughout this section ã, ā and $\tilde{b}$ denote an infinite input sequence, a finite input sequence and an infinite output sequence respectively. Also, *r* denotes a reaction function. For simplicity the interpretation representing a behavior is denoted by the behavior itself.

First, we define strong satisfiability.

Definition 4. *φ is strongly satisfiable if* $\forall \tilde{a} \exists \tilde{b}$, $\tilde{a} \sqcup \tilde{b} \models \varphi$ *holds.*

We now explain the meaning of strong satisfiability. In reactive systems, input events are made by the environment and not by the reactive system. If a reactive system is realizable, then for any infinite input event sequence, there is an infinite output event sequence made by the reactive system. Thus, this strong satisfiability is a necessary condition of realizability. We can show that strong satisfiability is not a sufficient condition as follows. We suppose that φ is strong satisfiable. For each infinite input event sequence, we can find an infinite output event sequence from the infinite event sequence such that φ is satisfied. However, the reactive system must produce an output event from the input event sequence until the current time but not from the infinite event sequence. Therefore strong satisfiability does not guarantee that reactive systems behave so that φ is satisfied. Later, we will explain strong satisfiability by using some examples.

Next, we define stepwise satisfiability and stepwise strong satisfiability.

Definition 5. *A reactive system RS preserves satisfiability of φ if it satisfies the following condition:*

$$\forall \bar{a} \exists \tilde{a} \exists \tilde{b}, \ \bar{a}\tilde{a} \sqcup behav_{RS}(\bar{a})\tilde{b} \models \varphi.$$

φ is stepwisely satisfiable if there is a reactive system which preserves the satisfiability of φ.

Definition 6. *A reactive system RS preserves strong satisfiability of φ if it satisfies the following condition:*

$$\forall \bar{a} \forall \tilde{a} \exists \tilde{b}, \ \bar{a}\tilde{a} \sqcup behav_{RS}(\bar{a})\tilde{b} \models \varphi.$$

φ is stepwisely strongly satisfiable if there is a reactive system which preserves the strong satisfiability of φ.

We now explain the meaning of stepwise satisfiability. If φ is stepwise satisfiable, then there is a reactive system $RS = \langle X, Y, r \rangle$ which preserves the satisfiability of φ. For any input event sequence, the reactive system RS can behave and there is always a possibility that φ is satisfied even though RS actually does not satisfy φ. The meaning of stepwise strong satisfiability is the same as that of stepwise satisfiability.

Now we show some examples of specifications to explain the properties above. See also Figure 1.

EXAMPLE 1. *Satisfiable but neither stepwisely satisfiable nor strongly satisfiable specification.*

1. $req_1 \rightarrow \Diamond res$.
2. $req_2 \rightarrow \Box \neg res$.

This example shows that a specification is neither stepwisely satisfiable nor strongly satisfiable if it could require conflicting responses at the same time.

EXAMPLE 2. *Stepwisely satisfiable but not strongly satisfiable specification.*

This example shows a part of a simple lift specification. In the specification below, an output proposition *Move* is intended to show when the lift can move. *Open* means that the lift door is open, and $Floor_i$ means that the lift is on the i-th floor. An input proposition B_{open} represents the request "open the door" and B_i represents the request "come or go to the i-th floor."

1. $\Box(\neg Move \wedge Floor_i \rightarrow Floor_i \, U \, Move)$.
   (if *Move* is not true when the lift is at the i-th floor, stay there until *Move* holds)
2. $\Box(Open \rightarrow \neg Move)$.
   (if the door is open, do not move)
3. $\Box\big(\neg B_{open} \wedge (\neg Move \, U \, B_{open}) \rightarrow [B_{open} \Rightarrow \neg B_{open}] \, Open\big)$.
   (if *Move* is not true, open the door while B_{open} holds)
4. $\Box(B_i \rightarrow \Diamond Floor_i)$.
   (if asked to come or go to the i-th floor, eventually arrive at the floor)

If B_{open} will be true forever after some state where both $\neg Move$ and $Floor_i$ hold, and $B_{j(\neq i)}$ will be true after this state, $\Diamond Floor_j$ could never be satisfied. This example shows that a specification is not strongly satisfiable if for some infinite input sequence a $\Diamond$-formula has no opportunity to hold.

EXAMPLE 3. *Strongly satisfiable but not stepwisely satisfiable specification.*

1. $(req_1 \, U \, req_2) \leftrightarrow res$.

This example shows that a specification is not stepwisely satisfiable if it could require a response depending on the future sequences of requests.

EXAMPLE 4. *Stepwisely satisfiable and strongly satisfiable but not stepwisely strongly satisfiable specification.*

1. $\Diamond req \leftrightarrow res$.

This example shows that a specification is not stepwisely strongly satisfiable if it could require a response to the future occurrence of a request. The difference between EXAMPLE 3 and EXAMPLE 4 is that the truth value of the negation of $\Diamond$ *req* in EXAMPLE 4 could not be known in the finite states while the truth value of both of req_1 U req_2 and its negation could be known in the finite states. In fact, in EXAMPLE 4, if the truth value of *res* is *true* in the first state, the satisfiability of the specification will be preserved against every finite input sequence since $\neg \Diamond$ *req* could not be known in the finite states.

EXAMPLE 5. *Stepwisely strongly satisfiable but not realizable specification.*
   This example describes a specification for a system intended to train dogs to respond to beep by barking.

1. $\Box \Diamond$ *bark* $\rightarrow$ (a) $\land$ (b) $\land$ (c) $\land$ (d), where
   (a) : $\Box \Diamond feed$.
   (b) : $\Box \Diamond beep \land \Box \Diamond \neg beep$.
   (c) : $\Box (beep \rightarrow \neg feed)$.
   (d) : $\Box \left(\left(beep \land \neg (beep\, U\, (\neg beep \land bark)) \right) \leftrightarrow [\neg beep \Rightarrow beep]\, \neg feed \right)$.

In the following structure, where *beep* holds at the states represented by • and not at the other states,

$$beep \land \neg (beep\, U\, (\neg beep \land bark)) \text{ ——— } (*)$$

in (d) holds at each • before $\otimes$ if and only if the dog does not bark at $\otimes$.

$$\cdots \rightarrow \circ \rightarrow \bullet \rightarrow \bullet \rightarrow \bullet \rightarrow \otimes \rightarrow \circ \rightarrow \circ \rightarrow \cdots$$

If $(*)$ holds, the system does not feed the dog as a penalty until the next trial. Note that the dog is not required to wait until *beep* becomes false. Barking before the end of *beep* is sufficient to be fed since *beep* is an output proposition and thus the value of *beep* at some state depends on the values of the input propositions (in this case, *bark*) at the same state. Recall the definitions of a reaction function and the behavior of a reactive system.
   If a dog will never bark after some state, the system can never satisfy the consequent of 1. $\Box \Diamond$ *bark* in 1 excludes such dogs[1].
   This specification is strongly satisfiable since for every input sequence, there *exists* a behavior that satisfies the specification. A reaction function that satisfies (c) and (d) preserves the strong satisfiability of the specification. Therefore, the specification is also stepwisely strongly satisfiable. It is not realizable, however, since for every reaction function, there is a dog that will never be trained, i.e., there exists an input sequence against which the behavior of the reactive system does not satisfy the specification.

---

[1] Without $\Box \Diamond bark$ in 1, the specification loses the strong satisfiability.

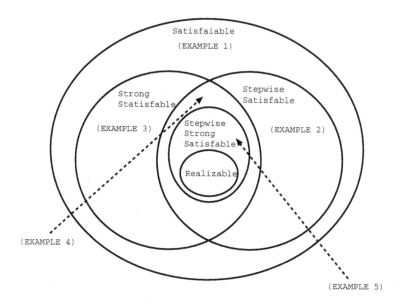

Fig. 1. The classifications of specifications: The figure also shows classes that the example specifications belong to

The difference between EXAMPLE 2 and EXAMPLE 4 is in the way that a $\Diamond$-formula loses the opportunity to hold. In EXAMPLE 2, $\Diamond Floor_i$ loses the opportunity depending *only on the input sequence*. In EXAMPLE 4, however, $\Diamond feed$ loses the opportunity depending on *both the input sequence and output sequence*. In other words, $\Diamond Floor_i$ always loses the opportunity against a specific input sequence, while $\Diamond feed$ does not always lose the opportunity against any input sequence.

5   Decision Procedures

In reference [12], judgment procedures of strong satisfiability, stepwise satisfiability and stepwise strong satisfiability were given, but they are not sound or complete. Especially, the procedure in reference [12] judges that some stepwise satisfiable formulae is not stepwise satisfiable. For example, $(y_1 U y_2) \vee x$ is stepwise satisfiable, however, the procedure in reference [12] judges it is not stepwise satisfiable, where y_1 and y_2 are the input propositions and x is the output proposition. In reference [12], the judgment procedures of stepwise satisfiability and stepwise strong satisfiability does not make a tableau deterministic by a set of input and output propositions. However, we think such a determination of a tableau is necessary for deciding stepwise satisfiability or stepwise strong satisfiability. This determination of a tableau is main difference between the procedures of this paper and those of reference [12].

Thus, this section gives the revised decision procedures of strong satisfiability, stepwise satisfiability and stepwise strong satisfiability.

These procedures are based on the tableau method for PLTL [12, 13]. To begin, we describe the tableau method. This tableau method is based in [2, 7].

5.1   Tableau Method

A tableau is a directed graph $T = \langle N, E \rangle$ constructed from a given specification, where

- N is a finite set of nodes. Each node is a set of formulas.
- E is a finite set of edges. Each edge is a pair of nodes. If $\langle n_1, n_2 \rangle \in E$, we say that n_2 is directly reachable from n_1.

If $\langle n_1, a_1 \rangle, \langle a_1, a_2 \rangle, \cdots \langle a_k, n_2 \rangle \in E$, we say that n_2 is reachable from n_1 or that n_1 reaches n_2 in a tableau $\langle N, E \rangle$.

Definition 7 (Decomposition Procedure). *A decomposition procedure takes a set S of formulas as input and produces a set Σ of sets of formulas.*

1. *Put $\Sigma = \{S\}$.*
2. *Repeatedly apply one of steps (a) – (e) to all the formulas f_{ij} in all the sets $S_i \in \Sigma$ according to the type of the formulas until no step will change Σ. In the following, $f_1 U^* f_2$ and $\neg(f_1 U^* f_2)$ are called marked formula. The marked formulae represents that the marked formulae have been applied by the decomposition produce. We use marked formulae to find that whether the formulae have been applied by the decomposition produce or not.*
   (a) *If f_{ij} is $\neg\neg f$, replace S_i with the following set: $(S_i - \{f_{ij}\}) \cup \{f\}$.*
   (b) *If f_{ij} is $f_1 \wedge f_2$, replace S_i with the following set: $(S_i - \{f_{ij}\}) \cup \{f_1, f_2\}$.*
   (c) *If f_{ij} is $\neg(f_1 \wedge f_2)$, replace S_i with the following two sets:*
       $(S_i - \{f_{ij}\}) \cup \{\neg f_1\}$,
       $(S_i - \{f_{ij}\}) \cup \{\neg f_2\}$.
   (d) *If f_{ij} is $f_1 U f_2$, replace S_i with the following two sets:*
       $(S_i - \{f_{ij}\}) \cup \{f_2\}$,
       $(S_i - \{f_{ij}\}) \cup \{\neg f_1, f_2, f_1 U^* f_2\}$.
   (e) *If f_{ij} is $\neg(f_1 U f_2)$ replace S_i with the following two sets:*
       $(S_i - \{f_{ij}\}) \cup \{\neg f_1, \neg f_2\}$,
       $(S_i - \{f_{ij}\}) \cup \{\neg f_2, \neg(f_1 U^* f_2)\}$.

Definition 8. *A node n of a tableau $\langle N, E \rangle$ is closed if and only if one of the following conditions is satisfied:*

- *n contains both an atomic proposition and its negation.*
- *n contains an eventuality formula [2] and all reachable unclosed nodes from n contain the same eventuality formula.*
- *n cannot reach any unclosed node.*

---

[2] An eventuality formula is a formula of the form $\neg(f_1 U f_2)$.

Next, we describe the tableau construction procedure that repeatedly uses the decomposition procedure. The tableau construction procedure takes a PLTL formula φ as input and produces a tableau $T = \langle N, E \rangle$. In the procedure, a function $temporal(n)$ is used and defined as follows.

$temporal(n) =$
$\{f_1 U f_2 \mid f_1 U^* f_2 \in n\} \cup \{\neg(f_1 U f_2) \mid \neg(f_1 U^* f_2) \in n\}$

Definition 9 (Tableau Construction Procedure). *The tableau construction procedure takes a formula φ as input and produces a tableau of φ.*

1. *Put $N = \{START, \{\varphi\}\}$ and $E = \{\langle START, \{\varphi\}\rangle\}$ (START is the initial node).*
2. *Repeatedly apply steps (a) and (b) to $T = \langle N, E \rangle$ until they no longer change T.*
   (a) *(decomposition of states) Apply the following three steps to all the nodes $n_i \in N$ to which these steps have not been applied yet.*
      i. *Apply the decomposition procedure to n_i (we refer to the output of the decomposition procedure by Σ_{n_i}),*
      ii. *Replace E by the following set:*
          $(E \cup \{\langle m, m' \rangle \mid \langle m, n_i \rangle \in E \text{ and } m' \in \Sigma_{n_i}\}) - \{\langle m, n_i \rangle \mid m \in N\},$
      iii. *Replace N with the following set: $(N - n_i) \cup \Sigma_{n_i}$.*
   (b) *(transition of states) Apply the following two steps to all the nodes $n_i \in N$ to which these steps have not been applied yet.*
      i. *Replace E with the following set:*
          $E \cup \{\langle n_i, temporal(n_i) \rangle\}.$
      ii. *Replace N with the following set:*
          $N \cup \{temporal(n_i)\}.$

In [2, 7], it is proved that a formula is satisfiable if and only if the initial node $START$ of the tableau of the formula is unclosed. Thus, we decide the satisfiability of the formula φ by the following procedure.

Definition 10 (Tableau Method). *The following procedure decides whether a formula φ is satisfiable.*

1. *By Tableau Construction Procedure, construct a tableau of a formula φ*
2. *If the tableau of the formula φ is unclosed, then we decide that the formula φ is satisfiable. Otherwise, we decide that the formula φ is unsatisfiable.*

Example: Figure 2 shows the tableau of the specification

$$\varphi : y \leftrightarrow x_1 \, \mathcal{U} \, x_2.$$

In this example, $START$ of the tableau is unclosed. Thus, $y \leftrightarrow x_1 \, \mathcal{U} \, x_2$ is satisfiable.

5.2   Decision Procedures for Several Properties

We describe here the decision procedures of strong satisfiability, stepwise satisfiability and stepwise strong satisfiability.

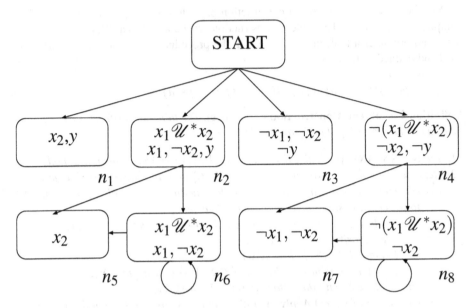

Fig. 2. The tableau of $y \leftrightarrow x_1 \, \mathcal{U} \, x_2$

In these procedures it is important to make a tableau deterministic. In order to judge strong satisfiability it is necessary to make a tableau deterministic by a set of input propositions. With respect to stepwise satisfiability and stepwise strong satisfiability, it is necessary to make a tableau deterministic by a set of input and output propositions.

To begin, we give some functions for a deterministic tableau.

Definition 11. *Let $T = \langle N, E \rangle$ be a tableau. The function $next(\mathbf{n})$ maps a subset of N to a subset of N, where $\mathbf{n}$ is a subset of N. The function $next(\mathbf{n})$ is defined as follows:*

$next(\mathbf{n}) \equiv \bigcup_{n \in \mathbf{n}} \{n' \mid \langle n, n' \rangle \in E\}$

The function atm and $\overline{atm}$ map an element of N to a set of atomic propositions. The function atm and $\overline{atm}$ are defined as follows:

$atm(n) \equiv \{f \mid f \in n \text{ and } f \text{ is atomic formula.}\}$
$\overline{atm}(n) \equiv \{f \mid \neg f \in n \text{ and } f \text{ is atomic formula.}\}$

Next, we define a deterministic tableau.

Definition 12 (Deterministic Tableau). *Let $\langle N, E \rangle$ be a tableau of specification φ. $\langle \mathcal{N}, \mathcal{E} \rangle$ is a deterministic tableau of φ and a set P of atomic propositions if and only if the following conditions are satisfied.*

- *$\mathcal{N}$ is a set of tableau node sets, that is $\mathcal{N} \subseteq 2^N$.*
- *Every element of $\mathcal{N}$ is not an empty set.*
- *$\mathcal{E}$ is a set of $\langle \mathbf{n}_1, a, \mathbf{n}_2 \rangle$ such that $\mathbf{n}_1, \mathbf{n}_2 \in \mathcal{N}$ and non-empty set $a \subseteq P$.*
- *If $\langle \mathbf{n}', a, \mathbf{n} \rangle \in \mathcal{E}$, then $a \cap \overline{atm}(\mathbf{n}) = \emptyset$ and $(P - a) \cap atm(\mathbf{n}) = \emptyset$*
- *If $\langle \mathbf{n}_1, a, \mathbf{n}_2 \rangle \in \mathcal{E}$, then for $n \in \mathbf{n}_2$, there is $n' \in \mathbf{n}_1$ such that $\langle n', n \rangle \in E$.*

We note that there are several deterministic tableaux for one specification. Next, we define a procedure for constructing a deterministic tableau that is used in the decision procedure of strong satisfiability, stepwise satisfiability and stepwise strong satisfiability. We note that the following tableau deterministic procedure constructs one of the deterministic tableaux of specification φ and a set P of atomic propositions, but not all of the deterministic tableaux.

Definition 13 (Tableau Deterministic Procedure). *The following procedure constructs a deterministic tableau* $\mathcal{T} = \langle \mathcal{N}, \mathcal{E} \rangle$ *of specification of* φ *and a set P of atomic propositions.*

1. *Construct tableau* $\langle N, E \rangle$ *of* φ *by the tableau construction procedure.*
2. *Set* $\mathcal{N} = \{START\}$ *and* $\mathcal{E} = \emptyset$.
3. *Repeat the following step until* $\mathcal{T}$ *no longer changes.*
   For $n \in \mathcal{N}$ *and* $a \in P$, *if* $next(n)/a$ *is not* $\emptyset$, *then add* $next(\mathbf{n})/a$ *into* $\mathcal{N}$ *and* $\langle \mathbf{n}, a, next(\mathbf{n})/a \rangle$ *into* $\mathcal{E}$, *where* $next(\mathbf{n})/a \equiv \{n \in next(\mathbf{n}) \mid a \cap \overline{atm}(n) = \emptyset, (P - a) \cap atm(n) = \emptyset\}$.

By using a deterministic tableau, we can judge whether there is a reactive system *RS* of φ such that *RS* behaves for an input event at any time, or whether there is an infinite output event sequence for any infinite input event sequence. However, we cannot judge satisfiability of φ using a deterministic tableau, and for checking the satisfiability of φ it is necessary to examine each part of a tableau included in the deterministic tableau. Next we define subtableau for this.

Definition 14. *Let* $\langle N, E \rangle$ *be the tableau of specification* φ. $\langle N', E' \rangle$ *is a subtableau of* φ *if and only if all of the following conditions are satisfied.*

1. $N' \subseteq N$,
2. $E' \subseteq E$,
3. *If* $\langle n_1, n_2 \rangle \in E'$, *then* $n_1, n_2 \in N'$,
4. $\langle N', E' \rangle$ *is strongly connected.*

Definition 15. *Let* $T = \langle N, E \rangle$ *be a subtableau of* φ *and* $\mathcal{T} = \langle \mathcal{N}, \mathcal{E} \rangle$ *be a deterministic tableau of* φ *and a set P of atomic propositions. We say that* $\mathcal{T}$ *includes T if and only if the following condition is satisfied.*

– *If* $\langle n, n' \rangle \in E$, *then there is a set a of propositions such that* $\langle \mathbf{n}, a, \mathbf{n}' \rangle \in \mathcal{E}$ *and that* $n \in \mathbf{n}$ *and* $n' \in \mathbf{n}'$.

A subtableau $\langle N, E \rangle$ *is closed if and only if all the elements of N include the same eventuality formula. If a subtableau is not closed, then we say that it is open.*

We consider that tracing the edges of a deterministic tableau corresponds to a behavior of a reactive system of φ. Since nodes and edges of a deterministic tableau are finite, each behavior of a reactive system of φ corresponds to a strong connected subgraph of a deterministic tableau of φ. In order to judge whether φ is satisfied in a behavior of a reactive system of φ, we obtain a strong connected subgraph of the deterministic tableau of φ corresponding to this behavior and check whether we can get an open subtableau included in this strong connected subgraph of the deterministic tableau. For this, we give the following definition.

Definition 16 (Same Path). Let $\mathcal{T} = \langle \mathcal{N}, \mathcal{E} \rangle$ be a deterministic tableau of specification φ, and $T_1 = \langle N_1, E_1 \rangle$ and $T_2 = \langle N_2, E_2 \rangle$ be subtableaux of $\langle \mathcal{N}, \mathcal{E} \rangle$. We say that T_1 and T_2 have the same path of $\mathcal{T}$ if and only if all of the following conditions are satisfied.

1. For each $n_1 \in N_1$, there are $\mathbf{n} \in \mathcal{N}$ and a node $n_2 \in N_2$ such that $n_1, n_2 \in \mathbf{n}$.
2. For each $n_2 \in N_2$, there are $\mathbf{n} \in \mathcal{N}$ and a node $n_1 \in N_1$ such that $n_1, n_2 \in \mathbf{n}$.
3. If $\langle n_1, n_1' \rangle \in E_1$, then there are $n_2, n_2' \in N_2$ and $\mathbf{n}, \mathbf{n}' \in \mathcal{N}$ such that
   - $n_1, n_2 \in \mathbf{n},\ n_1', n_2' \in \mathbf{n}'$,
   - $\langle n_2, n_2' \rangle \in E_2$ and
   - $\langle \mathbf{n}, a, \mathbf{n}' \rangle \in \mathcal{E}$.

Let T be a subtableau of a deterministic tableau $\mathcal{T}$. By definition, the behavior corresponding to the trace of T satisfies φ if and only if there is a subtableau T' such that T' is open and that T and T' have the same path of $\mathcal{T}$.

Next, we give decision procedures of strong satisfiability, stepwise satisfiability and stepwise strong satisfiability. The soundness and completeness of these decision procedures will be proved in the next section.

Definition 17 (Decision Procedure of Strong Satisfiability). *The following procedure decides whether a specification φ is strongly satisfiable.*

1. By the tableau deterministic procedure, construct a deterministic tableau $\langle \mathcal{N}, \mathcal{E} \rangle$ of specification φ and a set $\mathcal{X}$ of input propositions.
2. If for some $\mathbf{n} \in \mathcal{N}$ and some non-empty set $a \subseteq \mathcal{X}$, there are no $\mathbf{n}' \in \mathcal{N}$ and output event sets b such that $\langle \mathbf{n}, a \cup b, \mathbf{n}' \rangle \in \mathcal{E}$, then this decision procedure determines that φ is not strongly satisfiable. Otherwise, do the next step.
3. If there is a closed subtableau $\langle N, E \rangle$ included in $\langle \mathcal{N}, \mathcal{E} \rangle$ and if there is no open subtableau $\langle N', E' \rangle$ included in $\langle \mathcal{N}, \mathcal{E} \rangle$ such that $\langle N, E \rangle$ and $\langle N', E' \rangle$ have the same path, then this procedure determines that specification φ is not strongly satisfiable. Otherwise, this procedure determines that specification φ is strongly satisfiable.

Definition 18 (Decision Procedure of Stepwise Satisfiability).

1. By the tableau deterministic procedure, construct a deterministic tableau $\langle \mathcal{N}, \mathcal{E} \rangle$ of specification φ and a set $\mathcal{X} \cup \mathcal{Y}$ of input and output propositions.
2. Repeat the following operation until $\langle \mathcal{N}, \mathcal{E} \rangle$ no longer changes.
   For $\mathbf{n} \in \mathcal{N}$ and non-empty set $a \subseteq \mathcal{X}$, if there are no $\mathbf{n}' \in \mathcal{N}$ and non-empty set $b \subseteq \mathcal{Y}$ such that $\langle \mathbf{n}, a \cup b, \mathbf{n}' \rangle \in \mathcal{E}$, then delete $\mathbf{n}$ from $\mathcal{N}$. Delete elements such as $\langle \mathbf{n}, c, \mathbf{n}' \rangle$ or $\langle \mathbf{n}', c, \mathbf{n} \rangle$ from $\mathcal{E}$.
3. If $\mathcal{N}$ is not an empty set, then this procedure determines that φ is stepwise satisfiable. Otherwise, this procedure determines that φ is not stepwise satisfiable.

Definition 19 (Decision Procedure of Stepwise Strong Satisfiability).

1. By the tableau deterministic procedure, construct a deterministic tableau $\langle \mathcal{N}, \mathcal{E} \rangle$ of specification φ and a set $\mathcal{X} \cup \mathcal{Y}$ of input and output propositions.

2. *Repeat the following operation until $\langle \mathcal{N}, \mathcal{E} \rangle$ no longer changes.*
   For $\mathbf{n} \in \mathcal{N}$ and non-empty set $a \subseteq \mathcal{X}$, if there are no $\mathbf{n}' \in \mathcal{N}$ and non-empty set $b \subseteq \mathcal{Y}$ such that $\langle \mathbf{n}, a \cup b, \mathbf{n}' \rangle \in \mathcal{E}$, then delete $\mathbf{n}$ from $\mathcal{N}$. Delete elements such as $\langle \mathbf{n}, c, \mathbf{n}' \rangle$ or $\langle \mathbf{n}', c, \mathbf{n} \rangle$ from $\mathcal{E}$.
3. *If $\mathcal{N}$ is not an empty set, then this procedure determines that φ is not stepwise strongly satisfiable. Otherwise, do the next step.*
4. *For each $\mathbf{n} \in \mathcal{N}$, construct a deterministic tableau $\mathcal{T}' = \langle \mathcal{N}', \mathcal{E}' \rangle$ by the following procedure.*
   (a) *Construct tableau $\langle N, E \rangle$ of φ by the tableau construction procedure.*
   (b) *Set $\mathcal{N}' = \{\mathbf{n}\}$ and $\mathcal{E}' = \emptyset$.*
   (c) *Repeat the following step until $\mathcal{T}'$ no longer changes.*
      For $\mathbf{n} \in \mathcal{N}'$ and non-empty set $a \subseteq \mathcal{X}$, if $next(\mathbf{n})/a$ is not $\emptyset$, then add $next(\mathbf{n})/a$ into $\mathcal{N}'$ and $\langle \mathbf{n}, a, next(\mathbf{n})/a \rangle$ into $\mathcal{E}'$, where $next(\mathbf{n})/a \equiv \{n \in next(\mathbf{n}) \mid a \cap \overline{atm}(n) = \emptyset, (\mathcal{X} - a) \cap atm(n) = \emptyset\}$.

If there is a closed subtableau $\langle N_1, E_1 \rangle$ included in $\mathcal{T}'$ and if there is no open subtableau $\langle N_2, E_2 \rangle$ included in $\mathcal{T}'$ such that $\langle N_1, E_1 \rangle$ and $\langle N_2, E_2 \rangle$ have the same path of $\mathcal{T}'$, then this procedure determines that specification φ is not stepwise strongly satisfiable. Otherwise, this procedure determines that specification φ is stepwise strongly satisfiable.

6   Proof of Soundness and Completeness

This section proves the soundness and completeness of these decision procedures.

Theorem 1. *The decision procedure of strong satisfiability decides that a specification φ is strongly satisfiable if and only if φ is strongly satisfiable.*

Proof: ($\Rightarrow$) Let $\langle N, E \rangle$ be a tableau of φ. We suppose that the decision procedure of strong satisfiability determines that a specification φ is strongly satisfiable. By the definition of this procedure, there is a deterministic tableau $\mathcal{T} = \langle \mathcal{N}, \mathcal{E} \rangle$ of specification φ and a set $\mathcal{X}$ of input propositions such that for each $\mathbf{n} \in \mathcal{N}$ and each non-empty set $a \subseteq \mathcal{X}$, there are $\mathbf{n}' \in \mathcal{N}$ and non-empty set $b \subseteq \mathcal{Y}$ such that $\langle \mathbf{n}, a \cup b, \mathbf{n}' \rangle \in \mathcal{E}$. Therefore, for each infinite sequence of input event sets $\tilde{a}$, there are an infinite sequence $\tilde{b}$ of output event sets and an infinite sequence $\tilde{\mathbf{n}}$ of nodes of $\mathcal{N}$. For $i \geq 0$, we can obtain a node n_i of the tableau of φ such that $n_i \in \tilde{\mathbf{n}}[i]$ and that $\langle n_i, n_{i+1} \rangle \in E$ Since N is a finite set, there are a finite number of nodes in the infinite sequence $n_0 n_1 \cdots$. Let N' be a set of this finite number of nodes. Similarly, let E' be a set of $\langle n_i, n_{i+1} \rangle$ such that $n_i, n_{i+1} \in N'$. As a result, $E' \subseteq E$ and we can obtain the subtableau $\langle N', E' \rangle$.

The subtableau $\langle N', E' \rangle$ is included in $\mathcal{T}$. If $\langle N', E' \rangle$ is not closed, then the behavior $\tilde{a} \sqcup \tilde{b}$ satisfies φ. Otherwise, by the definition of the decision procedure, there is an open subtableau $\langle N'', E'' \rangle$ included in $\mathcal{T}$ such that $\langle N', E' \rangle$ and $\langle N'', E'' \rangle$ have the same path of $\mathcal{T}$. It then follows that the behavior $\tilde{a} \sqcup \tilde{b}$ satisfies φ. Therefore, for each infinite sequence $\tilde{a}$ of input event sets, there is an infinite sequence $\tilde{b}$ of output event sets such that $\tilde{a} \sqcup \tilde{b}$ satisfies φ.

($\Leftarrow$) We prove the contraposition. We suppose that a decision procedure of strong satisfiability decides that φ is not strongly satisfiable. Let $T = \langle \mathcal{N}, \mathcal{E} \rangle$ be a deterministic tableau constructed in the decision procedure of strong satisfiability. If $\mathcal{N}$ is an empty set, then for some infinite sequence $\tilde{a}$ of input event sets, there is no infinite sequence $\tilde{b}$ of output event sets such that $\tilde{a} \sqcup \tilde{b}$ satisfies φ. Thus, φ is not strongly satisfiable.

We suppose that $\mathcal{N}$ is not an empty set. By the definition of the decision procedure, there is a closed subtableau $\langle N, E \rangle$ included in $\mathcal{T}$ and there is no open subtableau $\langle N', E' \rangle$ included in $\mathcal{T}$ such that $\langle N, E \rangle$ and $\langle N', E' \rangle$ have the same path of $\mathcal{T}$. From $\langle N, E \rangle$, we obtain the infinite sequence of nodes of N. Let $n_0 n_1 \cdots$ be this infinite sequence. We also obtain the infinite sequence $\tilde{n}$ of elements of $\mathcal{N}$ by choosing $\tilde{n}[i]$ such that $n_i \in \tilde{n}[i]$. An infinite sequence $\tilde{a}$ of input event sets can be constructed such that $\langle \mathbf{n}_i, \tilde{a}[i], \mathbf{n}_{i+1} \rangle \in \mathcal{E}$. For $\tilde{a}$, there is no infinite sequence $\tilde{b}$ of output event sets because there is no open subtableau $\langle N', E' \rangle$ included in $\mathcal{T}$ such that $\langle N, E \rangle$ and $\langle N', E' \rangle$ have the same path of $\mathcal{T}$. Thus, φ is not strongly satisfiable.   □

Next, the soundness and completeness of the decision procedures of stepwise satisfiability and stepwise strong satisfiability are proven. To begin, we give the reaction function synthesis procedure for a deterministic tableau, which is used in these proofs.

Definition 20 (Reaction Function Synthesis Procedure). *If a deterministic tableau* $\langle \mathcal{N}, \mathcal{E} \rangle$ *of specification* φ *and a set* $\mathcal{X}$ *of input propositions satisfies the following conditions,*

- *$\{START\} \in \mathcal{N}$, and*
- *for $\mathbf{n} \in \mathcal{N}$ and non-empty set $a \subseteq \mathcal{X}$, there are $\mathbf{n}' \in \mathcal{N}$ and non-empty set $b \subseteq \mathcal{Y}$ such that $\langle \mathbf{n}, a \cup b, \mathbf{n}' \rangle \in \mathcal{E}$*

then we obtain the reaction function rec by the following steps.

1. *Q is a function which maps $\mathbf{n} \in \mathcal{N}$ and non-empty set $a \subseteq \mathcal{X}$ to $\mathcal{E}' \subseteq \mathcal{E}$. Q is defined as follows.*
   $Q(\mathbf{n}, a) \equiv \{\langle \mathbf{n}, a \cup b, \mathbf{n}' \rangle \mid \langle \mathbf{n}, a \cup b, \mathbf{n}' \in \mathcal{E}, b \subseteq \mathcal{Y}\}$
   In addition, we introduce some total order into $Q(\mathbf{n}, a)$ and define a function select based on this total order. The function select maps $\mathbf{n} \in \mathcal{N}$, non-empty set $a \subseteq \mathcal{X}$ and element g of $Q(\mathbf{n}, a)$ to element of $Q(\mathbf{n}, a)$. The function select$(\mathbf{n}, a, g)$ is defined as follows.
   (a) *If g is not a maximum of the total order introduced into $Q(\mathbf{n}, a)$, then select$(\mathbf{n}, a, g)$ is the next element of g on the total order.*
   (b) *Otherwise, select$(\mathbf{n}, a, g)$ is the minimum element of $Q(\mathbf{n}, a)$ on the total order.*
2. *The functions state, rec and sch are defined as follows.*
   - *The function state maps $\mathbf{n} \in \mathcal{N}$ and non-empty set $a \subseteq \mathcal{X}$ and sequence $\tilde{a}$ of input proposition sets to an element of $\mathcal{E}$. This function is defined as follows.*

$$state(\mathbf{n}, a, \tilde{a}) = \begin{cases} \text{the minimum element of } Q(\mathbf{n}, a), & \tilde{a} = \varepsilon \\ select(\mathbf{n}, a, state(\mathbf{n}, \tilde{a}[0] \cdots \tilde{a}[k-1])), & \mathbf{n} = sch(\tilde{a}[0] \cdots \tilde{a}[k-1]), \\ & a = \tilde{a}[k] \\ state(\mathbf{n}, a, \tilde{a}[0] \cdots \tilde{a}[k-1]), & otherwise \end{cases}$$

- *The function sch maps the sequence $\bar{a}$ of input proposition sets to $\mathbf{n} \in \mathcal{N}$. sch is defined as follows.*

$$sch(\bar{a}) = \begin{cases} \{START\}, \ \bar{a} = \varepsilon \\ \mathbf{n}', \quad \text{otherwise} \\ \quad \text{where } state(sch(\bar{a}[0] \cdots \bar{a}[k-1]), \bar{a}[k], \bar{a}[0] \cdots \bar{a}[k-1]) \\ \quad = \langle \mathbf{n}, \bar{a}[k] \cup b, \mathbf{n}' \rangle \end{cases}$$

- *The function rec maps the sequence $\bar{a}$ of input event sets to $b \subseteq \mathcal{Y}$. rec is defined as follows.*

$$rec(\bar{a}) = \begin{cases} \varepsilon, \ \bar{a} = \varepsilon \\ b, \ otherwise \\ \quad \text{where } state(sch(\bar{a}[0] \cdots \bar{a}[k-1]), \bar{a}[k], \bar{a}[0] \cdots \bar{a}[k-1]) \\ \quad = \langle \mathbf{n}, \bar{a}[k] \cup b, \mathbf{n}' \rangle \end{cases}$$

Next, we prove the soundness and completeness of the decision procedure of stepwise satisfiability.

Theorem 2. *The decision procedure of stepwise satisfiability determines that a specification φ is stepwise satisfiable if and only if φ is stepwise satisfiable.*

Proof:

($\Rightarrow$) We suppose that the decision procedure determines that a specification φ is stepwise. By the definition of this procedure, there is a deterministic tableau $\langle \mathcal{N}, \mathcal{E} \rangle$ satisfying the following condition.

- $\{START\} \in \mathcal{N}$
- For $\mathbf{n} \in \mathcal{N}$ and non-empty set $a \subseteq \mathcal{X}$, there are $\mathbf{n}' \in \mathcal{N}$ and non-empty set $b \subseteq \mathcal{Y}$ such that $\langle \mathbf{n}, a \cup b, \mathbf{n}' \rangle \in \mathcal{E}$.

Since this deterministic tableau satisfies the conditions of the reaction function synthesis procedure, we obtain a reaction function by applying this synthesis procedure. We call this reaction function *RS*.

RS determines the sequence of output proposition sets for any sequence of input event proposition sets and there is an element of $\mathcal{N}$ corresponding to each sequence of input event sets because of the definition of the function *state* in the definition of the reaction function synthesis procedure. For the finite sequence $\bar{a}$ of input proposition sets, we obtain a sequence $\bar{b}$ of output proposition sets and $\mathbf{n} \in \mathcal{N}$ by using *RS*. We can choose an element n of $\mathbf{n}$ and an open subtableau $T = \langle N, E \rangle$ of φ such that T is strongly connected and $n \in N$. This means that, for any sequence $\bar{a}$ of input event sets, there is a behavior which satisfies φ after $behav_{RS}(\bar{a})$. As a result, the reaction function *RS* preserves the satisfiability of φ. Therefore, φ is stepwise satisfiable.

($\Leftarrow$) We suppose that φ is stepwise satisfiable. By the definition, there is a reaction function *RS* which preserves the satisfiability of φ.

By the reaction function *RS*, we can inductively obtain a deterministic tableau $\langle \mathcal{N}, \mathcal{E} \rangle$ as follows.

1. Set $\mathcal{N} = \{START\}$ and $\mathcal{E} = \emptyset$.
2. For a non-empty set $a \subseteq \mathcal{X}$, let $\mathbf{n}$ be $next(\{START\})/(a \cup behav_{RS}(a))$. Add $\mathbf{n}$ into $\mathcal{N}$ and $\langle \{START\}, a \cup behav_{RS}(a), \mathbf{n} \rangle$ into $\mathcal{E}$. a is also a sequence of input proposition sets, and $\mathbf{n}$ is a node corresponding to the sequence a of input proposition sets.
3. Let $\mathbf{n}$ be a node corresponding to a finite sequence $\bar{a}$ of input proposition sets and let a be an input proposition set. Let $\mathbf{n}'$ be $next(\mathbf{n}/(a \cup behav_{RS}(a))$. Add $\mathbf{n}'$ into $\mathcal{N}$ and $\langle \mathbf{n}, a \cup behav_{RS}(a), \mathbf{n}' \rangle$ into $\mathcal{E}$. $\mathbf{n}'$ is a node corresponding to the sequence $\bar{a}a$ of input proposition sets.

In the following, we prove that the deterministic tableau $\langle \mathcal{N}, \mathcal{E} \rangle$ defined by these steps really exists.

Suppose that the node corresponding to the sequence $\bar{a}$ of input proposition sets is empty. Then there is no infinite sequence $\tilde{c}$ of input and output event proposition sets such that $behav_{RS}(\bar{a})\tilde{c}$ satisfies φ. This is inconsistent with the fact that RS preserves the satisfiability of φ. It follows that the node corresponding to sequence $\bar{a}$ of input proposition sets is not empty and that each element of $\mathcal{N}$ is not empty.

$\mathcal{N}$ and $\mathcal{E}$ are finite because the nodes and edges of the tableau of φ are finite. These steps construct $\mathcal{N}$ and $\mathcal{E}$ by using an infinite number of input event set proposition sequences, however, $\mathcal{N}$ and $\mathcal{E}$ no longer change after the input event set sequences have been used for some time in these steps because $\mathcal{N}$ and $\mathcal{E}$ are finite.

Therefore a deterministic tableau $\langle \mathcal{N}, \mathcal{E} \rangle$ defined by the above steps really exists.

By the definition, for $\mathbf{n} \in \mathcal{N}$ and non-empty set $a \subseteq \mathcal{X}$, there is $\mathbf{n}' \in \mathcal{N}$ and non-empty set $b \subseteq \mathcal{Y}$ such that $\langle \mathbf{n}, a \cup b, \mathbf{n}' \rangle \in \mathcal{E}$. This implies that the decision procedure of stepwise satisfiability decides that φ is stepwise satisfiable. $\qquad \square$

Next we prove the soundness and completeness of the decision procedure of stepwise strong satisfiability.

Theorem 3. *The decision procedure of stepwise strong satisfiability determines that a specification φ is stepwise strongly satisfiable if and only if φ is stepwise strongly satisfiable.*

Proof:

($\Rightarrow$) We suppose that the decision procedure of stepwise strong satisfiability determines that the specification φ is stepwise strong satisfiable. By the definition of this procedure, there is a deterministic tableau $\mathcal{T} = \langle \mathcal{N}, \mathcal{E} \rangle$ satisfying the following conditions.

- $\{START\} \in \mathcal{N}$
- For $\mathbf{n} \in \mathcal{N}$ and non-empty set $a \subseteq \mathcal{X}$, there are $\mathbf{n}' \in \mathcal{N}$ and non-empty set $b \subseteq \mathcal{Y}$ such that $\langle \mathbf{n}, a \cup b, \mathbf{n}' \rangle \in \mathcal{E}$.

Since this deterministic tableau satisfies the conditions of the reaction function synthesis procedure, we obtain a reaction function by applying this synthesis procedure. We call this reaction function RS.

RS determines the sequence of output proposition sets for any sequence of input event proposition sets and there is an element of $\mathcal{N}$ corresponding to each sequence of input event sets because of the definition of the function *state* in the definition of reaction function synthesis procedure. For a finite sequence $\bar{a}$ of input proposition sets, we obtain the sequence $\bar{b}$ of output proposition sets and $\mathbf{n} \in \mathcal{N}$ by using RS. By the definition of the decision procedure, there is a deterministic tableau $\mathcal{T}' = \langle \mathcal{N}', \mathcal{E}' \rangle$ satisfying the following conditions.

1. $\mathcal{T}'$ is strongly connected.
2. $\mathbf{n} \in \mathcal{N}'$
3. For $\mathbf{n}_1 \in \mathcal{N}'$ and non-empty set $a \subseteq \mathcal{X}$, there are $\mathbf{n}_2 \in \mathcal{N}'$ and non-empty set $b \subseteq \mathcal{Y}$ such that $\langle \mathbf{n}_1, a \cup b, \mathbf{n}_2 \rangle \in \mathcal{E}'$.
4. If there is a closed subtableau $\langle N_1, E_1 \rangle$ included in $\mathcal{T}'$, then there is an open subtableau $\langle N_2, E_2 \rangle$ included in $\mathcal{T}'$ such that $\langle N_1, E_1 \rangle$ and $\langle N_2, E_2 \rangle$ have the same path of $\mathcal{T}'$.

Therefore, for any infinite sequence $\tilde{a}$ of input proposition sets, there are an infinite sequence $\tilde{b}$ of output proposition sets and an infinite sequence $\tilde{\mathbf{n}}$ of nodes of $\mathcal{N}'$. For $i \geq 0$, we can obtain a node n_i of the tableau of φ such that $n_i \in \tilde{\mathbf{n}}[i]$ and that $\langle n_i, n_{i+1} \rangle \in E$ Since N is a finite set, there are a finite number of nodes in the infinite sequence $n_0 n_1 \cdots$. Let N' be a set of this finite number of nodes. Similarly, let E' be a set of $\langle n_i, n_{i+1} \rangle$ such that $n_i, n_{i+1} \in N'$. As a result, $E' \subseteq E$ and we can obtain the subtableau $\langle N', E' \rangle$.

Subtableau $\langle N', E' \rangle$ is included in $\mathcal{T}$. If $\langle N', E' \rangle$ is not closed, then the behavior $\tilde{a} \sqcup \tilde{b}$ satisfies φ. Otherwise, by the definition of the decision procedure, there is an open subtableau $\langle N'', E'' \rangle$ included in $\mathcal{T}$ such that $\langle N', E' \rangle$ and $\langle N'', E'' \rangle$ have the same path of $\mathcal{T}$. It then follows that the behavior $\tilde{a} \sqcup \tilde{b}$ satisfies φ. This implies that for each infinite sequence $\tilde{a}$ of input event proposition sets, there is an infinite sequence $\tilde{b}$ of output proposition sets such that $\bar{a}\tilde{a} \sqcup RS(\bar{a})\tilde{b}$ satisfies φ. Therefore, φ is stepwise strongly satisfiable.

($\Leftarrow$) We suppose that φ is stepwise strongly satisfiable. By definition, there is a reaction function RS which preserves the strong satisfiability of φ.

By the reaction function RS, we can obtain a deterministic tableau $\langle \mathcal{N}, \mathcal{E} \rangle$ as follows.

1. Set $\mathcal{N} = \{START\}$ and $\mathcal{E} = \emptyset$.
2. For non-empty set $a \subseteq \mathcal{X}$, let $\mathbf{n}$ be $next(\{START\})/(a \cup behav_{RS}(a))$. Add $\mathbf{n}$ into $\mathcal{N}$ and $\langle \{START\}, a \cup behav_{RS}(a), \mathbf{n} \rangle$ into $\mathcal{E}$. a is also a sequence of input proposition sets, and $\mathbf{n}$ is the node corresponding to the sequence a of input proposition sets.
3. Let $\mathbf{n}$ be the node corresponding to the sequence $\bar{a}$ of input proposition sets and let a be an input proposition set. Let $\mathbf{n}'$ be $next(\mathbf{n}/(a \cup behav_{RS}(a))$. Add $\mathbf{n}'$ into $\mathcal{N}$ and $\langle \mathbf{n}, a \cup behav_{RS}(a), \mathbf{n}' \rangle$ into $\mathcal{E}$. $\mathbf{n}'$ corresponds to the sequence $\bar{a}a$ of input event sets.

In the following, we prove that the deterministic tableau $\langle \mathcal{N}, \mathcal{E} \rangle$ defined by these steps really exists.

Suppose that the node corresponding to the sequence $\bar{a}$ of input proposition sets is empty. Then there is no infinite sequence $\tilde{c}$ of input and output event proposition sets such that $behav_{RS}(\bar{a})\tilde{c}$ satisfies φ. This is inconsistent with the fact that RS preserves the strong satisfiability of φ. It follows that the node corresponding to the sequence $\bar{a}$ of input proposition sets is not empty and that each element of $\mathscr{N}$ is not empty.

$\mathscr{N}$ and $\mathscr{E}$ are finite because the nodes and edges of the tableau of φ are finite. These steps construct $\mathscr{N}$ and $\mathscr{E}$ by using an infinite number of input event set sequences, however, $\mathscr{N}$ and $\mathscr{E}$ no longer change after the input proposition set sequences have been used for some time in these steps because $\mathscr{N}$ and $\mathscr{E}$ are finite.

Therefore, the deterministic tableau $\langle \mathscr{N}, \mathscr{E} \rangle$ defined by the above steps really exists.

For $\mathbf{n} \in \mathscr{N}$, we can obtain a deterministic tableau $\mathscr{T}' = \langle \mathscr{N}', \mathscr{E}' \rangle$ of the specification φ and a set $\mathscr{X}$ of input propositions satisfying the following conditions.

1. $\mathbf{n} \in \mathscr{N}'$
2. $\mathscr{T}'$ is strong connected.
3. For $\mathbf{n} \in \mathscr{N}'$ and non-empty set $a \subseteq \mathscr{X}$, there are $\mathbf{n}' \in \mathscr{N}'$ and output propositions sets b such that $\langle \mathbf{n}, a \cup b, \mathbf{n}' \rangle \in \mathscr{E}'$.
4. If there is a closed subtableau $\langle N_1, E_1 \rangle$ included in $\mathscr{T}'$, then there is an open subtableau $\langle N_2, E_2 \rangle$ included in $\mathscr{T}'$ such $\langle N_1, E_1 \rangle$ and $\langle N_2, E_2 \rangle$ have the same path of $\mathscr{T}'$.

In the following, we prove that this deterministic tableau really exists.

It is trivial that the first condition holds. Next, we prove that the second and third conditions hold. Suppose that for some $\mathbf{n} \in \mathscr{N}'$ and some non-empty set $a \subseteq \mathscr{X}$, there is no $\mathbf{n}' \in \mathscr{N}'$ and output propositions sets b such that $\langle \mathbf{n}, a \cup b, \mathbf{n}' \rangle \in \mathscr{E}'$. We can obtain a finite sequence $\bar{n}$ of elements of $\mathscr{N}'$ and a finite sequence $\bar{a}$ of input proposition sets such that the length of $\bar{a}$ is k, $\langle \bar{n}[i], \bar{a}[i], \bar{n}[i+1] \rangle \in \mathscr{E}'$ $(0 \le i \le k)$, $\bar{n}[0] = \mathbf{n}$ and $\bar{n}[k] = \mathbf{n}'$. Let $\tilde{a}$ be an infinite sequence of input proposition sets. Since $\langle \mathbf{n}', a \cup b, \mathbf{n}'' \rangle \notin \mathscr{E}'$ for any $\mathbf{n}'' \in \mathscr{N}'$ and output proposition set b, there is no sequence $\tilde{b}$ of output proposition sets such that $\bar{a}' \bar{a} \tilde{a} \sqcup \tilde{b}$ satisfies φ, where the length of $\bar{a}'$ is j, $\langle \bar{n}'[i], \bar{a}[i], \bar{n}'[i+1] \rangle \in \mathscr{E}'$, $\bar{n}'[0] = START$ and $\bar{n}'[j] = \mathbf{n}'$. This contradicts the fact that RS preserves strong satisfiability. Therefore, the third of the above conditions holds. Since this result and $\mathscr{N}'$ and $\mathscr{E}'$ are finite, the second of the above conditions holds.

Finally, we prove that the fourth condition holds. Suppose that there is a closed subtableau $\langle N_1, E_1 \rangle$ included in $\mathscr{T}'$ and that there is no open subtableau $\langle N_2, E_2 \rangle$ included in $\mathscr{T}'$ such that $\langle N_1, E_1 \rangle$ and $\langle N_2, E_2 \rangle$ have the same path of $\mathscr{T}'$. We can obtain an infinite sequence $\tilde{n}$ of elements of N_1. From $\tilde{n}$, we define an infinite sequence $\tilde{\mathbf{n}}$ of elements of $\mathscr{N}$ as follows:

– For $i \ge 0$, $n_i \in \tilde{\mathbf{n}}[i]$

From $\tilde{\mathbf{n}}$, we can also obtain an infinite sequence $\tilde{a}$ of input proposition sets as follows

– For $i \ge 0$, $\langle \mathbf{n}_i, a_i \cup b, \mathbf{n}_{i+1} \rangle \in \mathscr{E}'$

Let $\bar{a}$ be a finite sequence of input proposition sets such that $\mathbf{n}$ corresponds to $\bar{a}$. There is no infinite sequence $\tilde{b}$ of output proposition sets such that $\bar{a} \tilde{a} \sqcup RS(\bar{a}) \tilde{b}$ satisfies φ. This contradicts the fact that RS preserves strong satisfiability. Therefore, if there is a closed subtableau $\langle N_1, E_1 \rangle$ included in $\mathscr{T}'$, then there is an open subtableau $\langle N_2, E_2 \rangle$ included in $\mathscr{T}'$ such that $\langle N_1, E_1 \rangle$ and $\langle N_2, E_2 \rangle$ have the same path of $\mathscr{T}'$. Thus, we have proved that the fourth condition holds and $\mathscr{T}'$ exists.

Since $\mathscr{T}'$ exists, the decision procedure of stepwise strong satisfiability determines that the specification φ is stepwise strong satisfiable.   □

7   Conclusion

This paper presented the decision procedures of strong satisfiability, stepwise satisfiability, and stepwise strong satisfiability. We plan to implement these procedures and to apply them to reactive system specification description support and to reactive system program synthesis from formal specifications. This enables us to synthesize secure reactive system programs. We also plan to clarify the complexity of these procedures.

References

1. A. Pnueli, The Temporal Logic in Programs, in: *Proc. 18th Ann. IEEE Symp. on Foundations of Computer Science*, (1977) 46-57
2. E.A. Emerson, Temporal and Modal Logic, in: j. van Leeuwen, ed., *Handbook of Theoretical Computer Science, Vol. B* (North-Holland, Amsterdam, 1990) 995-1072
3. M. Abadi, L. Lamport, P. Wolper, Realizable and Unrealizable Specifications of Reactive Systems, *Lecture Note in Computer Science 372*, (1989) 1-17
4. A. Pnueli, R. Rosner, On the Synthesis of a Reactive Module, in: *Proc. 16th Ann. ACM Symp. on the Principle of Programming Languages*, (1989) 179-190
5. Z. Manna, P. Wolper, Synthesis of Communicating processes from Temporal Logic Specifications, *ACM Trans. Programming Languages and Systems* 6(1) (1984) 68-93
6. E.A. Emerson, E.M. Clarke, Using Branching Time Temporal Logic to Synthesize Synchronization Skeletons, *Sci. Comput. Programming* 2 (1982) 241-266
7. P. Wolper, Temporal Logic can be more expressive, *Informaition and Control 56*, (1983) 72-93
8. A. Pnueli, R. Rosner, On the Synthesis of an Asynchronous Reactive Module, *Lecture Note in Computer Science 372*, (1989) 652-671
9. A. Anuchitanukul, Z. Manna, Realizability and Synthesis of Reactive Modules, *Lecture Note in Computer Science 818* (1994) 156-168
10. Moshe Y. Vardi An Automata-Theoretic Approach to Fair Realizability and Synthesis, Computer Aided Verification, LNCS 939, (1995) 267-278
11. Ron van der Meyden and Moshe Y. Vardi Synthesis from Knowledge-Based Specifications CONCUR'98, LNCS1466, (1998) 34-49
12. R. Mori, N. Yonezaki, Several Realizability Concepts in Reactive Objects, in: *Information Modeling and Knowledge Bases*, (IOS, Amsterdam, 1993)
13. R. Mori, Y. Yonezaki, Derivation of the Input Conditional Formula from a Reactive System Specification in Temporal Logic, in: H. Langmaack, eds., Formal Techniques in Real Time and Fault Tolerant Systems, *Lecture Note in Computer Science 863*, (1994) 567-582.

A Model for Delimited Information Release

Andrei Sabelfeld[*,1] and Andrew C. Myers[2]

[1] Department of Computer Science, Chalmers University of Technology,
412 96 Gothenburg, Sweden
andrei@cs.chalmers.se
[2] Department of Computer Science, Cornell University, Ithaca, NY 14853, USA
andru@cs.cornell.edu

Abstract. Much work on security-typed languages lacks a satisfactory account of intentional information release. In the context of confidentiality, a typical security guarantee provided by security type systems is *noninterference*, which allows no information flow from secret inputs to public outputs. However, many intuitively secure programs do allow some release, or *declassification,* of secret information (e.g., password checking, information purchase, and spreadsheet computation). Noninterference fails to recognize such programs as secure. In this respect, many security type systems enforcing noninterference are impractical. On the other side of the spectrum are type systems designed to accommodate some information leakage. However, there is often little or no guarantee about *what* is actually being leaked. As a consequence, such type systems are vulnerable to *laundering attacks*, which exploit declassification mechanisms to reveal more secret data than intended. To bridge this gap, this paper introduces a new security property, *delimited release*, an end-to-end guarantee that declassification cannot be exploited to construct laundering attacks. In addition, a security type system is given that straightforwardly and provably enforces delimited release.

Keywords: Computer security, confidentiality, information flow, noninterference, security-type systems, security policies, declassification.

1   Introduction

A long-standing problem in computer security is how to verifiably protect the confidentiality of sensitive information in practical computing systems. One of the most vexing difficulties is that realistic computing systems do release some confidential information as part of their intended function. The challenge is how to differentiate between proper and improper release of confidential information.

For example, it is possible to learn a small amount of information about a user's password by attempting to log in; the attacker likely learns that the

---

[*] This work was partly done while the author was at Cornell University.

K. Futatsugi et al. (Eds.): ISSS 2003, LNCS 3233, pp. 174–191, 2004.

password is *not* the one guessed. How can this secure system be distinguished from an insecure system that directly reports the entire password to the attacker? This paper proposes *delimited release*, a new definition of security that helps make the distinction.

To protect confidentiality within a computing system, it is important to control how information flows so that sensitive information is not transmitted inappropriately to system outputs. One way to control these flows is to associate a *security level* with information in the system, and to prevent higher-level (more confidential) information from affecting lower-level (less confidential) information. Recently there has been much work embodying this approach in a language-based setting [37], where the system to be validated is a program and the security levels are types in that program [47, 19, 27, 2, 42, 45, 4, 38, 33, 39, 51, 5, 34]. A program written in this sort of *security-typed language* is considered secure only if it is well-typed, which rules out, for example, assignments from high-level variables to low-level variables.

This kind of static checking tends to be very restrictive, preventing practical programming. Typically these languages are intended to enforce some version of the *noninterference* [16] security property, which prevents low-level information from depending on high-level information. Yet many practical programs, such as the password checker mentioned above, do release information. Another example is aggregating data from a large database (such as an employee database) to compute a less confidential result (such as the average salary). And sometimes confidential information is released as part of a transaction or agreed-upon protocol, such as when information is purchased. All of these programs violate noninterference and would be rejected by the type systems of most current security-typed languages.

Assuming that the confidentiality of data is expressed as a security level, some additional mechanism is needed in order to express programs in which there is an intentional release of information. Some security-typed languages (e.g., [27, 33, 13]) have therefore added a *declassification* mechanism that coerces the security level of information downwards. Declassification serves as an escape hatch from the rigid restrictions of security type systems, but it (intentionally) violates noninterference.

A question that has not been addressed satisfactorily by earlier work is what security guarantees can be offered in the presence of declassification. Delimited release is such a guarantee. Like noninterference, it has the attractive property that it defines security in terms of the program semantics rather than in terms of non-standard mechanisms. Thus, it controls the *end-to-end* [40] behavior of the program: it is an *extensional* security property [26].

In the rest of the paper, we present an imperative language (Section 2), formally define delimited release security (Section 3), give a security type system that provably enforces delimited release (Section 4), discuss a password-checking example (Section 5), sketch related work (Section 6), and conclude (Section 7).

Fig. 1. A general security lattice $\mathcal{L}$ and the lattice $\mathcal{L}_{LH}$

2   A Security-Typed Language

To illustrate the security model, we consider a simple sequential language, consisting of expressions and commands. The language is similar to several other security-typed imperative languages (e.g., [47,4]), and its semantics are largely standard (cf. [48]).

The language syntax is defined by the following grammar:

$$e ::= val \mid v \mid e_1 \text{ op } e_2 \mid \texttt{declassify}(e, \ell)$$

$$c ::= \texttt{skip} \mid v := e \mid c_1; c_2 \mid \texttt{if } e \texttt{ then } c_1 \texttt{ else } c_2 \mid \texttt{while } e \texttt{ do } c$$

where val ranges over values $Val = \{false, true, 0, 1, \dots\}$, v ranges over variables Var, op ranges over arithmetic and boolean operations on expressions, and ℓ ranges over security levels.

We assume that the security levels of data are elements of a *security lattice* $\mathcal{L}$. The ordering specifies the relationship between different security levels. If $\ell_1 \sqsubseteq \ell_2$ then information at level ℓ_1 is also visible at level ℓ_2. However, if $\ell_1 \not\sqsubseteq \ell_2$ then information at level ℓ_1 is invisible at level ℓ_2. The join operation ($\sqcup$) of $\mathcal{L}$ is useful, for example, for computing an upper bound on the security level of an expression that combines sub-expressions at different security levels. An example is the security lattice $\mathcal{L}_{LH}$ with two elements *high* and *low* representing high and low confidentiality levels, respectively, with the ordering $low \sqsubseteq high$. A general security lattice $\mathcal{L}$ with a top element $\top$ and bottom element $\bot$ is depicted in Figure 1, along with the lattice $\mathcal{L}_{LH}$.

The *security environment* $\Gamma : Var \rightarrow \mathcal{L}$ describes the type of each program variable as a security level. The security lattice and security environment together constitute a *security policy*, which specifies that information flow from a variable v_1 to a variable v_2 is allowed only if $\Gamma(v_1) \sqsubseteq \Gamma(v_2)$. For simplicity, we assume a fixed Γ in the upcoming formal definitions.

The only language expression that is not standard is $\texttt{declassify}(e, \ell)$, a construct for declassifying the security level of the expression e to the level $\ell \in \mathcal{L}$. We require that declassify expressions are not nested. At the semantic level, $\texttt{declassify}(e, \ell)$ is equivalent to e regardless ℓ. The intention is that declassification is used for controlling the security level of information without affecting the execution of the program.

The semantics are defined in terms of transitions between configurations. A *configuration* $\langle M, c \rangle$ consists of a *memory* M (which is a finite mapping $M : Var \to Val$ from variables to values) and a *command* (or *expression*) c. If c is a command (resp. expression) then we sometimes refer to $\langle M, c \rangle$ as *command configuration* (resp. *expression configuration*). A transition from configuration $\langle M_1, c_1 \rangle$ to configuration $\langle M_2, c_2 \rangle$ is denoted by $\langle M_1, c_1 \rangle \longrightarrow \langle M_2, c_2 \rangle$. A transition from configuration $\langle M, c \rangle$ to a terminating configuration with memory M' is denoted by $\langle M, c \rangle \longrightarrow M'$. As usual, $\longrightarrow^*$ is the reflexive and transitive closure of $\longrightarrow$. Configuration $\langle M, c \rangle$ *terminates* in M' if $\langle M, c \rangle \longrightarrow^* M'$, which is denoted by $\langle M, c \rangle \Downarrow M'$ or, simply, $\langle M, c \rangle \Downarrow$ when M' is unimportant. We assume that operations used in expressions are total, and, hence, expression configurations always terminate (denoted by $\langle M, e \rangle \Downarrow val$).

3   A Delimiting Model for Confidentiality

The usual way of defining confidentiality is as *noninterference* [16], a security property stating that inputs of high confidentiality do not affect outputs of lower confidentiality. Various definitions of noninterference have been used by much recent work on language-based security (e.g., [47, 2, 19, 42, 45, 4, 38, 33, 39, 51, 5, 34]). However, noninterference cannot characterize the security of a program that is designed to release some confidential information as part of its proper functioning. We propose a new confidentiality characterization that delimits information release and precludes laundering attacks.

3.1   Noninterference

Noninterference is defined as follows for programs written in the language of Section 2: if two input memories are indistinguishable for an attacker at a security level ℓ then the behavior of the program on these memories is also indistinguishable at ℓ. Formally, two memories M_1 and M_2 are indistinguishable $M_1 =_\ell M_2$ at level ℓ if $\forall v. \Gamma(v) \sqsubseteq \ell \implies M_1(v) = M_2(v)$ (we assume a fixed Γ; hence the notation $M_1 =_\ell M_2$ is not parameterized by security environments). The behavior of two program configurations $\langle M_1, c_1 \rangle$ and $\langle M_2, c_2 \rangle$ is indistinguishable at ℓ (written $\langle M_1, c_1 \rangle \approx_\ell \langle M_2, c_2 \rangle$) if whenever $\langle M_1, c_1 \rangle \Downarrow M_1'$ and $\langle M_2, c_2 \rangle \Downarrow M_2'$ for some M_1' and M_2' then $M_1' =_\ell M_2'$. The behavior of two expression configurations $\langle M_1, e_1 \rangle$ and $\langle M_2, e_2 \rangle$ is indistinguishable (written $\langle M_1, e_1 \rangle \approx \langle M_2, e_2 \rangle$) if $\langle M_1, e_1 \rangle \Downarrow val$ and $\langle M_2, e_2 \rangle \Downarrow val$ for some val. We are now ready to formulate the noninterference security condition.

Definition 1 (Noninterference). *Command c satisfies* noninterference *if for all security levels ℓ we have*

$$\forall M_1, M_2. M_1 =_\ell M_2 \implies \langle M_1, c \rangle \approx_\ell \langle M_2, c \rangle$$

While noninterference is a useful dependency-based security specification, it is over-restrictive for programs with declassification. For example, suppose we need to intentionally release the parity of a secret variable h in such a way that no other information about h is leaked. The program performing such a release is below:

$$l := \texttt{declassify}(\texttt{parity}(h), low) \qquad \text{(Par)}$$

where $\Gamma(h) = high$ and $\Gamma(l) = low$ under the lattice $\mathcal{L}_{LH}$. In the above sense, this program is intuitively secure. However, noninterference flatly rejects the program because l does depend on h.

3.2   Escape Hatches and Delimited Release

In the example above, we want to express the requirement that only explicitly declassified data but no further information is released. Therefore, the specification of security must be relative to the expressions that appear under declassify operators. These expressions can be viewed as a part of the security policy, specifying the "escape hatches" for information release. To make this security policy explicit, one could require all escape hatch expressions to be declared in a separate interface. Because this is unimportant for the technical development, we omit this requirement. The new security specification *delimits* information release by only allowing release through escape hatch expressions:

Definition 2 (Delimited Release). *Suppose the command c contains within it exactly n declassify expressions* $\texttt{declassify}(e_1, \ell_1), \ldots, \texttt{declassify}(e_n, \ell_n)$. *Command c is secure if for all security levels ℓ we have*

$$\forall M_1, M_2. (M_1 =_\ell M_2 \ \& \ \forall i \in \{i \mid \ell_i \sqsubseteq \ell\}. \langle M_1, e_i \rangle \approx \langle M_2, e_i \rangle)$$
$$\implies \langle M_1, c \rangle \approx_\ell \langle M_2, c \rangle$$

Intuitively, this definition says that for all ℓ, M_1 and M_2 so that $M_1 =_\ell M_2$, if there is an information leak through one of the escape hatches $e_1, \ldots, e_n$ observable at level ℓ, i.e., $\exists i \in \{i \mid \ell_i \sqsubseteq \ell\}. \langle M_1, e_i \rangle \not\approx \langle M_2, e_i \rangle$, then this leak is allowed, i.e., no further conditions are imposed. However, if the difference between M_1 and M_2 is invisible at ℓ through all escape hatches, i.e., $\forall i \in \{i \mid \ell_i \sqsubseteq \ell\}. \langle M_1, e_i \rangle \approx \langle M_2, e_i \rangle$, then this difference must be invisible at ℓ through the entire execution of c, i.e., $\langle M_1, c \rangle \approx_\ell \langle M_2, c \rangle$.

One way of interpreting the delimited release definition is that a given program is secure as long as updates to variables that are later declassified occur in a way that does not increase the information visible by the attacker through the escape hatches. If no variables used in declassification are updated before the actual declassification, delimited release reduces to noninterference. This observation leads to a simple way of automatically enforcing delimited release, reported in Section 4.

It is instructive to compare delimited release to noninterference. Clearly, noninterference is stronger than delimited release:

Proposition 1. *If program c satisfies noninterference then c is secure.*

Furthermore, for a program without declassify primitives the two security properties coincide.

Proposition 2. *If* declassify *primitives do not occur in a secure program* c *then* c *satisfies noninterference.*

3.3   Examples

The security provided by delimited release can be understood from some simple examples: averaging salaries, an electronic wallet, and password checking.

Example 1 (Average Salary). Suppose variables $h_1, \ldots, h_n$ store the salaries of n employees. The average salary computation is intended to intentionally release the average but no other information about $h_1, \ldots, h_n$ to a public variable avg:

$$avg := \text{declassify}((h_1 + \cdots + h_n)/n, low) \tag{Avg}$$

We assume lattice $\mathcal{L}_{LH}$ so that $\forall i.\, \Gamma(h_i) = high$ and $\Gamma(avg) = low$. Clearly the program does not satisfy noninterference as there is a dependency from $h_1, \ldots, h_n$ to avg. However, the nature of information flow from high to low is limited. Although the low-level observer learns the average of the secret inputs, it is not possible to learn more information about them. For example, swapping the values of h_i and h_j is not visible at the low level. Allowing these limited flows, the program is accepted as secure by the delimited release definition.

On the other hand, consider a laundering attack on program Avg that leaks the salary of employee i to avg.

$$h_1 := h_i; \ldots h_n := h_i;$$
$$avg := \text{declassify}((h_1 + \cdots + h_n)/n, low) \tag{Avg-Attack}$$

This program does not satisfy delimited release. To see this, take $i = 1$, $M_1(h_1) = M_2(h_2) = 2$, $M_2(h_1) = M_1(h_2) = 3$, and $M_1(v) = M_2(v) = 0$ for all variables v different from h_1 and h_2. For $\ell = low$ we have $M_1 =_\ell M_2$ and $\langle M_1, (h_1 + \cdots + h_n)/n \rangle \approx \langle M_2, (h_1 + \cdots + h_n)/n \rangle$ because both expression configurations evaluate to $5/n$. But $\langle M_1, \text{Avg-Attack} \rangle \not\approx_\ell \langle M_2, \text{Avg-Attack} \rangle$ because the final value of the public variable avg is 2 and 3, respectively, which violates Definition 2. Therefore, the laundering attack is rejected as insecure.

Example 2 (Electronic Wallet). Consider an electronic shopping scenario. Suppose h stores the (secret) amount of money in a customer's electronic wallet, l stores the (public) amount of money spent during the current session, and k stores the cost of the item to be purchased. The following code fragment checks if the amount of money in the wallet is sufficient and, if so, transfers the amount k of money from the customer's wallet to the spent-so-far variable l:

$$\text{if } \text{declassify}(h \geq k, low) \text{ then } (h := h - k; l := l + k) \text{ else skip} \tag{Wallet}$$

We assume lattice $\mathcal{L}_{LH}$ so that $\Gamma(h) = high$ and $\Gamma(k) = \Gamma(l) = low$. As with program Avg, this program fails to satisfy noninterference but does satisfy delimited release. Below is an attack that abuses the declassification primitive and leaks[1] the secret variable h bit-by-bit to l (assuming h is an n-bit integer):

$l := 0$;
while $(n \geq 0)$ do
   $k := 2^{n-1}$;
   if declassify$(h \geq k, low)$ (Wallet-Attack)
     then $(h := h - k; l := l + k)$ else skip;
   $n := n - 1$

where $\Gamma(n) = low$. This is a laundering attack whose effect is magnified by the loop. It is not difficult to see that the attack is indeed rejected by the delimited release model.

3.4   Features and Extensions

An interesting feature of the delimited release is that it forces the programmer to be explicit about what information is being released. This is because the security policy, in the form of expressions under declassify, is simply a part of program text. For example, consider the following program:

$h := $ parity(h);
if declassify$(h = 1, low)$ then $(l := 1; h := 1)$ else $(l := 0; h := 0)$

where $\Gamma(h) = high$ and $\Gamma(l) = low$ under the lattice $\mathcal{L}_{LH}$. According to the security policy $h = 1$, whether or not the initial value of h was 1 is the information intended for declassification. Instead, however, the low-level observer learns the parity of the initial value of h. This is a laundering attack, which is rejected by the delimited release model. To produce a semantically equivalent secure version of the program above, the programmer may rewrite it to the following program:

if declassify(parity$(h), low)$ then $(l := 1; h := 1)$ else $(l := 0; h := 0)$

This is indeed a secure program according to Definition 2. That the parity of h is subject to intentional information release is now more evident from the security policy parity(h).

The desire to automate the above transformation leads to extensions based on *security ordering* for programs. A program c_2 is at least as secure as a program c_1 (written $c_1 \sqsubseteq_{sec} c_2$) if for all security levels $\ell \in \mathcal{L}$ and memories M_1 and M_2 we have whenever $M_1 =_\ell M_2$ and $\langle M_1, c_1 \rangle \approx_\ell \langle M_2, c_1 \rangle$ then $\langle M_1, c_2 \rangle \approx_\ell \langle M_2, c_2 \rangle$. The intuition is that c_2 leaks no more secret information than c_1, hence the security ordering. It is straightforward to see that security ordering $\sqsubseteq_{sec}$ is a preorder (reflexive and transitive). In the partial order, formed by equivalence classes of $\sqsubseteq_{sec}$, programs satisfying noninterference belong to the top-security

---

[1] Furthermore, this attack compromises the *integrity* of the customer's wallet variable. However, this is orthogonal to the confidentiality issues dealt with in this paper.

class (in the sense that the other programs are strictly less secure). A decidable approximation of this security ordering for driving security-enhancing program transformation is an attractive direction for future work.

The delimited release model has some limitations in describing security policies for information release, because all of the declassified expressions are assumed to be released. The model does not permit the expression of a security policy in which information should be released only under certain conditions. For example, consider a program that leaks either h_1 or h_2, but not both:

$$\texttt{if } l \texttt{ then } l := \texttt{declassify}(h_1, low) \texttt{ else } l := \texttt{declassify}(h_2, low)$$

where $\Gamma(h_1) = \Gamma(h_2) = high$ and $\Gamma(l) = low$ under the lattice $\mathcal{L}_{LH}$. This program is secure according to Definition 2. Both h_1 and h_2 appear under declassify, which, according to Definition 2, means that the program might leak the values of both. The requirement that only one of the two variables is released cannot be expressed using Definition 2. However, delimited release can be enhanced with *disjunctive policies* for representing finer policies as, e.g., "either h_1 or h_2 can be released but not both." Moreover, delimited release can be integrated with techniques based on *who* controls information release, such as *robust declassification* [50, 49, 30]. This integration can help specify whether the decision on which of h_1 and h_2 can be released may or may not be in the hands of an attacker. A remark on the combination of delimited release and robust declassification follows in Section 7.

4   A Security Type System for Delimited Release

This section presents a type system that statically enforces security. The typing rules are displayed in Figure 2. The general form of typing for an expression is $\Gamma \vdash e : \ell, D$ meaning that an expression e has type ℓ and effect D under an environment Γ. Typing for commands has the form $\Gamma, pc \vdash c : U, D$ meaning that a command c is typable with effects U and D under an environment Γ and a *program counter pc*. Program counters range over security levels; they help track information flow due to control flow. A program counter records a lower bound on the security level of variables assigned in a given program. The type system guarantees that if there is branching (as in if and while commands) on data at level ℓ then the branches must be typable under a program counter at least at ℓ, preventing leaks via assignments in the branches.

Besides tracking information flow through assignments and control flow (in the spirit of [11, 47]), the type system collects information about what variables are used under declassification (which is recorded in the effect D of an expression or a command) and what variables are updated by commands (which is recorded in the effect U of a command). For example, the D effect of a $\texttt{declassify}(e, \ell)$ expression is the set of variables appearing in e, written as $Vars(e)$. The key restriction guaranteed by the type system is that variables used under declassification may not be updated prior to declassification. This restriction is enforced

$$\Gamma \vdash val : \ell, \emptyset$$

$$\frac{\Gamma(v) = \ell}{\Gamma \vdash v : \ell, \emptyset}$$

$$\frac{\Gamma \vdash e : \ell, D_1 \quad \Gamma \vdash e' : \ell, D_2}{\Gamma \vdash e \text{ op } e' : \ell, D_1 \cup D_2}$$

$$\frac{\Gamma \vdash e : \ell, D}{\Gamma \vdash \texttt{declassify}(e, \ell') : \ell', Vars(e)}$$

$$\frac{\Gamma \vdash e : \ell, D \quad \ell \sqsubseteq \ell'}{\Gamma \vdash e : \ell', D}$$

$$\Gamma, pc \vdash \texttt{skip} : \emptyset, \emptyset$$

$$\frac{\Gamma \vdash e : \ell, D \quad \ell \sqcup pc \sqsubseteq \Gamma(v)}{\Gamma, pc \vdash v := e : \{v\}, D}$$

$$\frac{\Gamma, pc \vdash c_1 : U_1, D_1 \quad \Gamma, pc \vdash c_2 : U_2, D_2 \quad U_1 \cap D_2 = \emptyset}{\Gamma, pc \vdash c_1; c_2 : U_1 \cup U_2, D_1 \cup D_2}$$

$$\frac{\Gamma \vdash e : \ell, D \quad \Gamma, \ell \sqcup pc \vdash c_1 : U_1, D_1 \quad \Gamma, \ell \sqcup pc \vdash c_2 : U_2, D_2}{\Gamma, pc \vdash \texttt{if } e \texttt{ then } c_1 \texttt{ else } c_2 : U_1 \cup U_2, D \cup D_1 \cup D_2}$$

$$\frac{\Gamma \vdash e : \ell, D \quad \Gamma, \ell \sqcup pc \vdash c : U_1, D_1 \quad U_1 \cap (D \cup D_1) = \emptyset}{\Gamma, pc \vdash \texttt{while } e \texttt{ do } c : U_1, D \cup D_1}$$

$$\frac{\Gamma, pc \vdash c : U, D \quad pc' \sqsubseteq pc}{\Gamma, pc' \vdash c : U, D}$$

Fig. 2. Typing rules

in the rules for the sequential composition and the while loop. The overall programming discipline enforced by the type system ensures that typable programs are secure, which is formalized by the following theorem.

Theorem 1. $\Gamma, pc \vdash c : U, D \implies c$ *is secure.*

A proof by induction on the typing derivation is sketched in the appendix.

Note that the type system is more restrictive than necessary to enforce the security condition. For example, consider the program

$$h := \texttt{parity}(h); l := \texttt{declassify}(h, low)$$

where $\Gamma(h) = high$ and $\Gamma(l) = low$ under the lattice $\mathcal{L}_{LH}$. Although h is updated prior to declassification, the entire program actually leaks only the parity of the initial value of h, which is less information than the complete initial value of h leaked by the declassifying assignment alone. Indeed, according to Definition 2 the program is secure; however, it is rejected by the type system. Devising a more permissive type system for enforcing the delimited release security condition is a worthwhile topic for future work.

5   A Password-Checking Example

This section applies the delimited release model to password checking, illustrating how the type system gives security types to password-checking routines and also prevents laundering attacks.

We consider UNIX-style password checking where the system database stores the *images* (or the hashes) of password-salt pairs. *Salt* is a publicly readable string stored in the database for each user id, as a protection against dictionary attacks. For a successful login, the user is required to provide a query such that the hash of the string and salt matches the image from the database.

Below are typed expressions/programs for computing the hash, matching the user input to the password image from the database, and updating the password. We use arrows in types for expressions to indicate that under the types of the arguments on the left from the arrow, the type of the result is on the right from the arrow. The expression $\textbf{hash}(pwd, salt)$ concatenates the password pwd with the salt $salt$ and applies the one-way hash function $\texttt{buildHash}$ to the concatenation (the latter is denoted by $||$). The result is declassified to the level low.

$$\Gamma \vdash \textbf{hash}(pwd, salt) : \ell_{pwd} \times \ell_{salt} \to low$$
$$= \texttt{declassify}(\texttt{buildHash}(pwd||salt), low)$$

The expression $\textbf{match}(pwdImg, salt, query)$ checks if the password image $pwdImg$ is equal to the hash of the user query $query$ with the salt $salt$.

$$\Gamma \vdash \textbf{match}(pwdImg, salt, query) : \ell_{pwdImg} \times \ell_{salt} \times \ell_{query} \to \ell_{pwdImg} \sqcup low$$
$$= (pwdImg = \textbf{hash}(query, salt))$$

Notice that the expression is typable only if the security level of the result is no less confidential than both the security level of $pwdImg$ and low. The program $\textbf{update}(pwdImg, salt, oldPwd, newPwd)$ updates the old password hash $pwdImg$ by querying the old password $oldPwd$, matching its hash to $pwdImg$ and (if matched) updating the hashed password with the hash of $newPwd$.

$$\Gamma, \ell_{pwdImg} \vdash \textbf{update}(pwdImg, salt, oldPwd, newPwd) \; (low \sqsubseteq \ell_{pwdImg})$$
$$= \text{if } \textbf{match}(pwdImg, salt, oldPwd)$$
$$\text{then } pwdImg = \textbf{hash}(newPwd, salt)$$
$$\text{else skip}$$

Let us instantiate the typings above for the lattice $\mathcal{L}_{LH}$ and show that they capture the desired intuition.

- The honest user applying hash to a password and salt:
  $\Gamma \vdash \text{hash}(pwd, salt) : high \times low \rightarrow low$.
- The attacker hashing a password with the honest user's public salt:
  $\Gamma \vdash \text{hash}(pwd, salt) : low \times low \rightarrow low$.
- The honest user matching a password:
  $\Gamma \vdash \text{match}(pwdImg, salt, query) : low \times low \times high \rightarrow low$.
- The attacker attempting to guess a password by matching it to a legitimate password image and salt:
  $\Gamma \vdash \text{match}(pwdImg, salt, query) : low \times low \times low \rightarrow low$.
- The honest user modifying a password:
  $\Gamma, low \vdash \text{update}(pwdImg, salt, oldPwd, newPwd) : low \times low \times high \times high$.
- The attacker attempting to modify the honest user's password:
  $\Gamma, low \vdash \text{update}(pwdImg, salt, oldPwd, newPwd) : low \times low \times low \times low$.

These are all typable and hence secure programs. The rationale for considering these programs secure is that to succeed the attacker needs to guess the password, which is unlikely given a large password space and little prior knowledge.

That the programs are typable guarantees that the password-checking mechanism is not vulnerable to laundering attacks. For example, consider an attack that, similarly to Wallet-Attack, launders bit-by-bit the secret variable h to l (assuming h is an n-bit integer) via the declassification mechanism that is built in the hash expression.

$$
\begin{aligned}
&l := 0; \\
&\textbf{while } (n \geq 0) \textbf{ do} \\
&\quad k := 2^{n-1}; \\
&\quad \textbf{if } \text{hash}(\text{sign}(h - k + 1), 0) = \text{hash}(1, 0) \\
&\quad\quad \textbf{then } (h := h - k; l := l + k) \textbf{ else skip}; \\
&\quad n := n - 1
\end{aligned}
$$

where $\Gamma(k) = \Gamma(l) = \Gamma(n) = low, \Gamma(h) = high$ and sign returns $1, -1$ or 0 if the argument is positive, negative, or 0, respectively. That this attack might indeed leak h in a bit-by-bit fashion is easy to see because the inequality $h \geq k$ holds if and only if the inequality $h - k + 1 > 0$ holds, which, for a sensible hashing algorithm, is likely to be equivalent to $\text{hash}(\text{sign}(h - k + 1), 0) = \text{hash}(1, 0)$. Clearly, the program above is insecure according to Definition 2. Notice that the program is rightfully rejected by the type system. This is because variable h both occurs under declassification and is updated in the body of the loop.

Furthermore, observe that programs Avg and Wallet are typable whereas attacks Avg-Attack and Wallet-Attack are rejected by the type system.

6   Related Work

Policies for intentional information release have been an active area of research. Cohen's *selective (in)dependence* [8] security definition can be viewed as a precursor for our work. Cohen's definition is based on partitioning the secret input domain into subdomains requiring noninterference when secret variables are restricted to each subdomain. For example, program Par, revealing the parity of h to l, satisfies selective independence with respect to the partitioning of the domain of integers for h into odd and even numbers. However, the security policy of specifying *what* can be leaked relies on a semantic specification of subdomains. Recent incarnations of selective independence based on *abstract variables* [20], *equivalence relations* [39], and *abstract noninterference* [14] also need to be specified at the semantic level. In contrast, our escape hatches facilitate a syntactic way of specifying selective independence: two values are in the same subdomain if and only if the results of evaluating the expression under each `declassify` primitive on these two values are the same values. Moreover, the escape hatches provide the flexibility to condition the release of information on public values (cf. program Wallet), which cannot be represented by the original definition of selective independence. Finally, the syntactic escape-hatch policy mechanism leads us to a security type system that enforces security, whereas there appears no automatic enforcement mechanisms for (any variation of) selective independence.

Further related work is grouped into categories of *how* information is released, *how much* information is released, and *relative to what* information is released. For a more detailed overview of this area we refer to a recent survey [37].

How? A common approach to relaxing noninterference to account for intentional information release is based on *intransitive noninterference* [36, 32, 35, 24], which originated from early work on *conditional noninterference* [16, 17]. Mantel and Sands have recently addressed intransitive noninterference in a language-based setting [25]. Intransitive flows in the context of declassification-sensitive unwinding have been explored by Bossi et al. [6]. Intransitive noninterference accommodates policies where information might flow intransitively, e.g., from level ℓ_1 to ℓ_2 and from ℓ_2 to ℓ_3 but not from ℓ_1 to ℓ_3 directly. The goal is that information may only be declassified if it passes through a special declassifier security level. The assurance provided by this approach is that portions of computation between declassification actions are in a certain sense secure. However, no guarantees are given for the entire computation. Myers and Liskov's *decentralized model* [28, 29] offers security labels in which *selective declassification* [33] is permitted on the basis of a static analysis of process authority and relationships between principals. Security labels have additional structure that describes the entities capable of performing declassification. While the above policies help express *how* information is released, they fail to account for *what* has been released. In particular, neither intransitive noninterference nor selective declassification directly prevents laundering attacks.

How Much? A *quantitative* approach to information flow gives bounds on *how much* information may be released. For instance, this is useful for measuring how much information about the password is revealed on a login attempt during password checking. Based on Shannon's information theory [41], early ideas of quantitative security go back to Denning's work [10] which, however, does not provide automated tools for estimating the bandwidth. Clark et al. [7] propose syntax-directed inference rules for computing estimates on information flow resulted from if statements in an imperative language. Recent line of work by Di Pierro et al. [12] suggests *approximate noninterference*, which can be thought of as noninterference modulo probabilistically specified "noise" In a process-algebra setting, Lowe's quantitative definition of information flow [23] measures the capacity of information flow channels. However, tracking the quantity of information through program construct appears to be a daunting task. To date, there appears no static analysis with reasonably permissive rules for while loops.

Relative to What? In the rest of this section, we discuss models for information release relative to the attacker's power to observe and affect declassification. Volpano and Smith [46] have proposed a type system that allows password-matching operations and with the security assurance that (i) no well-typed program can leak secrets in polynomial (in the length of the secret) time, and (ii) secret leaks are only possible with a negligible probability. In subsequent work [44], Volpano proves that leaking passwords in a system where passwords are stored as images of a one-way function is not easier than breaking the one-way function. Both of these studies are, however, tailored to the password-checking scenario. Abadi gives a type system [1] in which declassification is connected to uses of encryption, for a calculus of cryptographic protocols, the spi calculus [3]. Secret keys and their usage are hidden by the security definition, allowing the result of encryption to be considered publicly visible. Sumii and Pierce [43] employ relational parametricity techniques for reasoning about cryptographic protocols involving encryption. Laud's complexity-theoretic security definition [21, 22] is also specific to declassification by encryption. This security definition ensures that a polynomial-time (in the length of the secret) adversary in an imperative language is not able to leak secrets by abusing the encryption-based declassification mechanism.

The idea underlying Dam and Giambiagi's *admissibility* [9, 15] is that the implementation of a specification satisfies admissibility if there are no other information flows than those described in a confidentiality policy of the specification. The relativity of information release here is with respect to information release in the specification.

Finally, Zdancewic and Myers have proposed a security condition called *robust declassification* [50], which captures the idea that an attacker may not learn more information than intended. The key idea is that attacker-controlled computation is not allowed to increase observations about secrets by causing misuse of the declassification mechanism. Robust declassification ensures that an active attacker (who can affect system behavior) cannot learn anything more than a passive attacker (who may only observe the system's behavior). Zdancewic has proposed a type system [49] intended to enforce robust declassification. Recently, Myers et al. [30] have generalized robust declassification as an enforceable end-to-end security property and introduced *qualified robustness* that provides untrusted code with a limited ability to affect information release.

7   Conclusion

We have presented a security model for intentional information release. Because this model delimits information flow by explicit policies, we are able to capture *what* information is released as opposed to *how* it is released. This approach enables us to track laundering attacks that are often undetectable by other models of information flow. Much work on information flow relies on *compartmentalization* (creating special security levels, or compartments, for data to restrict information flow) to fence against laundering attacks. However, as we have seen from the average-salary, electronic-wallet, and password-checking examples, compartmentalization is not a panacea. Our model can be viewed as another line of defense that prevents attacks missed by compartmentalization.

The delimited release model is in some ways orthogonal to robust declassification [50]; the former controls what may be declassified, and the latter ensures that the attacker cannot control decisions about when it is declassified. A synthesis of these security definitions in a language-based setting would further improve assurance that information is being released properly. Delimited release also opens up possibilities for using security-typed languages such as Jif [27,31] to write components of larger systems written in more conventional languages such as Java [18]. Delimited release security could guarantee that security-critical Jif code wrapped into Java programs would not disclose more information than is released by the Jif code alone.

Acknowledgment. Thanks are due to Fabio Martinelli, David Sands, Eijiro Sumii, and Steve Zdancewic for helpful comments.

This research was supported by the Department of the Navy, Office of Naval Research, ONR Grant N00014-01-1-0968. Any opinions, findings, conclusions, or recommendations contained in this material are those of the authors and do not necessarily reflect the views of the Office of Naval Research.

References

1. M. Abadi. Secrecy by typing in security protocols. *J. ACM*, 46(5):749–786, September 1999.
2. M. Abadi, A. Banerjee, N. Heintze, and J. Riecke. A core calculus of dependency. In *Proc. ACM Symp. on Principles of Programming Languages*, pages 147–160, January 1999.
3. M. Abadi and A. D. Gordon. A calculus for cryptographic protocols: The Spi calculus. *Information and Computation*, 148(1):1–70, January 1999.
4. J. Agat. Transforming out timing leaks. In *Proc. ACM Symp. on Principles of Programming Languages*, pages 40–53, January 2000.

5. A. Banerjee and D. A. Naumann. Secure information flow and pointer confinement in a Java-like language. In *Proc. IEEE Computer Security Foundations Workshop*, pages 253–267, June 2002.
6. A. Bossi, C. Piazza, and S. Rossi. Modelling downgrading in information flow security. In *Proc. IEEE Computer Security Foundations Workshop*, June 2004. To appear.
7. D. Clark, S. Hunt, and P. Malacaria. Quantitative analysis of the leakage of confidential data. In *Proc. Quantitative Aspects of Programming Languages*, volume 59 of *ENTCS*. Elsevier, 2002.
8. E. S. Cohen. Information transmission in sequential programs. In R. A. DeMillo, D. P. Dobkin, A. K. Jones, and R. J. Lipton, editors, *Foundations of Secure Computation*, pages 297–335. Academic Press, 1978.
9. M. Dam and P. Giambiagi. Confidentiality for mobile code: The case of a simple payment protocol. In *Proc. IEEE Computer Security Foundations Workshop*, pages 233–244, July 2000.
10. D. E. Denning. *Cryptography and Data Security*. Addison-Wesley, Reading, MA, 1982.
11. D. E. Denning and P. J. Denning. Certification of programs for secure information flow. *Comm. of the ACM*, 20(7):504–513, July 1977.
12. A. Di Pierro, C. Hankin, and H. Wiklicky. Approximate non-interference. In *Proc. IEEE Computer Security Foundations Workshop*, pages 1–17, June 2002.
13. D. Duggan. Cryptographic types. In *Proc. IEEE Computer Security Foundations Workshop*, pages 238–252, June 2002.
14. R. Giacobazzi and I. Mastroeni. Abstract non-interference: Parameterizing non-interference by abstract interpretation. In *Proc. ACM Symp. on Principles of Programming Languages*, pages 186–197, January 2004.
15. P. Giambiagi and M.Dam. On the secure implementation of security protocols. In *Proc. European Symp. on Programming*, volume 2618 of *LNCS*, pages 144–158. Springer-Verlag, April 2003.
16. J. A. Goguen and J. Meseguer. Security policies and security models. In *Proc. IEEE Symp. on Security and Privacy*, pages 11–20, April 1982.
17. J. A. Goguen and J. Meseguer. Unwinding and inference control. In *Proc. IEEE Symp. on Security and Privacy*, pages 75–86, April 1984.
18. J. Gosling, B. Joy, and G. Steele. *The Java Language Specification*. Addison-Wesley, August 1996.
19. N. Heintze and J. G. Riecke. The SLam calculus: programming with secrecy and integrity. In *Proc. ACM Symp. on Principles of Programming Languages*, pages 365–377, January 1998.
20. R. Joshi and K. R. M. Leino. A semantic approach to secure information flow. *Science of Computer Programming*, 37(1–3):113–138, 2000.
21. P. Laud. Semantics and program analysis of computationally secure information flow. In *Proc. European Symp. on Programming*, volume 2028 of *LNCS*, pages 77–91. Springer-Verlag, April 2001.
22. P. Laud. Handling encryption in an analysis for secure information flow. In *Proc. European Symp. on Programming*, volume 2618 of *LNCS*, pages 159–173. Springer-Verlag, April 2003.
23. G. Lowe. Quantifying information flow. In *Proc. IEEE Computer Security Foundations Workshop*, pages 18–31, June 2002.
24. H. Mantel. Information flow control and applications—Bridging a gap. In *Proc. Formal Methods Europe*, volume 2021 of *LNCS*, pages 153–172. Springer-Verlag, March 2001.

25. H. Mantel and D. Sands. Controlled downgrading based on intransitive (non)interference. Draft, July 2003.
26. J. McLean. The specification and modeling of computer security. *Computer*, 23(1):9–16, January 1990.
27. A. C. Myers. JFlow: Practical mostly-static information flow control. In *Proc. ACM Symp. on Principles of Programming Languages*, pages 228–241, January 1999.
28. A. C. Myers and B. Liskov. A decentralized model for information flow control. In *Proc. ACM Symp. on Operating System Principles*, pages 129–142, October 1997.
29. A. C. Myers and B. Liskov. Complete, safe information flow with decentralized labels. In *Proc. IEEE Symp. on Security and Privacy*, pages 186–197, May 1998.
30. A. C. Myers, A. Sabelfeld, and S. Zdancewic. Enforcing robust declassification. In *Proc. IEEE Computer Security Foundations Workshop*, June 2004. To appear.
31. A. C. Myers, L. Zheng, S. Zdancewic, S. Chong, and N. Nystrom. Jif: Java information flow. Software release. Located at http://www.cs.cornell.edu/jif, July 2001–2003.
32. S. Pinsky. Absorbing covers and intransitive non-interference. In *Proc. IEEE Symp. on Security and Privacy*, pages 102–113, May 1995.
33. F. Pottier and S. Conchon. Information flow inference for free. In *Proc. ACM International Conference on Functional Programming*, pages 46–57, September 2000.
34. F. Pottier and V. Simonet. Information flow inference for ML. In *Proc. ACM Symp. on Principles of Programming Languages*, pages 319–330, January 2002.
35. A. W. Roscoe and M. H. Goldsmith. What is intransitive noninterference? In *Proc. IEEE Computer Security Foundations Workshop*, pages 228–238, June 1999.
36. J. M. Rushby. Noninterference, transitivity, and channel-control security policies. Technical Report CSL-92-02, SRI International, 1992.
37. A. Sabelfeld and A. C. Myers. Language-based information-flow security. *IEEE J. Selected Areas in Communications*, 21(1):5–19, January 2003.
38. A. Sabelfeld and D. Sands. Probabilistic noninterference for multi-threaded programs. In *Proc. IEEE Computer Security Foundations Workshop*, pages 200–214, July 2000.
39. A. Sabelfeld and D. Sands. A per model of secure information flow in sequential programs. *Higher Order and Symbolic Computation*, 14(1):59–91, March 2001.
40. J. H. Saltzer, D. P. Reed, and D. D. Clark. End-to-end arguments in system design. *ACM Transactions on Computer Systems*, 2(4):277–288, November 1984.
41. C. E. Shannon and W. Weaver. *The Mathematical Theory of Communication*. University of Illinois Press, 1963.
42. G. Smith and D. Volpano. Secure information flow in a multi-threaded imperative language. In *Proc. ACM Symp. on Principles of Programming Languages*, pages 355–364, January 1998.
43. E. Sumii and B. Pierce. Logical relations for encryption. In *Proc. IEEE Computer Security Foundations Workshop*, pages 256–269, June 2001.
44. D. Volpano. Secure introduction of one-way functions. In *Proc. IEEE Computer Security Foundations Workshop*, pages 246–254, July 2000.
45. D. Volpano and G. Smith. Probabilistic noninterference in a concurrent language. *J. Computer Security*, 7(2–3):231–253, November 1999.
46. D. Volpano and G. Smith. Verifying secrets and relative secrecy. In *Proc. ACM Symp. on Principles of Programming Languages*, pages 268–276, January 2000.
47. D. Volpano, G. Smith, and C. Irvine. A sound type system for secure flow analysis. *J. Computer Security*, 4(3):167–187, 1996.

48. G. Winskel. *The Formal Semantics of Programming Languages: An Introduction.* MIT Press, Cambridge, MA, 1993.
49. S. Zdancewic. A type system for robust declassification. In *Proc. Mathematical Foundations of Programming Semantics*, ENTCS. Elsevier, March 2003.
50. S. Zdancewic and A. C. Myers. Robust declassification. In *Proc. IEEE Computer Security Foundations Workshop*, pages 15–23, June 2001.
51. S. Zdancewic and A. C. Myers. Secure information flow and CPS. In *Proc. European Symp. on Programming*, volume 2028 of *LNCS*, pages 46–61. Springer-Verlag, April 2001.

Appendix

This appendix presents a proof of Theorem 1.

Theorem 1. $\Gamma, pc \vdash c : U, D \Longrightarrow c$ *is secure.*

Proof. We sketch a proof by induction on the typing derivation for c. With the exception of the straightforward case for the subsumption rule (in the bottom of Figure 2), the induction is on the structure of c. Suppose c contains exactly n declassify expressions $\texttt{declassify}(e_1, \ell_1), \ldots, \texttt{declassify}(e_n, \ell_n)$. Suppose that for some security level ℓ and memories M_1 and M_2 where $M_1 =_\ell M_2$, we have $\forall i \in \{i \mid \ell_i \sqsubseteq \ell\} . \langle M_1, e_i \rangle \approx \langle M_2, e_i \rangle$. We need to show $\langle M_1, c \rangle \approx_\ell \langle M_2, c \rangle$. We assume that $\langle M_1, c \rangle \Downarrow M_1'$ and $\langle M_2, c \rangle \Downarrow M_2'$ for some M_1' and M_2' (the relation is obvious if one of the configurations diverges). It remains to be shown that $M_1' =_\ell M_2'$.

$\texttt{skip}$ Straightforward, because $M_1' = M_1 =_\ell M_2 = M_2'$.

$v := e$ Clearly, $M_1' =_\ell M_1 =_\ell M_2 =_\ell M_2'$ in case $\Gamma(v) \not\sqsubseteq \ell$. In case $\Gamma(v) \sqsubseteq \ell$, the typing rule for assignments ensures that the security levels of variables occurring in e—outside $\texttt{declassify}$ primitives—are below ℓ. Hence the values of these variables are the same in both M_1 and M_2. That the values of expressions under $\texttt{declassify}$ primitives are the same in both M_1 and M_2 is guaranteed by the assumption $\forall i \in \{i \mid \ell_i \sqsubseteq \ell\} . \langle M_1, e_i \rangle \approx \langle M_2, e_i \rangle$. (Note that declassification to level ℓ_j for some j so that $\ell_j \not\sqsubseteq \ell$ is not allowed by the typing rule for assignments.) To sum up, the values of variables outside declassification primitives are the same in both M_1 and M_2 and so are the values of expressions under $\texttt{declassify}$. Clearly, the application of $\texttt{op}$ operations to the subexpressions gives the same results for both M_1 and M_2. Therefore, $M_1' =_\ell M_2'$.

$c_1; c_2$ By the typing rule for sequential composition, both c_1 and c_2 must be typable. The set $I = \{i \mid \ell_i \sqsubseteq \ell \ \& \ \texttt{declassify}(e_i, \ell_i) \text{ occurs in } c\}$ can be viewed as the union of $I_1 = \{i \mid \ell_i \sqsubseteq \ell \ \& \ \texttt{declassify}(e_i, \ell_i) \text{ occurs in } c_1\}$ and $I_2 = \{i \mid \ell_i \sqsubseteq \ell \ \& \ \texttt{declassify}(e_i, \ell_i) \text{ occurs in } c_2\}$. As $\langle M_1, c_1; c_2 \rangle \Downarrow M_1'$ and $\langle M_2, c_1; c_2 \rangle \Downarrow M_2'$ there are M_1'' and M_2'' so that $\langle M_1, c_1 \rangle \Downarrow M_1''$ and $\langle M_2, c_1 \rangle \Downarrow M_2''$. Because $I_1 \subseteq I$, we can apply the induction hypothesis to c_1. We receive $M_1'' =_\ell M_2''$. In order to show $M_1' =_\ell M_2'$ we would like apply the induction hypothesis to c_2. However, this requires that we demonstrate $\forall i \in I_2. \langle M_1'', e_i \rangle \approx \langle M_2'', e_i \rangle$, which is different from what we know ($\forall i \in I_2. \langle M_1, e_i \rangle \approx \langle M_2, e_i \rangle$). But because the effect system ensures that no variable used in $\{e_i\}_{i \in I_2}$ is updated by c_1, we infer that for any variable v such that v occurs in $\{e_i\}_{i \in I_2}$ we have $M_1(v) = M_1''(v)$ and $M_2(v) = M_2''(v)$. This assures $\forall i \in I_2. \langle M_1'', e_i \rangle \approx \langle M_2'', e_i \rangle$, and hence, by the induction hypothesis, $M_1' =_\ell M_2'$.

if e then c_1 else c_2 Suppose $\Gamma \vdash e : \ell', D'$ for some ℓ' and D'. In case $\ell' \not\sqsubseteq \ell$, the pc-based mechanism of the type system ensures that only variables at or above ℓ' may be assigned to in c_1 and c_2. Thus, there are no assignments to variables at ℓ or below in either c_1 or c_2. Hence the memories M_1 and M_2 are unaffected below ℓ throughout the execution, which results in $M_1' =_\ell M_2'$. If $\ell' \sqsubseteq \ell$, then, because, $\forall i \in \{i \mid \ell_i \sqsubseteq \ell\}. \langle M_1, e_i \rangle \approx \langle M_2, e_i \rangle$, including all occurrences of e_i under **declassify** in e, we have $\langle M_1, e \rangle \Downarrow val$ and $\langle M_2, e \rangle \Downarrow val$ for some val. Hence, for both M_1 and M_2, the computation will take the same branch, i.e., c_1, if $val = true$, or c_2 otherwise. That $M_1' =_\ell M_2'$ follows by the application of the induction hypothesis to c_1 or c_2, respectively.

while e do d Suppose $\Gamma \vdash e : \ell', D'$ for some ℓ' and D'. Case $\ell' \not\sqsubseteq \ell$ is resolved in the same fashion as for **if**. If $\ell' \sqsubseteq \ell$, then

$$\forall i \in \{i \mid \ell_i \sqsubseteq \ell\}. \langle M_1, e_i \rangle \approx \langle M_2, e_i \rangle$$

which includes all occurrences of e_i under **declassify** in e. Therefore, we have $\langle M_1, e \rangle \Downarrow val$ and $\langle M_2, e \rangle \Downarrow val$ for some val. Hence, for both M_1 and M_2, either the computation proceeds with d, if $val = true$, or terminates otherwise. Because the **while** loop terminates for both M_1 and M_2, the computation can be represented as a sequential composition of a series of d commands. This case reduces to consequently applying the sequential composition case. Note that e keeps evaluating to the same value under both M_1 and M_2 after each iteration (the effect system ensures that no variable used under **declassify** is updated by d). Hence, when e becomes $false$, the loop terminates after executing the same number of d commands for M_1 and M_2. This implies $M_1' =_\ell M_2'$. □

The Interface Definition Language
for Fail-Safe C

Kohei Suenaga[†], Yutaka Oiwa[†], Eijiro Sumii[‡], and Akinori Yonezawa[†]

[†]Department of Computer Science, University of Tokyo
[‡]Department of Computer Science, University of Pennsylvania
{kohei, oiwa, sumii, yonezawa}@yl.is.s.u-tokyo.ac.jp

Abstract. Fail-Safe C is a safe implementation of full ANSI-C being developed by Oiwa and Sekiguchi. It uses its own internal data representations such as 2-word pointers and memory blocks with headers describing their contents. Because of this, calls to external functions compiled by conventional compilers require conversion of data representations. Moreover, for safety, many of those functions need additional checks on their arguments and return values. This paper presents a method of semi-automatically generating a wrapper doing such work. Our approach is to develop an Interface Definition Language to describe what the wrappers have to do before and after function calls. Our language is based on CamlIDL, which was developed for a similar purpose between Objective Caml and C. Our IDL processor generates code by using the types and *attributes* of functions. The attributes are additional information describing properties which cannot be expressed only by ordinary types, such as whether a pointer can be NULL, what range of memory can be safely accessed via a pointer, etc. We examined Linux system calls as test cases and designed a set of attributes required for generating their wrapper.

1 Introduction

The C language [2] is a programming language which was originally designed to develop UNIX. This language provides very flexible methods of memory access such as getting pointers to memory blocks, accessing memory via pointers, casting pointers into other types, and so on. Although these features enable programmers to write low-level operations efficiently and flexibly, they often cause critical security problems such as buffer overrun.

Fail-Safe C [11] is a full ANSI-C compatible compiler which makes programs written in C safe, preventing illegal memory accesses. Compared with previous studies [10, 14, 7, 1] which also make C programs safe, Fail-Safe C can accept a larger set of programs. For example, Fail-Safe C can safely deal with casts from pointers to integers.

The previous safe C compilers can guarantee safety when the source files of a program are available and can be compiled with these compilers. However,

K. Futatsugi et al. (Eds.): ISSS 2003, LNCS 3233, pp. 192–208, 2004.
© Springer-Verlag Berlin Heidelberg 2004

they cannot make the program safe when some functions it calls (e.g., library functions) are given as binaries compiled with usual C compilers such as gcc. Although some of the safe C compilers [14] provide method of writing wrapper for external functions, it is still too tedious to write wrappers for many external functions.

We present a method of semi-automatically generating wrappers of external functions for Fail-Safe C. We designed an interface definition language (IDL) and implemented an IDL processor which generates wrappers from interface definitions of external functions. As long as the generated wrappers are used in calling external functions (and the functions behave correctly in accordance with the interface definitions), programs are guaranteed to run safely even when these functions are executed. There are many IDLs which interface between safe languages and C. However, they are designed primarily to convert data representation of one language to another, and do not take the safety of the execution as an important aspect. Our purpose is not only interface between two languages, but to guarantee the safety of external function calls.

The wrappers' work is roughly categorized into two groups: checking preconditions and converting data representations. Because Fail-Safe C uses its original data representation, we have to convert representations of arguments and return values before and after calling external functions compiled by usual C compilers. Additionally, there are many functions which require some preconditions for safety before being called. Our IDL processor generates wrappers from given interface definitions which specify what preconditions have to hold, what kind of conversions are required, and so on. At execution time, the wrappers utilize the metadata that is added to arguments by the Fail-Safe C compiler to confirming preconditions like whether the passed memory block has sufficient size to call the function safely.

The rest of this paper is organized as follows: In Section 2, we briefly present how Fail-Safe C works. In Section 3, we examine by case study what wrappers have to do. After showing the syntax and semantics of our IDL in Section 4, we present the result of experiments in Section 5. Finally, we review previous work in Section 6 and discuss future work in Section 7.

2   Fail-Safe C

2.1   Data Representations

In this section, we briefly introduce the internal data representations used in Fail-Safe C. Further details are described in [11].

Memory Blocks. In the Fail-Safe C world, every memory block has a header. The header is a structure which contains size information of the memory block and a pointer to a structure called *TypeInfo*. Fail-Safe C performs boundary checks for every memory access by using the size information in the header. TypeInfo contains the name of the type of the memory block and a table of pointers to functions called *handler methods*.

Handler Methods. In the C language, one can arbitrarily cast a pointer into another type. This causes inconsistency between the static type of a pointer and the actual type of a memory block that it points to. Thus, in general, we cannot trust a pointer's static type. Rather, we have to access a memory block according to its actual type.

For this purpose, Fail-Safe C augments each memory block with functions for accessing it, called handler methods. To be more specific, the TypeInfo structure of a memory block contains a table of pointers to its handler methods. Fail-Safe C replaces every memory access with calls to these handler methods. When accessing memory, handler methods perform safety checks such as alignment checks according to the memory block's layout. By using handler methods in each memory block, we can safely access a memory block even if a pointer's static type is different from the actual type of the memory block.

Fat Pointers. In Fail-Safe C, every pointer is represented in two words. The upper word represents the base address of the memory block it points to, while the lower word represents an offset from the base address. By separating the offset from the base address, Fail-Safe C can perform boundary checks fast. In addition, headers of memory blocks can be accessed fast and safely, because all headers are placed just before the base address. Moreover, Fail-Safe C can detect invalid arithmetics between pointers to different memory blocks by comparing their base addresses.

The least significant bit of a base address is used as a *cast flag*. This flag is on if the pointer was cast from a pointer of another type. In this case, handler methods must be used to access memory via the pointer because the pointer's static type may be different from the memory block's actual type. On the other hand, if the flag is off, we can safely access the memory block in usual ways without using handler methods. By tracing whether a pointer is cast and by using handler methods according to need, Fail-Safe C can deal with cast pointers without sacrificing access speed of non-cast pointers. Fig. 1 illustrates the relation among a fat pointer, a memory block and TypeInfo.

Fat Integer. In usual C, one can cast a pointer to an integer whose size is not smaller than the pointer's size. To allow this, Fail-Safe C represents integers in two words. An usual integer is represented in two words with the upper word set to zero. (Thus, programs which use an arbitrary integer as a pointer does not work in Fail-Safe C.) When a pointer is cast to an integer, Fail-Safe C writes the pointer's base address in the integer's upper word and the pointer's offset in the integer's lower word. When an integer is cast to a pointer, Fail-Safe C inspects the header pointed to by the upper word of the integer, and checks the type of the memory block. If the type is different from the pointer's type we are casting to, the cast flag of the pointer is set. With these procedures, we can maintain safety even when we cast a pointer to an integer and cast the integer back to another pointer. Note that only integers whose size is big enough to retain pointers are represented in two words. Small integers like `char` are represented in the usual way.

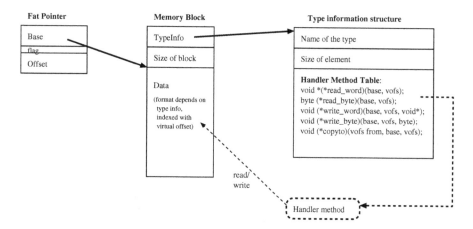

Fig. 1. Relation among a fat pointer, a memory block and a TypeInfo

2.2   Safety Guaranteed by Fail-Safe C

Most of unsafe behavior of C is caused by illegal memory accesses. Thus, the main focus of Fail-Safe C is on memory safety. However, not all of the unsafe behavior is caused by memory problems. For example, though integer overflow is not a memory problem, it is an unsafe behavior because it can cause buffer overrun [3]. As discussed in [12, pp. 7–8], a programming language can be considered safe when programs written in the language can never go wrong – that is, at every point during execution, their next behavior is predictable from the semantics of the language. From this point of view, we can take undefined behaviors in ANSI-C specification [2] as unsafe behaviors.

From the considerations above, we state the safety of Fail-Safe C as follows:

> Assume that a semantics of C is defined. Fail-Safe C always aborts a program when its next behavior is undefined in the semantics.

Although we have to formally define the semantics of C in order to make this statement exact, we do not argue about such formalism here and use the above statement to informally understand the safety Fail-Safe C guarantees.

3   Wrappers

3.1   Control Flow

Before explaining the details of wrappers, we briefly describe how wrappers generated from interface definitions work. Fig. 2 shows the flow of function calls. In this figure, a global variable g and three functions, main, wrapper_f and f are involved in an external function call. main is a function which is compiled by the Fail-Safe C compiler. f is an external function compiled by a usual C compiler.

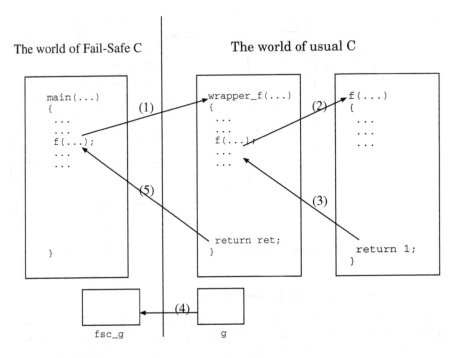

Fig. 2. Control flow of applications which use our IDL

wrapper_f is a wrapper generated from the interface definition (written in our IDL) of f.

First, main calls the external function f. Fail-Safe C replaces this call by a call of wrapper_f [(1) in Fig. 2]. After wrapper_f checking the preconditions specified by the interface definition of f, the representation of arguments are converted. Then, wrapper_f calls the external function f with converted arguments [(2)]. After f returns [(3)], wrapper_f converts the representation of the return value and side-effect on pointer-type arguments to Fail-Safe C's one. Besides, if the interface definition of f says that f updates global variables, say g, wrapper_f has to make this update visible from main. To achieve this, our IDL processor prepares two regions for global variables. One is to retain a value of the global variable for Fail-Safe C's representation (fsc_g in Fig. 2), and the other is for the usual C's representation (g in Fig. 2). After f returns, wrapper_f copies the values of g to fsc_g with converting its representation [(4)].

3.2   Safety Guaranteed by Our IDL

We will now explain what kind of safety is guaranteed by our IDL. Our IDL can guarantee the safety as long as two conditions stated in the following hold.

Firstly, Fail-Safe C's safety always holds in Fail-Safe C's world, especially just before the call to wrappers. This condition holds if Fail-Safe C does not contain bugs.

Secondly, each interface definition given to our IDL processor has to agree with the actual implementation of an external function. Thus, if an interface definition is wrong, our IDL cannot guarantee safety.

In short, we can state the safety of our IDL as follows.

A wrapper generated by our IDL safely calls an external function (in Fail-Safe C's sense) if the following conditions hold:

- The safety of Fail-Safe C holds before calling external functions.
- An interface definition agrees with the implementation of an external function.

3.3   Case Study: Linux System Calls

In this section, we describe the structure of wrappers. First, we explain by examples how wrappers should work. We use two linux system calls, read and accept, as examples.

read **System Call.** The Linux system call read is declared as follows:

```
int read(int fd, char *buf, int n);
```

fd is a file descriptor and n is the size of a memory block pointed to by buf. Data are written to the memory block that buf points to if the return value is not -1. In this case, the return value indicates the size of written data. The return value -1 means that data are not written due to some error. In this case, the global variable errno describes what the error is.

Preconditions. Firstly, we consider preconditions to call read safely. There are three preconditions that have to hold. First, because n is the size of a buffer, $n \geq 0$ has to hold. Second, buf cannot be NULL. This can be confirmed by checking that the upper word (base address) of buf is not zero. Last, the size of the buffer has to be actually more than n. This can be confirmed from the size information in the header of the memory block. read does not perform write accesses to buf beyond the region specified by n. So, as far as read is correctly implemented, buffer overrun does not occur by calling this function if preconditions above are checked.

Converting Data Representations (Before the Call). After checking preconditions, a wrapper converts the data representations of arguments from Fail-Safe C's to usual C's. The wrapper converts fd and n, which have two-word representation, into the usual representation. As for buf, because the memory block buf points to has different layout, only converting the representation of the value of buf is insufficient. Thus, buf is converted to a pointer which points to a n-byte memory block newly allocated as in the usual C.[1]

---

[1] Actually, in this particular case, the conversion is not required since the representation of char is the same between Fail-Safe C and usual C.

Converting Data Representations (After the Call). The wrapper converts the data representation of the return value, arguments and global variables from usual C's back to Fail-Safe C's. First, if the return value is not -1, the memory block buf points to has to be updated. To do this, the wrapper writes data from the memory block allocated before the function call (see above) back to the memory block pointed to by buf. Then the former memory block is deallocated.

If the return value is -1, a global variable errno is updated, indicating what error has occurred. In this case, the wrapper copies the value of the usual C's region to the Fail-Safe C's region converting its representation.

Accept System Call. Let us look into another example, the accept system call. It is declared as follows:

```
int accept(int socket,
           struct sockaddr *address,
           unsigned int *address_len);
```

where sockaddr is declared as follows:

```
struct sockaddr {
    unsigned short sa_family;
    char sa_data[14];
};
```

socket, address and address_len are, respectively, a socket descriptor, a pointer to sockaddr and a pointer to an integer which indicates the size of the structure address points to. Address may be NULL, in which case address_len is ignored.

A caller of accept passes address a pointer to sockaddr, which is casted from a pointer to a protocol specific struct. For example, if the caller uses the IP protocol, address is cast from a pointer to sockaddr_in defined as follows:

```
struct sockaddr_in {
    unsigned short sin_family;
    unsigned int sin_port;
    struct in_addr sin_addr; /* an IP address */
    unsigned char sin_zero[8];
};
```

It is guaranteed that such protocol specific structs contain an **unsigned short** member at the beginning. On the other hand, the static type of sa_data, an array of char, is usually different from its actual type.

If the return value of accept is not -1, the value is a descriptor of a newly created socket. In this case, the structure pointed to by address is updated, indicating the address with which the socket is connected. address_len is also updated, indicating the size of address. If the return value is -1, errno is updated to indicate what error has occurred.

Preconditions. We first see what preconditions are required to call this system call safely. The following four preconditions are to hold if `address` is not `NULL`:

- `address->sa_data` is not `NULL`.
- `address_len` is not `NULL`.
- `*address_len` $\geq$ 0.
- The size of the memory block `address` points to is more than `*address_len` bytes.

Among the above conditions, the first and second can be confirmed by checking that the upper word of `address->sa_data` and `address_len` is not zero. The fourth condition is confirmed from the header of the memory block `address` points to.

Converting Data Representations (Before the Call). After confirming preconditions, we convert data representations of arguments as we did in the case of `read`. Firstly, the wrapper converts `socket`'s representation from two-word to one-word.

Secondly, if `address != NULL`, the wrapper has to allocate `*address_len` bytes of memory block and copy the contents of the memory block pointed to by `address`. During the copy, the representation of each member of the structure has to be converted. `Sa_family`, whose type is `short` and its representation is the same in Fail-Safe C and usual C, can be copied directly. Although `sa_data`'s actual type may be different from its static type as we mentioned before, we can copy data safely using handler methods.

Finally, if `address_len` is not `NULL`, the wrapper newly allocates an integer in the usual C's representation, copies `*address_len` to the integer converting its representation, and makes a pointer to the integer.

Converting Data Representations (After the Call). After the function returns, the wrapper again has to convert back the representation of the return value and reflects side effects as in the case of `read`.

The return value and the global variable `errno` are converted completely in the same way as in `read`.

If the return value is not `-1`, the memory blocks pointed to by `address` and `address_len` may have been overwritten. Conversion of these values is done as follows. For `address_len`, the wrapper copies the value of the integer newly allocated before the call (see above) back to the memory block `address_len` points to. For `address`, the wrapper copies each member's value converting their representation. During the copy, the wrapper uses handler methods for `sa_data` as we did before calling.

3.4   Information Required by IDL

From the case study above, we now see that our IDL needs at least the following information to generate wrappers.

- Whether a pointer can be NULL.
- What region of a memory block can be accessed safely via a pointer.
- What kind of side effects, such as updates of memory blocks and global variables, occur during a function call.
- Conditions which have to hold before a function call (for example, n ≥ 0 in read).

3.5   Structure of Wrappers

On the basis of the case study in the previous sections, we split wrappers in the following five phases:

- Precondition Checking
- Decoding and Allocation
- Call
- Deallocation and Encoding
- Return

In the rest of this section, we explain what wrappers do in each phase.

Precondition Checking. In this phase, wrappers confirm that preconditions specified in interface definitions actually hold. For example, preconditions like whether a pointer is NULL and whether a specified region is safely accessible are confirmed, along with user-specified preconditions such as n ≥ 0.

Decoding and Allocation. In this phase, wrappers convert the representations of arguments from Fail-Safe C's to usual C's. Integers, which are represented in two words—base and offset—are converted to one-word representation by adding the offset to the base. As for pointers, wrappers allocate memory blocks with the size which is specified by the pointer's attribute. Then, wrappers copy the contents of original memory blocks to the allocated memory blocks, converting the data representation. The result of the conversion is a pointer to the newly allocated memory block.

Call. After the two phases above, a wrapper calls an external function. If the previous two phases have finished normally, and if the implementation of the external function matches the interface definition, the call should be safe. (Even if there are postconditions that have to hold, wrappers do not check those. As mentioned in section 3.2, our IDL assumes that an interface definition matches the implementation of the external function. Under this assumption, if the preconditions hold, the postconditions should also hold.)

Deallocation and Encoding. In this fourth phase, a wrapper (1) converts the representation of the return value and (2) reflects side effects caused by an external function call. The former work is exactly the reverse of the decoding and allocation phase. The latter work is as follows. Our IDL processor prepares memory that keeps Fail-Safe C's representation of each global variable. If an external function may have updated some global variables, the wrapper copies their values to the memory, converting their representation.[2]

Return. If there is a return value, the wrapper returns a value converted in the previous phase.

4   Fail-Safe C IDL

4.1   Syntax

In this section, we present the syntax of our IDL. Interface definitions written in our IDL almost look like C's header files which consist of declarations of functions, global variables and so on. One difference between our IDL and C's declaration is that types are annotated with *attributes* in our IDL. Attributes are additional information which cannot be expressed only with C's types, such as what region is accessible via a pointer.

Table 1 shows (part of) the syntax of our IDL.

The metavariable "type" is a type of C. "Ident" is a string which can be used as an identifier in C. "Pure-expr" is a C's expression which does not contain side effects. An identifier _ret is reserved to refer to a return value in "pure-expr".

"Attributes" is information added to types which is needed to generate a wrapper. An attribute with * is given to a value of pointer type. For example, if an attribute A* is given to a value of type T*, it means that the attribute A is given to the type T.

"Global-decl" is a declaration of a global variable which may be updated by external functions. It is a global variable declaration of C accompanied with attributes. "Struct-decl" is a declaration of a structure which is used by interface definitions. It consists of a structure declaration of C and attributes of each member. "Function-decl" is a interface definition of an external function. "attributes$_1$" is attributes of the return value and "attributes$_2$" is attributes of the function.

4.2   Attributes and Their Semantics

In this section, we present the attributes in our IDL, designed based on the case study described in Section 3.3.

always_null, maybe_null, never_null. These attributes are given to a pointer type variable, meaning the pointer has to be always NULL, can be NULL and must not be NULL, respectively. For example, for the **read** system call in Section 3.3, never_null is given to **buf**.

If these attributes are given, the generated wrapper confirms if these conditions actually hold in Precondition Checking phase.

---

[2] Conversely, in the decoding and allocation phase, we could copy the value of global variables from Fail-Safe C's memory into usual C's. However, this is not implemented so far, because we have never come across an external function which requires that.

Table 1. Syntax of our IDL (excerpt): { T } means a sequence of zero or more Ts. { T, } means a comma-separated sequence of zero or more Ts

attributes	::= ϵ | [{ attribute, }]
attribute	::= ident
	| ident ({ pure-expr, })
	| * attribute
global-decl	::= attributes type declarator
struct-decl	::= **struct** {
	{ attributes type declarator }
	}
declarator	::= { *[**const**] } direct-declarator
direct-declarator	::= ident
	| (declarator)
	| direct-declarator [[pure-expr]]
	| direct-declarator (param-list)
param-list	::= { attributes type declarator, }
function-decl	::= attributes$_1$ type { * [**const**] } ident (param-list) attributes$_2$

can_access_in_elem(e$_1$, e$_2$). This attribute is given to a variable of pointer type. It means that, if this attribute is given to a pointer argument p, the region from $p + e_1$ to $p + e_2$ must be readable and writable via p, where e_1 and e_2 are pure-exprs. In the case of **read** in Section 3.3, can_access_in_elem(0, n - 1) is given to **buf**.

If this attribute is given, the wrapper confirms that an indicated region is actually accessible from the header of the memory block in Precondition Checking phase. In Decoding and Allocation phase, the wrapper copies the contents of the given memory block to newly allocated one. In copying, the wrapper converts the representations of the contents of the memory block from the Fail-Safe C's one to the usual C's one.

can_access_in_byte(e). This attribute is given to a pointer type variable, meaning that e bytes from the pointer is accessible via the pointer. In the case of **accept** in Section 3.3, can_access_in_byte(*address_len) is given to **address**[3].

If this attribute is given, the wrapper confirms the indicated region is actually accessible from the header of the memory block pointed to by the pointer. The wrapper also copies the contents of the memory block to a newly allocated memory block in Decoding and Allocation phase.

string. This attribute is given to a pointer to **char**, meaning that the variable is a pointer to a null-terminated string. If this attribute is given, the wrapper

---

[3] Because **address_len** is dereferenced at this point, the precondtions of **address_len** have to be confirmed before those of **address** are confirmed. There may be dependencies among arguments as in this case. For now, our IDL ignores these dependencies and users have to resolve them manually.

confirms that the pointer is actually null-terminated in Precondition Checking phase and copies the string to a newly allocated memory block in Decoding and Allocation phase.

write_global(e_1, *ident*). This attribute is given to function declarations (specified at attributes$_2$ of Table 1.). Ident is a name of a global variable. This attribute means that if $e_1 \neq 0$ holds after the external function returns, ident is updated by the function. For example, write_global(_ret == -1, errno) is given to read. If this attribute is given, the wrapper copies the value of specified variable of the usual C's world to Fail-Safe C's one converting representation.

write(*e*, *ident*, e_1, e_2). This attribute is given to a function declaration. Ident is a pointer-type argument of the function which is not qualified by const. It means that, if $e \neq 0$ holds after the function returns, the region from ident $+e_1$ to ident $+e_2$ may be updated by the function. For example, write(_ret != -1, buf, 0, _ret - 1) is given to read. If this attribute is given, the wrapper writes back the contents of the specified region in Deallocation and Encoding phase. e_1 and e_2 can be omitted. In this case the wrapper writes back all of the accessible regions specified by other attributes.

precond(*e*). This attribute is given to a function declaration. It means that $e \neq 0$ has to hold before the external function call. For example, precond(n >= 0) is given to read. The specified condition is checked in Precondition Checking phase.

4.3   An Example of Interface Definition

Fig 3 shows an example of interface definition. We gave the interface definition of open, read, write and accept.

Note that each attribute can refer to every argument of the interface definition the attribute belongs to even if the attribute occurs before the argument it refers to. For example, although buf occurs before nbytes in read's interface definition, nbytes can be referred to by can_access_in_elem which is given to buf.

5   Experiments

5.1   Method and Results

We implemented our IDL processor described above in Objective Caml. Using this implementation, we measured the overhead caused by wrappers, comparing the time spent by programs which calls external functions in the following two cases:

- Programs compiled by Fail-Safe C and linked with Fail-Safe C run-time libraries. Of course it uses generated wrappers to call external functions.
- Programs compiled by gcc -O3 which calls external functions directly.

```
    int errno;

    struct sockaddr {
        unsigned short sa_family;
        [never_null] char *sa_data;
    };

    int open([never_null, string] const char *path, int flags)
      [write_global(_ret == -1, errno)];
    int read(int fildes,
                    [never_null,
                 can_access_in_elem(0, nbytes - 1),
                 write(_ret != -1, 0, _ret - 1)] char *buf,
                    int nbytes)
      [precond(nbytes >= 0), write_global(_ret == -1, errno)];
    int write(int fildes,
                    [never_null, can_access_in_elem(0, nbytes - 1)]
                const char *buf,
                    int nbytes)
      [precond(nbytes >= 0), write_global(_ret == -1, errno)];
    int accept(int socket,
              [can_access_in_byte(*address_len),
               write(_ret != -1)] struct sockaddr *address,
               [write(_ret != -1)] int *address_len)
      [precond(address == NULL || address_len != NULL),
       write_global(_ret == -1, errno)];
```

Fig. 3. An example of interface definition

We conducted experiments on machines with Sun UltraSPARC-II 400 MHz CPU with 13.0GB main memory.

Overhead of Converting Integers. First, we wrote a function succ as an external function. It receives one integer, adds 1 to it and returns. We also wrote a program which calls succ 10^7 times sequentially and compared the duration spent in the two cases mentioned before. The result of this experiment shows the overhead of converting integers. We show the result in Table 5.1. The overhead of the wrapper is only 6%.

Overhead of Converting Pointer-Type Arguments. Next, we wrote a function **arraysucc** and compiled it with gcc. It receives an array of 10^7 char and adds 1 to each element. We also wrote a program which calls **arraysucc** as an external function. The result of this experiment shows the overhead of converting pointer-type arguments. The result in Table 5.1 shows that the overhead of allocating memory and copying contents is very large, 199%, comparing with the overhead of converting integers.

Table 2. Overhead of each program

	succ	arraysucc	cp
with wrapper (msec)	234	597	144
without wrapper (msec)	220	200	91
overhead (%)	6	199	58

In this experiment, we also measured how much time is spent in each phase. We show the result in Table 3.

Table 3. Overhead of converting pointer-type arguments. P: Precondition Checking, D: Decoding and Allocation, C: Call, E: Deallocation and Encoding

	P	D	C	E	Total
Execution time (msec)	0	326	110	160	596
Ratio (%)	0	54.7	18.5	26.8	-

Overhead of a More Practical Program. Last, we wrote a program which copies files of 10^6 bytes using open, read, write as external functions, and measured overhead. The result is shown in Table 5.1. The overhead is 58% with wrappers.

Table 4. Time spent in each phase of read's and write's wrapper. P: Precondition Checking, D: Decoding and Allocation C: Call, E: Deallocation and Encoding

	P	D	C	E	Total
Execution time of read's wrapper (msec)	1	16	46	14	77
Execution time of write's wrapper (msec)	1	16	73	4	94

Also in this experiment, we measured the time spent in each phase. We present the result of read's and write's wrapper in Table 4. In this program, The time spent for Call phase is dominant because file access is performed in this phase. However, focusing on the execution time of the wrapper itself, the overhead of Decoding and Allocation phase is large as in the case of arraysucc.

5.2   Discussion

From the experiments above, we see that most of overhead is caused by Decoding and Allocation phase. Thus, to reduce overhead of a whole wrapper, we need to reduce the overhead of this phase.

There are two possible solutions. First one is to omit copying in Decoding and Allocation phase. For example, in the case of read, the contents of the memory block pointed to by buf is never read and always overwritten. In such case, wrappers do not have to copy contents of memory block in Decoding and Allocation phase.

Second one is to omit allocation of memory block in Decoding and Allocation phase if representations of memory blocks are the same in usual C and Fail-Safe C. For example, again in the case of `read`, if `buf` points to a memory block whose actual type is `char`, all the wrapper has to do is to convert a two-word representation to one-word one, without allocating a new memory block.

6   Related Work

Many functional languages have its own IDLs. For example, H/Direct [6, 5] and CamlIDL [9] are IDLs to call external functions from functional languages. The former is an IDL for Haskell [8] and the latter is for Objective Caml [13]. Although Chez Scheme [4] has no independent IDL, it can call external functions using `foreign-procedure` function. This function receives an interface definition of an external function and returns closure that calls the external function. These IDLs focus on conversion of data representation and pay less attention to safety checks than our IDL does. For example, although CamlIDL prepares `size_is` attribute which is a counterpart of our `can_access_in_elem`, wrappers generated by CamlIDL does not check buffer size even if the attribute specified. Because of this, if a buffer of insufficient size is passed to a generated wrapper, safety of an external function call is lost.

CCured [10, 14] is another safe implementation of C. This implementation analyses pointer usage statically and reduces needless dynamic checks. Because CCured also uses its own data representation, it also requires the data conversions before calling external functions. There are two methods to call external functions from programs compiled with CCured. The first one is to provide manually written wrappers of external functions. These wrappers check preconditions and converts data representation as ones which our IDL generates. The second one is to add the annotations that identify external function calls. With these annotations, CCured infers which data is used by the external functions. CCured separates the metadata of such data from the actual data, which is usually held in one memory block together with the actual data. Because the layout of the actual data is the same as the usual C's one, CCured can pass these data to external functions without converting representation. The latter method has a problem, however, that it cannot be applied to external functions that have side effects. Although CCured may have to change the metadata after calling such functions, there is no way to know what change has to be reflected. With our IDL, one can cope with external functions with side effects.

7   Conclusion and Future Work

In this paper, we proposed a method to semi-automatically generate wrappers to call external functions from Fail-Safe C. Using our implementation, we also measured overhead of generated wrappers.

For future work, we are planning to apply our approach to larger and more practical programs. Because the implementation of Fail-Safe C has not been completed yet, the amount of overhead for practical programs are yet to be seen. We are planning to examine all the system calls and library functions, extract common features and add new attributes. We will also examine the effectiveness of the optimization methods mentioned in Section 5.2 by applying it to sufficiently many functions.

Acknowledgment

We are grateful to the members of Yonezawa group, especially to Mr. Oyama Yoshihiro, for their comments on our work. Many ideas in this work stemmed from discussion with them.

References

1. Todd M. Austin, Scott E. Breach, and Gurindar S. Sohi. Efficient detection of all pointer and array access errors. In *Proceedings of the ACM SIGPLAN '94 Conference on Programming Language Design and Implementation*, pages 290–301, 1994.
2. Dennis M. Ritchie Brian W. Kernighan. *The C Programming Language (Second Edition)*. Prentice Hall, 1988.
3. CERT/CC. CERT Advisory CA-2003-10 Integer overflow in Sun RPC XDR library routines, April 2003. http://www.cert.org/advisories/CA-2003-10.html.
4. R. Kent Dybvig. *Chez Scheme User's Guide*, 1998. http://www.scheme.com/csug/index.html.
5. Sigbjorn Finne, Daan Leijen, Erik Meijer, and Simon L. Peyton Jones. H/Direct: A binary foreign language interface for Haskell. In *Proceedings of the third ACM SIGPLAN international conference on Functional programming*, pages 153–162, 1998.
6. Sigbjorn Finne, Daan Leijen, Erik Meijer, and Simon L. Peyton Jones. Calling hell from heaven and heaven from hell. In *Proceedings of the fourth ACM SIGPLAN international conference on Functional programming*, pages 114–125, 1999.
7. T. Jim, G. Morrisett, D. Grossman, M. Hicks, J. Cheney, and Y. Wang. Cyclone: A safe dialect of C. In *Proceedings of USENIX Annual Technical Conference*, June 2002.
8. Simon Peyton Jones. *Haskell 98 language and libraries: the Revised Report*, December 2002. http://www.haskell.org/definition/haskell98-report.pdf.
9. Xavier Leroy. *CamlIDL Users Manual*. INRIA Recquencourt, July 2001. http://camlidl.inria.fr/camlidl.
10. George C. Necula, Scott McPeak, and Westley Weimer. CCured: type-safe retrofitting of legacy code. In *Proceedings of the 29th ACM SIGPLAN–SIGACT symposium on Principles of Programming Languages*, pages 128–139, 2002.
11. Yutaka Oiwa, Tatsurou Sekiguchi, Eijiro Sumii, and Akinori Yonezawa. Fail-Safe ANSI-C Compiler: An approach to making C programs secure (progress report). In *Proceedings of International Symposium on Software Security, Tokyo, Japan, November 8–10, 2002*, volume 2609 of *Lecture Notes in Computer Science*. Springer-Verlag, February 2003.
12. Benjamin C. Pierce. *Types and Programming Languages*. MIT press, 2002.

13. Xavier Leroy Dmien Doligez Jacques Garrigue Didier Rémy and Jérôme Vouillon. *The Objective Caml system release 3.06 Documentation and user's manual.* Institut National de Recherche en Informatique et en Automatique, August 2002.
14. Jeremy Condit Matthew Harren Scott McPeak George C. Necula Westley Weimer. CCured in the real world. In *Proceedings of the ACM SIGPLAN '03 Conference on Programming Language Design and Implementation*, June 2003.

Lightweight Wrappers for Interfacing with Binary Code in CCured

Matthew Harren and George C. Necula

University of California, Berkeley,
Computer Science Division,
Berkeley, CA, USA 94720-1776
{matth, necula}@cs.berkeley.edu
(510) 642-8290   fax: (510) 642-5775

Abstract. The wide use of separate compilation and precompiled libraries among programmers poses a challenge to source-code based security and analysis tools such as CCured. These tools must understand enough of the behavior of precompiled libraries that they can prevent any unsafe use of the library. The situation is even more complicated for instrumentation tools that change the layout of data to accommodate array bounds or other metadata that is necessary for safety checking.

This paper describes the solution we use with CCured: a system of context-sensitive wrapper functions. These wrappers check that library functions are invoked on valid arguments, and also maintain the extra runtime invariants imposed by CCured. We describe the design of these wrappers and our experiences using them, including the case where complex data structures are passed to or from the library.

1   Introduction

Static program analysis tools, including those that detect or prevent security problems, usually rely on the availability of source code for the programs that they analyze. For interprocedural analyses, however, the practice of linking to precompiled libraries is a large hurdle. Tools that cannot analyze binary code need a way to model the behavior of these library routines.

There are a number of reasons why an analysis tool must deal with precompiled code. The most obvious reason is that the source code for a library may be proprietary. Even for open source libraries, however, many programmers will by default install only the binaries and header files; asking users to install the source code for each library is an undesirable burden. If software security analysis tools are to become more widely used, ease-of-use is an important consideration. Finally, modeling only the essential behavior of a library component allows natural support for dynamic linking. Users may choose alternate implementations of that component without having to reanalyze the program, provided the new implementation has the same preconditions and postconditions.

This paper presents a system that enables CCured [1], a source-based security tool, to interact with library code. Throughout this paper, we use "library

K. Futatsugi et al. (Eds.): ISSS 2003, LNCS 3233, pp. 209–225, 2004.

code" to refer to any binary code compiled without CCured to which we want to link CCured code. Because CCured uses run-time instrumentation in addition to compile-time analyses, the wrappers must support the maintenance and updating of CCured's runtime metadata, in addition to modeling the pertinent aspects of the library's behavior for the static analysis. One of the primary goals of CCured is ease of use on legacy code, and a convenient mechanism for wrappers is important when we use CCured on large legacy systems.

We begin with a brief overview of the CCured system and the difficulties in using precompiled libraries with CCured. Section 3 describes the wrapper functions we use to solve this problem. We discuss in Section 4 how these wrappers make use of the context-sensitivity feature of CCured.

Section 5 extends these wrappers to more complicated data structures. We provide examples of our wrappers in Section 6, and discuss related work in Section 7.

2   CCured

CCured is an interprocedural, flow-insensitive analysis and transformation tool that guarantees type and memory safety in C programs. By classifying pointers into "kinds" based on their usage, CCured is able to insert the necessary runtime checks to ensure memory safety. These runtime checks require that *metadata* be stored with many pointers to provide, for example, the bounds of the array being manipulated, or the dynamic type of an object.

In this paper, we will consider only the three CCured pointer kinds shown in Figure 1.

- A SAFE pointer is an ordinary, one-word C pointer that cannot be used with pointer arithmetic. SAFE pointers, if not null, point to valid memory locations of the appropriate type.
- A SEQ (sequence) pointer has a three-word representation: the pointer plus the bounds on the *home area* for this array. The pointer may be incremented or decremented, but the bounds do not change unless the pointer is over-written entirely. SEQ pointers use the following invariant: if the pointer is within the bounds it specifies, then dereferencing it will yield an object of the correct type.
- An FSEQ (forward sequence) pointer is an optimization for a common case of sequence pointers: when no lower-bound check is needed (because the pointer is never decremented), we need only a two-word representation. FSEQ pointers maintain the invariant that if the pointer value is less than the specified upper bound, then dereferencing it will yield an object of the correct type.

We prefer SAFE pointers to FSEQ, and FSEQ to SEQ, for performance reasons: SAFE pointers use less memory and require fewer checks at each access. Note that a SEQ pointer can be easily coerced to an FSEQ, and an FSEQ to a SAFE, by dropping unneeded metadata and performing the runtime checks.

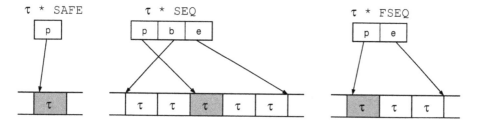

Fig. 1. SAFE, SEQ and FSEQ pointers, respectively, to the shaded memory locations

2.1   An Example

In the following code fragment,

```
1    char* a = (char*)malloc(mysize);
2    char* b = a;
3    b[5] = '.';
4    char* c = b;
5    char* d = c + 5;
```

CCured infers that variable b must carry an upper bound so that the array access on line 3 can be checked for safety at runtime. This requirement is transitively applied to variable a due to the assignment at line 2, since b must get its upper-bound from a. Similarly, variable c requires an upper bound because of the arithmetic on line 5, and this constraint also flows to b and a. We choose the best assignment of kinds that satisfies these constraints, and make variables a,b and c FSEQ. Variable d needs no bounds checks, so we make it SAFE.

Inferring these constraints requires a whole-program analysis. If lines 2 and 3 above are enclosed in a separate function "setFifth" (as shown below) we will need to pass the constraint that b requires an upper bound across the function boundary.

```
1    char* a = (char*)malloc(mysize);
2
3    char* c = setFifth(a);
4
5    char* d = c + 5;
     ...
6 char* setFifth(char* b) {
7    b[5] = '.';
8    return b;
9 }
```

Suppose setFifth is a precompiled library function, and its code is not visible to CCured. CCured will not know that it has to ensure that the argument b can be used in a memory operation. One solution is to write a wrapper function that understands the semantics of setFifth and will check that its argument has the right length. Because the library uses C-style pointers, the wrapper also needs to pass a one-word pointer to `setFifth`, and convert the return value back to a CCured pointer, as shown below:

```
1    char* a = (char*)malloc(mysize);
2
3    char* c = setFifth_wrapper(a);
4
5    char* d = c+5;
     . . .
6 char* setFifth(char* b); //Defined in a library.
7
8 char* setFifth_wrapper(char* b) {
9    if (LENGTH_OF(b) <= 5) { Error, abort the program ... }
10   //Call the real function:
11   char* retval = setFifth(CONVERT_TO_C(b));
12   return CONVERT_FROM_C(retVal);
13 }
```

However, this wrapper would need to be written in a kind-polymorphic way — the pointer kinds that a function uses may change depending how the function is used. For example, if line 5 in the example above were changed to

```
5    char* d = c - 10;
```

then variable c would need a lower bound. This requirement would force the return type of `setFifth_wrapper` to be a SEQ pointer, which in turn would force the argument to the wrapper to be SEQ so that we have a lower bound on b available for the operation labeled *CONVERT_FROM_C*. We would like to do this polymorphically, so that one such use of `setFifth_wrapper` does not force all uses of `setFifth_wrapper` to pass a SEQ value for b.

Our solution to the problem of library code in CCured is a system that makes writing these wrappers easy, and avoids the need to write separate wrappers for different pointer kinds. The wrappers we describe in this paper will:

1. Describe what constraints, such as buffer lengths, the external function requires on its inputs, and
2. Perform appropriate runtime actions to check these constraints, to convert CCured pointers to C, and to convert C pointers to CCured.

Although CCured cannot guarantee that the library functions are memory safe, the wrappers can guarantee that the function's preconditions are met, which will go a long way towards ensuring correct behavior.

3   Simple Wrappers for CCured

We present a mechanism for specifying wrapper functions that accomplishes both of the above points. At compile time, we generate constraints about what metadata should be carried with each pointer, and at runtime the specification is treated as a function that manipulates metadata, performs checks, and calls the underlying library code.

The wrappers are written as ordinary C code using a number of helper functions listed in Table 1. We can divide these helpers into two main groups:

- **Those That Operate on Wide Pointers.** (Group A in Table 1) Helper functions such as __ptrof ("pointer of") and __ensure_length read the metadata maintained in CCured's wide pointers and perform necessary checks. These functions also extract the data from a wide pointer for passing to the library.
- **Those That Operate on Standard Pointers.** (Group B in Table 1) Helper functions such as __mkptr ("make pointer") build wide pointers that CCured can use from the standard pointers returned by a library call.

Except for __check_string, which relies on a complete scan of the buffer, the operations shown here are constant-time functions requiring only a few simple instructions.

We use the type "void *" in Table 1 to denote helper functions that can be used on pointers of any type, but CCured's typechecking of helper functions is not as lax as these function signatures might imply. In fact, CCured will guarantee at compile-time that the arguments and return values at each call to a helper function have the same type. This prevents programmers from accidentally changing the apparent type of a pointer when passing it through a helper function, and it also allows CCured to maintain necessary invariants regarding the pointer base types that we do not discuss in this paper.

Figure 2 shows a wrapper specification for crypt, a function that returns a cryptographic hash of the key argument and the first two characters of the salt argument. The "#pragma ccuredwrapper" command tells CCured to replace all references to crypt in a program with crypt_wrapper, which has the same interface. Note that this replacement occurs also in the places where the address of the function is taken. This new layer of indirection provides a convenient encapsulation for the constraints and run-time actions needed when calling this external function.

This wrapper checks that the first argument to the function is a null-terminated string, and that the second argument is a sequence of at least two characters. Then we strip the metadata from the CCured pointers and call the library function using standard arguments. Finally, we trust the library function to return a null-terminated string (or a null pointer). So we invoke the helper function __mkptr_string; when thinResult is nonnull, this routine constructs a CCured pointer with a home area that starts at "thinResult" and ends at "thinResult + strlen(thinResult) + 1." If there is a bug in the library that causes it to return a pointer to a buffer that has no null character, the wrapper will read past the end of that buffer just as the original program would have. CCured offers no protection against bugs in external functions.

Table 1. Some of the helper functions provided by CCured for use in wrappers. Here, "void * SAFE" refers to a standard (one-word) pointer that is compatible with external functions, while all other uses of "void *" refer to an arbitrary CCured pointer

Group A. These functions are for use on *CCured pointers*:

- `void * SAFE __ptrof(void *ptr);`
  Type inference: no constraints.

  At run time: returns `ptr`'s underlying standard pointer.

  Asserts: `ptr` is either null or within bounds.
- `int __check_string(char *ptr);`
  Type inference: `ptr` must carry an upper bound (i.e. it must be FSEQ or SEQ, not SAFE).

  At run time: checks that `ptr` points to a valid string, and returns the length of the string.

  Asserts: `ptr` is nonnull, within bounds, and points to a buffer that has a terminating nul character.
- `void __ensure_length(void *ptr, unsigned int n);`
  Type inference: `ptr` must carry an upper bound.

  At run time: verifies that `ptr` is at least `n` bytes long.

  Asserts: `ptr` is nonnull, within bounds, and has at least `n` bytes between the pointer and the end of the home area.

Group B. These functions are for use on *standard pointers* (i.e. those returned by the library) and do not perform any checking:

- `void * __mkptr(void * SAFE p, void *phome);`
  Type inference: `phome` must have the same kind (SAFE, FSEQ, etc.) as the return type.

  At run time: returns a (possibly fat) pointer to `p` with the same metadata as `phome`.
- `void * __mkptr_size(void * SAFE p, int size);`
  Type inference: no constraints

  At run time: returns a (possibly fat) pointer to `p` with the end of the home area equal to `p + size`.
- `char * __mkptr_string(char * SAFE p);`
  Type inference: no constraints

  At run time: returns a (possibly fat) pointer to `p` with the end of the home area equal to `p + strlen(p) + 1`. Equivalent to `__mkptr_size(p, strlen(p) + 1)`.

3.1   Curing with Wrappers

We have implemented wrappers for about 120 commonly-used functions from the C Standard Library. CCured inserts these wrappers into the relevant header files so that calls to these functions are handled correctly with no further intervention required. For example, whenever a program imports the "crypt.h" header it will automatically import `crypt_wrapper` as well. Programmers who work with

```
char *crypt(char const *key, char const *salt);
  ...
#pragma ccuredwrapper("crypt_wrapper", for("crypt"))
__inline static
char *crypt_wrapper(char const *key, char const *salt)
{
  __check_string(key);
  __ensure_length(salt, 2);
  char* thinResult = crypt(__ptrof(key), __ptrof(salt));
  return __mkptr_string(thinResult);
}
```

Fig. 2. A wrapper for `crypt`, a function that computes a hash of its arguments. The wrapper verifies interface assumptions using the `__check_string` routine, removes CCured-specific metadata with `__ptrof`, calls the underlying function, and packages up the result using `__mkptr_string`. Note that `crypt_wrapper` has the same signature as `crypt`

their own libraries can insert the wrappers anywhere in the program — as long as CCured sees the `#pragma` it will substitute the wrapper globally.

Most of these wrappers have a very small footprint, so we declare them as "`inline`" to specify that the body of the wrapper should be inlined at the call site. One case where the wrapper cannot be inlined is with function pointers — instead of taking the address of the original function, we will take the address of the wrapper function.

When CCured processes wrapper code, it will add all of the usual safety checks and instrumentation, in addition to the checks that the programmer explicitly requested with the helper functions. From CCured's perspective, the only difference between a wrapper function and a normal function is that when it sees a call to a library function in a wrapper, it will allow the code to call the underlying library. In a regular function, a call to an external library will be replaced by a call to the appropriate wrapper.

4   Context Sensitivity

CCured's kind inference mechanism is flow and context insensitive. All call sites of a function will be treated as assignments of actual arguments to the same formal argument. This insensitivity means that the pointer kind associated with a formal argument is the most conservative required by any call site. For example, if there is a call to `setFifth` that requires a `SEQ` return value, then variable b in `setFifth` will be inferred to be `SEQ`, and every call site of the function will be required to pass a `SEQ` argument. This can cause undesirable `SEQ` pointers to spread throughout a program. This problem can become even worse when a function is called with incompatible types at different call sites. CCured is forced in this case to use a more expensive dynamically-typed pointer which we do not discuss here. In fact such problems would almost certainly occur for helper functions such as __ptrof that are intended to be used on any pointer type whatsoever.

To prevent this problem, CCured offers programmer-controlled context sensitivity. If the programmer declares a function to be context sensitive, CCured will treat each invocation of the function (or place where the address of the function is taken) independently.

Our wrappers use this context sensitivity for both the helper functions and the wrapper specifications themselves. This means that helper functions can operate on different pointer kinds when used in different contexts. We may infer that the argument and return type for __mkptr are SAFE in one location and SEQ in another. (Later, after the inference of kinds is complete, we replace the helper functions with code that actually performs the requested operation.) Similarly, the wrappers themselves can change depending on the call site.

CCured handles context-sensitive functions by creating a fresh copy of the function body for each call site, and then using its normal inference. When this is finished, CCured can coalesce any duplicate bodies back together, so that if some copies of setFifth use SEQ pointers and another group uses FSEQ, we need only two copies of setFifth in the final code — one for each kind. But coalescing can only go so far in preventing code bloat, so we usually disable context sensitivity for ordinary functions. We find that context sensitivity is more useful for wrappers than ordinary code because library functions (and hence their wrappers) tend to be used in multiple, unrelated parts of a program, making cross-contamination of constraints likely. Moreover, wrappers tend to be so small that they are often declared as "inline" already. By instantiating them at each call site early in the analysis, we can get the benefits of context sensitivity without further increasing the size of the code.

5   Deep-Copying Wrappers

The wrappers described so far work only when the library function accesses a single layer of pointers. Helpers such as __ptrof and __mkptr can manipulate metadata on the top layer, but are not enough when the library needs to access pointers to pointers. Because CCured changes the representation of pointers, data structures that include pointers are almost always incompatible with library code.

For most such data structures, we need a stronger wrapper mechanism. We therefore introduce *deep-copying wrappers*, which create a copy of the complex data structure in order to remove or add metadata. Deep-copying wrappers are regular wrapper that use some additional specification of how a data structure should be copied. When passing data to a library, we create a copy of the structure with no metadata; when retrieving data from a library we create a copy that has metadata to match its structure. (CCured's garbage collector insures that the newly-allocated copies are not leaked.) In exchange for breaking aliasing and adding a small performance cost, we have a means to exchange data between the two systems.

As an example, consider the following structure that is used for hostname lookups. For brevity, we show only three representative fields of the structure.

```
struct hostent {
    char    *       h_name;         /* official name of host */
    char    **      h_aliases;      /* alias list */
    short           h_addrtype;     /* host address type */
};
```

The library function **gethostbyname**, and related functions that perform domain name queries, return a pointer to a structure of this type. h_name points to a string containing the domain name and $h\_aliases$ points to a null-terminated array of string pointers representing other domain names for the computer.

CCured recognizes three pointer types for this structure, one for each use of "*". Each of these three pointer nodes may be given a different kind by the CCured inference depending on how they are used in the program. If all three pointers are inferred to be **SAFE**, then an ordinary wrapper will work fine. However, this outcome unlikely unless the h_name and $h\_aliases$ fields are never used, since reading any more than the first element requires array bounds information. If an ordinary wrapper were used when any of the pointers had a kind other than **SAFE**, a compilation error would occur to prevent the changed representation of **struct hostent** from causing bugs in the program.

We will consider the common case where each of these pointers becomes **SEQ**, reflecting the need for bounds to check the array accesses. This will change the shape of **struct hostent** in two ways, as shown in Figure 3:

1. The size of the struct itself will increase by four words, and the offsets of the fields will change, when the two top-level pointers are changed to wide pointers.
2. The inner pointers of $h\_aliases$ will also become wide pointers. This means that elements in the $h\_aliases$ array are now three words wide, so the array cannot be safely accessed by code that expects the array elements to be one word wide.

Either of these changes will pose a problem to our simple wrappers. Our solution is to define two versions of **struct hostent**: one that uses standard pointers, and one that uses wide. At runtime, we copy the data between the two representations.

5.1 Defining a Compatible Representation

Deep-copying wrappers use the **COMPAT** annotation to declare a type that should have no wide pointers. Figure 4 shows a wrapper that uses **COMPAT**.

When CCured sees this annotation, it creates two versions of the struct, which can be seen in Figure 5. The first, which keeps the name of the original struct (**hostent** in this case) has the default behavior for a type in CCured, and may be transformed to use wide pointers. The second definition will be given a new name

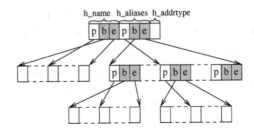

Fig. 3. Representation of **struct hostent** after the CCured transformation. Array-bounds metadata (gray) is interspersed with data (white)

```
#pragma ccuredwrapper("gethostbyname_wrapper", for("gethostbyname"));
__inline static
struct hostent* gethostbyname_wrapper(const char * name) {
  __check_string(name);
  struct hostent COMPAT * hcompat = gethostbyname(__ptrof(name));

  __DECL_NEW_FROM_COMPAT(hres, hostent, hcompat);
  return hres;
}
```

Fig. 4. A wrapper for **gethostbyname**, which performs a DNS lookup for the specified domain name. This wrapper validates its input, calls the underlying library function, and receives as a result a structure that uses standard pointers. __DECL_NEW_FROM_COMPAT allocates a new **struct hostent** called *hres* and populates it with the data in *hcompat*. (If *hcompat* is null, then *hres* will be too.) Section 5.2 describes how CCured generates the metadata needed by __DECL_NEW_FROM_COMPAT

(**hostent_COMPAT** in this case) and used wherever the programmer has specified the **COMPAT** declaration. The **COMPAT** version uses the same representation as C and never includes wide pointers, so this is the format that the library uses.

5.2   Generating Deep Wrappers

Now we need a mechanism to copy data between the wide and COMPAT structures. CCured generates a "deep copy" function to copy between the two representations when the wrapper author specifies, for each field of each struct, how such copying should be done. Depending on how the program interacts with the library, we may need to copy data from wide structs to standard, vice versa, or both.

For example, consider the standard-to-wide direction used for **gethostbyname**. Figure 6 shows the annotation that we give to CCured for this case.

- The **h_addrtype** field does not involve pointers, so CCured knows to copy this value directly without any annotation needed from the programmer.

```
struct hostent {                              struct hostent_COMPAT {
    char * SEQ        h_name;                     char *        h_name;
    char * SEQ * SEQ  h_aliases;                  char **       h_aliases;
    short             h_addrtype;                 short         h_addrtype;
};                                            };
```

Fig. 5. Possible definitions of **struct hostent** after CCured's transformations. **char * SEQ** is a wide pointer to an array of characters, and **char * SEQ * SEQ** is a wide pointer to an array of **char * SEQ**s

- We use the annotation on line 3 to say that the *h_name* field is a string. The generated deep copy function uses **__mkptr_string** to create a wide pointer to this buffer.
- We add the annotation on line 4 to say that *h_aliases* is a null-terminated array of strings. This is a fairly common data structure in C, and CCured includes code that will copy this specific case. For more complicated arrays, we would put C code in this function to do any copying or checking needed.

Similarly, CCured allows programmers to specify conversions for each field in a wide-to-standard deep copy. However, the wide-to-standard direction tends to be simpler, because we do not need the programmer to tell us how to create metadata. It is much easier to delete metadata than it is to invent it.

6   Experiences

The **libc** wrappers that are packaged with the CCured distribution are important for CCured's ease of use. Programmers who want to move new programs to CCured do not have to worry about modeling these library routines.

We can compare a hand-written wrapper with one generated automatically using our heuristics, but there is no truly sound way to verify the correctness of a wrapper. The programmer who writes a wrapper or checks the output of the generation tool may make a mistake; the documentation of the library may be incorrect; or a particular implementation of a library routine may be unsound. However, we have found that our system of wrappers works well in practice. The wrapper functions are simple and easy to read, and they have succeeded in

```
1  __inline static
2  __DEEPCOPY_FROM_COMPAT_PROTO(hostent) {
3      __DEEPCOPY_FROM_COMPAT_STRING_FIELD(h_name);
4      __DEEPCOPY_FROM_COMPAT_STRINGARRAY_FIELD(h_aliases);
5  }
```

Fig. 6. A specification that tells CCured how to do a deep copy of **struct hostent**. This specification must accompany the wrapper in Figure 4

finding several real-world bugs that involved improper invocations of a library routine.

In this section, we give examples of wrappers that are provided with CCured. Most of the wrappers we use are as simple as the examples we have shown so far, but we also give in this section some of our more complex wrappers, such as those for open and qsort.

```
1 #pragma ccuredwrapper("strchr_wrapper", for("strchr"))
2 __inline static
3 char* strchr_wrapper(char* str, int chr)
4 {
5     __check_string (str);
6     char* result = strchr(__ptrof(str), chr);
7     return __mkptr(result, str);
8 }
```

Fig. 7. A wrapper for strchr, a function that returns the first occurrence of character *chr* in string *str*

Figure 7 shows a wrapper for the strchr function. As before, we use a **pragma** command to specify that calls to strchr in the program should be replaced with calls to this wrapper. The __check_string helper function on line 5 checks that *str* is a null-terminated C string using a linear scan of the buffer. __ptrof strips the metadata from this pointer so that it can be passed to the underlying function. The result of strchr is a pointer to a character in the *str* buffer, so we use the __mkptr helper to create a new wide pointer by combining the return value of the library function with the metadata from *str*. Note that this helper function propagates constraints from the return value to the *str* argument, so CCured will ensure that the argument *str* has any metadata needed to construct the return value.

Figure 8 wraps the open function. open returns a handle for the file whose path is specified by the first argument. The second argument is a bit vector of options. If the O_CREAT option of oflag is set, then there is a required third argument: an integer specifying the permissions with which the new file should be created. Our wrapper for open matches the variable-argument interface of the library function, with the annotation on line 2 telling CCured that any additional arguments will be ints.

Our wrapper for open must do three things: check that the filename is a valid string, using __check_string; strip its metadata with __ptrof as usual; and check that the third parameter is present if it is required. We do this last check using the standard C macros for implementing variable-argument functions, as shown in lines 11–13 of the figure. However, when this wrapper is processed by CCured, the vararg macros will be replaced by typesafe code. The new version of va_arg checks that each argument was actually present at the call site before attempting to access it. This runtime check uncovered a bug in the OpenSSH daemon where the third parameter was missing from a certain call to open. C normally provides

```
1 #pragma ccuredwrapper("open_wrapper", for("open"));
2 #pragma ccuredvararg("open_wrapper", sizeof(int))
3 __inline static
4 int open_wrapper (char *file, int oflag, ...) {
5     __check_string (file);
6     if(oflag & O_CREAT){
7         //The O_CREAT flag is set, so the mode is required.
8         int mode;
9         va_list argptr;
10
11        va_start( argptr, oflag );
12        mode = va_arg( argptr, int );
13        va_end( argptr );
14
15        return open(__ptrof(file), oflag, mode);
16    } else {
17        return open(__ptrof(file), oflag);
18    }
19 }
```

Fig. 8. A wrapper for open

no mechanism for determining how many parameters are passed to a function, so the implementation of open simply reads the next word on the stack, and in this case was creating the file with garbage permissions.

For variable-argument functions that use a printf-like interface, we provide a special mechanism for checking the correctness of the argument list against the format string. This checking is done statically when possible, or at runtime if the format string is not a constant. The "%n" argument specifier is prohibited for security reasons [2], but all other features of printf are supported.

In Figure 9, we give a wrapper for the standard library's quicksort routine qsort. This function takes as input an array of values, and a pointer to a comparison function that will compare any two of the elements in the array. The library will make many calls to the comparison function for each array that it sorts.

This callback function makes wrapping qsort problematic. Since the comparison is user-defined, it will be processed by CCured and may need to use wide pointers, which it cannot get from the library. To fix this, we use a different sort of wrapper. The function "__qsort_compare_wrapper" takes standard arguments from a library and constructs fat pointers to pass to a CCured-processed function — the reverse of the usual process. In order to do this, we store a copy of the array pointer in global memory. Now we can use __mkptr inside the comparison wrapper to generate wide pointers.

The use of global variables to simulate a closure is a significant limitation of this wrapper, as it prevents the wrapper from having a polymorphic type. The qsort_wrapper and qsort_compare_wrapper functions can be made context sensitive, but there is no analogous mechanism for context sensitive global

```
1  static void *__qsort_base;
2  static int (*__qsort_compare)(void*, void*);
3
4  static
5  int __qsort_compare_wrapper(void * SAFE left, void * SAFE right)
6  {
7     // map the 'left' and 'right' lean pointers to the
8     // fat pointers we need
9     void* fatleft = __mkptr (left, __qsort_base);
10    void* fatright = __mkptr (right, __qsort_base);
11
12    // and call the user-supplied sorting function, which
13    // expects fat pointers
14    return __qsort_compare(fatleft, fatright);
15 }
16
17 #pragma ccuredwrapper("qsort_wrapper", for("qsort"));
18 __inline static
19 void qsort_wrapper(void* base,
20                    size_t nmemb,
21                    size_t size,
22                    int (*compare)(void *left, void *right))
23 {
24    __cleartags (base, nmemb * size);
25
26    // save the pertinent values
27    __qsort_base = base;
28    __qsort_compare = compare;
29
30    qsort(__ptrof (base), nmemb, size, __qsort_compare_wrapper);
31
32    __qsort_base = 0;
33 }
```

Fig. 9. A wrapper for qsort. While qsort is executing, two global variables store the metadata of the array being accessed and a reference to the user-defined comparison function, respectively. We pass "__qsort_compare_wrapper" to the library's qsort as the comparison function; when this intermediate function is called we use the global variables to reconstruct fat pointers for the relevant arguments and call the user's comparison function

variables. After all, code can be replicated without changing its behavior, but not so a variable. This wrapper will work so long as qsort is only used on arrays of one type and one kind, but any attempt to use it on multiple pointer types will result in a "bad cast" since CCured will notice that you assign arrays of different types to *__qsort_base*.

One solution would be to add a mechanism to CCured that would support true closures. However, we would prefer not to introduce that much complexity into the language solely for use by callback functions. Our current distribution offers programmers a choice of two wrappers for `qsort`: this one, which may be used whenever the program only sorts lists of a single type; and a version without the wrapper for the comparison function, which can be used if the programmer carefully structures his comparison function so that it takes SAFE pointers as arguments.

7   Related Work

Several other systems have used wrapper functions to check that library functions are used properly. For example, Vo et al. [3] use wrapper functions written in a custom specification language to test for safe use of libraries, particularly with respect to error return codes. Ignoring errors returned by library functions is a common source of software problems. Their wrappers can automatically retry library functions that fail due to transient problems such as insufficient resources.

Libsafe [4] is a set of wrapper functions for the standard C library that attempts to prevent stack smashing attacks. When a stack buffer is passed to a library function, the libsafe wrapper can use the frame pointer to detect whether the library is at risk of overwriting a return pointer. This does not protect heap locations, however, and still allows other locations in the same stack frame to be overwritten by a buffer overflow. Either of these could allow an attacker to gain control of a system.

Fetzer and Xiao [5] present HEALERS, a system of automatically generated library wrappers that check error return codes and certain preconditions. The tool can infer the preconditions for a function by testing it on a range of inputs. However, the set of checks that HEALERS can perform is limited by the unsound nature of C. In an earlier paper [6], these authors describe some ways in which bounds data can be found for heap objects when checking library preconditions. Together with the libsafe strategy for checking stacks, this system can prevent many buffer overflow attacks on the stack and in the heap. But these heap checks are more costly than ours, and the system provides no way to perform typechecking of variable argument functions. Nonetheless, HEALERS could overcome these limitations if it were used in the context of a runtime system such as CCured.

Suenaga et al. [7] present an interface definition language for a situation similar to ours. Fail-Safe C is a typesafe C compiler that increases the size of both pointers an integers to two words. Rather than writing wrappers as C functions, Fail-Safe C programmers annotate the declarations of library routines with the necessary constraints, and the compiler generates the wrapper. This has the nice property that wrapper specifications in Fail-Safe C can be more concise than in CCured, and they avoid some "boilerplate" aspects of CCured's specifications such as the `#pragma`. However, CCured's wrappers give wrapper authors the full power and flexibility of the programming language. This flexibility allows us to wrap functions like `open` and `qsort`, which Fail-Safe C cannot, even though we had not considered variable-argument functions or callback functions while we were initially designing our system.

Our deep-copying wrappers are unsatisfactory in some situations because the act of copying the data structures may break aliasing that is expected between the program and the library. An alternative to this copying is to store the meta-data separately from the regular data, so that the regular data is in a format that is already compatible with the library. Recently, we have devised a solution that does exactly that [1]. Although it is possible that this split representation may cause slight performance degradation, it has performed well in practice. Even with a split representation, however, it is still necessary to have a wrapper that checks pre- and post-conditions.

A second alternative to the simple deep copy we propose is a call-by-copy-restore implementation, such as in [8]. Our current implementation provides call-by-copy semantics, which may break aliasing. With call-by-copy-restore semantics, we would copy the data to a compatible representation, call the library, and then copy modified data back to the original locations, where appropriate. This is more expensive than our naïve copying, but so long as the library does not retain a pointer to the data that is passed to it, these function calls would behave the same way as the original library calls do.

8   Conclusions

CCured provides an easy-to-use mechanism for integration with precompiled libraries. This mechanism is needed because CCured only operates on source code, and most programs rely on libraries whose source code is not readily available. Our solution supports both compile-time constraints and run-time instrumentation, and handles complex structures.

This system has helped us use CCured with a large number of real-world programs. Currently, we rely on wrappers to provide bug-checking and run-time support for over 120 functions. We use deep-copying wrappers for over a dozen functions, including `glob`, `getpwnam`, `gethostbyname`, and related functions. We believe that using C syntax for wrappers makes them easy to write and understand, and gives them sufficient power to check a wide range of constraints.

We have found several memory bugs in existing programs using these wrappers. Our system takes advantage of CCured's memory safety to perform more precise checks of certain preconditions than would normally be possible in a library. Among other things, we can check buffer lengths, null-terminated strings, and the arguments passed to variable-argument functions, including `printf`-like functions.

With this system, it is quick and easy to write wrappers and hook them into the system. Deep wrappers require little debugging, while other wrappers often require none at all. In practice, we have found some bugs in wrappers after they are first used – both bugs that allow memory errors to slip through and those that cause false positives. However these are not common, and the cost of developing stable wrappers can be amortized over the many programs that use a library.

Acknowledgments

We would like to thank the other members of the CCured team — Jeremy Condit, Scott McPeak, and Westley Weimer — for their help with the development and testing of the system.

References

1. Condit, J., Harren, M., McPeak, S., Necula, G.C., Weimer, W.: CCured in the real world. In: Proceedings of the ACM SIGPLAN 2003 conference on Programming Language Design and Implementation, ACM Press (2003) 232–244
2. Newsham, T.: Format string attacks (2000) http://www.lava.net/~newsham/format-string-attacks.pdf.
3. Vo, K.P., Wang, Y.M., Chung, P.E., Huang, Y.: Xept: a software instrumentation method for exception handling. (1997) 60–69
4. Baratloo, A., Singh, N., Tsai, T.: Transparent run-time defense against stack smashing attacks. In: Proceedings of the USENIX Annual Technical Conference. (2000)
5. Fetzer, C., Xiao, Z.: An automated approach to increasing the robustness of C libraries. In: Proceedings of the 2002 International Conference on Dependable Systems and Networks, IEEE Computer Society (2002) 155–166
6. Fetzer, C., Xiao, Z.: Detecting heap smashing attacks through fault containment wrappers. In: Proceedings of the 20th IEEE Symposium on Reliable Distributed Systems. (2001)
7. Suenaga, K., Oiwa, Y., Sumii, E., Yonezawa, A.: The Interface Definition Language for Fail-Safe C. In: Proceedings of the 2003 International Symposium on Software Security. Lecture Notes in Computer Science, Springer (2004)
8. Tilevich, E., Smaragdakis, Y.: NRMI: Natural and efficient middleware. In: Proceedings of the 23rd International Conference on Distributed Computing Systems, IEEE Computer Society (2003) 252

Detecting Unknown Computer Viruses
– A New Approach –

Akira Mori

Japan National Institute of Advanced Industrial Science and Technology
amori@carc.aist.go.jp

Abstract. We give an overview of the tools to detect computer viruses without relying on "pattern files" that contain "signatures" of previously captured viruses. The system combines static code analysis with code simulation to identify malicious behaviors commonly found in computer viruses such as mass mailing, file infection, and registry overwrite. These prohibited behaviors are defined separately as security policies at the level of API library function calls in a state-transition like manner. The current tools target at Win32 binary viruses on Intel IA32 architectures and early experiments show that they can detect most email viruses that had spread in the wild in recent years.

1   Backgrounds

The damage caused by computer viruses is more serious than ever in today's society, where personal communication, corporate business, and social infrastructures heavily depend on computer networks. Unfortunately, email attachments have become a popular method of spreading malicious codes over the network. It has lead to the rise of anti-virus industry and it is now almost obligatory for us to have anti-virus programs on personal computers and/or email servers.

Yet we keep hearing reports on new viruses and warnings that we have to update pattern files to avoid infection and further spread. The main reason is that current anti-virus programs rely on byte-to-byte comparison between files, where binary strings taken from previously captured viruses are used as unique signatures. Since a file is recognized as a virus only if it contains matching signatures in the pattern file, it is impossible to detect previously unknown viruses.

A couple of methods have been proposed to tackle the problem, but both have shortcomings. **Sandboxing**, which runs suspicious programs in a virtual isolated computer environment, does not offer guarantee as it may not reveal random or environment specific behaviors while **heuristic scanner**, which does more than string matching by checking program structures common to virus programs, are prone to false positives.

Since further sophistication of computer viruses is not a remote threat, a new method of detecting unknown viruses is needed.

K. Futatsugi et al. (Eds.): ISSS 2003, LNCS 3233, pp. 226–241, 2004.

2   Technical Obstacle in Detecting Viruses

There is one major obstacle in detecting computer viruses, which is to detect **self-decrypting** and **polymorphic** viruses. A self-decrypting virus consists of a decoder part and an encrypted body. The malicious codes are hidden in the encrypted body and decoded on-the-fly when the virus file is executed to transfer control to the decoder, which is normally placed at the entry point of the executable file. When the decoder is finished, the control is transfered to the now decoded virus body, that may contain malicious codes for damaging computer systems, hiding codes on memory or in the hard disk for further activities, and spreading the virus through networks. See Figure 1.

Self-decrypting viruses are developed to make inspection based detection less effective. Since the encrypted part has little information as to what happens when the file is executed, one has to decide whether it is a virus or not by looking at the decoder part, which usually has an innocent appearance. One can still use signature based method, but preparing signatures that can discriminate between normal files and virus files becomes much more difficult. For examples, more than one binary strings may be needed for a signature, one for the decoder part and the other(s) for the encrypted part.

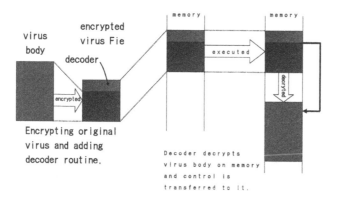

Fig. 1. Self-decrypting viruses

Polymorphic viruses are developed as a further counter measure to anti-virus programs. A polymorphic engine is included in the encrypted body that alters the encryption scheme when the virus spreads for the next victims (Figure 2). Since polymorphic viruses carry different decoders and hence different (if not infinitely many) appearances every time they travel, it gets even more difficult to prepare a consistent set of signatures coping with a large number of variation of the same virus. This is why anti-virus companies often say that their products cover tens of thousands of different viruses.

Together with another coding technique called **metamorphism**, which alters code appearances without changing operational meanings by inserting irrelevant

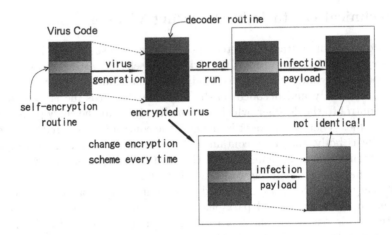

Fig. 2. Polymorphic viruses

instructions and/or permuting instructions not interfering with each other, one can write virus programs that are extremely difficult to detect with signature based methods. Zmist is an example of such sophisticated computer viruses [1].

The capability of signature based methods is limited to preventing previously known computer viruses of simpler kinds. For more secure protection, a new method has to be developed combining static inspection with dynamic emulation of the code.

3   A New Approach

Our goal is to check all possible execution paths of program files for malicious behaviors particular to computer viruses. The key observation here is, with the problem of self-decrypting/polymorphic viruses aside, one can identify program behaviors at the level of system calls to operating systems. The modern operating systems such as Unix and 32bit Windows (Win32) encapsulate application programs so that system resources such as files, shared memories, hardware devices and networks are only accessible through operating systems by way of system calls[1]. If the sequences of system calls in the program are enumerated, the chances of knowing the critical behaviors of the program are greater. This can be done with careful (static) inspection of the program. Figure 3 shows some malicious program behaviors and related system calls (**API calls** in the Win32 terms) for example.

---

[1] One can write a program that accesses system resources without asking the operating system, but such a program inevitably assumes the particular configuration of the target system and will not survive on other machines, which is not a good tactic for a computer virus at all.

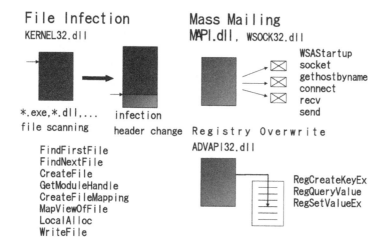

Fig. 3. API function calls associated with malicious behaviors

On the other hand, to deal with self-decrypting/polymorphic viruses, one has to consider dynamic emulation methods as it is best to let their decoders do the job. However, emulation techniques used in sandboxing is not suitable for our purpose as activating the emulator frequently in the process of analyzing virus files slows down the tool performance. In order to have seamless controls over both dynamic code emulation and static code analysis, we have developed an IA32 CPU simulator based on the observation that to detect malicious behaviors, it is sufficient to identify a series of API function calls in the target program and going into execution of library codes should be avoided. We need to trace what the target program does, and not to reproduce what the system does in the execution.

As in Figure 3, particular use of API functions characterizes prohibited malicious behaviors. We call such descriptions **policies** and are designing a language to define state transitions of mass mailing, file infection, and registry overwriting with vocabularies available at the level of API function calls. Policies can be viewed as semantic extensions to traditional signatures in the sense that they capture a wider variety of malicious codes. Having separate policy definitions makes the anti-virus tools flexible and customizable, too. Policies and the language for them will be touched upon in Section 3.7.

To summarize, our approach is to examine program files at the level of system calls to check if there is a malicious behavior specified in the policy definitions with the help of code simulation in decrypting virus bodies and gathering information available at runtime. In the followings, we will explain components built in the current tools.

3.1   Code Simulator

The core role of the code simulator is to simulate changes occurring to computational components of an IA32 (or X86) CPU such as registers, flags, and

memories when an instruction is executed. Figure 4 has a GUI appearance of
the simulator. The simulator runs both on Windows and Unix (including Linux)
platforms and has standard debugger capabilities such as step execution, breakpoints, and memory dumps. Instructions in the left panel are executed with display scrolling up. The upper-right panel holds the values of registers and flags
while the lower-right panel displays contents of the stack area. The simulator is
integrated with other components and can be used with or without GUI.

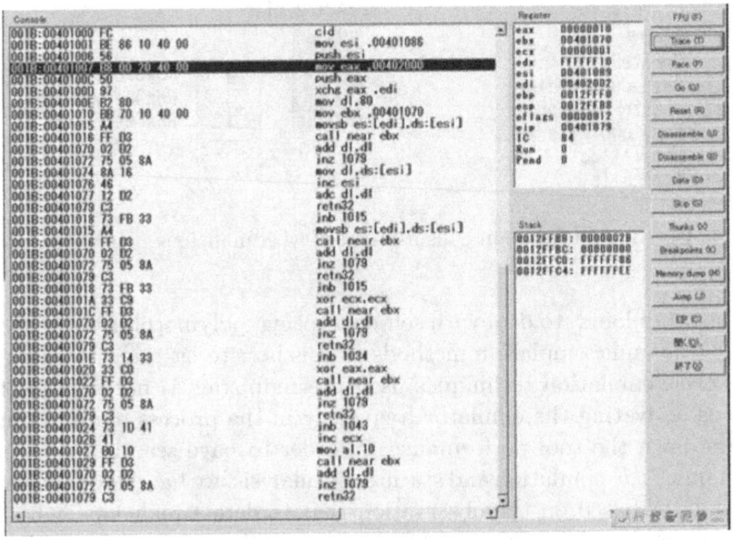

Fig. 4. Code simulator GUI snapshot

The tool does not depend on a particular simulator program. For example,
the current tool can use the code simulator of the open source IA32 emulation
called Bochs [2]. Since Bochs has longer development history and is portable and
more complete as a CPU simulator, we are leaning toward using Bochs simulator
when the license issue is cleared.

3.2   PE Loader

Code simulation is not sufficient for observing program behaviors in the working
environment. Executable files usually have extra information such as import
tables for externally defined functions including API functions, section tables
for sizes and relocation offsets of code segments, and entry points where the
control is first transfered when the file is executed. Such information needs to be
symbolically processed when the file is handed to the simulator. We have a loader
functionality for PE (Portable Executable) files, which is a binary executable
format on the Win32 platform.

For license concerns, we have created skeletal libraries files that have the same header information and function entries as the original Win32 library files. It is these skeletons that are loaded when the PE loader needs libraries referred in the target programs.

3.3   Identification of API Function Calls

As mentioned earlier, it is not necessary to follow the execution of API library functions to identify malicious behaviors of the programs. Instead, the simulator only manages addresses of externally defined functions by book-keeping their names and the memory locations where they are stored. In general, there are two such occasions:

- when the loader assigns addresses to external functions according to the information in the import tables as the program is loaded, and
- when the program assigns addresses to external functions at runtime by calling LoadLibrary and GetProcAddress API functions.

To handle the second case is important in our detection method since most viruses try to hide API functions they use and opt for runtime address assignment as opposed to loader assignment, in which function addresses are easily associated with function names prior to program execution. See Figure 5 for the difference between the two. Normal programs declare API functions they use in the import tables of their executable (PE) files in the form of triples of the library name, the address where the string of the function name is stored, and the address where the address of the function will be stored. The loader takes care of determining and filling the address of the function when it places the libraries on memory. On the other hand, the programs can load libraries by themselves by LoadLibrary and then use GetProcAddress to get function addresses. In the latter case, the function address is given in EAX register as a return value of GetProcAddress. It will be much more difficult to determine which function is called at the indirect subroutine call call ptr in the latter case since such binding information can only be obtained at runtime.

As static identification of API function calls is essential to our method, we perform data flow analysis during static code analysis (in Section 3.6). The simulator processes LoadLibrary and GetProcAddress symbolically utilizing the PE loader functionality of the tool (explained in Section 3.2) to record the pair of the function name and address, and the analyzer traces the use of the function address and determines which function is called at call ptr instructions that are marked in advance. This information is used to associate oracles (see Section 3.6) to branch instructions to guide the simulator in the later cycles.

3.4   Symbolic Simulation of API Function Calls

When the simulator encounters an indirect subroutine call call ptr, it checks if it is an API function call and if that is the case, it performs necessary symbolic manipulations according to the tasks of corresponding API functions, removes the arguments put onto the stack before the subroutines are called, stores the

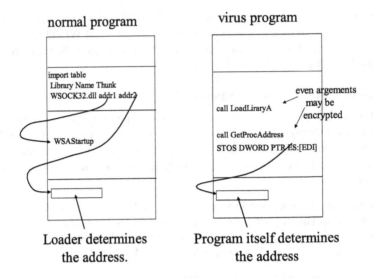

Fig. 5. API Function Addresses: Runtime vs Load Time

return value in EAX register, and finally goes on to the next instruction as if it has just returned from the subroutine. The arguments have to be removed since it is the callee's job in the Win32 library convention. Note that removing arguments from the stack requires knowledge of standard API functions as the numbers and bytes of the arguments vary from function to function. The same complication goes for the return value.

As is clear with LoadLibrary and GetProcAddress explained above, processing API functions requires large amount of symbolic manipulation when the simulator encounters indirect subroutine calls corresponding to them. To organize individual tasks in a modular manner, a **stub function** is used for each API function, which has codes for removing arguments from the stack and setting a return value in EAX in addition to individual tasks. These individual tasks may include the following virtual operations.

– heap manipulation
– file manipulation
– registry manipulation
– exception handling
– thread handling
– paging

The first three are necessary for the simulator to follow the activities of the target programs. For example, a virus may copy itself to a file and modifies the registry to execute the copy every time the machine wakes up. If one wishes to check such a behavior as it is, the simulator needs to recored which file is copied and check that the corresponding file is registered as a startup program in the registry. The similar treatment is required for the socket structure created in the heap when checking the mass mailing behavior.

The exception handling is needed to follow interruptions triggered by virus programs such as zero division. The program may dynamically insert an exception handler that takes the control flow to the decryption routine and cause exception by performing zero division in an obscure way. Such a dynamic transition can only be followed if exception handling is properly emulated. In fact, exploiting the Win32 exception mechanism called SEH (Structured Exception Handling [3]) is very popular in recent viruses as a way of cheating debugger and emulators as many of them still cannot handle SEH properly. Paging is needed for the same reason. Intentional page faults are often used as SEH triggers. Our tool is capable of emulating both SEH and paging.

Thread handling is another functionality often exploited in virus programs that needs dynamic emulation. Because there is very limited amount of documentation about Win32 thread handling (for example in [4]), it is very difficult to emulate full thread mechanism of the Win32 platform. Our current tool can emulate thread creation/synchronization in a serialized manner as well as TLS (Thread Local Storage) accesses, but is not capable of emulating multi-thread environments. Viruses only with distributed malicious actions that are collectively taken by several threads can not be detected by our tools at the moment[2].

Preparing stub functions for a large number of Win32 libraries (i.e., dll files) is a daunting task. Currently, we have stub functions contained in approximately 100 dll files. We have a tool support for generating stub files automatically by parsing dll files except for the return values. The return values in the Win32 libraries are not consistent and manual completion cannot be avoided. Note that the choice of the return values is heuristic and depends on stub implementation.

3.5   Win32 Virtual Environment Database

Although the simulator does not follow the API function codes in the external libraries, it is necessary to mimic certain functionalities to determine if the target program has virus-specific behaviors. For this purpose, a database of virtual Windows environments consisting of

- registry keys/values,
- file/directory structures, and
- environment variables

is maintained. The database is referred from stub functions to follow behaviors peculiar to computer viruses. A typical scenario is getting an SMTP server address from the registry key. Currently, the database covers all registry keys, all environment variables, and common file/directory names that viruses are likely to touch. For registry keys and environment variables, dummy values such as my.smtp.server for an SMTP server address are inserted where necessary.

---

[2] We have not seen such a sophisticated virus yet.

3.6   Static Code Analysis

Depending on a code simulator poses the same problem as the sandboxing method. However, covering all possible execution paths can be difficult when the program behaves like self-decrypting or polymorphic viruses. To cope with this problem, we use a static code analyzer to guide the simulator. When the simulator encounters a code that has not been visited by the analyzer, the analyzer takes control and starts scanning all reachable codes from there. When the analyzer encounters the API function calls related to given policies, it starts marking precedent branch instructions with **oracles** that tell the simulator which way to go. See Figure 6 for an intuitive illustration. Oracle marking is performed in a recursively way and codes are managed in segments separated by branch instructions and their target (landing) instructions. What the analyzer does is similar to dis-assemblers except that the analyzer may use runtime information provided by the simulator such as runtime API function addresses explained in Section 3.4.

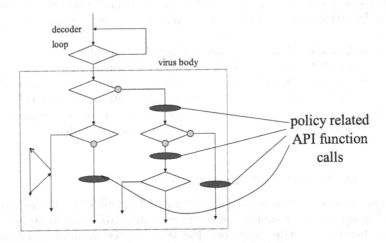

Fig. 6. Oracles for Guiding Analyzer

Another important role of the analyzer is to track data flow of the function addresses assigned by the PE loader and the pair of `LoadLibrary` and `GetProcAddress` as explained in Section 3.3. Since there is no perfect method of knowing effects caused by the program, the process of oracle marking and data flow analysis are inevitably heuristic.

We outline the internal of the analyzer in the following. The analyzer uses the following data structures.

– `landing_info`: containing information about landing points of branch instructions[3]

---

[3] Typically, a branch instruction has a couple of landing addresses, one for the next instruction and another for the one executed when branch condition is true.

- address
- list of branches leading to the current landing point
- pointer to the next branch in the control flow
- oracle information
- `branch_info`: containing information about branch instructions
  - address
  - list of landing points leading to the current branch
  - landing points associated to the current branch

The analyzer maintains a pair of hash tables of `landing_info` and `branch_info` that registers visited landing points and branches respectively, and a list `unanalyzed_list` of `landing_info` that marks the beginnings of the code segments to be analyzed. Then it repeats the following steps:

1. pick one landing point from the `unanalyzed_list` and start analysis from the instruction at the address; if the `unanalyzed_list` is empty, then return to the simulator;
2. if the instruction is a branch instruction, append its landing points to the `unanalyzed_list` and go back to Step 1;
3. if the instruction is invalid (i.e., cannot parse as a valid instruction), then set **breakpoints** at the current address and go back to Step 1;
4. if the instruction is an indirect subroutine call, then start data flow analysis backward from the current address;
   (a) if the indirect subroutine call is found to be a call to an API function related to given policies, then start oracle marking from the address;
   (b) if the indirect subroutine call has an indefinite call address, then set **breakpoints** at the current address and continue;
5. otherwise continue analysis instruction by instruction until it goes out of bound of the memory section assigned by the PE loader;

A few comments are in order:

- Subroutine calls are also treated as branch instructions.
- The reverse pointers of `landing_info` and `branch_info` are necessary for recursive oracle marking in Step 4a.
- The analyzer is invoked once when the target program is loaded in the simulator and called from the simulator when a branch instruction whose landing points are not included in the hash table of `landing_info`.
- The breakpoints are set to invoke the analyzer when the simulator happens to reach the addresses where there were invalid instructions or indefinite indirect calls since the situation might have changed.
- The choice in Step 1 is non-deterministic and one can control search strategy by choosing queue, stack or any other heuristic ordering among `unanalyzed_list`.
- Oracle marking can be also heuristic.

Data flow analysis in Step 4 traces back the value of the operand of an indirect subroutine call until it matches one of the function addresses previously assigned by the PE loader or the pair of LoadLibrary and GetProcAddress. If analysis goes out of the current code segment, the call is regarded as indefinite.

The method explained here is not complete by any means, however, it has been designed to reduce overheads such as instruction marking, explicit representation of control flows (i.e., flow charts), and backtracking while maintaining ability to analyze concrete application programs including virus programs.

3.7   Policy Definition and Policy Checker

As we mentioned earlier, a policy is an abstract description of a prohibited program behavior that is commonly found in computer viruses. In our case, a policy is defined by a state transition machine which leads to a final denial state, and whose transitions are annotated by certain API function calls with certain arguments. The role of a policy checker is to determine, by organized use of the simulator and the analyzer, if there is a possible execution sequence covered by the policy in the target programs or executable files. See Figure 7.

We are still in the process of designing a policy definition languages, but we have explored an idea of using formal specification language for this purpose. We have examined a number of virus samples to identify key API functions used for oracle marking that characterize policies, and registry keys/values, file/directory names, and environment variables often referred in those API function calls, and have defined about 25 policies.

The language we have used is CafeOBJ [5]. The following is the definition of the final step of the mass mailing behavior.

```
To(Buf) == MMAddr &
Addr(Sock) == MMSmtp &
stat(S) == MMConnect ->
stat(send(Sock,Buf,Len,Flags),S)
    = MMFinal.
```

It says that when send function in WSOCK32.dll is called, if the To field of the message composed in the second argument Buf contains a random mail address MMAddr taken from the registry, and the address of the socket assigned to the first argument Sock is an SMTP server address MMSmtp also taken from the registry, and the current state is the semi-final state MMConnect where the socket has been connected, then the next state is the final denial state MMFinal.

In checking the policy, the attributes such as MMAddr and MMSmtp must be determined when the simulator processes API function calls that read registry values/files at certain keys/directories where those addresses are usually found. The Win32 virtual environments mentioned in Section 3.5 are used in the stub functions corresponding to the API functions.

The current implementation does not have the separated policy language interpreter and policy checker. These functionalities are hard-coded in the body of the stub functions. We are going to built a **macro processor** that translates abstract policy definitions into executable codes (in our case C and C++) to be inserted in the body of the stub functions. See Figure 7 again for an illustration.

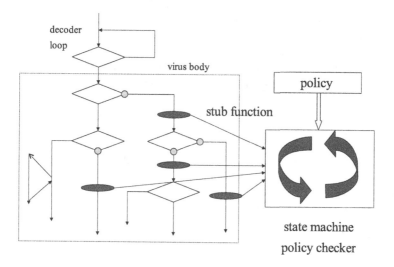

decoder
loop

virus body

policy

stub function

state machine
policy checker

Fig. 7. Policy Checking Mechanism

The policy set we have so far includes:

- **Mass Mailing:**
  using API functions in WSOCK32.dll, MAPI.dll or WININET.dll; gathering victim addresses from the WAB (Windows Address Book), the Outlook Express address books, or the Internet Explorer caches; SMTP protocol simulations is performed when using WSOCK32.dll functions.
- **File Infection:**
  modifying files after performing directory scan; tends to be quite diverse; currently only typical scenarios are defined.
- **Registry Modification:**
  modifying system registry, typically auto start programs; prefix list of protected registry keys is used to define the policy.
- **Network Connection:**
  connecting to unknown servers using protocols such as HTTP and FTP using functions in WSOCK32.dll or WININET.dll; protocol simulation is performed when checking the policy.
- **Process Scan:**
  enumerating processes in memory and obtain process ID's; should be extended to cover concrete process infection behaviors.
- **Self-Code Modification:**
  modifying own code especially the header information such as import tables; sometimes too strong as ordinary self-decrypting archive file are found illegal by this.

- **Anti-debugger/Emulation:**
  hiding itself from debuggers and emulators using various tricks.
- **Out of Bounds Execution (OBE):**
  executing code outside of the memory section declared in the PE header; very powerful but too strong sometimes as some self-decrypting execution files are found illegal by this.
- **System File Access:**
  accessing file in the system area such as `/WINDOWS/SYSTEM32`; the same prefix list as the registry modification policy is used.
- **External Execution:**
  invoking external programs/processes using `CreateProcess`, `ShellExecute`, and so on.
- **Illegal Address Call:**
  calls to addresses obtained by parsing export tables of library files; trying to bypass `GetProcAddress`.
- **Backdoor:**
  opening unauthorized ports.
- **Self Duplication:**
  making copies of itself; most common viral behavior.

4   Experiments

We have conducted experiments of virus detection using approximately 200 samples that had spread in the wild in recent months such as `Magistr`, `Badtrans`, `Klez`, `MyDoom`, `Bagle` and `Netsky` including their variants.

The result is quite positive and the current working policy set consisting of about 20 policies can detect all samples without issuing false positives for the randomly inserted normal applications and archives. About 50 samples have been examined to refine policies, so the rest 150 samples are detected in unknown status.

Average time needed to finish detection was 1.65 seconds on a very humble laptop computer with 800MHz Pentium III and 640MB memory. 3 variants of `Magistr` takes more than 40 seconds each, so excluding them results in 0.7 seconds in average. The programs size of the sample viruses ranges from 4096 bytes to 500KB and from 150KB to 1MB for inserted normal programs. We have also confirmed that oracles are essential in virus detection. About 40% of the samples are declared safe without oracle marking.

Based on the results, we feel that most viruses reported on a daily basis can be detected with no information about previous viruses. Especially, it is nice to note that all variants of `Netsky`, `MyDoom`, and `Bagle` have been detected in real time. The tools are designed to work on mail servers with enough computation power. We have set up an experimental mail server outside the firewall to evaluate effects on the throughput. An open source email filter called `AMaVis` [6] and a mail transport agent called `exim` are used. `AMaVis` checks emails passing through `exim`, strips attachments, sends them to virus detection tools, receives the result, and performs a series of tasks such as sending warnings to system administrators and original senders. Our tools have also been successfully integrated into the AnZenMail client [7] using its plug-in capabilities.

As for false positives, our method is algorithmic and deterministic in large part and programs without the code exhibiting behaviors specified in the polices are never judged illegal. In our case, false positive can be considered as having policies that are too strong (i.e., self-modification policy). Although there are some procedures relying on heuristics such as oracle marking, return values of stub functions, and the depth of data flow analysis, they work to increase or decrease "false negatives" instead. In other words, the heuristics are used to fine-tune detection rates.

Figure 8 shows the architecture of our tools.

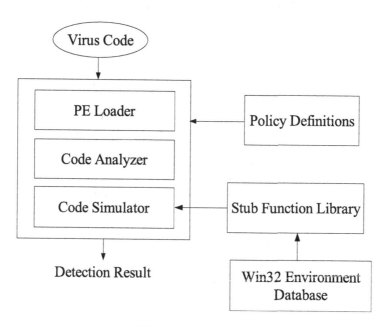

Fig. 8. Tool Overview

5   Concluding Remarks

In this paper, we have reported on a new method of detecting computer viruses without relying on specific information of previously captured viruses. The approach is unique in that it tries to identify program behaviors at the level of OS system calls by coordinated use of the static analyzer and the code simulator. Features include:

- It can check dynamic code behaviors such as self-decrypting and self-mutation.
- It does not depend on imprecise heuristics.

- It can fail safe; even when the complexity of the codes exceed the ability of the tools, one can still judge that the target is suspicious unlike in pattern based methods, where failure means little as to the potential threat.
- It is policy based. Users can design their own security policies.

Although there is no perfect method in computer virus detection, early experiments show that the tool actually can detect viruses that has spread in the wild recently treating them as if they were unknown.

As a matter of fact, there are very few researches focusing on the combination of static analysis and dynamic code emulation for binary programs as we do. [8] presents ideas of applying theoretical static analysis methods to restoration of code obfuscation in an attempt to detect malicious behaviors in metamorphic virus programs such as Zmist. The paper excludes self-decrypting viruses and only deals with a handful of samples. The system presented in the paper is still in a premature prototype status.

The Bloodhound scanner of Symantec [9, 10] combines sandbox emulation with heuristic scanner. An artificial threshold are posed on the number of program loops to determine when the decoder routine is finished, which is a serious limitation in practice. Also the detection method relies on heuristics and prone to false positives.

The Norman Sandbox [11] is a commercial anti-virus product based on a software emulator just like Bochs. They claim that all Win32 libraries are re-implemented in assembly language, so the same ideas of having stub functions might be pursued. However, it is an emulation based detection and it is difficult to check all execution paths as we do. Therefore, they only have 4 types of policies and does not leave users rooms for policy customization.

As for future research, we are planning on parallel processing where task forking takes place within a single policy checking besides the followings topics:

- development of policy language and its macro processor,
- implementation of full thread emulation,
- performance evaluation in real-life situations (a mail server hosting several hundreds of users), and
- constant refinement of tools and policies,

Other future topics that seem promising include applications to:

- vulnerability detection in binary programs, where system call identification and data flow analysis are used to bound check certain C functions;
- filtering shell code packets in IDS, where self-decrypting and polymorphic shell codes are analyzed in the same way as virus programs.

Acknowledgements

The author thanks Toshimi Sawada and Tadashi Inoue at SRA Key Technology Laboratory, Inc. and Tomonori Izumida at AIST, Japan for their heroic efforts in designing and implementing the tools. The part of the work presented in this paper was supported by the research and development funding from NiCT (National Institute of Information and Communications Technology), Japan.

References

1. Peter Ferrie and Péter Ször, Zmist Opportunities, VIRUS BULLETIN, (2001)
2. Bochs: The Open Source IA-32 Emulation Project, found at `http://bochs.sourceforge.net/`
3. Jeffrey Richter, Programming Applications for Microsoft Windows, Microsoft Press (1999)
4. David A. Solomon and Mark E. Russinovich, Inside Microsof Windows 2000, Third Edition, Microsoft Press (2000)
5. Kokichi Futatsugi and Răzvan Diaconescu, *CafeOBJ Report: The Language, Proof Techniques, and Methodologies for Object-Oriented Algebraic Specification*, World Scientific, AMAST Series in Computing, Vol.6 (1998)
6. A Mail Virus Scanner, available at `http://www.amavis.org/`
7. E. Shibayama, S. Hagihara, N. Kobayashi, S. Nishizaki, K. Taura, and T. Watanabe, AnZenMail: A Secure and Certified E-Mail System, *Software Security - Theories and Systems*, Lecture Notes in Computer Science, Springer-Verlag, Vol. **2609**, pp.201-216 (2003)
8. Mihai Christodorescu and Somesh Jha, Static Analysis of Executables to Detect Malicious Patterns, Proc. of *the 12th USENIX Security Symposium (Security'03)* (2003)
9. United States Patent 6,357,008, Dynamic heuristic method for detecting computer viruses using decryption exploration and evaluation phases.
10. United States Patent 5,696,822, Polymorphic virus detection module.
11. Norman SandBox Whitepaper, found at `http://www.norman.com` (2003)

Security Policy Descriptions Through the Use of Control Structure of a Target Program

Hirotake Abe[1] and Kazuhiko Kato[2,3]

[1] Doctoral Program in Engineering, University of Tsukuba,
1-1-1 Tennoudai, Tsukuba, Ibaraki 305-8573, Japan
habe@osss.is.tsukuba.ac.jp
[2] Institute of Information Sciences and Electronics, University of Tsukuba,
1-1-1 Tennoudai, Tsukuba, Ibaraki 305-8573, Japan
kato@is.tsukuba.ac.jp
[3] CREST, Japan Science and Technology Agency

Abstract. Running a program under surveillance by a reference monitor system is a promising approach to secure use of programs. However, with the existing reference monitor systems, it is difficult to make a security policy description that adequately conforms to the Least Privilege Principle. In this paper, we propose a novel mechanism of implementing reference monitor systems. Our mechanism utilizes information obtained by analyzing a target program before it is used. Our mechanism enables one to make security policy descriptions in a fine-grained manner, allowing persistence of the Least Privilege Principle. Our proposal includes a graphical user interface (GUI) tool that helps the user to describe the security policy. We describe implementation of a reference monitor system using our mechanism and implementation of the GUI tool. We measured the performance of our mechanism on a micro benchmark and macro benchmark.

1 Introduction

Many of the problems of computer security are caused by the vulnerabilities in the computer's software. Even if there are no security flaws in the design of a program, a seemingly insignificant flaw in implementation of the program may cause significant damage to computers all over the world. A typical "insignificant" flaw in an implementation is buffer overflow, which allows malicious users to do stack smashing attacks [1]. At present, the most common countermeasure to a found vulnerability in a program is to update the program. However, sometimes it is not possible to update the program quickly, since it may take time to prepare an update, or the update may involve side effects which causes problems.

To achieve secure use of programs, we propose a means of preventing security problems that does not require updates of vulnerable programs. The reference monitor concept is the approach we use to achieve this, and it involves checking all the references preformed by a subject whether the references are valid or not [2].

The main ideas of the proposal are threefold. First, we use the reference monitor concept to ensure that the execution of a program is compliant with the Least Privilege Principle [3]. Second, we use a security policy description specialized to a single

K. Futatsugi et al. (Eds.): ISSS 2003, LNCS 3233, pp. 242–261, 2004.

program. Third, we use a fine-grained form of the description utilizing the control structure of a target program.

The previously proposed reference monitor systems [4–7] are inadequate for our purpose since they focus on realizing generic descriptions of security policy which can be applied to many programs, and they use the coarse-grained descriptions for the security policy, which is not compliant to the Least Privilege Principle.

We developed a novel reference monitor mechanism. The mechanism utilizes information obtained by analyzing a target program beforehand. The mechanism enables one to make security policy descriptions in a fine-grained manner, thus complying with the Least Privilege Principle. Our mechanism is independent of specific programming language, architectures, or hardware. It is also applicable to various platforms.

Describing a security policy usually requires an in-depth understanding of the program in question. This may result in higher costs when describing a security policy in contrast with the existing systems. To reduce this cost, our proposal includes a graphical user interface (GUI) tool that helps the user to describe the security policy in a way that uses the control structure of the target program.

The rest of this paper is organized as follows. Section 2 describes the problems of existing reference monitor systems. Section 3 describes our solution to these problems. Section 4 describes an implementation of our reference monitor and our support tool for making a security policy description. Section 5 presents a quantitative evaluation of our mechanism. Section 6 describes related work to our proposal, and Section 7 concludes this paper with a brief summary and note on future work.

2   Problems with Existing Reference Monitor Systems

A reference monitor system intercepts each reference issued by a target program before the reference is actually processed. Each time a reference is captured, the system judges whether it is valid. This scheme can discover risks that cannot be discovered by the static approach, which include digital signatures and static analyses, involving compensation of total execution time of a monitored process.

The reference monitor system knows what references should be allowed according to a given security policy description. Existing reference monitor systems use simple security policy description forms. The form allows a security policy description to be general-purposed and does not require the writer to have an in-depth knowledge of a target program. However it is difficult to use these to make security policy descriptions which precisely reflect users' security policy.

We illustrate the problems by giving concrete examples. Although we use the notion of the Java Protection Domain [5] in the examples, we should note that the problems are not only inherent to the Java Protection Domain, but are common to all of the existing reference monitor systems.

The Java Protection Domain is a well-known reference monitor. It was designed for Java Applets, Java programs which can be embedded in web pages. A web browser puts an applet into a Protection Domain prepared for it. The applet is executed with more restricted authority than the web browser itself has. In general, applets cannot access files in a local file system.

All the classes, which are the building blocks of Java programs, have information about their signer (with a digital signature) and code base (the URL of where the class code was loaded). Java runtime determines which protection domain the class should be put in by referring to this information.

Here is an example of the policy descriptions used in the Java Protection Domain.

```
grant signedBy "Duke" {
  permission java.io.FilePermission "/tmp/*", "read,write";
};
```

In this example, the classes signed by Duke are granted the abilities to read and write files in /tmp directory. In the Java Protection Domain, a set of classes, which is defined by a signer or a codebase, is called a protection domain, or simply a domain.

The problem is that authority is given to a coarse-grained fragment of code. Ligating all the classes signed by the same person or which have been downloaded from the same directory is ambiguous. Each class in the ligated classes has its own purpose, different from any of the other classes. It also requires a different authority to accomplish its role. Making a general-purposed description of a security policy results in an ambiguous authority, which is union of the required authorities for each class. This means that unnecessary authority is often given to classes.

Even within a class, there can be functions with different purposes. Suppose that in the same class there is a function that accesses a file and another function that does not access any file. To give authority to allow both functions, the authors describing the security policy must give the union of both functions. As a result, the function which does not need access to any file is given authority to access one. This is regarded as going against The Least Privilege Principle and may cause a problem if the function which does not need to access to any file has a vulnerability.

Moreover, a function can have different roles depending on the situation, and thus, the function would require different authorities to fulfill each role. This problem often happens with wrapper functions. Which files should be allowed to be opened depends on the purpose, and the purpose depends on the caller of the function. Given a function which reads a data file and another function which writes logs, a general-purpose wrapper function used by both functions to access files should be executed with different authorities. In the case of the data reader, the wrapper function should be granted only to read data files, whereas in the case of the log writer, the wrapper function should be granted only to write log files. However, the existing systems cannot place such limitations because they do not take into account which function called the wrapper function.

A union of authorities is not only ambiguous; it may also be expensive. Figuring out an appropriate union of authorities for ligated code is usually performed in an iterative way as follows:

1. The author describing the security policy (the policy maker) makes the description which is thought to be most secure.
2. The policy maker runs a program under observation by a reference monitor system with the description. However, the execution often fails because the description issues a false positive alert, i.e., lack of authority to perform a normal operation.
3. If the execution stops by violating the description, the policy maker alters the description to avoid the false positive alert.

4. The policy maker repeats procedure 2 and 3 until no false positive alerts are issued.

It is hard to predicate how long this procedure continues. Certainly, for larger target programs, the procedure is likely to take longer.

3   Our Proposals

Our proposal is for making fine-grained and specialized descriptions of security policy. It consists of two major parts. One embodies a concept called dynamic security policy. The other is a GUI tool called VIP Builder.

3.1   Dynamic Security Policy

Overview. To solve the problems of Section Two, we propose a mechanism called *dynamic security policy*. A dynamic security policy is one that gives an authority which can be switched according to the control structure of the target program. With a dynamic security policy, a subject which is given authority is not a fragment of code like a class or an executable file, but a function call. A dynamic security policy enables one to switch to another authority at an arbitrary function call in a target program. The authority may be switched after performing the function call, and the target program would continue with the new authority. The reason why we call the mechanism dynamic security policy is that the point at which authority is switched can be changed many times after compilation of the target program.

Switching of authority itself is not a novel idea. The idea is already used in the Java Protection Domain and SubDomain [7]. In the Java Protection Domain, authority can be switched when control transits over a boundary between two domains. In SubDomain, authority switches when invoking another program with exec system calls. The difference between them and dynamic security policy is that a switch of authority in dynamic security policy depends on the switch. With the existing systems, it is impossible to realize such a description.

In a dynamic security policy, all the function calls in a target program are regarded as timings for switching authority. Arbitrary function calls can be used to switch authority. Whoever makes the description of the security policy can implement a description through the use of the control structure in the target program. When a function call is performed, the authority of the running program switches according to the given description. Until control returns from the callee function to the caller function, the program runs with the switched authority. The policy description consists of pairs of identifiers of the function call, and *rules* that describe the way to switch authority. The rules represent the differences between the old and new authorities. Therefore, authority which is not described in the rules is retained during a switch.

On a target program performing a reference (typically a system call) to access resources (e.g. file systems, network connections, etc), a monitor process checks the current authority and determines whether the operation is allowed or not. Because the authority for such a operation depends on the history of the calling functions, the check will not always result in the same decision.

Applications. Benefit from using a dynamic security policy as follows.

Forcing the Least Privilege Principle on Existing Programs. With the existing systems, careful design of a program is required in order to comply with the Least Privilege Principle because authority can only be given with a coarse-grained unit. To give different authorities to privileged and non-privileged code with the existing systems, the different codes must be clearly separated. With dynamic security policy, it is easy to comply with the principle even if the program is not so carefully designed; authority is given in a fine-grained manner and can be specialized for a single program.

Using Securely a Program in Which a Vulnerability was Found. Not only for a preventative use like the above, a dynamic security policy can avoid a known vulnerability in a program. If a place where the vulnerability exists is already pinpointed, we can deprive it of authority to invoke unnecessary system calls. The program can be run normally unless it is exploited. If it is exploited, our reference monitor will detect an unexpected system call and terminates further execution.

Countermeasure for Dynamically Loaded Plug-in Code. Some programs, including some web browsers and some web servers, have been made extensible to make their programs more useful. With the existing reference monitor systems, if one is to give different authorities to the main code of an extensible program and to the extension code, or to give different authorities to each of the extension codes, the extensible programs must be carefully designed to be able to separate their codes clearly. With a dynamic security policy, it is possible to give different authorities to extensible codes without the need for such careful design work.

Performance Improvements. Monitoring the execution of a program incurs temporal costs when examining each suspicious operation. Consequently, some users may want a trade-off between performance and security. Existing reference monitor systems do not allow for this, but ours does. The user can take away observations on a frequently executed part of code, while retaining the security of the other parts.

Example of a Description. The following is an example of a description of a dynamic security policy description.

```
default:
        allow_read /etc/ld.so.preload
        allow_read /etc/ld.so.cache
        allow_read /lib/tls/libc.so.6
100a0:
        allow_read /home/habe/secret.txt
100b0:
        disallow  /home/habe/secret.txt
```

This description consists of three sections, each with its name and rules. The name is usually a hexadecimal number, except for a special keyword `default`. The section named `default` contains default rules which will be automatically loaded when the execution of the target process starts. In the other cases, the name of a section indicates the address of its target function call. In the example, the second and third section contain rules which will be loaded at the execution of the function call at addresses of 100a0 and 100b0, respectively.

The directive *allow_read* gives permission to read files. If the argument of the directive is the path name of a file, it gives permission to read the file. If an argument is the path name of a directory, it gives permission to read all the files in the directory. The directive disallow prohibits all the operations on a specified resource.

Below is a scenario of an execution with the example 1.

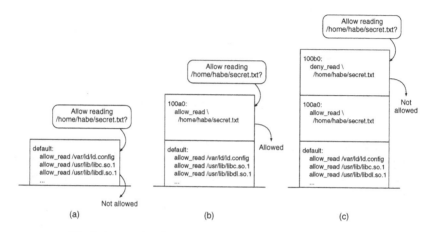

Fig. 1. A scenario of an execution with Dynamic Security Policy

1. Before starting the execution of the target program, the rules in the default section are loaded by the reference monitor (1(a)). If the program attempts to read the file secret.txt at this time, it fails because there are no rules allowing it to read secret.txt.
2. The execution reaches a function call at 100a0. At this time, a rule in a section 100a0 is loaded. As a result, the program gets permission to read secret.txt and becomes able to read it.
3. The execution reaches a function call at 100b0. At this time, a rule in a section 100b0 is loaded. As a result, the program loses permission to read secret.txt and becomes unable to read it.
4. The execution reaches a return in a function called by the function call at 100b0. At this time, the rule in a section 100b0 is annulled. As a result, the program gets permission to read secret.txt and becomes able to read it again.

3.2   Interactive Assistance Environment to Making Dynamic Policy Description

Compared with existing policy descriptions, describing a dynamic security policy requires a deeper understanding of the target program. Because making a security policy description is already quite difficult, it would be unrealistic to force the ordinary user to make an appropriate description of a dynamic security policy without aid.

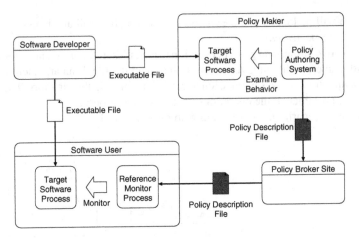

Fig. 2. Secure Software Circulation Model

We created a novel form of distribution called the *secure software circulation model* [8, 9]. Figure 2 shows the four kinds of participants in the model and their relationships. Note that in the ordinary case, there are only two kinds of participant; the *software developer* and the *software user*; the model adds the *policy maker* and the *policy broker*. The policy maker makes security policy descriptions and registers them on a policy broker site. The software user chooses an appropriate security policy description from the ones registered on the policy broker site.

We designed a tool to help policy makers make dynamic security policy descriptions. The tool is named *VIP Builder*. The design goal of the tool is to enable policy makers to save time and effort. The tool provides the following functional capabilities.

- Visualization of control structure in a program
- Debugging of dynamic security policy descriptions
- Architecture-independent graphical user interface

In this section, we describe these functional capabilities.

Visualization of Control Structure in a Program. To make a dynamic security policy description, the writer must have an understanding of the target program. The best way to understand it is to read its source code carefully. However, the source code is not always available. Even if the source code is available, reading the source code carefully is often difficult and time consuming. To make an appropriate description in a shorter time, it is important to obtain knowledge about the program as soon as possible.

Another difficulty in making a description is identifying where the corresponding call instruction is. Each instruction in a program's code is distinguished from others by its unique address. To point to a function call in a dynamic security policy description, a policy maker must find its address. Finding the address by hand is very time-consuming and should be avoided for quick development of the description.

VIP Builder provides a visualization of the control structure of the target program. The structure is shown as a control flow graph. Figure 3 shows a screen shot of the control flow graph of a function. Nodes in the graph represent function calls, jumps and

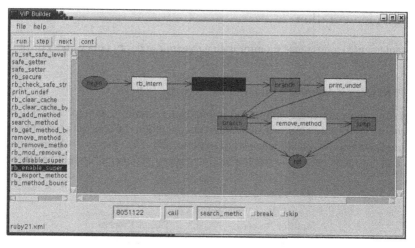

Fig. 3. A screen shot of VIP Builder

branches. Edges in the graph represent transitions of control between two instructions. Other instructions including add, sub, load or store are not shown in the graph. Therefore, a policy maker can see only essential information to understand the control structure. Furthermore, the visualization helps to point to an instruction without using the address. The policy maker thus does not write a dynamic security policy description by hand, but instead generates one automatically by using VIP Builder. If the policy maker clicks on a node, a dialog window appears, which is used to write switching rules.

Debugging of Dynamic Security Policy Description. VIP Builder also provides a capability of debugging dynamic security policy descriptions. The policy maker can run a target program under a dynamic policy description, viewing its progress. The program can be executed in various ways: single-step run, run until exit of function, and run until breakpoint.

This function helps the policy maker to make sure of whether the dynamic security policy description worked as intended. When an execution of a target program is about to violate the description, it is suspended automatically. The policy maker can then alter the description to avoid the violation. After altering the description, the policy maker can continue the execution without restarting the program from the beginning. This will help to reduce the cost of making a dynamic security policy description.

Architecture-Independent Graphical User Interface. A dynamic security policy description is architecture-specific because an executable file of its target program is dependent on the architecture. However, a task to make a policy itself is not essentially dependent on specific architecture. The task only depends on the control structure of the program and APIs to access resources. Therefore, we designed VIP Builder to be independent of any architecture as long as possible. Once a policy maker is accustomed to using VIP Builder on one architecture, he or she also should be able to use VIP Builder on any other architecture.

4   Implementation

We implemented a reference monitor with a dynamic security policy and VIP Builder.

4.1   Reference Monitor with Dynamic Security Policy

There are two essential mechanisms to implement a reference monitor with a dynamic security policy. One is a mechanism to intercept operations of accessing resources in the host environment. It typically consists of system calls. The other is to observe function calls and returns to determine whether an intercepted system call should be allowed or not.

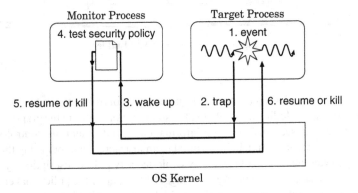

Fig. 4. Intercepting a system call

Intercepting System Calls. Recent unix-based or unix-like operating systems have a functional capability to monitor the activities of a process. The most common API with this capability is `ptrace`. `Ptrace` is available on many operating systems including Linux, *BSD and Solaris. `Ptrace` enables a process to control an execution of another process, and to investigate its memory and its registers.

To monitor a process of a target program with `ptrace`, another process is prepared before starting a monitored process. The other process is called the *monitor process*. The monitor process creates a target process, and begins monitoring it. Each time a system call is issued by the target process, the monitor process is notified. For each notification, the monitor process determines which system call was issued and what was the object of the call. Figure 4 shows the details of the interception and the investigation procedures.

Switching Authority. To implement switching authority, one must know the calling history of the functions in the target process. There are two approaches to learning the history. One is eager evaluation, and the other is lazy evaluation [10]. The former intercepts all the watched function calls. Each time a function call is intercepted, the monitor process determines the current authority of the target program. The latter determines the authority each time a system call is intercepted, by inspecting its runtime stack.

Eager Evaluation. Intercepting all the watched function calls is the key to implementing eager evaluation. Intercepting a system call is easily performed with support from an operating system. However, intercepting a function call is not simple because the function call is irrespective of the operating system.

We used a trap instruction to intercept a function call. This method is often used when implementing a program debugger. Our reference monitor also intercepts the return corresponding to the intercepted call. To intercept the return, we inserted the trap at the address of an instruction that executed just after the return. Here is the procedure to intercept calls.

1. Before starting execution of the target program, all the watched function calls are replaced with trap instructions. The replaced instructions are stored for the occasion of performing a call. The rules in the default section of the security policy description are put on top of the stack in the reference monitor process. After that, the execution starts.
2. If a trap is caused by executing a trap instruction, the reference monitor finds the address of the instruction that caused the trap.
3. The trap instruction is replaced with the original call instruction. After that, the reference monitor lets the target process perform single-step execution with the original function
4. The reference monitor replaces the call instruction with a trap instruction. Furthermore, the reference monitor replaces the very next instruction that will be executed after returning from the called function.
5. The reference monitor puts the rules of the trapped function call on top of the stack. After that, the reference monitor resumes the execution.
6. If the next trap is caused by a trap instruction replacing a call instruction, the reference monitor repeats steps 2-5. If the next trap is caused by a trap instruction that is the next instruction of the most recent intercepted call, the reference monitor replaces the trap instruction with the original instruction and resumes execution after removing the rules from the top of the stack.

Lazy Evaluation. To implement lazy evaluation, it is essential to inspect the runtime stack of a target process. The stack is in the memory of the process, and its location in memory is indicated by registers. The inspection can be achieved by using `ptrace` or similar interface, to access the contents of the memory and the registers.

The stack inspection gives a sequence of called functions at the timing of when a system call is issued. Lazy evaluation has three steps.

1. The reference monitor looks for the address of the most recent function call.
2. It checks if there is a switch of authority bound to the function call. If there is, the reference monitor checks the rules set in the switch. If there is a rule concerning a system call issued by the target process, the reference monitor decides its action based on the rule and finishes the evaluation. If there is no bound for switching the function call or rules concerning the system call, the reference monitor skips to the next function call.
3. The reference monitor repeats step 2 until all the function calls have been checked. If there are no rules concerning the system call, the reference monitor disallows it.

Discussions

Jumps and Branches Over a Boundary Between Functions. The design of the dynamic security policy mechanism assumes that leaps of control between functions are always caused by call instructions. This means that jumps or branches to the outside of a function are not treatable.

It is possible to enumerate all the jumps and branches over a boundary and to hook these in order to switch authority. However, a switch caused by a jump or a branch will never be annulled because it is not obvious, unlike a call, which authority should be applied and when the switch should be annulled.

In our design, such jumps and branches are not allowed. They can be found by analyzing the executable code of a program.

Indirect Addressing Using Registers. The destination address of a call, jump or branch is not always a constant. It may be a variable calculated from register values. This can be happen when a source code of a program is written using function pointers in C, or virtual functions in C++.

On an indirect call, the authority introduced by the switch bound with the call should be variable according to the destination of the call. The destination can be learned by analyzing the operand of the call instruction and register values.

On an indirect jump or an indirect branch, one should make sure that the destination address will not cross a boundary between functions. This can be achieved by analyzing in a way similar to that of analyzing the call instructions. Alternatively, one could use SFI [11] or memory protection with a memory paging mechanism [12, 13].

4.2   Implementation of VIP Builder

As shown in Figure 5, VIP Builder consists of three parts; (a) Control Flow Graph Generator, (b) User Interface, and (c) Reference Monitor. The Control Flow Graph Generator and Reference Monitor must be implemented for each architecture. The User Interface can be shared in all architectures.

Here is the process flow of using VIP Builder.

1. The Control Flow Graph Generator reads an executable file of the target program and generates a representation of the control structure in the program. The control structure is represented as control flow graphs for each function in the program. The representation is architecture-independent and interpretable to the User Interface.
2. The User Interface takes control flow graphs as input and displays the graphs to the policy maker. The graphs are shown as a set of directed graphs.
3. The policy maker makes a dynamic security policy description and debugs it by manipulating the User Interface. When debugging, the User Interface controls the target program via the Reference Monitor.
4. The Reference Monitor invokes the target program, intercepts system calls, manages current authority, and manages breakpoints set by the policy maker. The Reference Monitor intermittently reports on the state of the process.
5. When the policy maker finishes, the User interface outputs a dynamic security policy description to a file. The file is distributed to its user via a Policy Broker Site. The

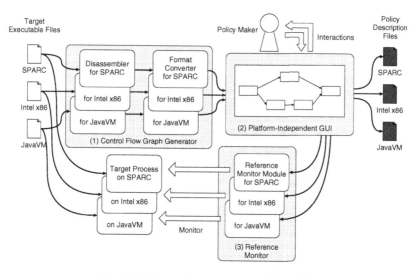

Fig. 5. Workflow of components in VIP Builder

user gives the description to a reference monitor and executes the target program under observation of the reference monitor.

Control Flow Graph Generator. The role of the Control Flow Graph Generator is to output control flow graphs, which are interpreted by the User Interface, by analyzing the executable file of the target program. In our implementation, the Control Flow Graph Generator utilizes an existing disassembler to analyze the executable. Control Flow Graph Generator manipulates an output from the disassembler and converts it into a form that can be interpreted by the User Interface.

First, the Control Flow Graph Generator invokes the disassembler program and lets it process a given executable file. Next, the Generator receives only the necessary information from the output of the disassembler. Unnecessary information, including arithmetic instructions and memory i/o instructions, are discarded at this time. After that, for each function, the Generator constructs a control flow graph based on the received information. While constructing the graph, some tasks, including boundary checks of jump and branch instructions and name resolution of dynamically-linked library functions, are performed. Finally, the Control Flow Graph Generator outputs the control flow graphs. The graph is in an abstract format which is independent of architecture. The format is defined with XML. Figure 6 shows an example of the graph.

At present, there are three implementations of the Control Flow Graph Generator: one for SPARC architecture, one for IA32 architecture and one for the Java Virtual Machine. In the SPARC and IA32 implementations, the objdump disassembler is utilized. It is a part of the binutils [14] package maintained by the Free Software Foundation. In the Java Virtual Machine implementation, the javap disassembler is utilized. It is a part of J2SDK developed by Sun Microsystems.

```
<function name="main">
<branch address="80487e3" target="[8048808]"/>
<call address="80487f3" target="fprintf"/>
<call address="8048800" target="exit"/>
<nop address="8048808" target="" label="[8048808]"/>
<call address="8048811" target="socket"/>
<branch address="8048826" target="[8048844]"/>
<call address="8048830" target="perror"/>
<call address="804883d" target="exit"/>
<nop address="8048844" target="" label="[8048844]"/>
<call address="804884d" target="bzero"/>
<call address="804886d" target="atoi"/>
<call address="8048886" target="htons"/>
<call address="80488b1" target="bind"/>
<branch address="80488c6" target="[80488e4]"/>
<call address="80488d0" target="perror"/>
<call address="80488dd" target="exit"/>
<nop address="80488e4" target="" label="[80488e4]"/>
<call address="80488ef" target="listen"/>
<branch address="8049904" target="[8048920]"/>
<call address="804890e" target="perror"/>
<call address="804891b" target="exit"/>
<nop address="8048920" target="" label="[8048920]"/>
<nop address="8048924" target="" label="[8048924]"/>
<call address="8048944" target="accept"/>
...
```

Fig. 6. Example of a control flow graph

User Interface. The User Interface constructs directed graphs from the control flow graphs and displays them to the user. The directed graph is automatically laid out for easy viewing. Figure 3 shows an example of displaying a directed graph. A node in the display can represent an entry, exit, call, jump or branch. Clicking on a node makes the color of the node change and makes information about the instruction visible at the bottom of the display window.

If the address of a call is undefined because it depends on dynamic information like memory and registers, the callee function cannot be determined. In this case, such calls are displayed as nodes without a destination.

The User Interface is written in the Java language. The major advantage of doing so is portability. For the display and automatic layout of the directed graphs, we utilized the Graph Foundation Classes for Java [15], which was developed by IBM.

Discussions

When a Target Program Cannot be Disassembled. VIP Builder utilizes a disassembler to extract the control structure of a program. However, most commercial programs prohibit reverse engineering, including disassembling, in the End User License Agreement. Our approach seems to be inapplicable to such programs.

We are considering an alternative method to analyze an executable file of such a program. It is a use of automata generation by observing a running program. This method was developed for use in an intrusion detection system [16]. The control structure of a program would be constructed from runtime stack information each time the program issues a system call.

Although this method is applicable to cases where disassembling is prohibited, it has the disadvantage of needing coverage of the constructed control structure. To completely cover the program's control structure, all run paths must be observed. Therefore, it requires much training for better coverage.

Labor and Skill Required to Make Security Policies. With our proposing system, much labor and much skill will be required to make security policies than other systems do. However, we suppose that these are not so high as impractical.

We have had experience in making security policy descriptions for experiments which are described in section 5. Largest software we have dealt with is Apache HTTP server, which has about 274 thousand lines of its source code. Before we dealt with it, we did not have knowledge of its structure. However, we have made the security policy used in the experiments in about an hour. Procedural steps of the work was as follows: Firstly, we traced normal executions. Secondly, we found the place where rules should be set on, and we made a policy description. Finally, we made sure by testing manually that the software still works with it. We suppose that these steps was not so difficult for ordinary programmers to perform.

Of course, it is not sufficient for objective judgement. In future, we would like to collect more experiences of many people in making security policy descriptions, in order to evaluate effectiveness of our system.

5   Evaluation

To assess practicality of our scheme, we evaluated the performance of a reference monitor we implemented. Our evaluation consisted of micro benchmarks and macro benchmarks.

5.1   Microbenchmark: System Calls

We performed microbenchmarks to examine runtime overhead when calling a system call with our scheme. We measured time periods when calling an open system call (1) without monitoring, (2) with monitoring according to a static security policy description, and (3) with monitoring according to a dynamic security policy. An open system call is a system call that causes an evaluation of authority by a reference monitor. A static description means a description without dynamic switching. In other words, a static description consists of only the default section. In both cases with monitoring, we measured cases (a) with eager evaluation and (b) lazy evaluation, as described in Section 4. We also measured the time periods when calling a getpid system call, which is a system call ignored by a reference monitor. Our implementation uses the ptrace system call to control and investigate the target program. Evaluations were performed on a Linux PC with a 2.8GHz Pentium4 and 1024MB RAM. The Linux distribution we used is RedHat 9.

Below is the dynamic security policy description used in the evaluations.

```
default:
        allow_read /etc/ld.so.preload
        allow_read /etc/ld.so.cache
        allow_read /lib/tls/libc.so.6
8048540:
        allow_read /home/habe/secret.txt
```

The default section gives the authority to read files when initiating execution of a program. The other section gives the target program the authority to open a file named "secret.txt", which is not allowed to be opened in the default section. The index number of the other section indicates the address of the call instruction which calls an open system call in the target program. The static policy we used in this measurement is a description consisting of only the default section and has a rule to allow to read secret.txt in the default section.

Table 1. Processing time on performing a system call (in μs)

	open	getpid
(1) no monitoring	0.978	0.395
(2-a) static, eager eval.	13.6	7.97
(2-b) static, lazy eval.	21.5	7.99
(3-a) dynamic, eager eval.	41.3	7.99
(3-b) dynamic, lazy eval.	21.5	8.00

Table 1 shows the result of the measurements. Our scheme increased the execution time of an open system call. With a dynamic security policy, lazy evaluation was approximately two times faster than eager evaluation. The reason why is that manipulation of the trap instruction took a lot of time. To perform an eager evaluation, a single-step run of a program involves context switches between the target process and the monitor process. On the other hand, lazy evaluation does not require single-step runs.

As for the static security policy, the magnitudes of temporal costs of eager evaluation and lazy evaluation were reversed, with eager evaluation being approximately two times faster than lazy evaluation. The reason is that eager evaluation required only investigation of registers in the target process, whereas lazy evaluation required investigation of the registers and also the runtime stack in the target process.

These results suggest a bifurcation between eager evaluation and lazy evaluation. If there are many switches in a target program, it is advantageous to use lazy evaluation because a switch of authority incurs less overhead than in eager evaluation. If there are few switches, it is advantageous to use eager evaluation because a system call like an open call incurs less overhead than in lazy evaluation.

It is worth mentioning about the overhead of the getpid system call, which is ignored by the reference monitor. The ptrace interface does not support selective interruption of system calls, like the proc file system in Solaris has. Therefore, all the system calls are intercepted by the reference monitor, and the reference monitor must find out which type of system call has been issued. Identifying the type of system calls

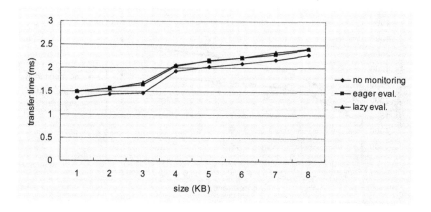

Fig. 7. Transfer Time

involves a context switch, which incurs very large overhead in comparison with a getpid system call.

5.2   Macrobenchmark: HTTP Server

To assess the performance of our mechanism in practical situation, we measured transfer time and throughput of a HTTP server without moniring, with eager evaluation, and with lazy evaluation. We deployed Apache 2.0.47 on the PC we used in the previous measurement. We measured performance of the server with "ab" benchmarking tool, which is included in Apache distribution. It was run on another PC, which has the same performance. These PCs were connected via a 100Base-TX switch.

The following is a description of dynamic security policy we used in the measurements. At `807f43e` and `809786b` in executable code of the server, there are call instructions to a function named `apr_file_open`, which is a wrapper function of `open` system call. With this description, the server can open files in `htdocs` only when calling a `open` system call via these two function calls. Otherwise, opening the files will always fail.

```
default:
           allow_read /opt/httpd-2.0.47/conf/
           allow_readwrite /opt/httpd-2.0.47/logs/
           allow_read ...
           ...
807f43e:
           allow_read /opt/httpd-2.0.47/htdocs/
809786b:
           allow_read /opt/httpd-2.0.47/htdocs/
```

Figure 7 shows the time periods when transferring files in various sizes. With our mechanism, the transfer time increases approximately 0.2 ms independently of the size of the transfered file.

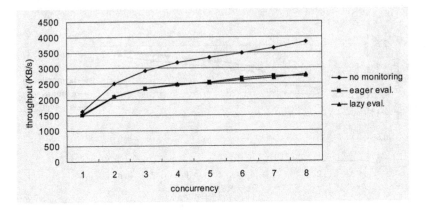

Fig. 8. Throughput

Figure 8 shows the throughput when transferring repeatedly a 2KB-sized file with various concurrency. With our mechanism, as throughput decreases there is a corresponding increase in concurrency. In the result, there are considerable decrements when transferring the file with high concurrency. The decrement will be alleviated in more practical situation, which has narrower bandwidth and higher latency.

In both measurements, there was no significant difference between eager evaluation and lazy evaluation.

6   Related Work

SecurePot [17] is a reference monitor system which enables its user to make a security policy description in an interactive way. If a target program tries to access a local resource, the reference monitor suspends its execution and asks the user whether the access should be allowed or not. The user's response is automatically cached in the reference monitor. When the execution has finished, the accumulated responses are written to a file as a security policy description. The description can be used in another execution of the same program. The design concept of VIP Builder is inspired by SecurePot. VIP Builder has improved features, including visualization of the control structure and detailed description of security policy, in comparison with SecurePot.

Janus [4] is a reference monitor system with a simple model. The security policy description of Janus gives constant authority to all programs being used by a user. MAPBox [6] extends the model of Janus. In MAPBox, program are classified depending on their functionalities. Security policy descriptions are prepared for each class. The approach of MAPBox is a good bet for improving security. However, as we stated before in Section 2, we think that a more fine-grained classification of subject to which authority is given is important to achieving higher security.

SubDomain [7] is a reference monitor that can switch authority each time a different program is loaded via an `exec` system call. While SubDomain developers had a similar motivation to ours, there are two major differences between their design and ours. One is the grain of switching authority. Our scheme allows one to switch authority in units of functions, a finer grain than units of programs. The other is the management of the transition between two different units. SubDomain does not care which `exec` system call causes a transition between one program to another. Our scheme allows switching authority depending on which function call causes the transition. In addition, there is no support for making a security policy description for SubDomain.

Recently, memory protection mechanisms using virtual memory have been proposed [12, 13]. These mechanisms are versatile and applicable to various systems. They aim to use extension code in a secure manner. They assign different authorities to each fragment of the code. We think that it is possible to combine the memory protection mechanism and our scheme and that it will bring better results in terms of both efficiency and security.

A GUI tool called "policytool", which is a part of J2SDK, is a tool which helps a policy maker to create a security policy description. The policy maker can generate a security policy description by choosing an appropriate permission from a list and typing the subject (signer's name or codebase URL) of the description and the object of the permission. This helps the policy maker to remember the correct names of the permissions and to avoid format errors in the description. Policytool only helps in writing a description, and does not help to make a policy. VIP Builder is designed to help both activities, providing the visualization and the debugging feature.

Visual Policy Editor [18] is a tool which helps to make a policy description for network security. Visual Policy Editor displays the topology of the network, and the user can deploy firewalls, VPN tunnels and so on by manipulating the display. A policy description is automatically generated by the Visual Policy Builder. VIP Builder and Visual Policy Editor have different targets, but they have similar objectives.

Naccio [19] is a system which enforces given security policies in a program. Naccio generates wrapper functions from a given security policy description. Naccio can generate wrapper functions for multiple platforms (Java and Win32, at present) from a single security policy description. The advantage of Naccio is expressiveness. However, its disadvantage is complexity of the description, which is thought to be attributable to the expressiveness. The reason for both the advantage and the disadvantage is that the security policy description for Naccio is procedural. Procedural descriptions can express virtually any type of security policy. However, making such a policy description is difficult. A policy maker must be skilled with the Platform Interface provided with Naccio.

7   Conclusion

In this paper, we proposed a scheme called dynamic policy description and described the implementations of a reference monitor with a dynamic security policy and a GUI tool called VIP Builder. We evaluated the performance of the reference monitor to show that our scheme would be of use in the real world.

Our future plans are as follows: First, we would like to implement an adaptation of our scheme to commercial applications that are prohibited from being disassembled. We are planning to apply a method to extract the control structure by observing a running program. Second, we would like to combine memory protection mechanisms and our scheme. The combination will enhance security and effectiveness. Other plans include application of dynamic security policy to checking the authority of normal (not system calls) functions and to dynamically loaded code and performance tuning. Finally, we are planning to integrate the reference monitor system and VIP Builder into the SoftwarePot system [8, 9].

Acknowledgments

Thanks to Wei Wang and Peter Suranyi for helping us to implement VIP Builder. Thanks to Yoshihiro Oyama for informative comments while writing this paper.

References

1. Aleph One: Smashing The Stack For Fun And Profit. Phrack **49** (1996) http://www.phrack.org/show.php?p=49&a=14.
2. Anderson, J.P.: Computer Security Technology Planning Study. Technical report, Hanscom AFB, Bedford, MA (1972)
3. Saltzer, J.H., Sheroeder, M.D.: The Protection of Information in Computer Systems. Proceedings of the IEEE **63** (1975)
4. Goldberg, I., Wagner, D., Thomas, R., Brewer, E.A.: A Secure Environment for Untrusted Helper Applications: Confining the Wily Hacker. In: Proceedings of the 6th USENIX Security Symposium, San Jose (1996)
5. Gong, L., Schemers, R.: Implementing Protection Domains in the Java Development Kit 1.2. In: In Proceedings of the Internet Society Symposium on Network and Distributed System Security, San Diego, California (1998)
6. Acharya, A., Raje, M.: MAPbox: Using Parameterized Behavior Classes to Confine Untrusted Applications. In: Proceedings of the 9th USENIX Security Symposium, Denver (2000)
7. Cowan, C., Beattie, S., Kroah-Hartman, G., Pu, C., Wagle, P., Gligor, V.: SubDomain: Parsimonious Server Security. In: Proceedings of the 14th Systems Administration Conference (LISA 2000), New Orleans (2000)
8. Kato, K., Oyama, Y.: SoftwarePot: An Encapsulated Transferable File System for Secure Software Circulation. Technical Report ISE-TR-02-185, Institute of Information Sciences and Electronics, University of Tsukuba (2002)
9. Kato, K., Oyama, Y., Kanda, K., Matsubara, K.: Software Circulation Using Sandboxed File Space - Previous Experience and New Approach. In: Proceedings of the 8th ECOOP Workshop on Mobile Object Systems. (2002)
10. Gong, L.: Inside Java2 Platform Security. Addison-Wesley (1999)
11. Wahbe, R., Lucco, S., Anderson, T.E., Graham, S.L.: Efficient Software-Based Fault Isolation. In: Proceedings of the 14th ACM Symposium on Operating System Principles (SOSP '93), Asheville (1993) 203–216
12. Takahashi, M., Kono, K., Masuda, T.: Efficient Kernel Support of Fine-Grained Protection Domains for Mobile Code. In: Proceedings of the 19th International Conference on Distributed Computing Systems (ICDCS '99), Austin (1999) 64–73
13. Tzi-cker Chiueh, Venkitachalam, G., Pradhan, P.: Integrating segmentation and paging protection for safe, efficient and transparent software extensions. In: Proc. of the 17th ACM Symp. on Operating Systems Principles. (1999)
14. Free Software Foundation: (binutils) http://www.gnu.org/directory/binutils.html.

15. IBM Corp.: (Graph Foundation Classes for Java) `http://alphaworks.ibm.com/tech/gfc`.
16. Sekar, R., Bendre, M., Dhurjati, D., Bollineni, P.: A Fast Automaton-Based Method for Detecting Anomalous Program Behaviors. In: Proceedings of the IEEE Symposium on Security and Privacy. (2001)
17. Oyama, Y., Kato, K.: SecurePot: Secure Execution System using System Call Hook. In: The 18th annual convention of Japan Society for Software Science and Technology (In Japanese). (2001)
18. Check Point Software Technologies Ltd.:   (Visual Policy Editor) `http://www.checkpoint.com/products/management/vpe.html`.
19. Evans, D., Twyman, A.: Flexible Policy-Directed Code Safety. In: Proceedings of the IEEE Symposium on Research in Security and Privacy, Oakland, CA, IEEE Computer Society, Technical Committee on Security and Privacy, IEEE Computer Society Press (1999) 32–45

Securing RPC with a Reference Monitor for System Calls

Yasushi Shinjo[1], Yoshinori Nakata[2], and Kozo Itano[1]

[1] Institute of Information Sciences and Electronics, University of Tsukuba,
Tsukuba, Ibaraki 305-8573, Japan
yas@is.tsukuba.ac.jp
http://www.is.tsukuba.ac.jp/~yas/
Phone: +81 29-853-6562, Fax: +81 29-853-5206
[2] College of Information Sciences, University of Tsukuba

Abstract. This paper proposes a method to improve access control for RPC by using a reference monitor for system calls. The proposed method uses a set of kernel extension modules. Unlike conventional packet filters, some kernel modules can handle RPC-level parameters, such as program numbers and procedure numbers for filtering RPC messages. Furthermore, these filtering modules can decode arguments of individual procedures based on virtual machine instructions. Another kernel module confirms a user identifier and group identifiers in the RPC request messages. Therefore, individual RPC servers can use those identifiers for improving security. The performance decline cased by those kernel modules is small and less than the variation of communication times over a 100Mbps LAN.

1   Introduction

Remote Procedure Call (RPC) is one of the most widely used techniques to implement distributed systems. For example, Network File System (NFS) and Network Information System (NIS) are build on SunRPC or ONC RPC [1]. Recently, RPC is also used within a single host, such as desktop environments of window systems [2]. RPC with objects is also known as Object Request Broker (ORB), and widely used in local and distributed systems.

As the use of RPC spreads, the attacks on RPC are also increasing [3, 4, 5, 6, 7]. A report by the SANS Institute and FBI ranks RPC as the top threat in Unix-based systems [8].

To protect programs that use networks, a packet filter is one of the most popular and effective mechanisms. However, conventional packet filters have the following problems when protecting RPC programs.

1. They cannot deal with RPC level parameters, such as RPC program numbers and RPC procedure numbers. Furthermore, it is very hard to build packet filters that can decode individual RPC message bodies in advance.
2. They cannot manipulate popular credentials, such as user identifiers (UIDs) and group identifiers (GIDs).

K. Futatsugi et al. (Eds.): ISSS 2003, LNCS 3233, pp. 262–280, 2004.

To address these problems, we propose a method to improve access control for RPC by using a reference monitor for system calls. In this method, we enable a user to describe access control policies as instructions of a virtual machine. The virtual machine interprets given instructions and decodes not only RPC message headers but also individual RPC message bodies. Therefore, we can adapt arbitrary RPC programs.

As a reference monitor for system calls, we use our own one, SysGuard. SysGuard uses a set of kernel extension modules called *guards*. In this paper, we show the design and implementation of guards for improving access control for SunRPC. By using these guards, we can prevent the attacks in [3–7].

In SysGuard, we define a guard (kernel module) as simple as possible, and we achieve sophisticated functions by composing multiple guards. Therefore, multiple guards for RPC often work together for a single process. Since such guards for RPC are independent of one another, a straightforward implementation requires duplicate decoding of RPC messages. To omit duplicate decoding, we share the decoding module among RPC guards for each process. We also use a lazy method to avoid unnecessary decoding of RPC messages.

The rest of the paper is organized as follows. Section 2 shows the mechanism of SunRPC and the overview of the SysGuard reference monitor. Section 3 describes the design and implementation of the kernel modules of SysGuard to improve access control for SunRPC. Section 4 describes modifications to clients and servers for securing RPC. We will show that modifying clients is easy and practical because it can be implemented by replacing a dynamic link library. Section 5 shows experimental results. Section 6 describes related work. Finally, Section 7 concludes the paper.

2   SunRPC and SysGuard

In this section, we describe the mechanism of SunRPC, one of the most popular RPC implementations briefly, and address the problems of access control. Next, we describe the overview of SysGuard, a reference monitor for system calls.

Finally, we show existing kernel modules of SysGuard and their limitations when we have to protect RPC programs.

2.1   The Mechanism of SunRPC and Access Control

Figure 1 shows the overview of the SunRPC mechanism. In this figure, a client on host1 is invoking the procedure `proc1()` of a server on host2. SunRPC uses TCP/IP or UDP/IP as message transport. In SunRPC, the port numbers of TCP or UDP are not fixed in advance, but they are fixed when a server starts up. On the server-side host, a server called a *port mapper* [1] is running. The port mapper translates a following triple to a corresponding port number:

---

[1] The name of its executable file is typically `portmap` or `rpcbind`.

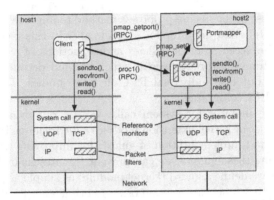

Fig. 1. The mechanism of SunRPC and access control facilities

- A program number
- A version number
- A protocol number (TCP or UDP)

In SunRPC, the following messages are exchanged among a client, a sever, and the port mapper:

1. When a server is executed, it invokes the procedure **pmap_set()** of the port mapper in the same host with RPC, and registers its port number. The port number of the port mapper itself is fixed to 111.
2. When a client is executed, it invokes the procedure **pmap_getport()** of the port mapper in the server's host with RPC, and gets the port number.
3. The client invokes the server with the port number that is obtained from the port mapper.

As discussed in Section 1, conventional packet filters cannot handle RPC-level concepts, such as program numbers, procedure numbers, and arguments of individual procedures. Furthermore, it is not simple to set up conventional packet filters for dynamically changeable port numbers. In this paper, we address these problems.

In the original design of SunRPC, access control is performed by RPC servers. On each procedure invocation, a server can get either of following types of client's credentials:

- AUTH_NONE: No credential is attached.
- AUTH_SYS (AUTH_UNIX): The credential includes a User Identifier (UID), a main Group Identifier (GID), and supplement group identifiers (groups).
- AUTH_DH and AUTH_KERB: The credential includes a digital signature based on the Diffie-Hellman (DH) or Kerberos cryptographic technology.

It is easy to spoof the credential of AUTH_SYS. Using digital signatures requires modifying both a client and a server and often running additional key servers. Therefore, many RPC programs have not used digital signatures. Furthermore, although we use digital signatures, we cannot prevent buffer overflow

```
result_t proc1(aug_t *arg, struct svc_req *rqstp)
{
  if ( rqstp->rq_cred.oa_flavor == AUTH_SYS )
  {
    struct authunix_parms *cred =
        (struct authunix_parms *)rqstp->rq_clntcred;
    if( permit(cred->aup_uid,cred->aup_gid,
                 cred->aup_len,cred->aup_gids,OPERATION1) )
    {
      task1();
    }
    ...
  }
  ...
}
```

Fig. 2. Access control in an RPC server using a credential of AUTH_SYS

```
cl = clnt_create(host,SERVICE_PROG, SERVICE_VERS, "tcp");
cl->cl_auth = authsys_create_default();
proc1( &arg, cl ); /* call stub and perform RPC */
```

Fig. 3. Sending a proper credential of AUTH_SYS by a legitimate client

attacks. In this paper, we show a method to prevent spoofing of the credential of AUTH_SYS with a reference monitor. We also describe how to prevent some buffer overflow attacks in Section 3.2.

Figure 2 shows usage of the credential of AUTH_SYS at the server side. Each procedure takes two parameters: the argument of the procedure and request information (`rqstp`). First, the procedure `proc1()` in Figure 2 confirms that the credential is of AUTH_SYS. Next, the procedure `proc1()` calls the function `permit()` to check if the client with the credential is permitted to perform the operation. If it is permitted, the procedure `proc1()` performs the corresponding task.

Figure 3 is a program fragment of an RPC client that sends a credential of AUTH_SYS. The library function `clnt_create()` allocates a structure and a socket for calling the specified RPC server. This library function creates a credential of AUTH_NONE by default. In this program fragment, this default credential is replaced with the result of the library function `authsys_create_default()`.

It is easy to spoof the credential of AUTH_SYS. Figure 4 shows a program fragment of a malicious client that sends a spoofed credential of AUTH_SYS. The second argument to the library function `authsys_create()` is a UID of the AUTH_SYS credential. The number 0 means the privileged user. In this paper, we show a mechanism to prevent this type of spoofing, so access control in the original RPC design becomes effective.

2.2   The Overview of the SysGuard Reference Monitor

SysGuard is a reference monitor for system calls [9]. SysGuard uses a set of kernel modules called *guards* to improve the system security. Figure 5 shows the

```
cl = clnt_create(host,SERVICE_PROG, SERVICE_VERS, "tcp");
cl->cl_auth = authsys_create("localhost", 0, 0, 0, NULL); /* spoofing */
proc1( &arg, cl ); /* call stub and perform RPC */
```

Fig. 4. Sending a spoofed credential of AUTH_SYS by a malicious client

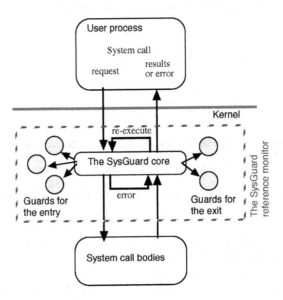

Fig. 5. The overview of the SysGuard reference monitor for system calls

system call processing in a SysGuard-enabled system. Guards are called from the SysGuard core that corresponds to the entry and the exit of the system calls. When a user process issues a system call with a trap instruction, the flow of control is transferred into the entry of the system call. In a conventional system, a global jump table of system calls is referred and the corresponding function is invoked. In SysGuard, the SysGuard core checks if some guards are attached to the system call for the process. If there are guards, the SysGuard core invokes each of them sequentially. Each guard decides whether the invocation of the system call is allowed or not. If all the guards for the system call in a process allow the invocation, the body of the system call is executed. Otherwise, the body of system call is not executed, and an error is returned to the user process. For example, a guard for the system call connect() can check the address of the communication peer in the argument of the system call and decide whether the invocation of the system call is allowed or not.

Some types of guards are invoked from the exit of system calls. For example, if a guard for the system call accept() needs to check the communication peer, the guard must be attached to the exit of system call. At the exit, if all the guards allow the invocation, the results of the system call are returned to the user process in a regular way. Otherwise, the effects of the system call are can-

Table 1. General guards restricting network access

Name	Description
NoRawSocket	This guard stops the system call `socket()` if its type is SOCK_RAW.
TCPClientOnly	This guard blocks the system call `accept()`, so the process can never be a server.
UDPClientOnly	This guard matches the requests and replies in UDP/IP communications by observing the system calls `sendto()`, `recvfrom()`, etc., and passes only the pattern "sending a request and then receiving a reply".
TCPServerPeerFilter	This guard examines the result of the system call `accept()`, and disconnects the established connection if the predefined rule sets do not allow the communication with the peer (client).
UDPServerPeerFilter	This guard is the UDP version of UDPServerPeerFilter. It differs in that this guard examines the result of the system call `recvfrom()` and `recvmsg()`.
TCPClientPeerFilter	This guard is a variant of TCPServerPeerFilter. This guard differs in that it works in the client side. It examines the second argument of the system call `connect()`, that is, the IP address and port number of the communication peer (a server).
UDPClientPeerFilter	This guard is the UDP version of TCPClientPeerFilter.

celed. For example, a newly opened file or connection is closed. Next, an error is returned to the user process, or the system call is executed again.

SysGuard has a scope facility for guards [9]. With this facility, scope of guards can be specified by using the process attributes, such as UID, GID, and PID. The guard scoping on a per-process basis improves composability of individual guards, and simplifies individual guards [9]. Unlike device drivers and the kernel programs in Linux Security Module [10], guard programs are portable if they use standard system call interfaces and guard support functions.

2.3   General Guards Improving Access Control for Networks

To improve access control for SunRPC, we can use general-purpose guards for networks [9]. Table 1 summarizes such general-purpose guards for networks. Since the guards in Table 1 do not interpret communication messages, they have the same limitations as conventional packet filters. For example, we cannot describe access control policies in terms of RPC. In the following sections, we show the guards that interpret RPC messages.

By using general-purpose guards, we can simplify guards for RPC. For example, with the guard NoRawSocket, we can build guards for SunRPC that do not have to observe raw sockets.

3 Improving Access Control for SunRPC with SysGuard

The existing guards described in Section 2.3 cannot understand RPC messages, so they are not enough for protecting RPC programs. In this section, we show the design and implementation of guards that analyze RPC messages to improve access control for SunRPC.

3.1 The Design of Guards for SunRPC

We settle the following design principles:

- Attach guards for clients as well as servers. It becomes important to protect clients from malicious servers, now [11]. As similar to NFS, it is effective to control clients within a local host or well-managed LANs.
- Block request messages instead of reply messages. The recovery from missing requests is much easier than the recovery from missing reply messages. Blocking request messages can be dealt with as missing of request messages.
- Keep a single guard as simple as possible, and compose multiple simple guards if a complex function is needed. Small and simple programs are easy to develop, and have less chance to include security vulnerabilities.

Based on these design principles, we have designed the following guards for SunRPC:

(1) RPCClientRequestFilter

This guard works in a client side, and performs filtering on request messages using PRC program numbers, version numbers, and procedure numbers. In addition to those numbers in RPC headers, this guard can decode individual request messages. An access control policy is written in instruction sequences of a virtual machine. When the policy is not satisfied, this guard blocks sending request messages in the system calls `sendto()`, `write()`, and so on.

(2) RPCServerRequestFilter

This is similar to the guard RPCClientRequestFilter, but it differs in that this guard works at a server side. This guard blocks receiving request messages in the system calls `recvfrom()`, `read()`, and so on.

(3) RPCClientReplyFilter and RPCServerReplyFilter

These guards work for the reply messages, and the other things are same as RPCClientRequestFilter and RPCServerRequestFilter, respectively.

(4) RPCClientConfAuthSys

This guard confirms that the credential of AUTH_SYS contains the true UIDs and GIDs of client process. If the credential contains a spoofed value, this guard blocks sending request messages. This guard makes it possible to build secure individual RPC servers as well as a secure port mapper.

In the following subsections, we show details of RPCClientRequestFilter and RPCClientConfAuthSys.

```
{
  prog 100004 eq
  proc 8 eq
  deny
}
```

Fig. 6. An example of access control policy (disallowing the procedure `ypall()`)

3.2   RPCClientRequestFilter, a Guard for RPC Request Messages by Using a Virtual Machine

RPCClientRequestFilter is a guard for RPC request messages at a client side. This guard decodes an RPC request message and determines whether or not it allows sending the message based on given policies. In this guard, access control policies are written in instructions of a virtual machine. Figure 6 shows a procedure in an assembly language of the virtual machine. This procedure disallows invocations of the procedure `ypall()` of NIS. This procedure is often used for stealing a password file.

The virtual machine has a typed stack a program counter. Its assembly language has a similar syntax as PostScript [12]. In this assembly language, each word separated by white spaces corresponds to a single instruction of the virtual machine. Numbers are assembled into literal instructions that push the corresponding immediate values to the stack. A pair of braces groups instructions, and makes a procedure. We can define named procedures in the following syntax as in PostScript:

/*name* { *word-sequece* } `def`

The last sequence of unnamed procedures describes access control policies. Each unnamed procedure is evaluated sequentially. Each procedure consists of a condition and an action. If the condition is satisfied, the action is executed. Otherwise, the next procedure is evaluated. An action is either `allow` or `deny`. If a procedure returns `allow` or `deny`, the evaluation of the procedure list is stopped at that point, and the result is treated as the return value of the guard. Finally, no procedure is matched, `allow` is assumed by default. This can be reversed by adding `deny` with an empty condition.

Figure 6 includes only a single procedure that observes the RPC program number and the RPC procedure number. The instructions `prog` and `proc` are instructions that push the program number and the RPC procedure number to the stack, respectively. The numbers `100004` and `8` are assembled into literals that push the corresponding immediate values to the stack. The instruction `eq` pops up two integer values from the stack and compares them. If these two values are same, the program counter of the virtual machine is advanced to the next instruction. Otherwise, the virtual machine stops the evaluation of the current procedure, and returns the default value, `allow`.

Although RPC headers are variable length structures, they can be decoded by a single program. On the other hand, individual RPC request messages have

```
{
  prog 100083 eq proc 7 eq
  param xdr_string strlen 64 gt
  deny
}
```

Fig. 7. Limiting the length of the string in the first argument of the procedure (ToolTalk)

their own specific formats, so it is not trivial to develop guards for individual messages.

To solve this problem, we describe decoders of individual messages in the virtual machine instructions. Figure 7 shows a procedure that can decode a request message of the ToolTalk service [2]. This procedure blocks sending a large string whose length is greater than 64, and prevents the attack to the ToolTalk service [3].

First, this procedure checks the program number and the procedure number. The instruction **param** initializes the cursor for decoding the argument of the request message. The instruction **xdr_string** decodes the parameter as a string and advances the cursor to the next parameter. The instruction **strlen** pops up the string value from the stack and pushes its length to the stack.

It is not difficult for RPC programmers to write access policies in our virtual machine language if they can access interface descriptions. It is a straightforward task to translate the interface descriptions of SunRPC to our virtual machine instructions. We have a plan to implement a compiler that generates machine instructions from the policy description at the level of the interface description language. Sometimes, we cannot obtain interface descriptions. For example, the ToolTalk service is a product, and its interface is not open. In the case [3], we can prevent the attack because it is a buffer overflow attack, the ToolTalk service uses strings in RPC messages, and it is easy to find strings in RPC messages. We need interface descriptions to write policies for complex RPC messages.

Note that conventional packet filters cannot deal with individual RPC messages without extension modules for SunRPC. The engine of our virtual machine can be embedded to extensible packet filters, such as Linux iptables/netfilter [13]. One limitation of this method is use of process attributes, such as UIDs and GIDs. It is hard for packet filters to get such attributes while it is easy for a reference monitor.

3.3   Observing System Calls in RPCClientRequestFilter

The guard RPCClientRequestFilter has to observe the following system calls:

- Before the execution of **send()**, **sendto()**, and **sendmsg()**.
- Before the execution of **write()**.
- After the execution of **connect()**.

Figure 8 shows a top-level function of the guard RPCClientRequestFilter. This function is invoked before the system call **sendto()** is executed. Each guard

```
before_sendto (struct guardhandle *ghp,
  int fd, const void *msg, int len, unsigned int flags,
  struct sockaddr *to, int tolen)
{
  work = (rpcvm_guard_t) ghp->work ;
  vm = rpcvm_guard_getvm( work );
  peer.to = to ; peer.tolen = tolen ;
  if( rpcvm_initenv(vm, (void *)msg, len,
        before_sendto_getpeername, &peer ) == 0 )
    return( GUARD_DENY );
  perm = rpcvm_proclist_eval( vm, work->proclist, work->proclist_len );
  return( perm );
}
```

Fig. 8. The function that is invoked before the system call sendto in the guard RPC-ClientRequestFilter

instance has a private work space that can be obtained from **ghp->work**. This function retrieves the work space and gets the pointer to an instance of virtual machine.

Next, this function calls the function **rpcvm_initenv()**, and makes a binding environment for evaluating virtual machine code. We will discuss the binding environment in Section 3.4. Those values are computed from the following arguments to the function **rpcvm_initenv()**:

– The address and length of the outgoing message.
– The closure (callback function) to extract the IP address and port number of the communication peer.

After initializing the binding environment, the function **before_sendto()** calls the function **rpcvm_proclist_eval()** and interprets the procedure list that is given as the instruction sequences of the virtual machine. The procedure list is stored in the private work space.

For the system call **write()**, this guard has the function **before_write()**, which is almost similar to **before_sendto()**. In the case of **write()**, there is a performance problem to be solved. Unlike **sendto()**, **write()** is one of the most frequently used system calls. This system call is also invoked for non-RPC interprocess communications including HTTP as well as for file output. Observing the system call **write()** may cause a large performance decline.

We reduce the overhead of **write()** by using the following methods:

1. We allocate a list of file descriptors for each process. When the system call **connect()** returns a success, the file descriptor is inserted to the list.
2. When the function **before_write()** is invoked, the function first searches the list. If the current file descriptor is not found in the list, the function returns allow immediately. Since the list does not contain the file descriptors that are gained by the system call **open()**, the function **before_write()**

Table 2. The values in the binding environment of the virtual machine

Mnemonic	Description
prog	The program number
vers	The version number
proc	The procedure number
rpcvers	The version of the RPC protocol
direction	The direction of the message. CALL(==0) or REPLY(==1).
ipaddr	The IP address of the peer
port	The port number of the peer
uid	The user identifier
gid	The group identifier
groups	The list of supplemental group identifiers

returns immediately for file output. Otherwise, the function tries to decode the message.

3. If the message is determined as a non-RPC message, such as HTTP, the function removes the file descriptor from the list.

To distinguish RPC messages from non-RPC messages, we use the following signatures in the RPC message:

- The direction field is 0 for request or 1 for reply.
- The version number of the RPC protocol is 2.

Note that these byte sequences include zeros, so they never appear in proper places when text based protocols, such as HTTP and SMTP, are used. If a malicious program puts these byte sequences in a text based protocol, and tries to cause performance degradation, the peer shutdowns the connection, immediately.

3.4   Building the Binding Environment

When procedures in the virtual machine instructions are evaluated, the values in Table 2 are available in *the binding environment*. These values are logically computed in the function rpcvm_initenv() by getting values from a user space memory or kernel data structures of the network protocol stack. At this time, we have to address the following issues:

- Not all the values in Table 2 are used to evaluate procedures. Analyzing unused values causes performance decline. Especially overhead in the system call sendto() is larger because the peer address should be taken from the obscure user space.
- Decoding RPC messages may be repeated for a single system call. Multiple instances of the guard RPCClientRequestFilter can be attached in a process. Furthermore, other RPC-related guards may be attached to the same process and repeat decoding.

To solve those problems, we use the following techniques:

- Delaying analysis of RPC messages until the values are actually used.
- Sharing the analysis results among several guards.

3.5   An Assembler and a Debugger

We have developed an assembler for the virtual machine. This assembler reads the program in the assembly language and produces object code. The assembler has a macro facility in the same syntax as definition in PostScript. The assembler performs a simple abstract interpretation and type checking.

We have also developed a user-level debugger of the virtual machine. This debugger accepts the same machine instructions as the guards in the kernel, and can execute a program through the dynamic link facility [2].

3.6   Other Guards Filtering RPC Messages

The guard RPCServerRequestFilter is very similar to RPCClientRequestFilter. The difference is that RPCServerRequestFilter works at a server side. The guard RPCServerRequestFilter mainly observes the system call `recvfrom()`, `read()`, and `accept()`.

The RPCServerRequestFilter can accept the same procedures as RPCClientRequestFilter. Unlike RPCClientRequestFilter, comparing program numbers can be omitted usually because a typical RPC server works for a single RPC program.

3.7   RPCClientConfAuthSys – Confirming a Credential of AUTH_SYS

As described in Section 2.1, it is easy to spoof a credential of AUTH_SYS. The guard RPCClientConfAuthSys works at a client side, and confirms a credential of AUTH_SYS in a request message. With this guard, a malicious client cannot spoof a credential of AUTH_SYS.

First, this guard decodes an RPC header and extracts the credential in the RPC header. The credential includes a UID, a main GID, and supplement GIDs (groups). Next, this guard compares these IDs with the attributes of the current process. If the credential includes an unknown ID, the guard blocks sending the request message.

We emphasize that it is easy for a reference monitor at the system call level to get process attributes, such as UIDs and GIDs. On the other hand, it is hard for packet filters to get such information.

Usage of the guard RPCClientConfAuthSys is simple. It can be instantiated and attached to the process without any parameter. The implementation of the guard uses the binding environment in Section 3.4.

---

[2] Unlike system calls, a dynamic link facility can be bypassed.

4   Modifying Clients and Servers for Securing SunRPC

As similar to packet filters, the RPC messages filters described in Section 3.1 do not require modifications to RPC programs. For example, we can protect the ToolTalk servers without modifying the server by the guard RPCServerRequest-Filter. On the other hand, we have to modify clients and servers for making use of the guard RPCClientConfAuthSys. We have described the general usage of the credential of AUTH_SYS in Section 2.1. In this section, we describe modifications to GNU Libc and ypserv, an NIS server.

4.1   GNU Libc

GNU Libc (also known as glibc) is a collection of library functions for the C programming language. This library includes both the client and server side support functions of SunRPC.

If we can modify GNU Libc, we can use the credential of AUTH_SYS without modifying any clients that are linked with GNU Libc. The client side code of SunRPC uses AUTH_NONE by default. It is easy to replace the part of AUTH_NONE with that of AUTH_SYS. Concretely, we can replace invoking `authnone_create()` with invoking `authsys_create_default()` in GNU Libc.

GNU Libc includes NIS access functions that also perform RPC to a remote NIS server. The credential including UID is useful for an NIS server.

Note that bypassing this modified GNU libc does not degrade safety. If a malicious client sends a request that contains AUTH_NONE, the server can refuse the request because the request does not contain AUTH_SYS.

4.2   ypserv

The server ypserv [14] is an implementation of the NIS server. The main purpose of NIS is to share a password file among Unix-based workstations. The current popular NIS server does not have an access control facility on a per-field basis, while an advanced replacement called NIS Plus has such facility. Therefore, current NIS cannot provide a facilty called *shadow password*. In shadow password, the password file /etc/passwd is public accessible and contains dummy hash values of passwords. The true hash values of passwords are stored in a separated file that can be accessed only by the privileged user.

If the client programs are changed as described in 4.1, and the guard RPC-ClientConfAuthSys is enabled, the shadow password facility can be implemented in NIS. We have modified a ypserv program for realizing the shadow password facility. Figure 9 shows the final part of the procedure `ypmatch()` in our modified ypserv. The sign + at the begging of lines means adding to the original code. In this program fragment, before ypserv returns the result, ypserv checks the map name and the UID in the credential. If the map is a password map (`passwd.byname` or `passwd.byuid`) and the UID is not the privileged user's one, then ypserv scrambles the password field in the result.

```
bool_t
ypproc_match_2_svc (ypreq_key *argp, ypresp_val *result,
                    struct svc_req *rqstp)
{
    ...
        result->stat = YP_TRUE;
        result->val.valdat_len = rdat.dsize;
        result->val.valdat_val = rdat.dptr;
+       if( is_passwd(argp->map) && !is_root(rqstp) )
+           passwd_scramble(result->val.valdat_val,result->val.valdat_len);
    ...
    return TRUE;
}
```

Fig. 9. The function that is invoked before the system call sendto in the guard RPC-ClientRequestFilter

5   Experiments

We have implemented the guards RPCClientRequestFilter, RPCServerRequest-Filter, and RPCClientConfAuthSys. We have also implemented the ypserv program that supports password shadowing. We are now implementing the other guards. In this section, we show the experimental results confirming functions of those guards. In addition, we present that the performance decline by those guards is small.

Currently, SysGuard is available in the following systems.

- i386 Linux 2.2
- Alpha Linux 2.2
- i386 FreeBSD 4.7

We made experiments using SysGuard for i386 Linux 2.2. All experiments were performed on a PC with a Pentium III 1GHz, with 384k bytes of external cache and 384M bytes of main memory.

We measured the execution times in the success cases. In other words, we measured the execution times when all the guards allowed the execution of the system call. If at least a single guard disallows the execution of a system call, a benchmark program does not work or the apparent execution times become shorter because the system calls are not executed and errors are returned soon.

5.1   Request Filters

We have confirmed that the guard RPCClientRequestFilter and RPCServerRequestFilter effectively blocks some suspicious activities.

First, we ran a client program yp-all in the environment where the guard RPCClientRequestFilter is enabled with the procedure in Figure 6. The program yp-all invokes the procedure ypall() of ypserv and takes three arguments: the host name where ypserv is running, the domain name of NIS, and the map name.

The following script shows that invoking the procedure `ypall()` is blocked by
the guard RPCClientRequestFilter.

```
% ./yp-all $host $domainname passwd.byname
yp_all: clnt_call: RPC: Unable to send; errno = Permission denied
% _
```

The error message means that sending the request message was blocked by
the guard in the local host.

Next, we started the server ypserv in the environment where the guard RPC-
ServerRequestFilter is enabled with the procedure in Figure 6. After that, we
run the same client program yp-all with no guard. The result follows.

```
% ./yp-all $host $domainname passwd.byname
yp_all: clnt_call: RPC: Unable to receive;
errno = Connection reset by peer
% _
```

The client had sent the request message with the system call `write()`. After
that, the client tried to receive the reply message with the system call `read()`.
At the server side, ypserv tried to receive the request message with the system
call `read()`. However, this receiving is blocked by the guard RPCServerRequest-
Filter, so the server closed the connection of TCP/IP. Therefore, at the client
side, an error (`ECONNRESET`) was returned in the system call `read()`.

5.2   Modified ypserv and RPCClientConfAuthSys

As described in Section 4.2, we have modified ypserv that sends true hash values
of passwords only if the client sends the UID of a privileged user. We ran this
ypserv, and executed a client program yp-match that invokes the procedure
ypmatch(). In the following script, we ran the program yp-match twice with no
guard:

```
% ./yp-match $host $domainname passwd.byname yas
yas:*************:1231:40:Yasushi SHINJO:/home/yas:/bin/tcsh
% ./yp-match -u 0 $host $domainname passwd.byname yas
yas:A3zByrCCux20w:1231:40:Yasushi SHINJO:/home/yas:/bin/tcsh
% _
```

The first execution of yp-match sent a request with the AUTH_NONE credential (default). The program takes the host running ypserv, the domain name
of NIS, the map name, and the search key. In the result line, the password field is
filled with the character '*'. The second execution of yp-match sent a request
with the AUTH_SYS credential with the UID 0. The result contains the true
hash value of the password.

Next, we ran the same program in the environment where the guard RPC-
ClientConfAuthSys is enabled. The result follows.

```
% ./yp-match -u 0 $host $domainname passwd.byname yas
host: RPC: Unable to send; errno = Operation not permitted
% _
```

This error message means that sending the request message with a spoofed
credential is blocked by the guard.

5.3   Micro Benchmarks

To measure the overheads of the guards, we use the following programs:

yp-match This program invokes the procedure ypmatch(), repeatedly. This program uses the system call sendto() and recvfrom(). The sizes of request and reply messages are about 128 bytes.

udp-echo This program sends and receives packets of UDP/IP, repeatedly. This program uses the system call sendto() and recvfrom(). The size of a message was set to 128 bytes.

file-write This program writes data to a file, repeatedly. This program uses the system call write(). The size of output data was set to 128 bytes.

In this experiment, we use the guards RPCClientRequestFilter and RPCClientConfAuthSys. For the guard RPCClientRequestFilter, we give the procedure in Figure 6.

The programs yp-match and udp-echo send and receive 10000 UDP packets, and get the best results. To eliminate uncertain characteristics of networks, we ran the programs locally. In other words, both clients and servers were executed in a single host.

Table 3 shows the execution times of procedures in microseconds. In Table 3, the first column of each program contains the shortest execution times, and the second column contains the differences with that in the normal kernel. If we ran yp-match over the 100Base-TX Ethernet, the 90%-range of the execution times was 145–342 microseconds. The differences to the execution times were smaller than this variation. Therefore, it is hard to observe the performance decline of NIS access in a real life. The udp-echo program yielded an almost same trend as yp-match.

In the cases of the program file-write, those guards increased the execution times by 0.71 microseconds. This overhead is smaller than that of yp-match and udp-echo. This result means that the optimization described in Section 3.3 works well.

5.4   An Application Benchmark

Table 4 shows another result of an application benchmark, the compilation of a program (the patch command). We chose this application because this benchmark works in all environments, and it includes many invocations of the system

Table 3. The minimum execution times of procedures in microseconds

Environment		Benchmark programs					
		yp-match		udp-echo		file-write	
		time	diff	time	diff	time	diff
Normal (localhost)		42.4	0	12.5	0	1.62	0
Sys-Guard	no guard	43.4	1.0	12.9	0.4	1.68	0.06
	RPCClientRequestFilter	47.2	4.8	16.8	4.3	2.33	0.71
	RPCClientConfAuthSys	46.7	4.3	15.8	3.3	2.33	0.71

Table 4. Average execution times of compiling the `patch` command in seconds

Environment		time	diff
Normal (localhost)		5.33	0
Sys-Guard	no guard	5.33	0.00
	RPCClientRequestFilter	5.38	0.05
	RPCClientConfAuthSys	5.34	0.01

calls `write()` and `fork()`. The memory for the virtual machine is copied at `fork()`. The patch program consists of 24 program files, 17 header files, and mounts to 12,000 lines. We repeated the experiment 100 times, and measured the average execution times. Since we repeated experiments, all the file contents are expected on disk cache.

The results of the experiment are shown in Table 4. We observed a small performance decline (less than 1%).

6   Related Work

Some packet filters use virtual machines to describe access control policies [15]. Our virtual machine differs from those systems in that our virtual machine is dedicated to RPC and works in a reference monitor for system calls. Therefore, it is easier to write access control for RPC using process attributes such as UID and GID.

The Eternal System [16] provides fault tolerance for CORBA objects [17]. CORBA enables to modify messages through the concept of *interceptors*. The Eternal System implements reliable multicast and replication management with the interceptor. Compared with the Eternal System, our system differs in that our system deals with malicious code and uses a reference monitor for system calls.

Some reference monitors for system calls invoke user-level modules [18] [19] [20]. Our method is faster than such user-level modules.

In Generic Software Wrappers [21], system administrators can use a high-level language, called WDL (Wrapper Description Language) to describe access control policies. A program in WDL is translated into C programs by the WDL compiler, and the C programs are translated loadable kernel modules. This system does not include a virtual machine.

PivodVM is a virtual machine that uses a sparse instruction space for defending machine code injection attacks, such as buffer overflow attacks [22]. PivodVM has obfuscation tools that change instructions. Unlike PivodVM, our virtual machine is protected, so no obfuscation tool is needed.

7   Conclusion

In this paper, we have proposed a method to improve access control for SunRPC. In this method, we use a reference monitor for system calls. We have designed and implemented a set of kernel modules for the reference monitor. The most important modules are RPC messages filters that take access control policies as instruction sequences of a virtual machine. Unlike conventional packet filters, those RPC message filters can manipulate RPC-level concepts, such as RPC program numbers and procedure numbers. Furthermore, those message filters can decode parameters of individual RPC procedures. Therefore, our method can prevent the attacks on RPC in [3, 4, 5, 6, 7] that cannot be handled by conventional packet filters.

In addition to the filters, a kernel module enforces correct use of the credential including UID and GID. This module enables to realize access control in individual RPC servers. To use this module, we have to modify clients. In this paper, we have shown that modifying clients is easy and practical because it can be implemented by replacing a dynamic link library.

The overheads caused by the kernel modules are very small and less than the variation of communication times over a 100Mbps LAN. With this experimental evidence, we have shown the advantage of our method to improve access control for RPC.

References

1. RFC1831: RPC: Remote Procedure Call Protocol Specification Version 2. (1995)
2. The Open Group: CDE 2.1 - Programmer's Overview and Guide. (1997)
3. CERT Advisory CA-1998-11: Vulnerability in ToolTalk RPC Service. (1998)
4. CERT Advisory CA-1999-08: Buffer Overflow Vulnerability in Calendar Manager Service Daemon, rpc.cmsd. (1999)
5. CERT Advisory CA-2000-17: Input Validation Problem in rpc.statd. (2002)
6. CERT Advisory CA-2001-27: Format String Vulnerability in CDE ToolTalk. (2001)
7. CERT Advisory CA-2002-10: Format String Vulnerability in rpc.rwalld. (2002)
8. The SANS Institute and FBI: The Twenty Most Critical Internet Security Vulnerabilities. (October 2002) http://www.sans.org/top20/oct02.php.
9. Shinjo, Y., Eiraku, K., Suzuki, A., Itano, K., Pu, C.: Enhancing access control with sysguard, a reference monitor supporting portable and composable kernel module. In: IEEE 2002 Pacific Rim International Symposium on Dependable Computing (PRDC 2002). (December 2002) 167–176
10. Wright, C., Cowan, C., Morris, J., Smalley, S., Kroah-Hartman, G.: Linux security modules: General security support for the linux kernel. In: USENIX Security Symposium. (2002)
11. OpenSSH Security Advisory (adv.channelalloc): Off-by-one error in the channel code. (2002)
12. Adobe Systems: PostScript(R) Language Reference (3rd Edition). (1999)
13. Russell, R.: Linux 2.4 Packet Filtering HOWTO. http://www.netfilter.org/. (2002)
14. Kukuk, T.: The manual page of ypserv 2.8. (2003) ftp://ftp.kernel.org/pub/linux/utils/net/NIS/.
15. McCanne, S., Jacobson, V.: The BSD packet filter: A new architecture for user-level packet capture. In: USENIX Winter 1993 Conference. (1993) 259–270
16. Narasimhan, P., Moser, L.E., Melliar-Smith, P.M.: Using interceptors to enhance corba. IEEE Computer **32** (1999) 64–68
17. Object Management Group: CORBA v2.4.2. (2001)

18. Takahashi, M., Kono, K., Masuda, T.: Efficient kernel support of fine-grained protection domains for mobile code. In: 19th IEEE International Conference on Distributed Computing Systems. (1999) 64–73
19. Acharya, A., Raje, M.: MAPbox: Using parameterized behavior classes to confine untrusted applications. In: USENIX Security Symposium. (2000)
20. Kato, K., Oyama, Y., Kanda, K., Matsubara, K.: Software circulation using sandboxed file space previous experience and new approach. In: Proceedings of 8th ECOOP Workshop on Mobile Object Systems. (2002)
21. Fraser, T., Badger, L., Feldman, M.: Hardening COTS software with generic software wrappers. In: Proceedings of the 1999 IEEE Symposium on Security and Privacy. (1999) 2–16
22. Osawa, N.: An adaptive security mechanism based on dynamic instruction customization. In: The 6th IASTED International Conference Software Engineering and Applications (SEA 2002). (2002) 222–227

UML Scrapbook and Realization of Snapshot Programming Environment

Osamu Sato[1], Richard Potter[2],
Mitsuharu Yamamoto[2], and Masami Hagiya[1]

[1] Graduate School of Information Science and Technology, University of Tokyo
[2] JST CREST, Faculty of Science, Chiba University

Abstract. We have developed SBUML (Scrapbook for UML), an extension of UML (User-Mode Linux), by adding checkpointing functionality to UML. In this paper, we first describe the design and implementation of SBUML, and then propose a new snapshot programming environment, which is realized by the SBUML programming interfaces. The intended applications of SBUML include intrusion detection and sandboxing for network security, and software model checking for verifying multi-threaded programs. In particular, using snapshot programming, one can enumerate state spaces of programs actually running under Linux.

1 Introduction

Today, the virtualization of system software is drawing a great deal of attention. VMware[11] is a typical example of a so called "virtual computer system". With a virtual computer system, we can construct various virtualized hardware resources inside a real computer (host computer), and make multiple independent virtual computers inside a single host computer.

Some virtual computer systems have a functionality called *checkpointing*, i.e., saving its own runtime state as a snapshot. For instance, the "suspend" functionality provided by VMware allows the user to save and restore snapshots of the VMware machine at any time.

In general, the most important functionality of a virtual machine is to behave as multiple machines using only one physical machine. Most virtual computers have the checkpointing functionality only as an additional feature. But if we look this feature more thoroughly, we can expect it to support various solutions.

1. Recovering server systems from abnormal states
   In most of the Internet services widely used today, the lack of good administrators increases the time to recover from troubles. We can minimize the recovering time by saving snapshots before such troubles and restoring them.
2. Making environments for education
   It is very difficult to prepare completely the same environments for educating server administrators or software engineers. If we distribute saved snapshots of environments prepared well for education, such a problem will be solved.

K. Futatsugi et al. (Eds.): ISSS 2003, LNCS 3233, pp. 281–295, 2004.

3. Increasing the convenience of desktop environments
   Today, the performance of our personal computers has been greatly increased. So it is practical to use virtual computers for saving desktop environments. We can save snapshots of computers in the office and continue our work at home.
4. Making intrusion detection systems (IDS) and honeypots
   Because snapshots include all the runtime information of the machines we can analyze snapshots statically and extract various kinds of information from them. So we can apply the checkpointing functionality to construct IDS and honeypots, and find out how the states of the machines have been changed by malicious attacks.
5. Applying it to sandboxing technologies
   Generally, access from virtual machines to resources of their host machine is restricted. So we can regard virtual machines as sandboxes. Unlike Java sandboxing, we can execute native machine codes. Files and network resources are also virtualized. Moreover, we can migrate runtime snapshots of the sandboxes.

In this study, we made extensions to User-mode Linux (UML). We call the extended UML "Scrapbook for UML" (SBUML). It enables us to do checkpointing in UML easily.

Table 1. Functionalities provided by SBUML

command name	functionality
sbumlfreeze	Freeze all UML processes
sbumlcontinue	Resume all UML processes
sbumlsave	Save UML state as a snapshot
sbumlrestore	Restart UML with specified saved snapshot
sbumlanalyzesnapshot	Analyze a UML snapshot statically and extract some information
sbumlschedule	Register a process for external scheduling
sbumldonext	Execute a particular UML process until the state is changed
sbumlenumeratestate	Make a snapshot tree by enumerating states of a specified UML processes

In addition to implementing the checkpointing functionality, we made external interfaces that provide all SBUML functionalities (Fig.1) to command-line programs. With these interfaces, we can manipulate SBUML in a script language (such as /bin/sh), and construct systems that do complex snapshot manipulations. In other words, we provide a programming environment for SBUML snapshots. It can also be regarded as generalization of ideas demonstrated in SBDebug[5], which provides a debugging environment for snapshots of Emacs Lisp.

The reason why we use UML is as follows. If we used existing commercial virtual computers such as VMware, the implementation based on them would be restricted because their internal implementation must be treated as a black box. Of course, some of the solutions we described before can be realized using them. But the use of open source virtual computers is more suitable for flexible extensions of the system and its checkpointing functionality.

In the last part of the paper, we describe a real-environment model checking system as an example of snapshot programming. In this model checker, a shell script integrates some of the functionalities of SBUML so that it can enumerate the possible states of a set of processes by running them in a virtual computer. For realizing this, we have to extract some "interesting" parts of the process states from the snapshot and control execution of the processes. These functionalities are difficult to implement if they are based on existing virtual computers with the "suspend" functionality. Our use of UML is essential for this application.

In this section, we have explained the background of our work. In Section 2, we introduce the implementation of UML itself to give preliminary knowledge for understanding SBUML. In Section 3, we describe SBUML's implementation in detail. In Section 4, we explain additional functionalities for making the model checker, such as analyzing snapshots and controlling UML processes. In Section 5, the realization of the SBUML real-environment model checking system is the main subject. And in Section 6, we present some future work including SBUML optimization and features to make the model checker applicable to wider areas.

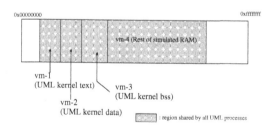

Fig. 1. Address spaces of the UML process

2   User-Mode Linux

In this section, we introduce User-mode Linux as a virtual operating system and some important features in its implementation.

User-mode Linux is an extended Linux kernel developed by Jeff Dike[1]. UML runs inside a real Linux machine as a collection of user-mode processes. This means that UML can be regarded as a virtual operating system. We can execute multiple instances of the virtual OS, called the *guest OS,* inside the real OS, called the *host OS.* Most of the UML extensions are implemented as architecture-dependent codes in the Linux kernel source. So the mechanisms of UML as an operating system (e.g., process management and memory management) are almost the same as those of the general Linux kernel.

2.1   Virtual Memory

In UML, the physical memory is simulated by several files in the host OS. The following four files are created on the host when we invoke a new instance of UML:

- Text areas of the kernel binary (vm-1)
- Data areas of the kernel binary (vm-2)
- Bss areas of the kernel binary (vm-3)
- Rest of the simulated physical memory (vm-4)

All four files are mapped to the kernel address area of all UML processes. In addition, parts of vm-4 are mapped to areas in the kernel virtual memory and process address spaces using the normal page allocation mechanism of the guest Linux kernel. (Fig.1).

2.2   UML Processes

In a real operating system, the address space of a process is constructed on some memory regions allocated by the kernel. On the other hand, the address space of a UML process is constructed as a part of the address space of a host process. When one new process is created inside UML, the host OS creates one process corresponding to the UML process. UML then allocates UML virtual memory regions, which are text, data, and bss of "UML executable", inside the process. Parts of the vm-4 file are also allocated and mapped as userspace regions in the process.

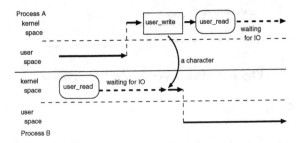

Fig. 2. Context switching mechanism in UML

As we described before, areas of "kernel executable" (vm-1, vm-2, vm-3, vm-4) are shared by all UML processes. It enables UML to run each process in kernel mode. UML sets its own signal hander for SIGUSR1 to the UML kernel-mode stack. This means that the UML kernel-mode is implemented as a signal handler.

2.3   Context Switching of UML Processes

As we described before, one UML process is constructed inside one host process address space. However, this means the UML kernel cannot directly switch context from one UML process to another. For doing this, UML uses a special technique that makes use of pipes on the host.

Each task_struct structure of UML includes a pair of host pipe file descriptors (switch_pipe). When a UML process is not active, it waits by reading from its switch_pipe. The current active process writes a character to the pipe of the next process when it is chosen by the scheduler. Then, the next process exits from its reading and becomes active.

We explain this technique with Fig.2. User_read and user_write are the internal functions of the UML context switcher. User_read only reads a character from the switch_pipe, and user_write only writes. All processes except for the one active process are waiting for the pipes, such as Process B. If the context is going to be switched from Process A to B, Process A calls user_write and writes a character to the switch_pipe of Process B. And because Process B can now read a character, it changes to the active state. On the other hand, Process A calls user_read at the next step, and begins to wait.

Using such a method, UML can simulate a physical computer where only one process is running at a time.

2.4   UML Filesystems

Like the UML virtual memory files, the filesystems of UML are also constructed as host files. For emulating disk accesses to the virtual disks, UML uses a separate process for called the *"IO thread"*.

2.5   Tracing Thread

UML intercepts systems calls by using a special process called the *"tracing thread"*. The tracing thread works by calling ptrace() for all UML processes when they are created so that control will pass to the tracing thread whenever a UML process makes a system call. Then the tracing thread can manipulate the internal process state so that the system call is redirected to the UML kernel instead of the host kernel. The UML process actually starts processing the system call when the tracing thread sends it a signal, which the UML process handles on a signal stack in its user-mode kernel area.

3   Implementation of SBUML Core Methods

Building on top of the features described in the previous section, we added the checkpointing functionality based on UML, which we call the SBUML core. In this section, we explain the internal implementation of the SBUML core in detail.

3.1   Checkpointing Requirements

For checkpointing UML, we must save several kinds of information about UML.

1. UML virtual memory files
   As we described before, the UML virtual memory is implemented as host files. We can save these files, so saving the state of the memory can be done easily.
2. UML filesystems
   UML filesystems can be easily saved because they are also constructed on the host files. But their size is several GBytes, and it is waste of resources on the host to save the whole disks.
   For solving this problem, we use the copy-on-write filesystem mechanism (COW) provided by the original UML. COW enables us to make deltas of UML filesystems, and these deltas are sparse files on the host. So we can save the large number of snapshots that are required for the implementation of the model checker.
3. Runtime states of UML processes
   The host processes for each UML process also contain some state that must be saved for checkpointing.
   – Process address space
     As the vm-4 file contains user process address space regions and is separated into many pages, which are mapped to the UML process address space, we have to save how each page in vm-4 is mapped. The most direct method is to get the mapping information from the /proc directory of the host. However, because the mapping only depends on the UML paging mechanism, we can also obtain this information from the UML kernel. To make the implementation concise, we chose the latter method.
   – Contexts of host processes
     All UML processes run as user-mode processes on the host, so we also have to save the runtime contexts of the host processes. For implementing this, we use setjmp() and longjmp() functions for saving and restoring the runtime contexts inside a snapshot, respectively.
4. Host file descriptors used by UML
   UML uses many host file descriptors for virtual memory, virtual disks, xterm windows, etc. So we made an extension to UML that saves a file descriptor information each time UML opens a new one. And when SBUML makes a snapshot, the descriptor information is also included inside it.

3.2 Control Thread

The first problem in implementing SBUML was about its external interfaces. We must tell UML to do various operations such as freezing and continuing machine execution. The original UML has an interface called "mconsole" and we can manipulate UML through it. But if we use the mconsole for SBUML, it causes some troubles, because the mconsole is processed by UML processes and uses virtual socket connections to the host. Extending the tracing thread is another idea, however its interactions with the other processes are complex and adding new functionality to it seemed risky. Therefore, we introduced the "control thread", a new process to handle the overall checkpointing functionality.

The control thread is a process with the shared UML kernel image, but it runs independently of the UML scheduling and it does not have its own task_struct. The major functionalities of the control thread are as follows:

– Accepts and processes checkpointing operations from outside,
– Creates new UML processes with itself as their templates (described later).

We implemented these important roles of SBUML inside the control thread for making the implementation clearer. (Fig.3)

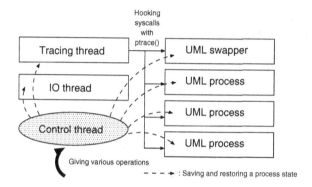

Fig. 3. UML process and control thread. The control thread does SBUML checkpointing compositely

3.3   SBUML Core

Now, we describe the core functionalities of SBUML. These are all implemented with their command-line interfaces for shell scripts.

1. Suspending and resuming (sbumlfreeze, sbumlcontinue)
   When making UML snapshots, we have to make sure that every UML process is in a "safe state", which means that no process writes any data to the memory or disks during snapshot saving.
   For solving this problem, we have to make all UML processes safe. As described before, all UML processes share the UML kernel images. So we add a flag inside the UML kernel, and the control thread changes its value according to the operations from outside. If the flag is active, each UML process gets trapped into a loop where it can not write any data. Since most UML processes are waiting on a read from a pipe, they are actually in host kernel mode. To force them back to user mode, a special character is sent to every thread's wait pipe. Suspending is implemented in this way. Resuming is implemented simply by resetting the flag so that all processes exit the safe loop.
2. Saving snapshots (sbumlsave)
   With sbumlfreeze and sbumlcontinue, we can make UML in a safe state. Then we only have to save all information described in Section 3.1.

3. Restoring snapshots (`sbumlrestore`)

The most complex functionality in SBUML is restoring snapshots. The new instance of UML created by this functionality must be the same as the old one. In our implementation, the following methods are used.

(a) Recovering the file descriptors as soon as making the new UML kernel.
(b) Making the control thread and some other special processes from the tracing thread which will be made in the next phase. The UML swapper process and the IO thread are independent of the UML scheduling and have different memory mapping from the others. So they must be made separately.
(c) The control thread calls the clone() system call of the host for each UML process that must be recreated. Because the control thread has the UML kernel image inside, it can serve as an initial template for all UML processes.
(d) Each process made by the control thread recovers its own address space with the kernel information. Then the process tells the tracing thread to do ptrace() itself through a variable inside the kernel. Finally, the created process calls longjmp() with a jmp_buf that was preserved in the snapshot.

As a whole, the saving and restoring functionality has been implemented successfully. The SBUML implementation adds approximately 5500 lines of C and 1800 lines of shell script to the UML source code.

For the prototype used in this study, saving and restoring snapshots with 32MB of virtual RAM and a 1.1GB file system could be done in 10–20 seconds in the laptop PC environment (Pentium 4 2GHz, 1GByte RAM) used in our development. A recent rewrite of SBUML addresses some of the inefficiencies of the original implementation and reduced this time to 1–12 seconds. Most of the time is spent copying the COW files, so the time varies greatly depending on whether the disk pages are in the host's cache. The time also depends on how the COW files are copied, because they are sparse file that contain mostly zeros. We use the -S option on the tar command which writes sparse files in a fraction a second. However, it still takes around 10 seconds to read a COW file because Linux requires that it read all the zeros on the 1.1GB file system. Since information about the used blocks is actually coded into the COW file's header, doing efficient reading of COW files is straightforward and will be easy to add to SBUML. Once we implement this, it will be possible to save and restore snapshots in less than a second.

For further optimization, note that only a small part of the information in a snapshot will be used for model checking. It is only necessary to copy the blocks of memory and disks pertaining to one state transition. So instead of copying several dozen megabytes per snapshot as we do now, it possible to copy only a few tens of thousands of bytes. We are currently investigating how fast this will make SBUML for actual model checking use.

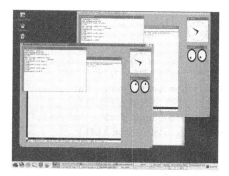

Fig. 4. Saving VNC desktops using SBUML. In SBUML, we can make multiple virtual computers with completely the same state from one snapshot

And we also made some tests of saving desktop environments using VNC[12], by checkpointing SBUML running the VNC server inside (Fig. 4). It takes 10–20 secs to save and restore such snapshots.

4 Additional Methods for the Model Checker

We have described the checkpointing mechanism of SBUML. In this section, we illustrate several additional functionalities for making the snapshot programming environment. They enable us to control and analyze UML processes of interest and provide the core functionality for the SBUML model checker.

4.1 Manipulating UML Scheduler

Because result of a multi-threaded program can depend on how the operating system schedules the processes, we added functionality so that an external script can specify the scheduling order. First, the `sbumlschedule` command was added to allow a script to specify which processes should be scheduled externally, and the UML scheduler was modified to never schedule these processes by default. Then the `sbumldonext` was added to allow a script to force the UML scheduler to schedule one of these processes next. By default, all the externally scheduled processes are forced back to the scheduler after every system call. This gives enough scheduling granularity for the demonstrations in this paper.

4.2 Extracting Snapshot Information Statically

Since we know the format of SBUML snapshots, we can extract information about the UML kernel and its processes without running UML. We call this functionality "static extraction". The following is an example code we used for testing the functionality. It is a program for the so called "Dining Philosopher Problem".

```
void *philo(void *arg)
{
    /* ... */
    while (1) {
        read(pipes[i%NUM].fd[0], &c, 1);
        printf("%d takes his left fork...\n", i);
        read(pipes[(i+1)%NUM].fd[0], &c, 1);
        printf("%d takes his right fork...\n", i);
        printf("%d waiting...\n",  da->id);
        sleep(1);
        write(pipes[i%NUM].fd[1], &c, 1);
        printf("%d leaves his left fork...\n", i);
        write(pipes[(i+1)%NUM].fd[1], &c, 1);
        printf("%d leaves his right fork...\n", i);
        sleep(1);
    }
    return 0;
}
```

As for the processes made from this code, we restrict our attention to:

− Location of the program counter
− Pipe information shared by all the processes

Such information can be obtained from the memory images inside the snapshot. For this example, we made a program specialized for static extraction of the dining philosophers. This means that this extractor program represents our notion of "interesting" parts of the dining philosophers' states. If we generalize this method, we will be able to obtain any kernel and userspace information from UML snapshots by using the mapping information inside task_structs.

4.3   Step Execution per One State Transition

Using the two functionalities described above, we implemented a method for step execution per a process. This "step execution" does not mean the ordinary function provided by a debugger, but it continues execution of the specified process until transition in the "interesting" parts of the state takes place. With this method, we can construct a state transition graph of the "interesting" processes.

The technique is,

1. Save a snapshot of SBUML.
2. Execute our specified process prior to the others. This execution continues until the SBUML scheduler is invoked.
3. Compare the snapshot with the present machine using the static extraction. If their results are the same, we continue scheduling the same process using the scheduler manipulation above.

With this simple technique, we can do step execution for one state transition of a process.

5   An Application : SBUML Real-Environment Model Checker

Using these functionalities, we developed the SBUML real-environment model checker as an example of snapshot programming that demonstrates new potential for checkpointing systems.

Model checking is a technique for automatic verification, which checks whether a finite state system satisfies some kinds of properties by exhaustively searching its state space. In traditional model checkers, target systems are described in special languages at some abstract level, and such abstract descriptions are verified. Therefore, traditional model checking has succeeded only in finding mistakes in the specification stage.

But nowadays, especially in the field of software verification, many people are trying to apply the model checking techniques not only to the specification stage but also to the implementation stage. Such model checkers deal with bytecodes or programs written in generic programming languages as their targets. For example, VeriSoft[2] and CMC[3] execute binaries compiled from C source code and enumerate possible states for model checking.

The system we aim at in our study is also a real-environment model checker. It executes compiled binaries inside the virtual computer for model checking. As in CMC, it remembers paths of state transitions of the target processes for re-execution. But because SBUML can be checkpointed at any time, the cost for the re-execution is reduced and there is potential for faster checking.

The following code is the core of the SBUML model checker, written in a shell script using the SBUML command-line interfaces. It shows that we can easily write complex systems (such as model checkers) using the snapshot programming interfaces.

```
#!/bin/sh
#
# sbumlenumeratestate
#

mname=$1
hashfile=$2
parentss=${3:-0}
pname=${4:-0}

list='sbuml--choices $mname'
[ -z "$list" ] && exit

ntime='date +%s'
sbumlsave $mname $ntime -c -f
```

```
OLDIFS=$IFS
IFS=,
for i in $list ; do
    sleep 1
    sbuml--donext-unless-changing-state \
        $mname $i
    hash=`cat sshash.tmp`
    rm -f sshash.tmp
    echo "$parentss", "$pname" > ssinfo

    if grep $hash $hashfile > /dev/null
    then
        exit 0
    else
        echo $hash >> $hashfile
        sbumlenumeratestate \
            $mname $hashfile $ntime $i
    fi
    sbumlrestore $mname $ntime -c -f
done
IFS=$OLDIFS
```

In brief, this script gets an initial snapshot from its argument, does step execution until state transition occurs for each executable process, saves a snapshot after the step execution, and calls the script recursively. For instance, if we assume that there are two executable processes, A and B. From the initial snapshot, we can obtain two more snapshots. One is after A's one-step execution and another is B's. From the former snapshot, two more snapshots can be obtained, and for the latter the same method can be applied. Repeating this, an infinite state tree is constructed in general. But if we focus on the "interesting" parts of the states inside a snapshot, we can obtain a snapshot tree with a finite size using pruning methods (Fig.5).

We have succeeded in making the snapshot tree of the Dining Philosopher code described in Section 4.2, using the SBUML model checker.

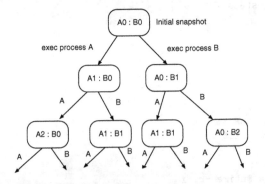

Fig. 5. State enumeration with making a snapshot tree

We have also succeeded in finding states that lead to deadlock in the tree.

6   Related Work

Since our model checker is still a prototype, it is too early to compare it with existing software model checkers like VeriSoft and CMC. Instead, we give a brief comparison and discuss a possible combination of our approach with others.

In CMC, hashed values of states are computed and stored for detecting duplicated states. It also keeps a stack of states for state enumeration. We basically take the same approach as that of CMC but under the environment of a real operation system.

VeriSoft takes a different approach called the "state-less approach". It does not store states (or their hash values), but only keeps a history of state transitions. For state enumeration, it replays the history of transitions up to a branching point, and then try another state transition. VeriSoft has succeeded in verifying or testing various kinds of existing software. Using special libraries for process scheduling, it can execute a set of communicating processes.

Our approach is considered to have the following advantages.

- Unlike VeriSoft or CMC, the target processes are executed under a self-contained, realistic environment (i.e., Linux), and therefore we can potentially verify or test more properties of the target application more faithfully.
- In VeriSoft, executions are always replayed up to a branching point. For those applications that require long a initialization step, or always execute some intermediate steps that are purely deterministic, this approach introduces compounding inefficiencies.

However, the approach of VeriSoft is very attractive in its performance on both time and space. Since we also enumerate states by controlling process scheduling, it is possible to combine our checkpointing approach and that of VeriSoft. The possible scenario is as follows. We checkpoint the entire operating system when the target application starts up. We then control and record the schedule of the application processes and checkpoint the entire operating system occasionally. In order to enumerate states, we replay the processes from a checkpointed snapshot. As the performance of saving and restoring snapshots improves, the above combination will work better, and the entire performance of state enumeration will also improve.

Except for our study, there have been proposed many ideas for checkpointing UML: porting a software-suspend extension of Linux kernel (swsusp)[6] to UML, using existing checkpointing system (cf. CRAK[8]) from outside of UML, etc. However, these ideas have not reached completion. It may be partly because the speed of the development of Linux and User-mode Linux has been too fast to follow.

We can list the study on Network Transferable Computer[7] as one of our related work. They use VMware, Linux and swsusp for checkpointing, and construct network transferable Linux inside VMware. SoftwarePot[9] makes archives of software and its virtual filesystems and realizes saving and migrating virtual environments, but does not migrate checkpointed process state.

SBDebug[4, 5] is a Computation Scrapbook system for checkpointing runtime states of Emacs Lisp. It shows solutions for applying checkpointing to reading, writing, debugging, testing, and documenting programs.

7   Conclusions and Future Work

In our study, we designed and implemented the SBUML checkpointing system and its command-line interfaces. It includes not only functionality for checkpointing but also for manipulating the scheduler and analyzing snapshots. We also gave an example of snapshot programming using SBUML.

Currently, we have the following future work in mind.

1. Optimization of SBUML
   Although SBUML checkpointing is reasonably efficient, the model checking directions of our research will benefit from any improvements that can be made to its time and space efficiency. Fortunately there are many obvious ways to improve the efficiency. One is simply by parallelizing the model checking on multiple computers, since we can already migrate SBUML snapshot to other machines. However, even on one machine there are many improvements that can be made. For example, although the COW files do not take up much space on disk, the copy command still reads several hundreds of megabytes of zeros, an inefficiency that can easily be removed. Also, there is opportunity to use a COW mechanism on the virtual memory files, which has potential to greatly increase the speed for model checking, where very few memory blocks are changed between snapshots.
2. More implementation of the SBUML model checker
   Now, we are continuing implementation of the SBUML model checker. In this paper, it is shown only as one of the examples of snapshot programming. But finding concrete bugs of existing server programs is proposed as our next work. For doing this, we have to extend our static extraction to be able obtain values of internal variables of programs, etc. An appropriate method to define "interesting" parts of states and state transition is also future work.
3. Explore other Computation Scrapbook applications
   SBDebug[4, 5] has demonstrated for Emacs Lisp how Computation Scrapbooks can be useful for various programming activities. If we can transfer these applications to SBUML, it may be possible to apply them to almost any programming language that runs in Linux.

Acknowledgements

This work was supported in part by a Grant-in-Aid for Precursory Research for Embryonic Science and Technology (PRESTO), from Japan Science and Technology Agency (JST). We would like thank to Kazuhiko Kato and Yasushi

Shinjo at University of Tsukuba, for giving us many beneficial comments about this paper.

References

1. The User-mode Linux Kernel Home Page
   [http://user-mode-linux.sourceforge.net/]
2. Patrice Godefroid. "Model Checking for Programming Languages using VeriSoft", Proceedings of the 24th ACM Symposium on Principles of Programming Languages, pages 174-186, Paris, January 1997.
3. M. Musuvathi, D. Park, A. Chou, D. Engler, and D. Dill. "CMC: A Pragmatic Approach to Model Checking Real Code", Usenix Association, OSDI 2002.
4. Richard Potter, "Computation Scrapbook of Emacs Lisp Runtime State", Symposia on Human-Centric Computing Languages and Environments, September 2001.
5. Richard Potter and Masami Hagiya, "Computation Scrapbooks for Software Evolution", Fifth International Workshop on Principles of Software Evolution, IWPSE 2002, 143–147, May 2002.
6. Software Suspend for Linux
   [http://swsusp.sourceforge.net/]
7. Network Transferable Computer
   [http://staff.aist.go.jp/k.suzaki/NTC/]
8. Hua Zhong and Jason Nieh, "CRAK: Linux Checkpoint/Restart As a Kernel Module", Technical Report CUCS-014-01, Department of Computer Science, Columbia University, November 2001.
9. Kazuhiko Kato and Yoshihiro Oyama, "SoftwarePot: An Encapsulated Transferable File System for Secure Software Circulation", Software Security — Theories and Systems, Volume 2609 of Lecture Notes in Computer Science, Springer-Verlag, February 2003.
10. Edmund M. Clarke, Jr., Orna Grumberg and Doron A. Peled, "Model Checking", The MIT Press, 1999.
11. VMware [http://www.vmware.com/]
12. Tristan Richardson, Quentin Stafford-Fraser, Kenneth R. Wood & Andy Hopper, "Virtual Network Computing", IEEE Internet Computing, Vol.2 No.1, Jan/Feb 1998 pp33–38.

Managing Information Technology Security Risk

David P. Gilliam

Jet Propulsion Laboratory, California Institute of Technology,
4800 Oak Grove Dr., MS 144-210,
Pasadena, CA 91109
david.p.gillliam@jpl.nasa.gov

Abstract. Information Technology (IT) Security Risk Management is a critical task for the organization to protect against the loss of confidentiality, integrity, and availability of IT resources and data. Due to system complexity and sophistication of attacks, it is increasingly difficult to manage IT security risk. This paper describes a two-pronged approach for managing IT security risk: 1) an institutional approach, that addresses automating the process of providing and maintaining security for IT systems and the data they contain; and 2) a project life cycle approach that addresses providing semi-automated means for integrating security into the project life cycle. It also describes the use of a security template with a risk reduction/mitigation tool, the Defect Detection and Prevention (DDP) tool developed at the Jet Propulsion Laboratory (JPL).

1 Introduction

Engineering Information Technology (IT) security is a critical task to manage in the organization. With the growing number of system security defects being discovered and as the impact of malicious code escalates, Security Engineering (SE) of IT security is increasingly critical both organizationally and in the project life cycle [1]. Organizations have suffered significantly over the last few years due to the loss of Confidentiality, Integrity, and Availability (CIA) of IT resources due to malicious code attacks and breakins. Understanding and mitigating these risks is paramount in protecting organizational resources. The problem has been noted by the United States (US) Government Accounting Office (GAO) showing that US federal agencies are at high risk. "Specifically, the Inspector General found security lapses relating to access to data, risk assessments, sensitive data identification, access controls, password management, audit logs, application development and change controls, segregation of duties, service continuity, and system software controls, among others" [2]. A single compromise can put an entire organization at risk of loss of IT resources whether it is from a system breakin, a worm infection, or an unintended exposure.

Understanding and managing IT security risk becomes paramount in protecting organizational resources—systems, data, facilities, and most of all people. Controls to identify and manage IT security risks are available, but they are generally applied non-uniformly as a reaction to a threat. Few organizations formally analyze IT security risks and the effectiveness of mitigations to the threats. As systems grow more com-

K. Futatsugi et al. (Eds.): ISSS 2003, LNCS 3233, pp. 296–317, 2004.
© Springer-Verlag Berlin Heidelberg 2004

plex and distributed, managing the IT environment and resources securely is increasingly problematic. A concerted approach to Security Engineering (SE) is needed to understand the extent of risks, available mitigations, and their relative value versus costs. There are two key areas that IT security engineering should address: 1) managing IT security risk corporately; and 2) managing IT security risk in the system development life cycle (SDLC). Anything that is produced and consumed needs to have security 'built-in' as opposed to being 'bolted-on.'

SE and IT security risk management has a significant impact on corporate survival and requires a formal approach to addressing it. SE is a continuous life cycle process that extends from the organization to the project. Risks at the institutional level impact projects and risks at the project level impact the institution. Both areas must be managed through an SE approach. All too often approaches to managing IT security either address the enterprise environment or address the project life cycle singularly. What may be appropriate for the enterprise (implementation of firewalls, patch management, etc.) may not directly relate to the project life cycle, especially the system development life cycle (SDLC) which is more concerned with implementation of security controls and reducing vulnerabilities and exposures in systems and software. A risk in the enterprise is a risk to a project and its resources. Likewise, a project may expose the enterprise to risk through developing and using insecure systems or software (often referred to as 'eating your own dogfood' or 'dogfooding', where a software development firm will be the first to test and use its own products). [3]

This paper describes an approach at JPL for security engineering and managing IT security risk. It identifies tools and instruments that can be used in the life cycle to identify and reduce or mitigate IT security risks. Section 2 discusses risk management and a model for calculating risk and risk mitigations. Section 3 describes a Defect Detection and Prevention (DDP) risk assessment and analysis tool used in the project life cycle and the capability for extending it to IT security risk assessment. Section 4 describes the specific application of the DDP tool to IT security risk in the project life cycle. Section 5 describes the use of the tool enterprise-wide. Section 6 concludes with a summary of the need for integration of both project and institutional risk management. Effective risk management should have a coordinated approach that addresses both areas, and identifies their interactions and impact of risks and mitigations.

2 IT Security Risk and Risk Management

Understanding IT security risk and its impact in terms of potential loss to the organization will help to identify the level of risk that the organization must manage. First, the System Security Engineer (SSE) must understand the nature of risks in terms of vulnerabilities and exposures and their likelihood of being used against the organization along with their impact if realized. Second, the SSE must have a good grasp of mitigations, the extent to which risks are mitigated by various technologies and their relative costs. Third, the SSE must be able to provide critical information to management to obtain needed resources to implement and manage security controls.

2.1 Security Risk

Security risk impacts organizational IT resources. The impact extends to the SDLC in the production of goods and services for consumption either by a client/customer or by the organization. System and software security defects can be reduced significantly through risk management. When risk is used in reference to IT security, the discussions generally focus on defining and describing security risk and mitigations in terms of protection of data and systems. IT security risk is characterized in terms of Confidentiality, Integrity and Availability (CIA). These terms are commonly understood as:

- *Confidentiality*: Assuring information will be kept secret, with access limited to appropriate persons. For Intellectual property or medical information, confidentiality is a critical issue.
- *Integrity*: Assuring information will not be accidentally or maliciously altered or destroyed. Loss of Integrity is a critical issue for data on which decisions are based.
- *Availability*: Assuring information and communication services will be ready for use when expected. An attack can impact a critical system that is dependent on high availability.

Security risk is similar to other identified key risk areas such as safety and reliability. The National Aeronautics and Space Administration (NASA) Continuous Risk Management (CRM) web site defines risk as "characterized by the combination of the probability that a project or other enterprise will experience an undesired event with unacceptable consequences, impact, or severity." Starting with this definition, risk management is defined as "a proactive, continuous and iterative process to manage risk to achieve the planned objectives. The process involves identifying, analyzing, planning, tracking, controlling, documenting, and communicating risks effectively." [4] It is illustrated by CRM as a continuous process as shown in Figure 1.

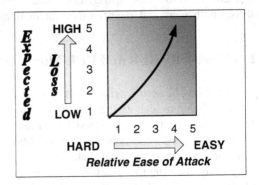

Fig. 1. Risk Assessment Process   **Fig. 2.** Exploit Attack Probability

A risk assessment methodology is needed to aid in and guide this process. The National Institute of Standards and Technology (NIST) "Risk Management Guide for Information Technology Systems," presents a nine step process to risk assessment: 1) System Characterization, 2) Threat Identification, 3) Vulnerability Identification, 4) Control Analysis, 5) Likelihood Determination, 6) Impact Analysis, 7) Risk Determination, 8) Control Recommendations, 9) Results Documentation, with each step having specified inputs and outputs that lead to the succeeding step. [4]

A risk assessment methodology must quantify the cost of a risk occurrence (loss of CIA), and the cost to mitigate risks such as used in Probability Risk Assessment [5]. In application to security, risk is a function of the *impact* an adverse event would have were it to succeed in breaching defenses, its *likelihood of succeeding*, and the *frequency* at which such events are perpetrated. Quantifying risk in these terms depends on the relative value of the potential loss or disruption should the risk event occur. A simple algorithm to quantify IT security risk can be defined as:

$$Risk = impact * likelihood * frequency \qquad (1)$$

where:

*Impact = damage * recovery time*

- Damage can be characterized as the criticality of the data and IT resources along with the degree and extent of their destruction or loss – that is, the criticality of the data and resources and the degree and extent of the loss or compromise.
- Recovery time is the length of time to recover needed data and IT resources from a compromise.

Likelihood = potential success of an attack

- Likelihood is the potential that if the attack succeeds it leads to loss or compromise of CIA.

*Frequency = number / time, where number = ease * likelihood * impact*

- Number is the number of events occurring over a time interval
- The frequency of an exploit being perpetrated is based on three factors: how easy it is to originate an attack, how likely that attack will succeed, and how much impact it will have if it does succeed.

More complex algorithms can be used. However, the added complexity can also impede the assessment by too many variables to weight and factor easily into the process.

The key characteristic of SE (compared to safety engineering) is the malicious intent of the attackers, who deliberately favor attacks that they perceive have a greater potential for success and a greater potential impact (see Figure 2). Attack sophistication and complexity are unpredictable and these must factor into risks and their mitigations. Damage is premised on the fact that attacks that are easier to carry out and that result in greater harm will occur more often. However, it is difficult to predict new attacks and attack types. System complexity factors and sophistication of attacks create events must be evaluated as they occur. For this reason IT security risk management must be a persistent process. Security risks will change over time as more 'hacking' tools are made available to attackers. In addition, the attackers are persistent in their attacks. As the climate changes these security risks must undergo re-evaluation, sometimes which must be undertaken on the fly such as the exposure of systems to the 'Blaster Worm' attack.

2.2 Security Risk Management

Effective IT security risk management requires collaboration between management, IT security professionals, system engineers, and other stakeholders. It requires knowing and understanding customer needs, government regulations, stakeholder requirements, the organizational environment, etc. Identifying IT security risks, providing a means to manage, and mitigating or accept risks, is resource intensive. It is not the responsibility of just one or two people. The SSE must have the support and involvement of management, system engineers, system administrators, contracts and procurement officers, legal affairs, even the general users.

It is requisite in security engineering to decompose governing policies, standards, and requirements from the customer and stakeholders into their basic constituent elements to assess security requirements, risks, and develop a risk management plan. However, as shown above, the complexity of the IT environment and the sophistication of attacks impact manage these risks. Use of a risk assessment tool like DDP will aid the SSE in identifying and managing these risks. Additionally, a risk tool that provides a graphical representation of the cost of risks versus the cost of mitigating risks will enable informed decisions on risks that are critical and require mitigation, those that should be mitigated depending on the available resources, and those that can be accepted as residual risks.

Not all risks can be mitigated due to cost, resource, or other issues. However, awareness of the residual risks and the cost to the organization should they be realized, is essential for management to make informed decisions on the extent of resources to apply to IT security risk management and mitigations. Trade-off analysis should be undertaken of the various mitigations for both their costs and effectiveness. Additionally, this process must be revisited as new technologies become available and costs for technology decreases.

2.3 Related Work

The Gartner Group in identifying the cornerstones of an InfoSec (Information Security) risk management program makes the point that "IT assets that put an enterprise at risk must be identified through an IT risk assessment inventory that covers multiple domains in an organization." [6] Not directly included in their assessment is IT SSE in the SDLC. Other security risk management approaches also address enterprise security risk management from a system or site qualification perspective [7, 8, 9]. Both ISO9000 and the Capability Maturity Model Integration (CMMI) address the importance of managing risk. The CMMI web site provides models for improvement and management of the development life cycle. [10, 11] The Carnegie Mellon University (CMU), Software Engineering Institute (SEI), provides several publications and a method for security risk management called "Octave" [12]. The method provides detailed processes, worksheets and guides for an analysis team to conduct a risk evaluation for their organization.

Recently, the National Institute of Health's (NIH) Center for Information Technology (CIT) has taken the problem of IT risk management to another level by providing an application/system security plan template that identifies several types of security controls. [13] The template provides guidance to security personnel, project managers, and system engineers in the steps to integrate security into the institutional processes and the project life cycle and can be used along with the security risk template identified here.

Security engineering is now just beginning to be addressed in the SDLC as depicted by the number of works on the subject being published. [1, 3, 14, 30, 31] These works present a system life cycle approach that addresses requirements, design, development, operations and maintenance. However, many approaches do not cover the relationship and integration of the SDLC and institutional risk management processes. Additionally, the process of phasing out software and systems often is not addressed. When they are phased-out, security exposures and vulnerabilities may be introduced, especially if other systems are dependent on receiving data from them and those people responsible for these other systems have not been notified.

3 Defect Detection and Prevention Risk Management Instrument

A risk management instrument has been developed by Steve Cornford and Martin Feather at the Jet Propulsion Laboratory (JPL) called Defect Detection and Prevention (DDP). [15, 16] DDP is a risk assessment instrument that is analogous to a blank spreadsheet. Inputs into this instrument are templates. The goal of DDP is to "facilitate risk management over the entire project life cycle beginning with architectural and advanced technology decisions all the way through operation" [16]. "The name reflects its origins as a structured method for planning the quality assurance of hardware systems. Since then its scope has expanded to also encompass decision-making earlier in the development lifecycle, and to be applicable to software, hardware and systems." [15] DDP has proven to be effective as a risk management instrument as shown by the results of its use on a JPL flight project subsystem [17]. Early project life cycle risk management and mitigation is the core of DDP. Whereas most risk and cost models take time to develop and provide results over the project life cycle, DDP begins early in the life cycle and attempts to provide risk costs and tradeoffs early when initial design decisions are being made.

DDP assists system engineers in identifying risks, the relative cost of mitigating the risks and the trade-offs in risk mitigation and acceptance. "DDP explicitly represents risks, the objectives that risks threaten, and the mitigations available for risk reduction. By linking these three concepts, DDP is able to represent and reason about the cost-effectiveness of risk reduction alternatives" [17]. The DDP process brings together stakeholders in the project who are domain experts and who represent the life cycle phases from inception to retirement. According to Feather, "The single most important aspect of the DDP approach is that it supports multiple experts [who] pool their knowledge" allowing them "to take the sum total of their pooled knowledge into account as they make decisions" [15]. In addition, it allows users and domain experts to assign relative weights to risks and risk mitigations. This process represents a multi-disciplinary approach to risk management in the project life cycle—one of the strengths of the DDP process.

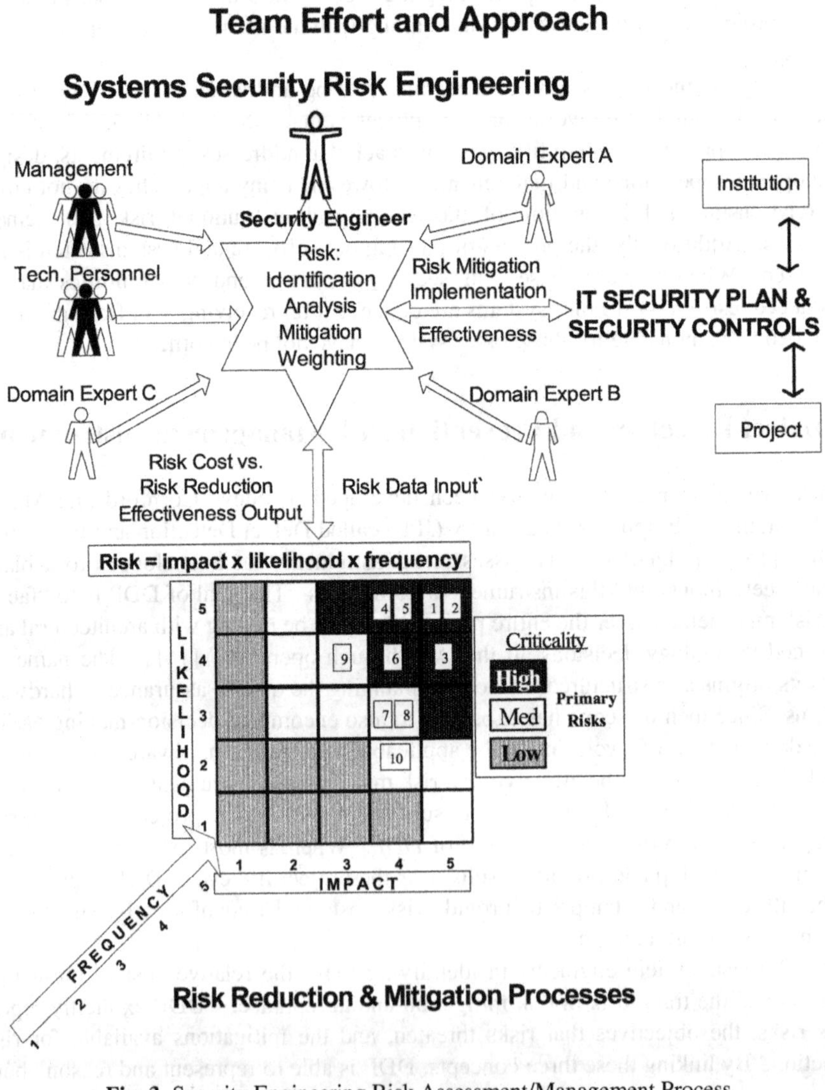

Team Effort and Approach

Systems Security Risk Engineering

Fig. 3. Security Engineering Risk Assessment/Management Process

The application of DDP to security as a risk management instrument allows an SE more effectively to assess and manage risks whether it is for the enterprise or for the SDLC. Both enterprise and project risks and their mitigations need to be evaluated together for a full risk impact/mitigation assessment. The security engineer needs to work closely with the system engineer and domain experts in this process. Figure 3 depicts the process that facilitates providing weighted inputs into the DDP instrument.

The process pools the combined inputs of the domain experts and performs calculations over the entire body of gathered information providing aggregate risk calculation information and searches for near-optimal solutions for mitigating risks. It then provides coherent visualizations back to the domain experts so well-informed decisions can be made. The process can be refined until an optimal solution is achieved. [15] Figure 4 is a graphical representation of the iterative process that identifies the optimal area for costing risks.

The results of a DDP risk assessment/mitigation analysis are output in a graphical representation of the mitigated risks and the residual risks as shown in Figure 5 [18]. Inputs to DDP generate the visualization charts of risks, mitigations to the risks, and associated weightings for risk and risk mitigations. Each of the areas of risk can be reviewed through the instrument's drill-down capabilities.

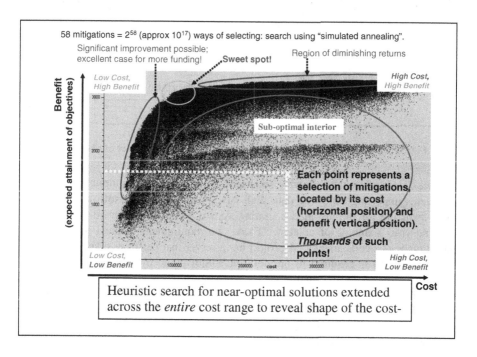

Fig. 4. Cost/Benefit trade-off analysis

Identification of risks and their mitigations is a critical activity when addressing the matrix of institutional and project risk mitigations and the impact of the risk requirements and various mitigations. Examples 1 and 2 describe the impact and why it is important on an enterprise scale to use a tool such as DDP to help identify the areas of concern.

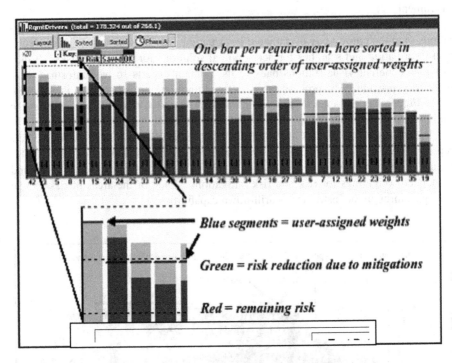

Fig. 5. Graphical presentation of risks sorted into descending order of risk levels

Example 1: Consider the following situation: An institutional requirement states that all systems importing/exporting data shall have Anti-Virus (AV) software protection where available for the installed operating system. The AV software shall perform real-time virus scanning of content. These two requirements protect the institution against malicious code attacks. A project has a server that performs a large number of file transfers and is required to provide upload/download of files in near real-time. The negative impact of the real-time AV scanning on CPU cycles and the ability of the system to process file requests within the specified timeframe must be identified and addressed. Recognition of this potential conflict and alternative means to address it is facilitated early in the life cycle through the use of the risk management process described above. In this example, an alternative, previously identified mitigation would be the installation and maintenance of an AV gateway server that processes all file downloads to the server. Each of the mitigation alternatives has a cost factor— one on availability of CPU cycles, the other in equipment and support. Both factors need to be weighted for the trade-off analysis [19].

Example 2: An institutional firewall has a positive impact in mitigating some risks in attack scenarios by preventing external port exploits. However, the firewall packet inspection may have an impact on a project requiring high throughput availability for its data. This problem can be compounded in a distributed enterprise that must pass data across the Internet.   The problem is further compounded if data encryption is required by the organization. These factors must be carefully weighed and balanced. The risks must first be identified and mitigations to them provided to the project so that they can be included in the project requirements specifications. A project systems engineer may be unaware of the institutional requirement. Use of a risk management tool can help identify these types of issues for the environment.

Advantage of DDP: DDP provides the capability to semi-automate the risk management process. It also provides the ability to track risk and to update the assessment as the requirements and environment change.   Auditing security risk and mitigation processes is significantly aided by using a risk management tool like DDP. Management decisions and traceability for those decisions as well as their impact can be made more easily with the risk analysis available to them. A rollup for risks over subsystems, systems, projects, and at the institutional level can be plotted using DDP to provide a management view of the overall state of risk [20]. For the life cycle, a risk baseline can be maintained. As the project's requirements and needs change over time, and as better mitigation tools are identified, the new technology and potential new threats can be compared against the baseline. This is especially useful during the SDLC maintenance phase.

4 IT Security Risk Management in the Project Life Cycle

In the project life cycle, the focus is on integrating security in the production of goods, such as software systems, and services such as Internet services (web or email hosting). Project resources may be spread across several systems which may not be co-located—potentially spread across large distances over the Internet. The System Administrator (SA) may or may not know the content or purpose of data supported by the systems. This is especially true for systems hosting distributed file sharing and enterprise project tools, including document libraries, requirements management tools, and groupware such as application development tools. Communication between project stakeholders and management is essential in the area of project life cycle security risk management. A process for addressing IT security risk in the SDLC is a requirement imposed on US federal agencies [21]. The Federal Information Processing Standards Publication, "Guidelines for Security of Computer Applications," gives guidance in identifying risks in the SDLC. However, it does not address give guidance on identifying and mitigating risks. [22]

4.1 Security Risk Management and System Engineering

Managing security risk in the project life cycle is a critical function for the enterprise as a number of the applications that are developed by the organization will be used within the institutional environment. Further, organizations that develop applications for public use or profit infuse the technology into their own environment [3]. This practice *does* provide additional testing and validation of the software as the organization will likely be the first to experience any problems associated with an application or system. However, there may be an adverse impact in that an immature product or one that has not been carefully controlled and managed could pose a high risk to the environment. Engineering risk assessment and management in the project life cycle becomes even more critical in these cases. A recent report identifies the fact that "most operating systems and commercial software applications are known to have more than 2 defects per KSLOC, or 2,000+ defects per million SLOC" (thousand - source lines of code) If security defects or concerns comprise only 5% of these defects, the report explains, there are still 100 security related defects per million SLOC. [23] Since major applications and operating systems are even more extensive, this number can be a significantly larger. For middleware (also referred to 'glueware'— software interfaces between applications), the security defect rate may be even higher.

4.2 Managing IT Security in the Project and SDLC Life Cycle

The value of SSE and risk management for the SDLC is that it brings together domain experts to address risk early on. Due to the fact that most IT environments are highly volatile, risk management of the SDLC must be a persistent process. The IT environment changes over time which affects risks and mitigations either positively with new tools, instruments and processes, or negatively such as when there is a major organizational change. The phases for coding, testing, validation, operations and maintenance must continue to have risk assessment performed. Formal tools to mitigate security risks have been developed at JPL to address the SDLC. These tools provide a unified approach to addressing SDLC vulnerabilities and exposures and are being integrated into DDP to provide an SDLC security risk management process. The approach includes a Security Checklist (SC), a vulnerability matrix, model-based verification, property-based testing, a list of Security Assessment Tools (SAT), and training. A two-phased SC that addresses the project life cycle and the external release of software has already been developed for NASA (Figure 6) [24]. The SC identifies critical areas of risk in the SDLC that need to be addressed. The SC includes verification and validation of requirements as they flow from specification through the design, development, operations and maintenance phases. A vulnerability matrix that classifies vulnerabilities and exposures, and a list of security assessment tools is currently hosted by the University of California at Davis [25]. Figure 6 depicts the use of these tools in the SDLC and a unified process for risk management/mitigation.

4.3 Model Checking and the Flexible Modeling Framework

Recently delivered to NASA is a software Model Checking (MC) technique, the Flexible Modeling Framework (FMF), for use in the software specification phase of the SDLC. MC offers the benefit by identifying problems early in the SDLC where it is less costly and easier to correct them. MC can aid in identifying vulnerabilities and undesired exposures in software. These often arise from a number of development factors that can often be traced to poor software development practices, new types of attacks, unsafe configurations, and unsafe interaction between systems and/or their components. MC offers a means for examining component interaction in relation to critical system properties such as safety and security. The use of MC as means of verification to mitigate vulnerabilities during the life cycle suffers from some practical limitations, including:

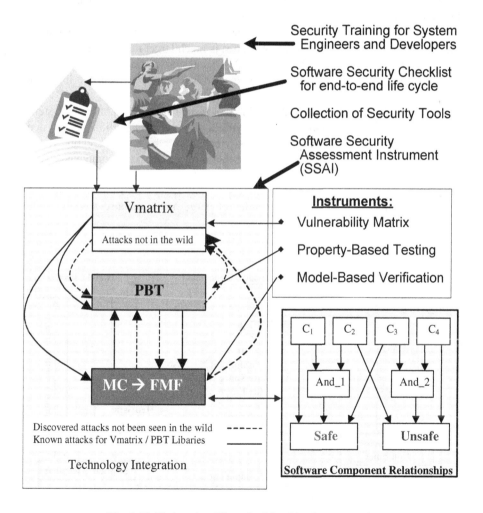

Fig. 6. Unified project life cycle risk mitigation approach

- The frequency of an exploit being perpetrated is based on three factors: how easy it is to originate Limits on the size and complexity of systems that may benefit from MC given reasonable computer memory resources
- Difficulty in rapid development, modification and verification of models in a timely manner during the early life cycle when systems tend to change and evolve quickly [27].

Traditionally, software model checkers automatically explore all paths from a start state in a computational tree that is specified in an MC model. The computational tree may contain repeated copies of sub-trees. State of the art Model Checkers such as SPIN exploit this characteristic to improve automated verification efficiency. The objective is to verify system properties with respect to models over as many scenarios as feasible. "Since the models are a selective representation of functional capabilities under analysis, the number of feasible scenarios is much larger than the set that can be checked during testing" [27]. FMF employs MC as its core technology and provides a means to bring software security issues under formal control early in the life cycle [26].

The MC FMF seeks to address the problem of formal verification of larger systems by a divide and conquer approach by verifying a property over portions of a system and then incrementally inferring the results over larger subsets of the entire system [27]. As such, the FMF is: 1) a system for building models in a component based manner to cope with system evolution over time and, 2) an approach of compositional verification to delay the effects of state space explosion. This methodology allows property verification results of large and complex models to be examined. [25]

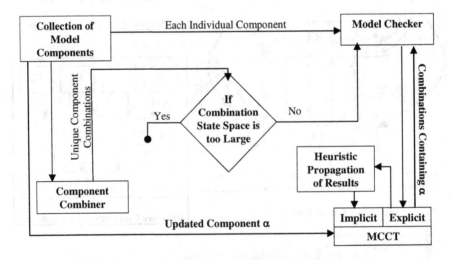

Fig. 7. Illustration of the Flexible Modeling Framework process

Modeling in a component-based manner involves building a series of small models, which later will be strategically combined for system verification purposes. This strategic combination correlates the modeling function with modern software engineering and architecture practices whereby a system is divided into major parts, and subsequently into smaller detailed parts, and then integrated to build up a software system (Figure 7). An initial series of simple components can be built when few operational specifics are known about the system. However, these components can be combined and verified for consistency with properties of interest.

4.4 Property Based Testing

Property Based Testing (PBT) is different from formal verification. It recognizes that implementation difficulties, and environment considerations, may affect conformance to the properties (and hence the security of execution). A key observation is that testing does not validate that a program will always meet the properties, unless all possible paths of execution are traversed. But it does provide additional assurance that the implementation is correct, and does satisfy the properties, when execution follows the tested control and data flow paths.

Many control and data flow paths are irrelevant to the program's satisfying the desired properties. A technique called slicing [28] creates a second program that satisfies the properties if, and only if, the original program satisfies those properties. The second program contains only those paths of control and data flow that affect the properties. This focuses the testing on paths of execution relevant to the security properties, rather than on all possible paths of execution.

Figure 8 captures the PBT verification process: given a knowledge of security and an accurate specification of the security model (which says what is and is not allowable), the software is analyzed to determine the level of assurance, or belief that the program does what it is intended to do. The properties being tested are directly taken from the security properties of the model. The expectation is that the code honors these. The program is then *sliced* to derive the smallest program equivalent to the original with respect to the stated properties. The program is then instrumented and tested. The testing either validates the properties or shows the do not hold. The tester helps determine the level of assurance of the program.

Implementation and operations also have special needs attached as well, such as removal of installation files which can be used to overwrite current configuration settings, or leaving configuration settings in an unsecured state after installation (usually settings are left at the default which generally has few security controls). Assignment of personnel responsibilities and setting up accounts and access control lists to the system and data is another issue in this phase. In particular, the maintenance phase is where a number of problems can arise where hardware and/or software is replaced or patched. When modules are replaced, the modules and interacting modules, at a minimum must be re-verified, and the system itself must be re-validated to process data. Often modifying the original system can inadvertently create vulnerabilities or unwanted exposures. For example, some modules that previously had been tested and verified as 'safe'. When they receive input that has changed due to changes in another module, a potential for an unintended weakness may now exist. Additionally, documentation must be updated to reflect the change, particularly when it affects operations and operational processes. When decommissioning a system to which another system has a dependency it may leave the related system in a vulnerable state. For example, an open port may exist which is waiting for data from a non-existent system. This is a high-risk problem as it provides an avenue for compromise. Performing a risk assessment whenever there is a significant change to the system environment especially when a network aware application or a system is shut-down is essential. Use of the described modeling and property based testing are useful preventatives in mitigating these risks.

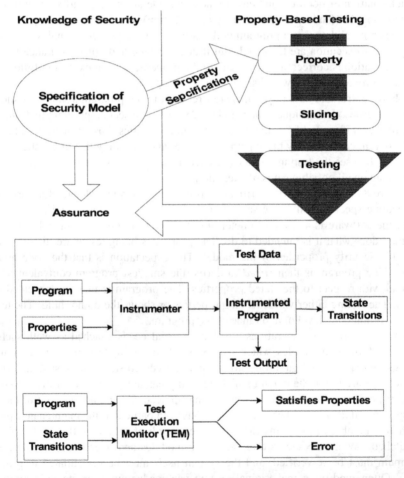

Fig. 8. PBT Process and Model

5 Enterprise-Wide IT Security Risk Management

Managing IT security institutionally must be an enterprise-wide effort. Not only does it require management support, but it also needs to be coordinated with the project life cycle. There is a mutual impact for managing and mitigating risks. Paramount is identification of IT resources, data and processes with the goal of protecting them. Results of an institutional risk assessment at JPL show that the following activities provide a high degree of mitigation at a favorable cost to the entire organization [29]:

- Use of an IT Security Database (ITSDB)
- Ability to test, disseminate and apply patches quickly (automated or semi-automated)
- Use of an intrusion detection system (IDS) that monitors traffic on the network
- Scanning systems to verify that IT computer systems are not vulnerable to attacks
- An automated security problem tracking system to ensure that systems are not vulnerable
- Firewalls

5.1 Security Plan Database (ITSDB)

Managing IT security risk in the organization at the enterprise level must account for both the institution as a single entity and the individual components and projects within the institution. To manage a process of this magnitude, use of an IT Security Database (ITSDB) containing the elements to be managed facilitates the ability to automate risk assessment and mitigation activities. Identification of IT resources and collecting the information in an ITSDB facilitates the ability to manage these resources. The ITSDB should include processes that provide input into it to capture requirements from the various sources such as standards, guidelines, policies, etc. [30, 31]. It can also serve as the focal point for centrally controlling management of IT risk, risk mitigations and IT resources. Without some form of semi-automated processes and control points, managing IT security and risk in the enterprise is virtually impossible for large organizations. An institutional approach developed at JPL to managing IT security risk at the enterprise level is shown in Figure 9 where the ITSDB and risk management process identifies and controls security risks [29]. Results of the analysis feed into processes that provide input and receive output from the ITSDB. (Fig. 9)

The JPL ITSDB includes following major elements: A security plan template for aiding in writing security plans for IT systems and resources, IT security policies and requirements for identifying lines of responsibilities, system and data protection, protective measures for operating systems, user, system administrator, cognizant management assigned responsibility for the IT resources, configuration control information for critical assets, identified security problems for any IT resources. The ITSDB process also outputs metrics, produces plans from the information entered, has email communication processes that alert managers and cognizant personnel to address security problems identified with the IT resources. JPL has successfully instituted an ITSDB and its associated process as described here along with the other technologies (patching services, IDS and Scanning, Security Problem Log, and Firewalls among other technologies).

In the ITSDB management process, enterprise IT security policies and directives require the implementation and control of security plans for the IT resources. These are formalized into requirements and protective measures, in particular protective measures for computer systems. This practice allows for the auditing of systems based on requirements and implementations that meet those requirements, including the continued updating of systems to meet the requirements for a secure computing system as new vulnerabilities are discovered.

The ITSDB process includes authentication roles and secure communications and is considered a critical asset to the organization. If centralized management of security is used, then the resource must be well-protected itself and provide redundant modes of access to ensure its confidentiality, integrity and availability.

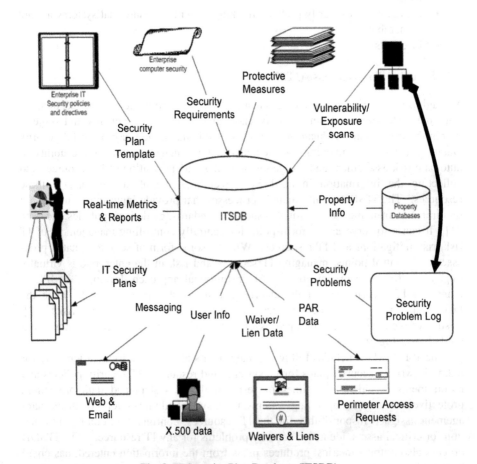

Fig. 9. IT Security Plan Database (ITSDB)

5.2 Security Problem Log (SPL)

Another security risk control/mitigation system developed and used at JPL is a security problem tracking system to ensure that security patches and controls are applied to systems within a specified period. The JPL ITSDB is integrated with a Security Problem Log (SPL) database (Fig. 10). The SPL is a database of computer system level IT security problems. If a vulnerability is identified for a system, an automated process creates an SPL ticket and emails are sent to key people to take corrective action. If a security problem ticket is not closed within a specified timeframe (noted in the ticket), the problem is escalated to management. The IT security group verifies the corrective action. If the corrective action is not verified, the SA is notified. The clock for the time to fix does not restart during this process. If a system presents a risk to the environment due to identified vulnerabilities and has not been corrected, it may be taken off the network. This decision is made by the IT security group with management.

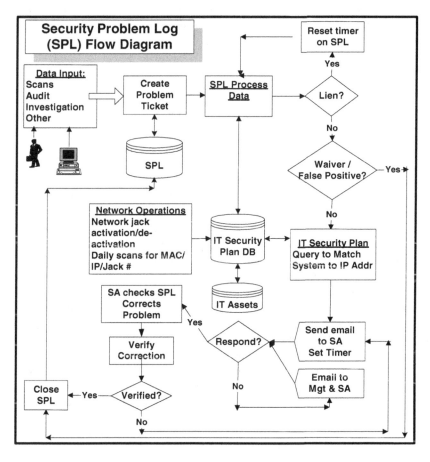

Fig. 10. Security Problem Log (SPL)

The JPL SPL has the following elements and processes:

- Records security problems found during internal on-site audits and electronic vulnerability scans
  - Issues tickets to be closed by expiration date
  - Notifies responsible personnel by email, with escalation to line managers for expired tickets
- Supports viewing and updating SPL tickets
  - Provides detailed vulnerability description and specific instructions for the preferred corrective action
  - One-click corrective action response, if preferred fix was applied
  - Accommodates rejection requests and requests to delay expiration date (liens)
  - Prevents creation of new tickets when there are previous false positives, waivers, liens, or duplicate open tickets
  - Closes open tickets when corrective action is verified, if a waiver is approved, or a false positive is confirmed

6 Conclusion

These risk management activities at JPL that address both institutional and project life cycles have shown that formalizing the process is highly effective and beneficial to both. Effective security risk management must be a proactive and persistent activity that involves the organization at both the institutional and the project levels. It requires the cooperation of everyone in the organization. An SSE can manage security risks by working with domain experts and management to identify the risks and their mitigations. Use of a risk management instrument can help provide objective control of the risk elements and their interactions both institutionally and in the SDLC.

The approach presented here attempts to join together the IT security risks faced together in the enterprise at both institutionally as a whole and in the SDLC. It is recognized that the approach does not cover the totality of security risks faced by organizations. However it does attempt to address two key areas. Additionally, the approach to risk management must take into account that security risks are in constant flux as exploits of vulnerabilities and attackers are becoming increasingly sophisticated, especially as new attack tools become available on the internet. Security risks must undergo continual evaluation, thus the persistence in the process to reassess risks, exposures, vulnerabilities, and the likelihood that an attack will succeed.

While the institutional risk mitigation process may benefit the life cycle, it must be carefully weighed and balanced against other risks and the potential impact of mitigations, especially in the interface with the project life cycle. Institutional risk abatement activities for the enterprise provide mitigations for the project life cycle and should be accounted for as part of the risk assessment and mitigation analysis process. Further, Integrating risk mitigations provided by the institution into the project life cycle helps to identify risks that may already be costed independently. The projects may rely on institutional mitigation for risks identified in its own processes which could reduce its overall security risk mitigation costs while providing higher security as well. Consequently, some of the mitigations, even though more costly when provisioned independently, may actually be cheaper as the costs are shared across the organization and are already factored into the project costs for institutional support. For this additional reason, it is more cost effective to implement an institutional risk assessment and mitigation program as described above. Spreading the cost of providing risk mitigation across projects actually reduces the cost for each project of providing its own support and tools independently.

A comprehensive architecture to manage IT security risk enables organizations to understand these risks better, including the likelihood of success, the potential for damage if successful, the effectiveness and cost of mitigations. It gives managers the capability to make informed decisions on mitigating risk and awareness and acceptance of the residual risk, along with the associated costs. It provides a pro-active approach that allows for continual risk assessment. Such a methodology applied as a systems engineering practice both institutionally and in the SDLC enables the organization to respond quickly and more effectively to new threats as the environment and technology change over time. For both the institution and projects performing risk assessment as part of an IT security plan process helps the organization to understand the security needs of the organization and provide the capability for better cost accounting. The risk management activities identified above have benefited JPL in its efforts to take proactive and cost effect steps in managing IT security risks.

Acknowledgement

The research described in this paper was carried out at the Jet Propulsion Laboratory, California Institute of Technology, under a contract with the National Aeronautics and Space Administration. Reference herein to any specific commercial product, process, or service by trade name, trademark, manufacturer, or otherwise, does not constitute or imply its endorsement by the United States Government or the Jet Propulsion Laboratory, California Institute of Technology.

References

1. Anderson, R. J., Security Engineering: A Guide to Building Dependable Distributed Systems, John Wiley & Sons; (2001)
2. GAO-03-98, Government Accounting Office (GAO) Audit: "Major Management Challenges and Program Risks: Department of Defense," GAO-03-98, January 2003 (available on the Internet at: http://www.gao.gov/pas/2003/)
3. Howard, M. and LeBlanc, D., Writing Secure Code, Second Edition, Microsoft Press, December, 2002
4. NASA CRM Resource Center website http://www.crm.nasa.gov/knowledge /default.html, accessed 09-15-2003
5. Stamatelatos, M.G., "Risk Assessment and Management, Tools and Applications," PowerPoint Presentation, available on NASA CRM Resource Center: http://www.crm.nasa.gov/papers/presentation_1.pdf (accessed 09-20-03)

6. Witty, R., "Successful Elements of an Information Security Risk Management Program," Gartner Symposium ITxpo, U.S. Symposium/ITxpo, Orlando, Florida, 6–11 October 2002.
7. ArcSight, "TruThreat Visualization Software", 2003, available at http://www. arcsight.com/.
8. RiskWatch, "Security Risk Management (SRM) software solutions for government and industry", information downloaded from the Internet on 10-10-03, http://www.riskwatch.com/.
9. McGraw, G., "Software Risk Management for Security", Citigal White Paper, 1999, available at http://www.cigital.com/whitepapers/.
10. ISO, International Organization for Standardization, ISO 9000:2000 family, Quality Management Systems, http://www.iso.ch/iso/en/iso9000-14000/iso9000/ selection_use/ iso9000family.html, accessed 09-19-2003
11. Carnegie Mellon University (CMU) Software Engineering Institute (SEI) Capability Maturity Model® Integration (CMMI^{SM}), available on the Internet at http://www.sei.cmu.edu/cmmi/general/ (accessed 09-20-03).
12. SEI, Carnegie Mellon University Software Engineering Institute, "OCTAVE Method," 11-11, 2003, available at http://www.cert.org/octave/methods.html.
13. NIH CIT (National Institute of Health, Center for Information Technology), "NIH Application/System Security Plan Template for Major Applications and General Support Systems," 1994.
14. Bishop, M., "Computer Security: Art and Science", Addison-Wesley Pub Co.; (2002).
15. Feather, M.S., Cornford, S. L., and Moran, K., "Risk-Based Analysis And Decision Making In Multi-Disciplinary Environments," Proceedings of IMECE'03 2003 ASME International Mechanical Engineering Congress & Exposition Washington, D.C., November 16–21, 2003.
16. Cornford, S. L., Feather, M. S., and Hicks, K. A., "DDP – A tool for life-cycle risk management," IEEE Aerospace Conference, March 2001, (available on the web at: http://ddptool.jpl.nasa.gov)
17. Cornford, S. L., Feather, M.S., Dunphy, J., Salcedo, J., and Menzies, T., "Optimizing Spacecraft Design – Optimization Engine Development: Progress and Plans," IEEE Aerospace Conference, March 2003, (available on the web at: http://ddptool.jpl.nasa.gov)
18. Feather, M.S., Cornford, S. L., and Dunphy, J., "A Risk-Centric Model for Value Maximization," Proceedings, 4th International Workshop on Economics-Driven Software Engineering Research, Orlando, Florida, May 21 2002, pp. 10-14
19. Feather, M.S., Hicks, K.A., Johnson, K.R., and Cornford, S. L., "Software Support for Improving Technology Infusion," Proceedings of the 1st International Conference on Space Mission Challenges for Information Technology (SMC-IT), Pasadena, California, July 2003, pp. 359-367; JPL Publication 03-13A, Jet Propulsion Laboratory, California Institute of Technology
20. Cornford, S., "Defect Detection and Prevention (DDP): A Tool for Life Cycle Risk Management: Explanations, Demonstrations and Applications," DDP Tool Training Seminar presented at JPL at the Jet Propulsion Lab, March 23, 2001
21. Swanson, M., "Guide for Developing Security Plans for Information Technology Systems," NIST Special Publication 800-18, 1998
22. FIPS PUB 73, Federal Information processing Standards Publication, "Guidelines for Security of Computer Applications," 1980
23. Heinz, L., "Preventing Security-Related Defects," news@sei interactive, 2Q, 2002, downloaded from the Internet at: http://interactive.sei.cmu.edu, August 19, 2003.

24. Gilliam, D., Wolfe, T., Sherif, J., and Bishop, M., "Software Security Checklist for the Software Life Cycle," Proc. of the Twelth IEEE International Workshops on Enabling Technologies: Infrastructure for Collaborative Enterprises, Linz, Austria, pp 243-248.

25. Gilliam, D., Kelly, J. Powell, J., Bishop, M., "Development of a Software Security Assessment Instrument to Reduce Software Security Risk" Proc. of the Tenth IEEE International Workshops on Enabling Technologies: Infrastructure for Collaborative Enterprises, Boston, MA, pp 144-149.

26. D. Gilliam, J. Powell, J. Kelly, M. Bishop, "Reducing Software Security Risk Through an Integrated Approach," 26th International IEEE/NASA Software Engineering Workshop, 17-29 November, 2003, Greenbelt, MD.

27. Component Based Model Checking, J. Powell, D. Gilliam, Proceedings of the 6th World Conference on Integrated Design and Process Technology, June 23-28, Pasadena CA, p 66 & CD

28. Weiser, M., "Program Slicing," IEEE Transactions on Software Engineering SE-10(4) pp. 352–357 (July 1984).

29. Miller, R. L., "JPL's Infrastructure for Managing IT Security: The Processes and Custom Toolset," presentation to the NASA IT Security Managers' Workshop, April, 2003.

30. Stoneburner G., Goguen, A., and Feringa, A., "Risk Management for Information Technology Systems," The National Institute of Standards and Technology Special Publication 800-30, 2001

31. Stoneburner, G., Hayden, C., and Feringa, A., "Engineering Principles for Information Technology Security (A Baseline for Achieving Security)," NIST Special Publication 800-27.

SEAS: A Secure E-Voting Applet System*

Fabrizio Baiardi[1], Alessandro Falleni[2], Riccardo Granchi[2,**],
Fabio Martinelli[2], Marinella Petrocchi[2], and Anna Vaccarelli[2]

[1]Dipartimento di Informatica, Università di Pisa, Italy
baiardi@di.unipi.it
[2]Istituto di Informatica e Telematica - CNR - Pisa, Italy
{alessandro.falleni, fabio.martinelli, marinella.petrocchi,
anna.vaccarelli}@iit.cnr.it

Abstract. This paper presents SEAS, the Secure E-voting Applet System, a protocol for implementing a secure and private system for polling over computer networks, usable in distributed organizations whose members may range up to dozens of thousands. We consider an architecture requiring the minimum number of servers involved in the validation and voting phases. Sensus, [7], a well known e-voting protocol, requires only two servers, namely a validator and a tallier. Even if satisfying most of the security requirements of an e-voting system, Sensus suffers of a vulnerability that allows one of the entities involved in the election process to cast its own votes in place of those that abstain from the vote. SEAS is a portable and flexible system that preserves the *lightness* of Sensus, but it avoids the mentioned weakness. We propose a prototype implementation of SEAS based on Java applet and XML technology.

1 Introduction

The growing interest on e-voting systems in the last two decades is due to the appealing benefits that could be achieved from such a technology. One of the main factors of interest is that these systems enable the users to easily express their preferences from whatever location. This hopefully may help to increase the number of voters in public elections. Other advantages are the exact interpretation of ballots and the virtually immediate publication of the results.

Although there have been several attempts to apply e-voting systems to public elections, there are still several doubts on their application to real elections, [16]. We may briefly recall two kinds of problems. On the one hand, the voter is not in a controlled precinct and this may increase the possibility of coercion; on the other hand, there are the usual computer security threats, *e.g.*, the user's PC may be unreliable due to the presence of virus, Trojan horses, *etc*. These problems represent serious obstacles to the application of e-voting systems to large scale public elections, given the unquestionable nature that these elections must have. Thus, an e-voting system for public elections

---

* Work partially supported by MIUR Project: "Strumenti, Ambienti e Applicazioni Innovative per la Società dell'Informazione", sottoprogetto SP1: Reti INTERNET: "efficienza, integrazione e sicurezza".
** This author is currently working at TradeSoft Technologies, Pisa, Italy.

K. Futatsugi et al. (Eds.): ISSS 2003, LNCS 3233, pp. 318–329, 2004.

should be not only secure, but also perceived as secure by its users. Because of these considerations, several researchers still consider the application of e-voting systems to large scale elections premature.

Nevertheless, we believe that e-voting solutions may be successfully applied for specific scenarios, *e.g.,* for e-polling systems. A successful outcome in these specific areas could increase the user confidence in such technologies. In this paper, we thus consider elections/polling in distributed organizations, whose members may range up to dozens of thousands and we suppose them to have digital certificates, following the directives of the proposed standard [10]. We investigate the adoption of the Sensus protocol [7], because it exploits a very limited number of distinct servers (basically two entities, namely the *validator* and the *tallier*). This makes the protocol more manageable w.r.t. other solutions adopting many servers, like the one proposed in [11].

Sensus suffers from a vulnerability that allows one of the entities involved in the election process to cast votes of eligible users that, although registered in the election process, abstain to vote. These illegitimate votes would fall into the final tally.

The main contribution of this paper is the design of SEAS, the Secure E-voting Applet System. SEAS has been defined by modifying the Sensus protocol, to avoid its well-known vulnerability, while preserving its other security properties. Further, we propose a prototype implementation of SEAS based on Java applet technology and XML, in order to define a flexible e-voting package.

Structure of the paper. Section 2 recalls the main goals of the e-voting protocols. Section 3 introduces notation and assumptions on which we rely throughout the paper. Section 4 describes the Sensus protocol and Section 5 introduces the SEAS protocol, our proposed variant of Sensus. Section 6 briefly sketches our prototype implementation. In Section 7 we discuss related work in the secure e-voting area. Finally, Section 8 offers some conclusions.

2 E-Voting Protocol: Goals

A comprehensive survey of the goals of an e-voting protocol has been proposed in [9]. Here, we recall some of the main properties only. Roughly speaking, any e-voting system should assure voter privacy while avoiding opportunities for fraud. Again, to be useful and acceptable by the voters community, it should be, at least, as secure as a traditional system. In particular, a set of criteria may be addressed as prudent guidelines for implementing a generic system.

- *Soundness, Unreusability, Completeness.* These three properties are strictly related. Soundness requires that no elector can invalidate the election (or the survey). This implies that either the final tally is correct or that any error in the final tally can be detected and consequently corrected. Unreusability and Completeness can be seen as sub-properties of soundness. The former requires that nobody can vote twice. As far as the latter is concerned, a system is complete if it is not possible to i) forge a vote; ii) remove a valid vote from the final tally; iii) add an invalid vote to the final tally. In practice, the property of completeness requires that *all and only* the valid votes get counted.

- *Privacy.* Neither the election authorities at stake nor anyone else can link any ballot to the voter who cast it.
- *Eligibility.* The system should allow all and only the eligible and registered electors to vote.
- *Fairness.* At any time, the voters must not know the partial results of the election. As a consequence, all the voted ballots should be kept secret until the end of the voting session. This property is required because a partial knowledge of the results may influence who, among the eligible electors, have not voted yet.
- *Verifiability.* Several alternative definitions of this property have been given in the literature. A strong notion of verifiability is: a system is verifiable if anyone can independently verify that all votes have been counted correctly, [7]. A weaker definition only requires that each voter can verify its own vote, [9].
- *Uncoercibility.* No voter can prove to have voted in a particular way. This requirement is important for the prevention of vote buying and extortion, see [3].

As a starting point of the development of Sensus, further properties have been considered. They are *flexibility, i.e.,* alternative ballot formats are available including open-ended questions, and *mobility, i.e.,* voters can cast their votes from any location.

3   Notation and Assumptions

Throughout the paper, we will use the following notation:

$$pk_i, pk_i^{-1} := \text{asymmetric pair of public/} \qquad \{...\}_{pk_i} := \text{message encrypted by}$$
$$\text{private keys of party } i \qquad \qquad \text{public key of party } i$$
$$ek, dk := \text{asymmetric pair of} \qquad \qquad \{...\}_{ek} := \text{message encrypted by}$$
$$\text{encryption/decryption keys} \qquad \text{encryption key } ek$$
$$\{...\}_{pk_i^{-1}} := \text{message signed by party } i \qquad (...)_{blind} := \text{blinded message}$$
$$h(m) := \text{digest of message } m$$

Typically, a digital signature is applied to the fingerprint of a message and then both the message itself and the signature are sent. For instance, to digitally sign message m at first $h(m)$ is computed and then it is encrypted by a private key pk_i^{-1} to produce the signature, *i.e.,* $\{h(m)\}_{pk_i^{-1}}$. Finally, the pair: $m, \{h(m)\}_{pk_i^{-1}}$ is sent. For readability, we adopt a lighter notation, where $\{m\}_{pk_i^{-1}}$ stands for both the cleartext and the signature.

E-voting protocols make often use of blind signatures, a cryptographic mechanism introduced in [5] that basically makes it possible to sign a message without being aware of its content. The classical little story of the carbon paper helps in understanding the mechanism: suppose to put a document and a sheet of carbon paper inside an envelope. Signing the outside part of the envelope will sign also the document. Further, upon removing the envelope, the signature will remain on the document. Thus, by means of a blind signature scheme a third party can validate the votes by digitally signing them even without knowing their values.

With regard to blind signatures, the following *qualitative* equation could be given:

$$\{m\}_{pk_i^{-1}} \leftarrow \{(m)_{blind}\}_{pk_i^{-1}}$$

where $(m)_{blind}$ is message m upon applying some algorithm (indeed the blind signature algorithm) making m not understandable. By signing $(m)_{blind}$, you obtain $\{(m)_{blind}\}_{pk_i^{-1}}$. Then, who first applied the blind signature algorithm can also remove (notation $\leftarrow$) the blinding, though maintaining the signature.

The following assumptions are required for both Sensus and SEAS:

1. IP packets cannot be analyzed in order to pair the elector identity with its messages. We assume to use anonymous communication channels, *e.g.*, a chain of World Wide Web forwarding servers, as suggested by Cranor and Cytron in [7].
2. The physical machinery from which an elector is casting its vote cannot be entered to read the ballot before the encryption. Furthermore, problems related to ballots being intercepted or delayed while in transit are not addressed here.
3. Cryptographic algorithms are robust enough to guarantee that an encrypted message can be decrypted only through the correspondent decryption key.
4. It is not possible that two (or more) electors generate two identical identifiers and two identical pairs of encryption/decryption keys.
5. Messages from voters will not arrive at the entities devoted to validate and count the voted ballots in the same order, allowing them to collude to link ballots with the voters who cast them. Further, messages from the whole community will arrive in a random order to the entity devoted to count the final tally. These features could be achieved by introducing a random delay between two consecutive transmissions by the same elector. Further, considering a community large enough that voters are likely to vote at approximately the same time can let the assumptions valid.

We also assume reliability of communication. Finally, in developing SEAS we assume the presence of an administrator of the whole election, trusted for each entity at stake. We call $cert_{CA}$ the digital certificate of this administrator.

4   The Sensus Protocol

In [7] Cranor and Cytron presented Sensus, a protocol implementing a secure and private system for polling over computer networks, where polling is a generic term that covers both surveys and elections. The protocol is based closely upon a scheme previously proposed by Fujioka *et al.*, [9]. Sensus is implemented through three modules:

– the pollster P, willing to ballot in a secure and private way. The pollster is a set of hardware/software modules through which a voter can cast its ballot. Throughout the paper, the terms *voters* and *pollsters* will be used interchangeably;
– the validator V, a server that first checks the eligibility of the pollster P and the uniqueness of its submission, and then it validates the submitted vote;
– the tallier T, a server devoted to count all the validated votes.

A preliminary phase of the protocol requires the involvement of another entity, the registrar R. The registrar implements the registration task, concerning with the compilation of a list of people both eligible and registered to vote. We call this list RVL.

RVL pairs the identifier of a voter with a public key[1]. It follows the formalization of the
Sensus protocol, basically consisting of five messages exchanged over the net. Note that
all the communications are intended to be encrypted with the public key of the receiver,
i.e., the outer part of the message is encrypted by pk_V, pk_P, pk_T when it is intended for
the validator, the pollster, the tallier respectively. For the sake of readability, we refrain
from explicitly denoting this layer of encryption. It is also understood that each receiver
i will first decrypt the received message by using its own private key pk_i^{-1}.

$$1) \quad P \rightarrow V : \{(h(\{B\}_{ek}))_{blind}\}_{pk_P^{-1}}, I$$
$$2) \quad V \rightarrow P : \{(h(\{B\}_{ek}))_{blind}\}_{pk_V^{-1}}$$
$$3) \quad P \rightarrow T : \{h(\{B\}_{ek})\}_{pk_V^{-1}}, \{B\}_{ek}$$
$$4) \quad T \rightarrow P : rec\#, \{\{B\}_{ek}\}_{pk_T^{-1}}$$
$$5) \quad P \rightarrow T : rec\#, dk$$

To guarantee the voter privacy steps 3 and 5 assume the use of anonymous communication channels (examples for anonymous communication can be found in Chaum's
mix-net [4], in Chaum's dc-net [6], in Onion Routing [21] and in [14]). [7] suggests the
use of a chain of World Wide Web forwarding servers.

1. The pollster P prepares a voted ballot B, encrypts it with a randomly generated secret
   encryption key ek. Then, P blinds the digest of the encrypted message, $h(\{B\}_{ek})$,
   and it digitally signs it with its private key pk_P^{-1}. Finally, P sends it to the validator,
   together with the identifier I.
2. The validator checks the credentials of the aspirant pollster. It first verifies the signature by applying the public key paired with pk_P^{-1}. After verifying the signature,
   it checks if i) I belongs to the list RVL of eligible and registered voters; ii) it is the
   first time that the voter identified by I sends a vote. If all these checks succeed, V
   applies its digital signature to the digest and it returns the signature to P.
3. P can remove the blinding from the validator signature. Then P sends the signed
   digest and the encrypted ballot to T.
4. The tallier T can now check the honesty of the pollster, by verifying that the encrypted
   ballot $\{B\}_{ek}$ has been validated by V. To this aim, T first verifies the signature by
   applying pk_V, then it computes an own digest on $\{B\}_{ek}$ and verifies its equality
   with what received. Then, T inserts $\{B\}_{ek}$ into a list of valid ballots, say RL. Finally,
   T signs the encrypted ballot and sends it back to P with a receipt number, to pair
   the ballot decryption key with the ballot itself. T also updates RL by inserting the
   receipt number.
5. Upon verifying that message 4 has been signed with the private key correspondent
   to pk_T, P sends the ballot decryption key dk to the tallier. The key does not travel
   as a cleartext, because all the messages are encrypted with the public key of the

---

[1] The protocol assumes that a public identifier and a secret token have been previously sent to
each voter. Again, each voter should have previously generated a pair of private/public keys. In
order to register, a voter should send three values to the registrar: an identifier, a secret token
and a public key. The registrar checks the token validity and subsequently updates the list with
the voter identifier and its public key.

receiver. The tallier uses the key to decrypt the ballot, adds the vote to the final tally and it pairs the decryption key with the correspondent entry in RL.

At the end of the voting session, the tallier publishes RL and the final tally.

Sensus (like its forerunner [9]) suffers from the following vulnerability: suppose someone among the eligible and registered voters abstain to vote. In our formalization, this implies that the first two steps are not performed. Then, the validator V could maliciously act, by replacing the votes of who abstained and by inserting its own votes:

$$3) P(V) \longrightarrow T \ \{h(\{B_V\}_{ek_V})\}_{pk_V^{-1}}, \{B_V\}_{ek_V}$$

where $P(V)$ is the validator pretending to be the pollster, B_V and ek_V are, respectively, a voted ballot prepared by the validator and the validator encryption key. Sensus does not entirely satisfy the *completeness* requirement, because the validator can introduce its own ballots in the final tally. In [7, 9] the authors themselves noticed this drawback and suggested that voters willing to abstain submit at least blank ballots. The misbehavior could be detected even without modifying the Sensus architecture. Assume that the validator publishes, at the end of the whole voting session, a list of the blinded encrypted ballots signed by each elector and RVL. Then, each voter could verify the signatures of all the encrypted ballots. As a result, the number of the illegitimate ballots could be detected, however there would still be no possibility to correct the final tally.

The remaining properties of Section 2 are satisfied except for: 1) *verifiability* in its strong notion. Indeed, a voter may find its entry in RL thanks to *rec#* and verify the integrity of the correspondent encrypted ballot. This leads to the fulfillment of weak verifiability; 2) *uncoercibility*. Indeed, a voter, by maintaining its receipt number, can pair *rec#* with its encrypted ballot (and decryption key) in the published list RL. Individual pollsters can close out their voting session before the whole election is close. This might be seen as a *fairness* violation, by leading a corrupted tallier, that knows partial results, to let them know to the community.

The work in [11] uses six central facilities, a larger number than the ones used in [7, 9]. In [11] the voter's browser informs the distributor module that a certain ballot, with a certain ID, has been casted. By doing this, the distributor module knows that all and only the ballots with certain IDs must fall into the final tally. This prevents any facility from generating votes for unused ballots. Our goal is to develop an electronic voting system that, while preserving the simple architecture of Sensus, *i.e.,* less modules than the ones required by [11], avoids the above-mentioned vulnerability.

5   The SEAS Protocol: Design

We take into account the needs of small communities of users, say up to dozens of thousands. Several private and public organizations fall into this spectrum of patterns. Given the considered relatively small scenario, we thought it right to adopt a protocol requiring a minimum number of modules. Our choice is justified both by the will to implement a low cost system and by the awareness that in an environment like the depicted one it is not always possible to locate many central facilities while simultaneously avoiding the risk of collusion among them.

Each voter belonging to the community is assumed to: 1) have the access to either a local or global net devoted to election activities; 2) be the owner of a digital certificate according to the directives of the proposed standard [10]. We also assume that a list RVL1 of the eligible and registered electorate is available before the election takes place. More specifically, our list must contain the following three items: name and digital certificate of each eligible and registered voter plus an identifier ID^1, unique for each voter. Further, there is another available field to be filled in a subsequent phase. The certificate certifies pk_P^1 and it is signed by the election administrator. Both the validator and the tallier know RVL1.

The system should be able to verify the validity of the ballots and to prevent illegitimate ballots from being included in the final tally. We introduce a new phase of registration, feasible contextually to the voting session. To take part in this phase, each voter generates a second identifier ID^2 and a second pair of keys, $pk_P^2, pk_P^{2\,-1}$, that will be used by the voter to sign the ballot sent to the tallier.[2] The new phase of registration relies on three initial steps, as follows:

$$
\begin{aligned}
0a) \quad & P \rightarrow T : \{(h(pk_P^2, ID^2))_{blind}, ID^1\}_{pk_P^1 {}^{-1}} \\
0b) \quad & T \rightarrow P : \{(h(pk_P^2, ID^2))_{blind}\}_{pk_T^{-1}} \\
0c) \quad & P \rightarrow T : \{h(pk_P^2, ID^2)\}_{pk_T^{-1}}, pk_P^2, ID^2
\end{aligned}
$$

All the communications are assumed to be encrypted with the public key of the receiver. Consequently, all the receivers have at first to retrieve the plaintexts by applying their own private keys to the received messages. Steps 0c, 3 and 5 assume the use of an anonymous communication channel. This is required to avoid that the tallier establishes a link between the pollster and its sensitive information by a simple traffic analysis. Note that steps 0a, 0b, 1, 2 and 4 do not strictly need an anonymous communication. Indeed, steps 0b, 2 and 4 involve messages coming from the election authorities. Further, messages 0a and 1 contain by themselves information denoting the sender identity (*i.e.*, ID^1).

0a P registers the public key pk_P^2 and the identifier ID^2 with T. To do this, P blinds the digest of the pair pk_P^2, ID^2, it adds the first identifier ID^1, it signs everything and it sends the result to T.

0b Upon receiving message *0a*, T retrieves pk_P^1 through the list RVL1 and ID^1 and it verifies the signature. Then, it signs $(h(pk_P^2, ID^2))_{blind}$ and it returns it to P. To trace the electors whose blind pairs have been signed, T updates RVL1.

0c The pollster removes the blinding, obtaining a message digest digitally signed by the tallier, and sends it back to T, along with the pair as a plaintext. The tallier verifies the validity of its own signature. If the verification succeeds, then T records the pair (pk_P^2, ID^2) in the special list RVL2, a newly introduced list designed to contain pairs (pk_P^2, ID^2) plus a further field to be filled in a subsequent phase.

---

[2] ID^2 should be unique, at least with high probability. To give an example, $P_{50000}^{id(63)} = 10^{-10}$, where $P_{50000}^{id(63)}$ is the probability that in a community of 50000 electors at least two electors randomly generate two identical 63 bits identifiers.

$$1) \quad P \rightarrow V : \{(h(\{B\}_{ek}))_{blind}\}_{pk_P^{1}{}^{-1}}, ID^1$$

$$2) \quad V \rightarrow P : \{(h(\{B\}_{ek}))_{blind}\}_{pk_V^{-1}}$$

$$3) \quad P \rightarrow T : \{h(\{\{B\}_{ek})\}_{pk_V^{-1}}\}_{pk_P^{2}{}^{-1}}, \{B\}_{ek}, ID^2$$

$$4) \quad T \rightarrow P : rec\#, \{\{B\}_{ek}\}_{pk_T^{-1}}$$

$$5) \quad P \rightarrow T : rec\#, dk$$

After the validation of the voted ballot (steps 1, 2, same steps as the first two steps in Section 4, where the identifier in message 1 is ID^1), the pollster sends its vote to the tallier (step 3). In particular, the digest of the encrypted ballot is signed by the validator and by the pollster too, through its second private key, $pk_P^{2}{}^{-1}$. To complete message 3) the pollster adds its second identifier ID^2. Upon the reception of message 3), the tallier must verify that ID^2 belongs to the list RVL2 and that it is the first vote issued by the voter identified by ID^2. It verifies the outer signature through the public key associated to ID^2 in RVL2. Note that this signature does not allow the tallier to know the voter identity, since ID^2 was first registered through blind signatures (0a, 0b, 0c). Then, it verifies the validator signature. If these checks succeed, all the remaining interactions follow the original Sensus scheme. At the end of the whole voting session, the validator publishes RVL1, the tallier publishes RL, RVL1, RVL2 and the final tally.

We briefly discuss the rationale for our construction. Let us suppose that the validator sends its own ballot to the tallier. This ballot will be signed with a private key, say $pk^{x}{}^{-1}$. The tallier will be able to accept the signature on the ballot and, consequently, the ballot itself if and only if the correspondent public key, say pk^x, has been previously been registered. The identity of who supplied that public key can be verified through the tallier signature, see step 0b. Hence, the only way for the validator to have its vote accepted is to be a registered user, but this is not possible because we assume that the entity in charge of the registration phase is trusted. The *completeness* property is satisfied. Note that we achieve also a strong notion of *verifiability*. Indeed, every message for which the validator/tallier signature is required is first signed by the elector itself. After the publication of the lists, each elector can verify the correct tally of all the votes by means of the lists themselves. The property of *uncoercibility* is not satisfied. As regards *fairness*, the same remarks valid for Sensus hold. Along with these informal arguments, we plan a more formal investigation, in order to provide a high confidence in SEAS.

6   Implementation

For our prototype implementation, we assume available RVL1. Its generation is extremely dependable from the environment. Broadly speaking, to build up the list a secret token, unique for each elector, should be distributed, possibly over a channel different from the one used during the voting session. In corporate environments, the token may be delivered together with the pay packet. Generically, we may think to home delivery.

To build up a portable system not dependable from the underlying platform, we choose Java as the implementation language. Further, given the huge diffusion of browsers supporting the Java language, we realize the pollster module, *i.e.*, the module running at the elector's side, as a Java applet. The applet can be executed over whatever platform supporting a Java Virtual Machine, *e.g.*, laptops, PDAs, and even cell phones. Actually, the pollster module consists of two basic components, an user friendly interface, realized with Java Swing API and Xerces, an XML parser, ([1]), and the module that let the user cast its vote. After an initialization phase, the second module starts to interact with the validator and tallier servers.

The validator and tallier modules are realized as Java servlets running in an application server AS, interfaceable with the database manager. This solution is a way out to delegate AS to manage any problem related to the database access, as well as to the replication of the database, in order to guarantee some system scalability. Further, each servlet instance does not individually enters the database, but asks to AS. In turn, AS can manage a pool of open connections to the database and can assign a free connection to the servlet who asked for it. When the servlet releases the connection, this remains open and can be-reassigned by AS to another servlet. This solution avoids the overhead of creating a TCP connection to handle each request.

All communications between the modules are encrypted and signed, thus we do not rely on any further secure communication layer, such as the Secure Socket Layer protocol. We are currently investigating the impact of the newly introduced cryptographic operations on the performance of the whole structure. Likely, the more cryptographic operations are introduced, the more the system is overloaded.

Further, in the proposed infrastructure, the tallier acts as a bottleneck for the whole system. Indeed, in order for the pollster to cast one vote, the tallier is involved in four operations, w.r.t. just one operation by the validator. This could be avoided by parallelizing the tallier. In particular, we aim at replicating the tallier by exploiting the so called *farm parallel paradigm*, [13], in order to reduce the tallier service time.

A note on the use of signed Java Applets. We exploit the technology of the signed Java applet to allow the applet to connect to the validator and tallier. The applet is signed by the election administrator. The main advantages of using a signed applet are: 1) the elector may download the applet wherever it is; 2) the applet is signed by the private key correspondent to the public key certified by $cert_{CA}$. By verifying the signature, the elector may be reasonably sure about the integrity of the applet code and the identity of the sender; 3) the applet may be validated, by a trusted third party, before downloading it. This validation acts as a further guarantee, by assuring that the applet only implements the SEAS protocol in a correct way.

A note on the use of the XML technology. The structure of the ballot is defined by a XML document. This makes it very flexible. For instance, we may easily implement elections with multiple and nested choices. Let us consider a survey where the electors are asked to tell their preferences about their favourite athletes. The system could present a first level of choice, asking for the selection of the favourite sports activity. Then, the system could reach deeper levels of details, by increasing its granularity. For example, the voter may select the particular team and finally the favourite athlete. A summary of the voting is presented finally to the elector.

Finally, we remark the usage, where possible, of open source tools and packages.

7 Related Work

Many electronic voting systems have been proposed in the past recent years. We recall the main features of some of them. As already discussed, Sensus was born from the ashes of the scheme proposed by Fujioka *et al.*, [9]. A relevant difference is that in Sensus the tallier can process votes before the end of the whole voting session. In practice, upon receiving the encrypted ballot, the tallier returns the receipt to the voter that may immediately submit the decryption key. Thus, the voters can close out their voting session even if the whole election is not closed yet.

In [11] the authors present a secure e-voting system for large scale elections. The proposed protocol differs from [7, 9] because it does not exploit blind signatures and anonymous communication channels. It introduces six servers, or modules. To prevent collusions among the modules and to guarantee integrity and privacy, a complex protocol is adopted for the communication among modules. In practice, when module A is about to transmit something to module B, it first sends data to module C, randomly chosen. Data are encrypted with the public keys of all the modules. C may decrypt data with its own private key and check the message integrity, at least as far as its dimension and its structure is concerned, and it randomly sends the message again to another module. The chain of forwarding messages continues until the data arrives to B. The fraud probability is low because, even if a module may alter a message without changing its original dimension and structure, the other modules can discover the fraud because each of them maintains a particular piece of information in a private file. The authors assume a very low probability of associating a vote to the identity of the elector, since this event would require collusions of all the modules at stake.

An e-voting system should verify the authenticity of the messages without violating the privacy about their origin. The above-mentioned protocols are examples of typical solutions occurring in the literature, some of them by making use of anonymous communication channels [7, 9], others exploiting the mechanism to forward messages, [11]. The protocol in [15] offers an alternative to the problem of privacy: it exploits a FTP server to satisfy the requirement on the *non-traceability* of the IP addresses during the voting phase. The protocol involves three servers and it does not require their trustiness, because possible collusions may be traced.

Given the specific scenario we take into account, *i.e.,* distributed organizations whose members may range up to dozens of thousands, we favour a protocol requiring the minimum number of authorities managing servers. Consequently, we choose Sensus as a starting point for SEAS. Finally, some related work address the problem of guaranteeing *uncoercibility* in e-voting systems, one among all, we refer to [12].

8 Concluding Remarks and Future Work

In this paper we have presented a variant of the Sensus protocol that fixes one well known vulnerability still preserving its good features. No new module has been introduced, since we rely on the tallier module already present in the original Sensus. We have developed an implementation based on Java applets and XML technologies that shown the feasibility of our e-voting protocol. To the best of our knowledge, this is the first implementation of a variant of Sensus with Java applets. Performance analysis are being performed to evaluate the impact of the newly introduced phase of registration. As future work, we plan to stress the nice feature of SEAS, *i.e.,* allowing "mobility" of the voter. In particular, we plan to implement SEAS by using the Java API for Mobile Phones developed in [2]. Moreover, we aim at producing a formal verification of the protocol correctness w.r.t. common e-voting requirements (*e.g.,* see [17, 19]). We plan to use one of the well-known approaches for formal verification developed in [8, 18, 20].

Acknowledgments

We are very grateful to Luca Bechelli for his careful feedback and advice on both the desigh and implementative phase of this work. We would also like to thank the anonymous referees for their useful comments.

References

[1] http://xml.apache.org/xerces-j/.

[2] I. G. Askoxylakis, D. D. Kastanis, and A. P. Traganitis. M-commerce api package for mobile phones. *ERCIM newsletter 54*, 2003. Special Theme: Applications and Service Platforms for the Mobile User.

[3] J. Benaloh and D. Tuinstra. Receipt-Free Secret-Ballot Election. In *Proc. of ACM STOC'94*, pages 544–553, 1994.

[4] D. Chaum. Untraceable Electronic Mail, Return Addresses, and Digital Pseudonyms. *Communications of the ACM*, 24(2):84–88, 1981.

[5] D. Chaum. Blind Signatures for Untraceable Payments. In *Proc. of Crypto'82*, pages 199–203. Plenum, NY, 1983.

[6] D. Chaum. The Dining Cryptographers Problem: Unconditional Sender and Recipient Untraceability. *Journal of Cryptology*, 1(1):65–75, 1988.

[7] L. Cranor and R. K. Cytron. Sensor: A Security-Conscious Electronic Polling System for the Internet. In *Proc. of HICSS'97*, 1997.

[8] R. Focardi, R. Gorrieri, and F. Martinelli. Non Interference for the Analysis of Cryptographic Protocols. In *Proc. of ICALP'00, LNCS 1853, 354-372*, 2000.

[9] A. Fujioka, T. Okamoto, and K. Ohta. A Practical Secret Voting Scheme for Large Scale Election. In *Proc. of Auscrypt'92*, volume LNCS 718, pages 244–260, 1992.

[10] R. Housley, W. Ford, W. Polk, and D. Solo. RFC 2459: Internet X.509 Public Key Infrastructure Certificate and CRL Profile, IETF, 1999. http://www.ietf.org/rfc/rfc2459.txt.

[11] J. Karro and J. Wang. Towards a Practical, Secure, and Very Large Scale Online Election. In *Proc. of ACSAC'99*, pages 161–169. IEEE Computer Society Press, 1999.

[12] E. Magkos, M. Burmester, and V. Chrissikopoulos. Receipt-Freeness in Large-Scale Elections without Untappable Channels. In *I3E*, pages 683–694, 2001.

[13] S. Pelagatti. *Structured development of parallel programs*. Taylor & Francis London, 1997.

[14] A. Pfitzmann, B. Pfitzmann, and M. Waidner. SDN-MIXes: Untraceable Communication with Small Bandwidth Overhead. *Kommunikation in Verteilten Systemen*, pages 451–463, 1991.

[15] I. Ray, I. Ray, and N. Narasimhamurthi. An Anonymous Electronic Voting Protocol for Voting over the Internet. In *Proc. of WECWIS '01*, pages 188–191. IEEE Computer Society Press, 2001.

[16] A. D. Rubin. Security Considerations for Remote Electronic Voting. In *Proc. of 29th Research Conference on Communication, Information and Internet Policy (TPRC01)*, 2001.

[17] P. Ryan and J. Bryans. Security and trust in digital voting systems. pages 113–120, 2003. Proc. of FAST'03, IIT TR-10/2003.

[18] P.Y.A. Ryan, S.A. Schneider, M.H. Goldsmith, G. Lowe, and A.W. Roscoe. *Modelling and Analysis of Security Protocols*. Addison-Wesley Publishing Co., 2000.

[19] S. Schneider and A. Sidiropoulos. CSP and anonymity. In *Proc of ESORICS'96*, pages 198–218, 1996.

[20] V. Shmatikov. Probabilistic model checking of an anonymity system. *Accepted to Journal of Computer Security (selected papers of CSFW-15)*, 2004.

[21] P.F. Syverson, D.M. Goldschlag, and M.G. Reed. Anonymous Connections and Onion Routing. In *IEEE Symposium on Security and Privacy*, pages 44–54, 1997.

The Design of a Secure Distributed Devices System Based on Immunity

Hiroyuki Nishiyama, Yukinobu Mine, and Fumio Mizoguchi

Information Media Center, Tokyo University of Science,
Noda, Chiba, 278-8510, Japan
{nisiyama, mine, mizo}@ia.noda.tus.ac.jp

Abstract. We designed a secure control system for distributed and co-operative systems, including robots and information appliances, by integrating network security based on the natural immune system. Although most network security systems are independent, we designed a device control level and a security level within the same agent's framework. This design defines the immunity cell agent as the process group that monitors the communication and operation of the network computer that is the controlling device. It defines the device agent as the process group that controls and manages devices. Each agent monitors a computer and controls devices individually. The immunity cell agent functions as an authentication system during negotiation between the device agents and the information exchange of cooperative processing when a request is received. We incorporate an immunity system into a multiagent robot system, using robots and sensors, and demonstrate its effects.

1 Introduction

The construction of distributed control systems for robots and information appliances with networks has recently increased. This is especially true in the construction of smart houses and smart offices supporting human activities and incorporating large-scale systems containing several sensors [8][11]. For example, Sato et al. installed several sensors in the floor and the bed, and installed a handling robot on the surface of a wall to support patients in a sickroom [11]. In their research, sensors recognize a patient's position and condition, and each device provides support accordingly. Mizoguchi et al. used mobile robots, handling robots, and several sensors in an office environment to deliver printed paper to users [8]. In these instances, the control software operating on the tip of each device or on the terminal through a serial cable was provided for each robot or sensor. A system connecting each tip and terminal through the existing local area network is commonly used to realize cooperation between devices. However, these distributed control systems must be built in a closed network. Users in an external network or environment are thus not considered to be using a system network. As a result, security in the communication protocol between the control software of the devices and sensors is not considered. Although ideally a control system would be built with a dedicated network, system configurations

K. Futatsugi et al. (Eds.): ISSS 2003, LNCS 3233, pp. 330–344, 2004.

using an available LAN environment are the norm. Therefore, in order to use a distributed control system for general purposes, we must satisfy the security requirements on a normal network through the software. Ferraiolo and others manage devices using Role-Based Access Control (RBAC) in a similar situation [2]. Although their research imposes use restrictions on the devices installed in the environment by user authentication, communication between devices is not considered.

Considering this background, we integrated the concept of a natural immunity system into the distributed cooperative system in order to strengthen the security of the system on a typical network. The human immunity system consists of trillions of immunity cells that detect and eliminate intruders, such as viruses, and cells are attacked by the intruder as "non-self." Processing efficiency is increased because immunity cells cooperate when detecting and excluding non-self. Research utilizing the concept of an immunity system has been introduced in autonomous robot control [7], unusual value extraction in a sensor network [6], and network security [3] [9]. In particular, Forrest et al. focused on designing a mechanism for detecting "self" and "non-self" in an immunity system that enables response to a strange intrusion [3]. Nishiyama et al. designed a multi-agent security system that detects intruders and reacts in a network computer the same way that the immunity cell group works in the body [9]. This system features real-time generation of many immunity cell agents for monitoring the operation of a computer and the information that flows in through a network, and for detecting and eliminating intruders.

In our research, we designed a secure distributed system for cooperative use between devices, integrating the framework of these immunity systems into a multiagent robot system. This system monitors accesses from other devices and the exchange of messages during cooperation between devices, and detects any illegal access. In this system, we prepare a device agent for every robot, device, and sensor; then we enable the exchange of messages with other agents. A device agent then enables a cooperating partner's selection, and information is exchanged between agents. In this communication process, a device agent recognizes information on the terminal of a partner's device agent by cooperating with an immunity cell agent, clarifying the terminal information of the device agent for communication. Our research prepares an immunity agent that monitors a network individually, rather than creating a new security implementation in the communication protocol between device agents. A device agent should perform only one request to an immunity agent for security, as when cooperation is requested of other devices. Thus, the existing distributed cooperation system can be upgraded to a secure system.

This paper is organized as follows. Section 2 explains the immune security system built into a multiagent robot system based on our research. We also briefly explain the natural immunity system and related research on the application of such an immunity system to computer software. Section 3 describes the structure for incorporating the immunity system into a multi-robot control system. Section 4 presents a demonstration of the system. Section 5 contains our conclusions.

2   Security System Based on Immunity

2.1   Immunity in Nature

An immunity system distinguishes self and non-self inside the body and eliminates the non-self [12]. In this system, two kinds of cells, "B-cells" and "T-cells," eliminate the non-self objects.

All immunity cells are lymphocyte cells generated from a single atomic cell, a hematopoietic stem cell. Cells originating from bone marrow are called "B-cells," and cells originating in the Thymus, "T-cells." Man's immunity system consists of two trillion lymphocyte cells, 20 to 30% of which are B-cells and 70% are T-cells.

A B-cell generates antibodies that distinguish and react with the non-self protein or "antigen," such as a virus, which is then eliminated. The B-cell itself is not capable of eliminating antigens. However, a B-cell has an antibody molecule like an antenna on its surface; the antibody corresponding to the antigen is compounded in large quantities by catching an antigen with the antenna. The B-cell is capable of memorizing the distinguished antigen and then generating many antibodies in a short time if the antigen is distinguished again (a secondary immunoreaction).

A T-cell distinguishes a self cell that is degraded by the antigen as non-self and eliminates it. A T-cell is generated in the thymus, where it is strictly educated to discriminate between self and non-self. Specifically, the T-cell is severely tested within the thymus and programmed to die. A few T-cells that distinguish only the self are converted into non-self and do not destroy the self, can go away besides the thymus. Forrest et al. conducted research on security that focused on the educational function of this thymus. Their research enables the detection of illegal entry (non-self) without infringing on regular access (self) [3].

2.2   Immunity System as a Super-Distribution System

These immunity cells, mutually activated by stimulating one another, efficiently eliminate cells polluted by the invasion of an antigen as well as the antigen itself. For example, if a T-cell detects a cell converted to non-self with the antigen, the T-cell eliminates that cell and orders the B-cell to generate antibodies for quickly eliminating the antigen. Thus, an immunity system eliminates not only self cells polluted with the antigen from the outside, but also the antigen itself as non-self. In this mechanism, two trillion cells comprising the immunity cell group cooperate among themselves in a super distribution.

The immune system efficiently distinguishes and eliminates intruders that enter the body because some immunity cells perform their own tasks as they cooperate with each other. An important feature of the immune system is that the system can eliminate intruders as they enter, as well as eliminating and restoring infected cells after the intruders have entered the body and infected some cells. The purpose of this system is to protect the body as a self. It enables man to survive in a degraded environment. We focused our attention on the robustness and toughness of such an immune system for network security. In particular, cooperation among immune system cells enables the cells to distinguish an intruder and an infected cell that a single immunity cell would have difficulty distinguishing. The mechanism can then efficiently eliminate them. These cooperation mechanisms are useful in intrusion detection and in specification of an intrusion route for network security.

2.3   Previous Research on Immunity-Based Security Systems

Forrest et al. realized a network security system based on an immunity system [3][5][4]. This model generates a unique pattern of illegal entry and assists in the detection of an illegal intrusion. The intrusion pattern randomly generates a candidate pattern consisting of combinations of various actions. Next, an action set of self is matched with this candidate pattern. If one portion of the action set is matched, the candidate is regarded as a "self" action and is canceled. Conversely, if a portion is not matched, the candidate is used as a detector (illegal intrusion pattern) of "non-self." To detect an intruder, all the generated patterns are checked for matches when a user action has been recognized through the network. When a pattern is matched, it is judged to be non-self. However, the detectors do not cooperate with the immunity cells, so each detector in the system independently performs intrusion detection. Moreover, the burden becomes excessive if a human administrator manages the situation after detection based on the number of targets in a computer and the access situation.

Ishiguro et al. proposed a method of applying an immunity system to an action-selection mechanism for realizing high robustness to environmental changes in autonomous control of a mobile robot [7]. In their proposal, the information about the external and internal environments that a robot's sensor detects is considered as an antigen, and an elemental action is considered as an antibody. They describe the model of the "action-mediation mechanism" that chooses suitable actions according to the robot's present situation through interaction between the antibodies via the immunity network. In another research study that applied the immunity network, Ishida et al. designed a diagnostic system for a dynamic relation network in a sensor network [6]. In a sensor network that uses some sensors in the same environment, this system detects a faulty sensor that is sensing an unusual value by checking the value in every other sensor in the immunity network.

2.4   Network Security System Based on Immunity

When an immune system concept is applied to computer security, "self" means access and a file created regularly by a regular user. In the "non-self," antigens eliminated by B-cells are accessed by illegal intruders and viruses; degraded self cells eliminated by the T-cell are files (processes) that are executed irregularly.

The human immunity system is a super-distribution system consisting of an immunity cell group. It performs intrusion detection and exclusion efficiently because the immunity cells cooperate. Nishiyama et al. emulate such a distributed system and cooperative mechanism to efficiently detect and exclude illegal intrusion [9]. Figure 1 depicts the concept of network security based on an immune system.

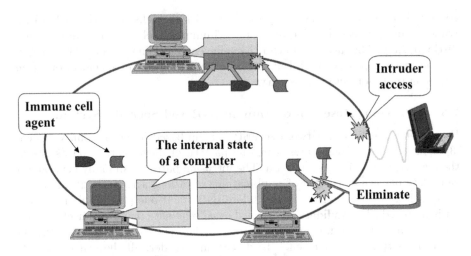

Fig. 1. Image of network security based on an immune system

Incorporating the functions of both a T-cell and B-cell, this immunity system is designed as a security system for all computers in a LAN. In this system, each immunity cell's role as an agent is defined as follows.

- B-cell agent ... Monitors the message information that flows in through a network. Specifying the port number to be monitored enables the monitoring of every network service using this agent.
- T-cell agent ... Monitors the process information currently performed within the computer.

Each cell agent model is described below.

B-Cell Agent

$$b\_cell_i(AccessInfo, AccessLog, Rule, Channel)$$

- $AccessInfo$ ... Information to monitor accesses, such as an IP address of a partner computer and a port number. This information is received from a network monitoring tool.
- $AccessLog$ ... Message information received from the candidate for monitoring.
- $Rule$ ... The action rule base for detecting non-self.
- $Channel$ ... The communication channel for recognizing self or non-self.

T-Cell Agent

$$t\_cell_j(ProcInfo, ProcLog, Rule, Cha, B_{cell}ID)$$

- $ProcInfo$ ... Information in the process for monitoring, such as Process ID and parent process ID. This information is received from a process-monitoring tool.

- *ProcLog* ... Information of the performed process.
- *Rule* ... The action rule base for detecting non-self.
- *Channel* ... The communication channel for recognizing self or non-self.
- $B_{cell}ID$ ... B-cell agent's ID code connected with itself.

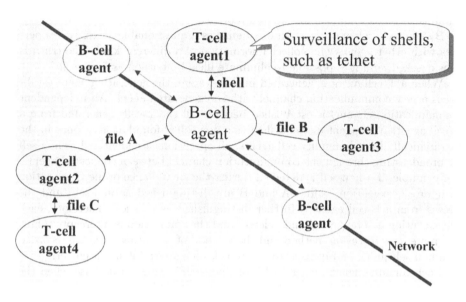

Fig. 2. Connection between immune agents

Connection Between Immune Agents. When access from another computer via a network is recognized or a new file (process) is detected, an agent is dynamically generated by a B-cell or a T-cell generator agent. For example, when files A and B are executed from a connecting access watched by a B-cell agent, the T-cell agents (No. 2 and No. 3) that watch each file are generated in Fig. 2. Moreover, when file C is executed during execution of file A, a T-cell is generated to watch file C. The relation of the parent process and child process in the T-cell agent that monitors these processes is realized as shown in Fig. 2. The generated immunity cell agent monitors the access or process, and the generated immunity cell eliminates the access or process when the agent detects an intruder-based rule base and judges the access or process as non-self. Additionally, cooperation among immunity cells enables the cells to distinguish an intruder and specify the intrusion route that would be difficult for a single immunity cell to distinguish and specify. After the intruders are identified, this mechanism can then efficiently eliminate them on all computers in the LAN.

In this system, all processes performed continuously by external operation are monitored as a set of a T-cell agent. Furthermore, when this system is mounted on each computer and an intruder accesses a computer via some other computers, it is possible to specify the access course by the relation between B-cell agents (refer to Fig. 2).

Cooperation Between Immune Agents. Each agent receives information about the monitored accesses or files and refers to a rule base to judge whether a cell is a self or non-self. Although this function is the same as that of conventional security systems, specifying an illegal intrusion based on only log information is difficult. Therefore, questionable accesses are also designated as detection targets in conventional systems, and final judgment is entrusted to the human administrator to whom the results are reported.

By contrast, when our system distinguishes a questionable access, it cooperates with other agents who collect information of a different kind. The truth is thus checked, and it is possible to eliminate illegal intrusion as "non-self."

When a T-cell agent is generated in this system, the generating agent establishes a new communication channel with the generated agent. An independent communication channel is established between all the T-cells generated from a B-cell agent. If an agent distinguished as a non-self is found at least once in the hierarchically built immunity cell agents, all operations are identified as non-self by broadcasting through the communication channel between connected agents. For example, if a non-self is detected during the surveillance of file C operation in figure 2, execution of files A and B are distinguished as non-self, and the access from a B-cell agent is further distinguished as non-self. Therefore, each file execution is interrupted and deleted, and the connection is intercepted. Furthermore, this intrusion method and the method of executing a file are recorded in a non-self judge and utilized to create rules for a new intrusion pattern.

Each immune agent judges "self" or "non-self" using a rule base when the agent receives information from the monitor target. This mechanism is the same as usual security systems; however, it is difficult for these systems to detect an intruder using only one type of log information. Therefore, in most systems a doubtful access is also a candidate for detection; these systems leave the final judgment to the administrator to whom they send the information. In contrast,

Table 1. Comparing typical security systems with immune security systems

	Typical security systems	Immune security systems
The rule of the illegal intrusion	Only a rule prepared in advance is used. The rule is updated by an update program.	A rule corresponding to a strange illegal intrusion can be created based on the assumption that self is not attacked. The rule is automatically updated when an illegal intrusion is detected.
Detection method	Matching process using the rule. The detection processing is performed as the top priority.	The matching process is performed using the rule, and immunity agents cooperatively detect the intruder. The detection processing can be performed using the free time of a computer, so the conventional calculation processing is not affected.
Correspondence after detection	Report to the administrator or block access only.	Block the access, and block all accesses and processes in the network of the intruder by cooperation among immunity agents.

in this system, when an immunity cell agent recognizes doubtful access, the agent sends a message to other immunity cell agents. All immunity cell agents receiving the message exchange behavior information about the access and cooperatively verify whether an illegal intrusion has been executed. Consequently, when an illegal intrusion is detected, each immunity cell agent eliminates the whole access as "non-self." Our immune security system detects and eliminates the illegal intrusion to the root authority based on some kinds of overflow hacking[9]. Here, the new viewpoint that compares an immunity concept with usual security can be summarized in table 1.

3   Secure Distributed Cooperative Control Based on Immunity

The immune security system explained above was researched for only network security. In our research, we integrated these immunity cell agents into a multiagent robot system that is a cooperative system for distributed device control. This takes into consideration the security of a robot system that works cooperatively by exchanging information through a network. Using the immune security system, the robot system can eliminate illegal use of the device by an intruder, and accurately identify the computer of the device that is exchanging information.

3.1   Structure of Device Agent

In our research, we apply an agent structure such as in Fig. 3 for cooperation between distributed devices. A device agent consists of a "Control agent" that controls a device via "Control software" and a "Negotiation agent" that negotiates with other device agents. Each agent is defined below.

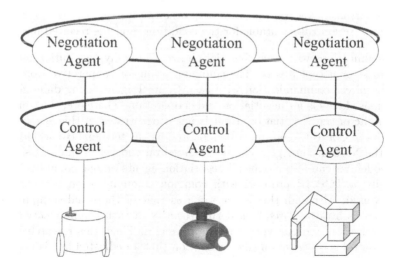

Fig. 3. Structure of device agent

Control Agent. A Control agent sends a command to the device and receives information such as sensing data from the devices through "Control software." The model of a Control agent is shown below.

$$control(ID, Task, Action, Rule, ActInfo)$$

- ID ... ID code
- $Task$ ... The task that should be performed
- $Action$ ... An executing action in order to perform $Task$
- $Rule$ ... Action rules suitable for the condition and the received message
- $ActInfo$ ... State information of the controlling device

A Control agent is able to open a direct communication channel with another Control agent and exchange messages with it while cooperating. For example, these communication channels are used in cooperative tasks, when location information is continually sent to a mobile robot from camera robots in order to guide the mobile robot exactly, or when performing synchronous processing between robots in order to deliver an object to a mobile robot from a manipulator.

Negotiation Agent. A Negotiation agent receives task requests from another Negotiation agent or user in the environment. When a Control agent requests a cooperative task, the Negotiation agent negotiates with another Negotiation agent to select a cooperative partner. As a result of negotiation, a Negotiation agent that is committed to a task sends a description of the task to its own Control agent. The model of a Negotiation agent is described below.

$$negotiation(ID, Task, Negotiation, Rule)$$

- ID ... ID code
- $Task$ ... The task that should be performed
- $Negotiation$ ... Negotiation state with other agents
- $Rule$ ... Action rules suitable for the conditions and the received message

Communications with each Negotiation agent are only negotiation messages that request or accept a task. The communication for cooperative work is executed by direct communication with each Control agent, using different communications channels for negotiation and cooperation. Therefore, the communication traffic of the Negotiation agent is not concentrated in this agent model. Although the Control Agent must be mounted on the terminal connected to the device, the Negotiation Agent can be mounted on another terminal. Using this agent model, we can also mount all negotiation agents on one computer.

Usually, a TCP/IP protocol with common communication between these agents is used. Although this is the same as that of the usual computer network, there is little research considering security in each communication, such as authentication and encryption of the messages. Thus, this research in such devices control is designed on the assumption that a dedicated line is used, and processing that degrades processing speed is not desirable for realizing real-time control.

With this background, we are including an immune security system in the mechanism of the conventional devices control systems, and enabling safe device control using the usual network.

3.2   Multiagent Robot System Based on Immunity

We integrated the immune security system described in Section 2 into the above multiagent system to realize a secure, distributed, cooperative system such as in Fig. 4. In this figure, a device agent has two B-cell agents; one monitors the flow of messages to other device agents, while the other monitors the flow of messages from other device agents. The T-cell agent monitors device control. We integrate these agent systems by using a multiagent robot language MRL [10] for each system design.

3.3   Confirming Cooperation Between Devices Based on Immunity

In negotiation and cooperation, the Negotiation agent and Control agent, which are device agents, cooperate with an immunity cell agent since a communication partner is specified. The device agents and immunity cell agent cooperate through the following steps.

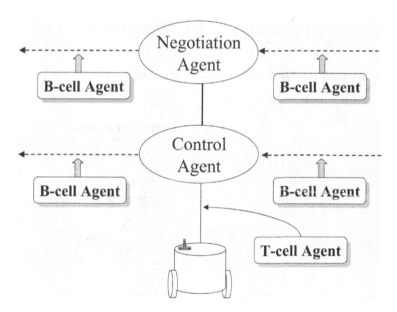

Fig. 4. Immune security system integrated into the multiagent robot system. The dashed lines mean the flow of messages. Each B-cell agent monitors these messages

Step 1. When a device agent is generated, the agent requests a B-cell generator agent to monitor a port number that the agent opens (refer to Fig. 5(a)). The B-cell agent that monitors the message transmission of the requesting

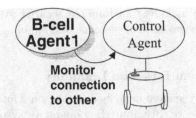

(a) Request for monitoring connection to other

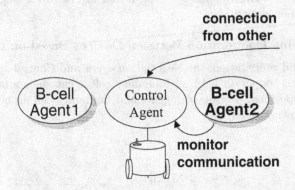

(b) Generate a new B-cell agent for monitoring communication

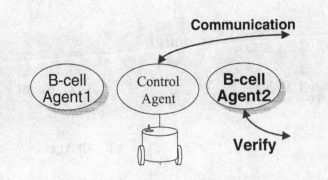

(c) Verify the communication between B-cell agents

Fig. 5. Flow of authentication among device agents based on immune agents. First, a device agent sends a request to the immune system; then a B-cell agent1 is generated for monitoring the connection to other device agents (in Fig. (a)). When the device agent is connected with other agents, a B-cell agent2 is generated for monitoring communication of the connection (in Fig. (b)). B-cell agent2 verifies a B-cell agent1 that monitors other device agent, and authenticates each message (in Fig. (c))

agent is also generated at this time. This B-cell agent monitors the contents of communication when the device agent connects or sends messages to other device agents.

Step 2. When the B-cell generator agent detects access to the monitoring port, the agent generates a B-cell agent to monitor the access (in Fig. 5(b)).

Step 3. The generated B-cell agent receives information concerning the IP address, port number, etc. of the accessing terminal, and monitors the message from the access until the access is terminated.

Step 4. The device agent accessed in step 2 requests confirmation of the accessing terminal from the B-cell agent generated by step 3, to confirm that the accessing terminal has the device agent of the cooperative partner.

Step 5. The B-cell agent requested in step 4 checks for the device agent on the accessing terminal with the B-cell agent generated by step 1 on the accessing terminal, and the agent accesses the device agent accessed in step 2 (in Fig. 5(c)).

Step 6. After confirmation of step 5, the B-cell agent confirms from whom the message is sent when the device agent accessed in step 2 receives a message from the accessing terminal.

Step 7. When the communication channel is closed by completion of cooperation, the B-cell agent generated by Step 2 disappears.

This system can check from which terminal the partner agent has made a connection when a communication channel of a device agent is opened during negotiation or cooperation.

Even if this system does not confirm conditions among device agents, confirmation between terminals is performed by communication between immunity agents, and the confirmation is obtained during cooperation.

4   Implement Experiment

The experiment environment for this research was an office space such as depicted in Fig. 6 used as a smart office, and we used various robots and sensors. This office had 12 rooms, and a user in the office could request service from the robots in each room.

Four mobile robots and two handling robots were used in this smart office. We also used camera, infrared, human-detection, and laser sensors. The control form of each robot and sensor system differed. For example, a mobile robot performed control from an internal computer, while the handling robot, the camera robot, and the laser sensor were connected to the terminal through a serial cable or video cable. The human detection sensor and the infrared sensor formed a network that was independent of the usual network provided by the LON unit group.

In this environment, we connected all robots and sensors through the LAN network, as depicted in Fig. 7, and integrated these various devices. The terminal of each sensor was connected directly to the LAN; each mobile robot used the

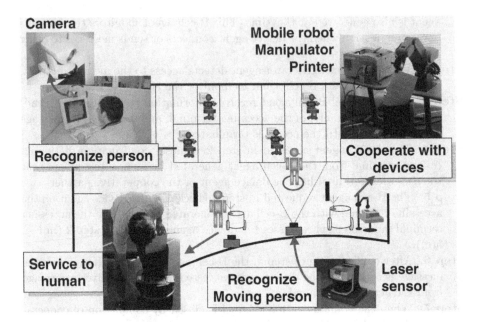

Fig. 6. Image of a smart office. This office can recognize and serve each person using several sensors and robots

access point of a wireless LAN, and the LON network was connected to the LAN network using HEXABINE as a bridge. Information was thus exchanged through each terminal.

We integrated and implemented the immunity system into a printed document delivery system that delivered printed documents to a user. We used Multi-agent Robot Language (MRL) [10] to implement the device agents and immunity cell agents. MRL introduced the functions of synchronization and asynchronous control that parallel logical language KL1[1] has, as well as stream communication; therefore, parallel processing of two or more agents, communication between agents, and dynamic generation and deletion of agents were possible. The cooperative work of the implemented system is as follows.

- Cooperation between a handling robot and a mobile robot
  The handling robot puts the document on the printer into the box on the mobile robot.
- Navigating cooperation between a camera robot and a mobile robot
  When the mobile robot moves to the printer position, the camera robot navigates the mobile robot using picture analysis for exact movement.
- Location cooperation between several sensors and a mobile robot
  When a mobile robot moves in the passage within the environment, the robot collects location information, using the information acquired from the infrared sensor installed on the ceiling and a wide-range laser sensor installed on the floor.

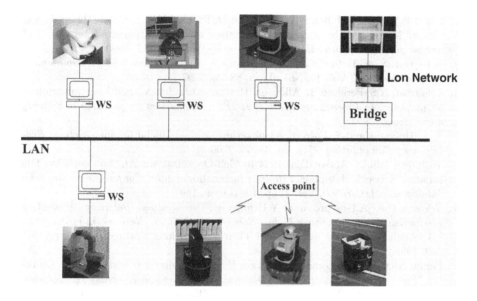

Fig. 7. Connection of devices via a network

In each cooperative task, the device agent of the requester selects its own cooperation partner by negotiation between agents. Immunity cell agents trace communication between device agents. Each device agent exchanges messages after confirming a partner agent by cooperation with an immunity cell agent when accessing a communication channel with other device agents for cooperation. We integrated an immunity system agent and realized secure communication between agents for cooperative control of distributed devices including robots.

5   Conclusion

We designed a secure control system for distributed and cooperative systems, including robots and information appliances, by integrating network security based on the immune system found in nature. Specifically, we designed a device agent that controls a device, and an immunity cell agent that performs network security as a multiagent system within the same framework, thus strengthening the security of communication between the device agents in cooperative work. We consider that the immunity agent system in this research can be applied not only to distributed device control, but also to GRID computing, P2P, etc. as a cooperative security system functioning throughout the network.

References

1. T. Chikayama: "A KL1 Implementation for Unix Systems", New Generation Computing, Vol.12, pp.123-124, 1993.

2. David F. Ferraiolo, Johon F. Barkley and D. Richard Kuhn, A Role Based Access Control Model and Reference Implementation within a Corporatre Internet, *ACM Transactions on Information System Security*, Vol. 1, No. 2, 1999.
3. S. Forrest, S. A. Hofmeyr and A. Somayaji, Computer Immunology, *Communications of the ACM*, Vol. 40, No. 10, pp. 88–96, 1997.
4. S. Forrest, A.S. Perelson, L. Allen and R. Cherukuri, Self-Nonself Discrimination in a Computer, *In Proceedings of the 1994 IEEE Symposium on Research in Security and Privacy*, 1994.
5. S. A. Hofmeyr and S. Forrest, Architecture for an artificial immune system, *Evolutionary Computation*, 7(1), pp. 45–68, 2000.
6. Yoshiteru Ishida, Active Diagnosis by Self-Organization: An Approach by The Immune Network Metaphor, *Fifteenth International Joint Conference on Artificial Intelligence (IJCAI'97)*, Vol. 2, pp. 1084–1089, 1997.
7. Y.Watanabe, A.Ishiguro and Y.Uchikawa, *Decentralized Behavior Arbitration Mechanism for Autonomous Mobile Robot Using Immune Network*, in D.Dasgupta Ed., Artificial Immune Systems and Their Applications, Springer-Verlag, pp.187–209, 1998
8. Fumio Mizoguchi, Anomaly Detection Using Visualization and Machine Learning, *Proc. of the Ninth IEEE International Workshops on Enabling Technologies: Infrastructure for Collaborative Enterprises (Workshop: Enterprise Security)*, pp. 165-170, 2000.
9. Hiroyuki Nishiyama and Fumio Mizoguchi: Design and Implementation of Security System Based on Immune System, *Software Security - Theories and Systems Lecture Notes in Computer Science*, Hot Topics No.2609 Springer-Verlag, February 2003.
10. H. Nishiyama, H. Ohwada and F. Mizoguchi, A Multiaget Robot Language for Communication and Concurrency Control, *International Conference on Multiagent Systems*, 206–213, 1998.
11. Tomomasa SATO and Taketoshi MORI, Robotic Room: Its concept and realization, *In Intelligent Autonomous Systems*, IAS-5, pp. 415–422, 1998.
12. Tomio Tada, Semantics of immunology (in Japanease), Seidosha, 1993.

Author Index

Lecture Notes in Computer Science

For information about Vols. 1–3201

please contact your bookseller or Springer

Vol. 3251: H. Jin, Y. Pan, N. Xiao, J. Sun (Eds.), Grid and Cooperative Computing - GCC 2004. XXII, 1025 pages. 2004.

Vol. 3250: L.-J. (LJ) Zhang, M. Jeckle (Eds.), Web Services. X, 301 pages. 2004.

Vol. 3249: B. Buchberger, J.A. Campbell (Eds.), Artificial Intelligence and Symbolic Computation. X, 285 pages. 2004. (Subseries LNAI).

Vol. 3246: A. Apostolico, M. Melucci (Eds.), String Processing and Information Retrieval. XIV, 332 pages. 2004.

Vol. 3245: E. Suzuki, S. Arikawa (Eds.), Discovery Science. XIV, 430 pages. 2004. (Subseries LNAI).

Vol. 3244: S. Ben-David, J. Case, A. Maruoka (Eds.), Algorithmic Learning Theory. XIV, 505 pages. 2004. (Subseries LNAI).

Vol. 3243: S. Leonardi (Ed.), Algorithms and Models for the Web-Graph. VIII, 189 pages. 2004.

Vol. 3242: X. Yao, E. Burke, J.A. Lozano, J. Smith, J.J. Merelo-Guervós, J.A. Bullinaria, J. Rowe, P. Tiňo, A. Kabán, H.-P. Schwefel (Eds.), Parallel Problem Solving from Nature - PPSN VIII. XX, 1185 pages. 2004.

Vol. 3241: D. Kranzlmüller, P. Kacsuk, J.J. Dongarra (Eds.), Recent Advances in Parallel Virtual Machine and Message Passing Interface. XIII, 452 pages. 2004.

Vol. 3240: I. Jonassen, J. Kim (Eds.), Algorithms in Bioinformatics. IX, 476 pages. 2004. (Subseries LNBI).

Vol. 3239: G. Nicosia, V. Cutello, P.J. Bentley, J. Timmis (Eds.), Artificial Immune Systems. XII, 444 pages. 2004.

Vol. 3238: S. Biundo, T. Frühwirth, G. Palm (Eds.), KI 2004: Advances in Artificial Intelligence. XI, 467 pages. 2004. (Subseries LNAI).

Vol. 3236: M. Núñez, Z. Maamar, F.L. Pelayo, K. Pousttchi, F. Rubio (Eds.), Applying Formal Methods: Testing, Performance, and M/E-Commerce. XI, 381 pages. 2004.

Vol. 3235: D. de Frutos-Escrig, M. Nunez (Eds.), Formal Techniques for Networked and Distributed Systems – FORTE 2004. X, 377 pages. 2004.

Vol. 3234: M.J. Egenhofer, C. Freksa, H.J. Miller (Eds.), Geographic Information Science. VIII, 345 pages. 2004.

Vol. 3233: K. Futatsugi, F. Mizoguchi, N. Yonezaki (Eds.), Software Security - Theories and Systems. X, 345 pages. 2004.

Vol. 3232: R. Heery, L. Lyon (Eds.), Research and Advanced Technology for Digital Libraries. XV, 528 pages. 2004.

Vol. 3231: H.-A. Jacobsen (Ed.), Middleware 2004. XV, 514 pages. 2004.

Vol. 3230: J.L. Vicedo, P. Martínez-Barco, R. Muñoz, M. Saiz Noeda (Eds.), Advances in Natural Language Processing. XII, 488 pages. 2004. (Subseries LNAI).

Vol. 3229: J.J. Alferes, J. Leite (Eds.), Logics in Artificial Intelligence. XIV, 744 pages. 2004. (Subseries LNAI).

Vol. 3226: M. Bouzeghoub, C. Goble, V. Kashyap, S. Spaccapietra (Eds.), Semantics of a Networked World. XIII, 326 pages. 2004.

Vol. 3225: K. Zhang, Y. Zheng (Eds.), Information Security. XII, 442 pages. 2004.

Vol. 3224: E. Jonsson, A. Valdes, M. Almgren (Eds.), Recent Advances in Intrusion Detection. XII, 315 pages. 2004.

Vol. 3223: K. Slind, A. Bunker, G. Gopalakrishnan (Eds.), Theorem Proving in Higher Order Logics. VIII, 337 pages. 2004.

Vol. 3222: H. Jin, G.R. Gao, Z. Xu, H. Chen (Eds.), Network and Parallel Computing. XX, 694 pages. 2004.

Vol. 3221: S. Albers, T. Radzik (Eds.), Algorithms – ESA 2004. XVIII, 836 pages. 2004.

Vol. 3220: J.C. Lester, R.M. Vicari, F. Paraguaçu (Eds.), Intelligent Tutoring Systems. XXI, 920 pages. 2004.

Vol. 3219: M. Heisel, P. Liggesmeyer, S. Wittmann (Eds.), Computer Safety, Reliability, and Security. XI, 339 pages. 2004.

Vol. 3217: C. Barillot, D.R. Haynor, P. Hellier (Eds.), Medical Image Computing and Computer-Assisted Intervention – MICCAI 2004. XXXVIII, 1114 pages. 2004.

Vol. 3216: C. Barillot, D.R. Haynor, P. Hellier (Eds.), Medical Image Computing and Computer-Assisted Intervention – MICCAI 2004. XXXVIII, 930 pages. 2004.

Vol. 3215: M.G.. Negoita, R.J. Howlett, L.C. Jain (Eds.), Knowledge-Based Intelligent Information and Engineering Systems. LVII, 906 pages. 2004. (Subseries LNAI).

Vol. 3214: M.G.. Negoita, R.J. Howlett, L.C. Jain (Eds.), Knowledge-Based Intelligent Information and Engineering Systems. LVIII, 1302 pages. 2004. (Subseries LNAI).

Vol. 3213: M.G.. Negoita, R.J. Howlett, L.C. Jain (Eds.), Knowledge-Based Intelligent Information and Engineering Systems. LVIII, 1280 pages. 2004. (Subseries LNAI).

Vol. 3212: A. Campilho, M. Kamel (Eds.), Image Analysis and Recognition. XXIX, 862 pages. 2004.

Vol. 3211: A. Campilho, M. Kamel (Eds.), Image Analysis and Recognition. XXIX, 880 pages. 2004.

Vol. 3210: J. Marcinkowski, A. Tarlecki (Eds.), Computer Science Logic. XI, 520 pages. 2004.

Vol. 3209: B. Berendt, A. Hotho, D. Mladenic, M. van Someren, M. Spiliopoulou, G. Stumme (Eds.), Web Mining: From Web to Semantic Web. IX, 201 pages. 2004. (Subseries LNAI).

Vol. 3208: H.J. Ohlbach, S. Schaffert (Eds.), Principles and Practice of Semantic Web Reasoning. VII, 165 pages. 2004.

Vol. 3207: L.T. Yang, M. Guo, G.R. Gao, N.K. Jha (Eds.), Embedded and Ubiquitous Computing. XX, 1116 pages. 2004.

Vol. 3206: P. Sojka, I. Kopecek, K. Pala (Eds.), Text, Speech and Dialogue. XIII, 667 pages. 2004. (Subseries LNAI).

Vol. 3205: N. Davies, E. Mynatt, I. Siio (Eds.), UbiComp 2004: Ubiquitous Computing. XVI, 452 pages. 2004.

Vol. 3204: C.A. Peña Reyes, Coevolutionary Fuzzy Modeling. XIII, 129 pages. 2004.

Vol. 3203: J. Becker, M. Platzner, S. Vernalde (Eds.), Field Programmable Logic and Application. XXX, 1198 pages. 2004.

Vol. 3202: J.-F. Boulicaut, F. Esposito, F. Giannotti, D. Pedreschi (Eds.), Knowledge Discovery in Databases: PKDD 2004. XIX, 560 pages. 2004. (Subseries LNAI).